Palgrave Shakespeare Studies

Series Editors
Michael Dobson
The Shakespeare Institute
University of Birmingham
Stratford-upon-Avon, UK

Dympna Callaghan
Syracuse University
Syracuse, NY, USA

Palgrave Shakespeare Studies takes Shakespeare as its focus but strives to understand the significance of his oeuvre in relation to his contemporaries, subsequent writers and historical and political contexts. By extending the scope of Shakespeare and English Renaissance Studies the series will open up the field to examinations of previously neglected aspects or sources in the period's art and thought. Titles in the Palgrave Shakespeare Studies series seek to understand anew both where the literary achievements of the English Renaissance came from and where they have brought us. Co-founded by Gail Kern Paster.

Editorial Board Members
Margreta de Grazia
Peter Holland
Michael Neill
Lois D. Potter
David Jonathan Schalkwyk

More information about this series at
http://www.palgrave.com/gp/series/14658

Rory Loughnane · Edel Semple
Editors

Staged Normality in Shakespeare's England

palgrave
macmillan

Editors
Rory Loughnane
School of English
University of Kent
Canterbury, UK

Edel Semple
School of English
University College Cork
Cork, Ireland

Palgrave Shakespeare Studies
ISBN 978-3-030-00891-8   ISBN 978-3-030-00892-5 (eBook)
https://doi.org/10.1007/978-3-030-00892-5

Library of Congress Control Number: 2018958729

© The Editor(s) (if applicable) and The Author(s) 2019
This work is subject to copyright. All rights are solely and exclusively licensed by the Publisher, whether the whole or part of the material is concerned, specifically the rights of translation, reprinting, reuse of illustrations, recitation, broadcasting, reproduction on microfilms or in any other physical way, and transmission or information storage and retrieval, electronic adaptation, computer software, or by similar or dissimilar methodology now known or hereafter developed.
The use of general descriptive names, registered names, trademarks, service marks, etc. in this publication does not imply, even in the absence of a specific statement, that such names are exempt from the relevant protective laws and regulations and therefore free for general use.
The publisher, the authors and the editors are safe to assume that the advice and information in this book are believed to be true and accurate at the date of publication. Neither the publisher nor the authors or the editors give a warranty, express or implied, with respect to the material contained herein or for any errors or omissions that may have been made. The publisher remains neutral with regard to jurisdictional claims in published maps and institutional affiliations.

Cover illustration: The Merry Wives of Windsor, Shakespeare play. Act II, Scene ii Falstaff and Mistress Quickly
Cover credit: Chronicle/Alamy Stock Photo

This Palgrave Macmillan imprint is published by the registered company Springer Nature Switzerland AG
The registered company address is: Gewerbestrasse 11, 6330 Cham, Switzerland

Acknowledgements

The editors would like to thank each of the scholars who contributed so generously to this volume; it has been our pleasure to work with such a talented and collegial group. Loughnane would like to thank his colleagues at the University of Kent, and those working on *The New Oxford Shakespeare*, for giving him the research time to undertake and complete this project. He would also like to thank colleagues and friends who responded with insight and good cheer to various queries: Sarah Dustagheer, William E. Engel, Bernhard Klein, Ivan Lupić, Carla Mazzio, and Catherine Richardson. Semple completed some of the work on this volume while on research leave, and she would like to thank her colleagues at University College Cork for their support during this time. Both editors would also like to thank Darragh Greene and Andrew J. Power for their many keen insights about the project. We would also like to express our gratitude to Dympna Callaghan and Michael Dobson for supporting the idea for this volume from the very beginning, and for their insightful feedback about the project as it developed. We are also deeply grateful to Ben Doyle, who commissioned the project, and to Camille Davies who was instrumental in getting the volume in shape for publication. Finally, this volume, like our previous, is dedicated to our families and loved ones—thanks for keeping us 'normal', so to speak, as we worked on this project.

Contents

1 Introduction: Stages of Normality   1
  Rory Loughnane

Part I   Discourses of Normality

2 Circling the Square: Geometry, Masculinity,
  and the Norms of *Antony and Cleopatra*   33
  Carla Mazzio

3 Normal School: *Merry Wives* and the Future of a Feeling   69
  Elizabeth Hanson

4 Regulating Time and the Self in Shakespearean Drama   89
  Kristine Johanson

5 Under the Skin: A Neighbourhood Ethnography
  of Leather and Early Modern Drama   109
  Julie Sanders

Part II Negotiating Normality in Performance

6 Shakespeare's Strange Conventionality 129
   Brett Gamboa

7 Transgressive Normality and Normal Transgression
   in *Sir Thomas More* 151
   Edel Semple

8 'So like an old tale': Staging Inheritance
   and the Lost Child in Shakespeare's Romances 173
   Michelle M. Dowd

9 'Proper' Men and 'Tricksy' Spirits: The Eunuch
   in Disguise in *Twelfth Night* and *The Tempest* 193
   Brinda Charry

Part III Staged Normality and the Domestic Space

10 Everyday Murder and Household Work
    in Shakespeare's Domestic Tragedies 215
    Emma Whipday

11 Children, Normality, and Domestic Tragedy 237
    Emily O'Brien

12 Feminine Transgression and Normal Domesticity 259
    Stephen Guy-Bray

13 Afterword 277
    Frances E. Dolan

Author Index 287

Subject Index 295

Notes on Contributors

Brinda Charry is Professor of English at Keene State College, NH, USA. She has worked on early modern constructions of alterity and cross-cultural relations. Her publications include *Emissaries in Early Modern Literature and Culture* (with Gitanjali Shahani) (2009), *The Tempest: Language and Writing* (2014) and *The Arden Guide to Renaissance Drama* (2017), along with several articles and book chapters. Brinda is also a writer of fiction and has published two novels and a collection of short stories.

Frances E. Dolan is Distinguished Professor of English at the University of California, Davis. She is the author of numerous articles and five books, most recently the award-winning *True Relations: Reading, Literature, and Evidence in Seventeenth-Century England* (2013), which includes chapters on reading depositions, plays, and conduct books as literary texts and historical evidence. Other books particularly pertinent to this volume's topic include *Dangerous Familiars: Representations of Domestic Crime in England, 1550–1700* (1994); and *Marriage and Violence: The Early Modern Legacy* (2008). Her current project, through chapters on composting, local food, wine, and hedgerows, examines how the seventeenth-century England continues to shape both hands-on practice and popular anglophone ways of imagining and describing what farming should be and do.

Michelle M. Dowd is Hudson Strode Professor of English and Director of the Hudson Strode Program in Renaissance Studies at the University of Alabama. She is the author of *Women's Work in Early Modern English Literature and Culture* (Palgrave, 2009), which won the Sara A. Whaley Book Award from the National Women's Studies Association, and of *The Dynamics of Inheritance on the Shakespearean Stage* (Cambridge, 2015). Her current book project is tentatively titled *Shakespeare's Working Words*.

Brett Gamboa is Assistant Professor of English at Dartmouth College, where he teaches Shakespeare and other dramatic literature, and sometimes lyric poetry and contemporary television. His essays appear in several journals and books, and he authored performance-oriented introductions and commentaries for *The Norton Shakespeare*. His first book *Shakespeare's Double Plays* (2018) is available from Cambridge University Press. Brett is also a theater director and dramaturge, having mounted productions professionally and on campus, including ten plays by Shakespeare.

Stephen Guy-Bray is Professor of English at the University of British Columbia, where he specializes in Renaissance poetry and queer theory. He has published books, articles, and co-edited collections, chiefly in those fields, and is now beginning a study of queer representation.

Elizabeth Hanson is Professor of English at Queen's University, Canada. Her publications include *Discovering the Subject in Renaissance England* (Cambridge University Press, 1998), and articles and book chapters on a range of subjects including school and university culture and the drama in early modern England, law, and literature, and the relation between literary text and social field. She is currently working on a book on the drama and the social place of learning in Shakespeare's England.

Kristine Johanson teaches and researches at the University of Amsterdam, where she is Assistant Professor of English Renaissance Literature and Culture. She is the editor of *Shakespeare Adaptations from the Early Eighteenth Century: Five Plays* (2014) and the *Parergon* special issue 'Approaches to Early Modern Nostalgia' (2016), and she is currently finishing her first monograph, *Golden Ages: Shakespeare and Nostalgia in Early Modern England*.

Rory Loughnane is Senior Lecturer in Early Modern Studies at the University of Kent. An Associate Editor of the *New Oxford Shakespeare*

(2016–), he edited over ten plays for the edition and co-authored with Gary Taylor a book-length study about the 'Canon and Chronology of Shakespeare's Plays' (2017). He is the co-editor of four essay collections, including *Late Shakespeare, 1608–1613* (2012), *Celtic Shakespeare* (2013), and *Staged Transgression in Shakespeare's England* (2013), as well as the co-editor of the anthology, *The Memory Arts in Renaissance England* (2016). He is currently editing the Works of Cyril Tourneur for the Revels Plays series, and co-edits with Laurie Maguire the 'Studies in Early Modern Authorship' book series for Routledge.

Carla Mazzio teaches in the Department of English at the University at Buffalo, SUNY. She is the author of *The Inarticulate Renaissance: Language Trouble in an Age of Eloquence* (awarded the Roland H. Bainton Prize, 2010), co-author of *Book Use, Book Theory: 1500–1700* (2005), and editor or co-editor of *Shakespeare & Science* (2009), *Historicism, Psychoanalysis and Early Modern Culture* (2000) and *The Body in Parts*, awarded the Beatrice White Book Prize in 1999. Mazzio's current project is entitled *The Trouble With Numbers: The Drama of Mathematics in the Age of Shakespeare*.

Emily O'Brien lectures and teaches in the School of English at Trinity College Dublin, where she recently completed an IRCHSS Postdoctoral Fellowship, and in the School of English, Drama and Film at University College Dublin. She has published on domestic tragedy, and is currently completing a monograph on early modern murder narratives in print and performance.

Julie Sanders is Professor of English Literature and Deputy Vice-Chancellor at Newcastle University in the UK. She has authored several books including scholarly editions of Jonson, Brome, and Shirley. *The Cultural Geography of Early Modern Drama, 1620–1650* (Cambridge University Press, 2011) won the British Academy Rose Mary Crawshay Prize. She is currently working on a study of 'Making Spaces in Seventeenth-Century London' and co-edits with Garrett A. Sullivan Jr. the 'Early Modern Literary Geographies' series for Oxford University Press.

Edel Semple is Lecturer in Shakespeare Studies at University College Cork, Ireland. She is co-editor of *Staged Transgression in Shakespeare's England* (Palgrave Shakespeare Studies series, 2013) with Rory Loughnane, and of 'European Women in Early Modern Drama', a special issue of *Early Modern Literary Studies* (2017), with Ema Vyroubalová. Edel has published on Shakespearean drama, Shakespeare on film and TV, prostitution in Elizabethan literature, and the critical history of early modern drama. She is also a coordinator of the 'Shakespeare in Ireland' scholarly blog, promoting and reporting on early modern events and research across the island.

Emma Whipday is Lecturer in Renaissance Literature at the University of Newcastle. She holds a Leverhulme Early Career Fellowship, working on brother–sister relationships on the early modern stage. Her monograph, *Shakespeare's Domestic Tragedies*, is forthcoming from Cambridge University Press; she has also published on domestic murder, *Arden of Faversham*, the RSC Roaring Girls season, and practice as research.

List of Figures

Fig. 2.1 Geoffroy Tory, The Roman letter "H", *Champ fleury* (Paris, 1529). The Huntington Library, San Marino, CA ... 33

Fig. 2.2 Geoffroy Tory, The letter "O", *Champ fleury* (Paris, 1529). The Huntington Library, San Marino, CA ... 38

Fig. 4.1 "To Time Wasters", in A Person of Quality, *Emblems divine, moral, natural, and historical expressed in sculpture, and applied to the several ages, occasions, and conditions of the life of many* (London, 1673; By permission of the Huntington Library, San Marino, CA) ... 92

Fig. 10.1 Guillaume de la Perrière, *The Theater of Fine Devices Containing an Hundred Morall Emblems* (London, 1614), Emblem XVIII. By permission of University of Glasgow Library, Special Collections ... 226

CHAPTER 1

Introduction: Stages of Normality

Rory Loughnane

When we see in everyday life things that are petty, ordinary, and banal, we generally fail to remember them, because the mind is not being stirred by anything novel or marvellous.[1]

Anonymous, *Rhetorica ad Herennium*

The aspects of things that are most important for us are hidden because of their simplicity and familiarity. (One is unable to notice something – because it is always before one's eyes.)[2]

Ludwig Wittgenstein, *Philosophical Investigations*

Writing nearly two thousand years apart, an anonymous Roman schoolteacher and an Austrian–British philosopher both articulate a universal truth: what is perceived as normal or everyday rarely draws or sustains interest. The schoolteacher finds this situation entirely understandable. Outlining the rules and methods for *memoria*, the fourth canon of rhetoric, he thinks it is only natural that when 'we see or hear something exceptionally base, dishonourable, extraordinary, great, unbelievable, or laughable, that we are likely to remember a long time'.[3] The everyday

---

R. Loughnane (✉)
School of English, University of Kent, Kent, UK
e-mail: R.Loughnane@kent.ac.uk

© The Author(s) 2019
R. Loughnane and E. Semple (eds.), *Staged Normality in Shakespeare's England*, Palgrave Shakespeare Studies,
https://doi.org/10.1007/978-3-030-00892-5_1

is forgettable and therefore of little use for practices of mnemonics; it is taken for granted. Wittgenstein, for his part, is investigating questions of philosophical psychology, specifically how we see things as something or other. (In medieval psychology, this is the power of apperception.) Writing about epistemology, he opined that not only was the everyday taken for granted, but also that it was less well understood because it was so taken.

As both men highlight, there is no reason for one to recall (and log) the unremarkable, but that does not mean there is not something therein concealed that deserves our attention.[4] Before our Roman schoolteacher, Heraclitus had observed that 'man is estranged from that with which he is most familiar'.[5] This notion of attentiveness and the attenuation of attention have been recently theorized with relation to the 'pursuit of the everyday' in contemporary poetics and culture. Andrew Epstein, drawing upon the musings of Max Weber about 'the disenchantment of the world' (i.e., industrial and scientific revolutions coinciding with increased secularization) and setting up the Romantic treatment of celebrating the everyday, argues that there emerged 'a newfound recognition that the everyday, the here and now, is perhaps *the* primary arena of human experience'.[6] While Epstein concedes that the everyday has been a 'perennial concern' of literary and artistic engagement, name-checking the works of Shakespeare alongside those written by Homer, Chaucer, and others, he firmly grounds this in a twentieth-century codification and reification (his terms) of the phenomena of 'the ordinary', 'the everyday', and 'the nature of attention'.[7]

This volume seeks to pay very careful attention to that which otherwise slips from the span of accumulated attentiveness, and it does so by analysing staged English drama of the early modern period. It is unlikely that Heraclitus, the rhetoric teacher, or Wittgenstein were thinking of the ordinary and the familiar in relation to drama of any period. An obvious explanation for this is that performance, as a mode of entertainment, tends towards the abnormal, the not-everyday, the extraordinary, and the uncommon. Drama, in our modern non-theatrical sense, is always put in contrast with the quotidian realities of existence. So, too, 'drama' can seem opposed to normality; the clue is in the Greek etymology of the word—'doing', 'action', 'deed'.[8] Drama, in the sense of plays and their performance, is rarely associated with tedium or routine. Not even the hardiest of Beckett fans would pay to see a play in which truly nothing happens.[9]

Stage plays entertain. Audiences may have always wanted to find themselves and their own lives reflected on stage (the mimetic correspondence leading to catharsis), but merely by putting action on stage it becomes extraordinary through exhibition, observation, and the dynamics of the staged performance experience. It is, of course, representation rather than presentation. *Staged* and *Normality* might seem therefore unlikely bedfellows. If an action is staged, it overturns and denies expectations and conventions of normality; regardless of content, a staged act is performative, and that act of staging calls attention to itself as a site of performance. For the stage, which could take any form, demarcates the space where the performance act (speech, song, movement) takes place from where it does not. An associated meaning of staged—that an event or action has been staged so as to mean that it is artificially produced in some way that is reminiscent of a performance—discloses the word's innate connoted abnormality.

In this volume, we are looking at normality through a very specific lens: performance, which simultaneously permits the imitation of normality (a subjective idea, as discussed below) and undoes it because it is recognizably imitative of normal behaviour rather than the recognized behaviour itself. But, as noted, that which is normal can easily drift from our attention, can be taken for granted. We are seeking, then, an analysis of the nature of drama apropos Carlo Ginzburg's analysis of the nature of clues.[10] He compares the methods and reasoning process of Morelli (a nineteenth-century art historian), Freud, and Doyle's Sherlock Holmes, to argue that what they had in common was a focus on the seemingly irrelevant detail rather than on the eye-catching centre of an artwork, a life, or a criminal case. (Thus, to identify the artist, the viewer must attend to the mundane feature—the painted ears and fingers—rather than the arresting focus of the work—the figure's enigmatic smile or ecstatic response to heaven; the same principles apply for investigating the psyche and crime.) What is normal may occupy a similar kind of place in early modern drama as the slip of the tongue for Freud, or the scratches on a watch for Holmes; it is that which does not grab and retain our attention, but that which is assumed, understated, unremarkable, overlooked, or, in essence, deemed to be normal, that merits and rewards improved understanding. The chapters in this volume, identifying and analysing passages of staged normality in plays by Shakespeare and his contemporaries, seek to see test the veracity of this hypothesis.[11]

Attention and Drama

> The middle of humanity thou never knewest, but the extremity of both ends.[12]
>
> *Timon of Athens* (14.299–300)

Staged normality may not be a concept one readily associates with pre-modern drama, and perhaps especially not with the drama of Shakespeare and his contemporaries. Asked for a recommendation of plays of the normal type, we might think of the 'naturalism' and 'realism' of later dramatists like Strindberg, Ibsen, Chekhov, Miller, and O'Neill, with their everyman antiheroes and scenes of domestic interaction.[13] With early modern English drama, reflecting upon the plays of Marlowe, Kyd, Middleton, Webster, and Ford, we might identify a tendency towards the extremes of human experience, action, and thought. Apemantus's remark to Timon, quoted above, seems especially apt in this context. In our earlier cognate volume, *Staged Transgression in Shakespeare's England* (2013), contributors sought to consider the function of staged performances of transgressive behaviours. In that volume's Introduction, I questioned whether 'the transgressive actions (and punishments) that are mimetically represented onstage are an edifying simulacrum of the governing and regulating mechanisms of the elite, or a potentially mobilizing revelation of socially destructive heterodoxy for the subordinate and marginalized' (16). Contributors to that volume addressed such ideas in various ways, some pointing to early modern drama's innate radicalism and others to its ultimate conservatism. The volume sought to draw together some of the strands of criticism surrounding performances of transgression, disorder, deviancy, and the 'other' in the drama of Shakespeare and his contemporaries, noting how the idea of transgression had formed the basis for a range of important studies about identity, race, nationality, the law, gender, and sexuality.[14] The present volume directs our attention to many of the same themes and topics but does so by analysing those passages and moments in early modern performance that seem so normal, so quotidian, so conventional, that they have escaped our span of critical attention or only rarely invited consideration or commentary.

The idea that a play's action could be sustained by the normal interactions of everyday life would also have been anathema to early modern playgoers.[15] So, too, for the fiercest opponents of the theatre, who highlighted the most transgressive elements of stage performances:

But if there were no euill in them, saue this, namely, that the arguments of tragedies is anger, wrath, immunitie, crueltie, iniurie, incest, murther & such like: the Persons or Actors, are Goddes, Goddesses, Furies, Fyends, Hagges, Kings, Quéenes, or Potentates. Of Commedies, the matter and ground is loue, bawdrie, cosenage, flattery, whordome, adulterie: the Persons or agents, whores, queanes, bawdes, scullions, Knaues, Curtezans, lecherous old men amorous yong men, with such like of infinit varietie: If I say there were nothing els, but this, it were sufficient to withdraw a good christian from the vsing of them.[16]

Philip Stubbes' litany of drama's horrors calls our attention to the conventions at work here; indeed, it would be difficult to find an early modern play entirely devoid of these sorts of character actions and behaviours. Stubbes is claiming, essentially, that the plays' most dreadful elements are also their most normal. William Prynne, in his typically fevered style, rails against exactly this 'ordinary stile':

[...] Stage-Playes are thus odious, vnseemely, pernicious, and vnlawfull vnto Christians in all the precedent respects: so likewise are they such in regard of their ordinary stile, and subiect matter; which no Christian can, or dares to patronize: If we survay the stile, or subiect matter of all our popular Enterludes; we shall discouer them, to bee *either* Scurrilous, Amorous, and Obscene: or Barbarous, Bloody, and Tyrannicall: or Heathenish, and Prophane: or Fabulous, and Fictitious: or Impious, and Blasphemous: or Satyricall, and Inuectiue: or at the best but Frothy, Vaine, and Friuolous: If then, *the composure, and matter of our popular Stage-Playes, be but such as this, the Playes themselues must needes be euill,* vnseemely, and vnlawfull vnto Christians.[17]

The many particulars in the complaints of Stubbes and Prynne are so overwhelming as to assure the reader of the transgressive nature of stage plays. Yet for those of a puritanical bent it is not simply what is performed but the act of performance itself which generates intense ire. Performance is simultaneously a mode of simulation, pretending to be that which you are not, and dissimulation, pretending not to be that which you are.[18] Two sides of the same coin, perhaps, but the anti-theatrical viewpoint, radical though it may be, yields some significant insights into the authenticity of normality in the context of a stage performance. We shall return below to this idea of the authentic and inauthentic in relation to the experience of normality. But for now, we can note that this present project and volume was motivated by this *totalizing* notional transgression of early modern theatre as identified by contemporary anti-theatrical complaints against performance as a mode of entertainment. The anti-theatricalists' taxonomy of the sins of stage plays reinforces the idea that early modern plays simply comprise one shocking moment of violence and horror after another; that the normal state of drama is an extreme action. But is this true?

Here is the rub. Early modern plays often took upwards of three or more hours to perform (continuously if in the outdoor theatres). Dramatists could not sustain playgoer interest and attention by simply writing one moment of sensational stage action after another. For a dramatic moment to be truly tense, touching, or meaningful, that moment must be sufficiently prepared for and distinguished from that which precedes it.[19] As the chapters in this volume demonstrate, early modern drama often relies upon the juxtaposition of the everyday and the extraordinary, between what is perceived as normal and abnormal; indeed, they show how it is the recognition of how, when, and why normality has been established and then disrupted that makes key dramatic moments striking and memorable. Staged normality may have been largely unattended to by early modern playgoers, but that does not mean it was not experienced by them, or, indeed, written by dramatists with that playgoer experience in mind.

Indeed, while early modern drama frequently showcases the extraordinary, we should not disregard how often characters in these plays advert to the extraordinariness of their present circumstances. What is happening right now, they protest, is not normal. Consider, for example, Shakespeare's favourite sun mythology. Again and again, his characters make mention of the sun-God Phoebus (Apollo), alluding to his daily journey across the sky (some nineteen times across fifteen plays). In beginning or ending his journey Phoebus brings, respectively, the dawn or sunset. So, just as the moment a 'lark at heaven's gate sings' in *Cymbeline*, 'Phoebus 'gins arise' to mark the dawn, while Juliet, awaiting the sunset that will bring Romeo to her, wishes that the 'fiery-footed steeds', bearing Phoebus in his chariot, would bring the sun-God to his journey's end (14.1–2). Juliet wishes to speed up time, to disrupt the natural order of things. But this is, of course, impossible, unnatural; in that play, obsessed with tempo and temporality, she is fated to endure time's natural progression. In contrast, then, consider Ross's interaction with the Old Man in *Macbeth*, where though 'by th' clock 'tis day … yet darkness does the face of earth entomb' (11.6, 9). Or the terrifying scene at Battle of Poitiers in *Edward III*, where a 'sudden fog' hangs over the battlefield and 'made at noon a night unnatural' (12.32, 34).[20] We see here how Shakespeare makes distinct the diurnal, the regular, from its antithesis. The characters expect daylight but they instead encounter darkness. This is not simply about the extraordinary that is experienced but the ordinary it disrupts. Recalling Apemantus' comment to Timon, we can also connect this concern with the middle-ground ordinariness to characterization: psychological equilibrium as opposed to the 'agon' of the tragic hero or the laughter of the fool. This is about a sense of equanimity—an emotional condition as much as social one—what the early moderns called 'order', which is to say there was no rebellion or other disruption. In other words, the experience and condition of abnormality is only understood through the lens of normality.

The present volume thus seeks to open up a new field of inquiry in studies of early modern performance. Contributors have sought to provide an answer to the following questions: what constituted normality in the early modern period, how was it staged, and what does its staging achieve? Given the political and evaluative valence of the term 'normal' and its opposite term, 'abnormal', can or should we use it as an umbrella term for what is customary? Have we as critics fetishized what *we* consider to be aberrant, different, or disorderly? In other words, might we, similar to playgoers and anti-theatricalists, have directed our eye exactly to where the dramatists have pointed us towards, and, in doing so, been less attentive to that which the transgressive actually transgresses? In offering answers to these kinds of questions the volume seeks to shift the weight of our critical attention towards an analysis of the significance of the early modern performance of the unremarkable, the ignorable, the forgettable, the everyday, the normal.

The Idea of Normality

What constitutes normal is, of course, highly problematic. The word seems to have drifted into English in the late sixteenth-century—derived from the Latin *normalis*, meaning right-angled or conforming to a rule—though it only enters regular usage in the eighteenth and nineteenth centuries (see Elizabeth Hanson's chapter for more on the word's etymology).[21] Neither Shakespeare nor any of his fellow dramatists ever use the term. Normality, the term for the state of being normal, is only first used in the nineteenth century. Auguste Comte and Emile Durkheim both contributed significantly to its modern conceptualization. Comte, writing from the perspective of sociological positivism, which proposes that society can be studied scientifically so as to yield valid and reliable evidence about how it operates and the laws that govern it, sought to identify and calculate criteria for normality as a measure of people and their societies. Durkheim, influenced by Comte's scientific approach but distancing himself from his predecessor's philosophy, described phases of social behaviour that can be observed objectively as 'social facts' and categorized these into two groups: the normal (everyday behaviours which help keep society integrated) and the pathological (abnormal behaviours which are socially disintegrative). Georges Canguilheim's mid-twentieth century medico-philosophical study, *The Normal and the Pathological* (originally published in 1943; reprinted and expanded 1963–1966), remains the most influential study of the emergence of normal as a form of classification.[22] Writing principally from a medical perspective, again distinguishing normality from pathology, he described 'the normal' as a means to classify 'the scholastic prototype and the state of organic health'.[23] He challenged the medical classification of disease as simply a deviation from an established norm, an abnormality. Rather, as the anthropologist Paul Rabinow notes, Canguilheim argued that 'suffering, not normative measurements and standard deviations, established the state of disease'.[24] Canguilheim had thus insisted upon the subjective nature of 'the normal', which he described as a 'dynamic and polemical concept' that is neither 'static' nor 'peaceful':

> A norm, or rule, is what can be used to right, to square, to straighten. To set a norm (*normer*), to normalize, is to impose a requirement on an existence, a given whose variety, disparity, with regard to the requirement, present themselves as a hostile, even more than an unknown, indeterminant. [...] The norm, by devaluing everything that the reference to it prohibits from being considered normal, creates on its own the possibility of an inversion of terms.[25]

Canguilheim observed that the setting of a norm automatically creates a category for all which does not adhere to this norm—the abnormal. In a recent response to Canguilheim's work, and drawing also on the writings of François Ewald, Mariano Croce and Andrea Salvatore neatly summarize this earlier proposed concept of normality:

> Normality is the outcome of a knowledge production process that homes in on a given aspect of reality – such as a practice, a profession, or more generally an activity or role within a practical context – to single out and objectify the elements which are claimed to characterize it.[26]

This argument, with its far-reaching implications for scientific thought, knowledge production, and cultural and anthropological studies about transgression and discipline, influenced the work of a generation of emerging French phenomenologists, including Louis Althusser and Michel Foucault. The latter—who would write a glowing introduction to the expanded edition of Canguilheim's treatise, where he described his elder's area of study as concerned with the 'formation of concepts', moving the study far beyond its disciplinary bounds—would turn his attention to the arbiters of what constitutes normality in *Discipline and Punish*, again asserting its innate subjectivity:

> The judges of normality are present everywhere. We are in the society of the teacher-judge, the doctor-judge, the educator-judge, the 'social-worker'-judge; it is on them that the universal reign of the normative is based; and each individual, wherever he may find himself, subjects to it his body, his gestures, his behaviour, his aptitudes, his achievements.[27]

Though ostensibly writing about the evolution of punitive systems, Foucault revealed his interest in how norms are constructed and instituted. He would next write and present a series of lectures about the Abnormal (in 1974–1975), in which he discusses the medical, judicial, and societal powers of processes of normalization (and thereby also the assertion of abnormality).[28] The later work focuses more on the modern concept of norms as averages (rather than simply ideals or expectations) that informed biopolitical control over populations.

The idea of normality, seen through the lens of the everyday, preoccupied twentieth-century thinkers from Martin Heidegger to Henri Lefebvre to Stanley Cavell. In Heidegger's analysis of the temporal character of 'alltäglichkeit' or 'everydayness', set out in *Sein und Zeit* (Being and Time), he asserts that Dasein (or people) are subject to the everyday conditions with which they attempt to make sense of the world in which they exist.[29] These conditions are explained and understood by people in various ways, depending upon the particulars of time of their experience of everydayness, resulting in ideologies (e.g., religious, political, cultural) upon which they 'fall' back upon as a sort of 'inauthentic' existence. Heidegger offers three key observations about 'everydayness' that I wish to highlight: that it explains how people live daily with 'the comfortableness of the accustomed, even if it forces [them] to do something burdensome and "repugnant"'; that 'in everydayness everything is all one and the same, but whatever the day may bring is taken as diversification'; and that 'everydayness is a way *to be* – to which, of course, that which is public manifestly belongs'.[30] Across all three points, we can recognize Heidegger's emphasis on the temporal tension between notional 'everydayness', past and future, and what is individually experienced in the everyday on a daily basis. But we will note that Heidegger is also asserting that despite an individual's agency to determine and understand the conditions of her/his own existence, he/she becomes subject to a series of conventional behaviours by his/her experience of the past, and expectation of the future, 'everydayness'.

Taking a similar argument into more archly political territory, Lefebvre sets out to critically analyse the quotidian realities of modern existence in *Critique de la vie quotidienne* (Critique of Everyday Life), and, by doing so, to define a role or goal of Marxist analysis as 'the critical knowledge of everyday life'.[31] Lefebvre was particularly interested in the 'estrangement' of people from themselves—reminding us of the earlier reading from Heraclitus—and especially in the context of the alienation of labour, returning us to the Heideggerian concept of the burdened workforce accepting that everyday burden.[32] But Lefebvre distanced himself from Heidegger's concept of the 'inauthentic' existence of everyday life. In a preface to Lefebvre's work, Michel Trebitsch identifies an optimistic streak in the philosopher's reading of the everyday:

> [...] his critique of everyday life is a dual reading, at once a rejection of the inauthentic and the alienated, and an unearthing of the human which still lies buried therein.[33]

This recuperation of the human element in the everyday can also be identified in Cavell's writings. Responding to Paul Ricoeur's negative assessment of the historians in the *Annales* School's interest in, and emphasis upon, what Ricoeur dismisses as 'eventless', Cavell counters that rather those historians are interested in demonstrating the value to be found in analysing what seems normal:

such a history is interested not in what Ricoeur calls the *eventless*, as though it seeks, as it were, what is not happening; such a history is interested rather in the *uneventful*, seeking, so to speak, what is not out of the ordinary.[34]

Timothy Gould's analysis of Cavell returns us full circle to the quotation from Wittgenstein that opens this chapter. Gould acknowledges that 'many commentators' have focused on 'the difficulty of seeing the obvious and everyday', and that for Wittgenstein 'it is everydayness itself that we have to overcome in order to allow ourselves to be struck by the importance of the everyday'.[35] For Cavell, interested in how philosophical writing can disclose the 'obvious', 'the demand that we show, in words, how the obvious can be obvious (and therefore how it can have remained obscure) is part of what makes philosophy philosophy'.[36] In other words, the task of philosophers is to use language, writing, to 'register the obviousness of the ordinary world'.[37]

However, as John Austin argues in *Sense and Sensibilia*, this registering of the obvious with language is complicated by the tool of language itself:

> [...] our ordinary words are much subtler in their uses, and mark many more distinctions, than philosophers have realized; and that the facts of perception, as discovered by, for instance, psychologists but also as noted by common mortals, are much more diverse and complicated than has been allowed for.[38]

Drawing upon Austin's work and discussing the 'elusiveness of the ordinary', Stanley Rosen thus argues that:

> [...] the very "ordinariness" of ordinary words is in large part an illusion. The ordinary is accessible, but it has the disconcerting feature of turning into the extraordinary even as we grasp it. [...] The ordinary is something that we pursue.[39]

Let us attempt to follow Rosen in his pursuit. Moving, as we have, from normality and its origins in studies of pathology, to theoretical analyses of the habitual nature of everyday existence, to a questioning of how the obvious and the ordinary can be identified and articulated, we can readily recognize the difficulty, if not impossibility, of providing an objective definition of normality that reveals itself in behaviours, activities, situations, language, etc. But still, *a la* Ginzburg and his clues, Canguiheim and his outcomes, and Rosen and his pursuits, we can attempt to qualify and analyse that which we do experience with relation to the semblative normality that is created or destroyed.

Nowhere is this process more fundamental than in the theatre, a mode of entertainment reliant upon the actors' dissimulation, a form of play based upon make-believe. Whatever notional normality is present, from the playgoer's perspective, is a combination of that which is artificially created and imagined. This would be sufficiently problematic in analysing a modern play in a modern setting by a modern dramatist. But the contributors to this volume seek to identify normality in four-hundred-year-old play-texts, each subject to their own contingencies of authorial production and textual transmission. Recalling Heidegger's analysis of temporality and everydayness, our threshold for normal may be radically different from those who first encountered such moments in the performance. Still, we persist in our pursuit of the normal in early modern England, that which has evaded our span of accumulated attentiveness, that which we have taken for granted in our reading, and, in doing so, we turn next to studies of early modern life outside the walls of the theatre.

Normality in Early Modern England

Despite its late emergence as a form of classifier, normality, as a concept, is historically unbound. Norms, normality, and practices of normativity and normalization all existed in early modern England, but these concepts were at least partially expressed in different, albeit inexact, ways. The chapters in the present volume are interested in how normality is established, classified, and understood in a performance context. Shakespeare, for instance, alternated between 'common' and 'ordinary' to express what we might understand in part as normal.[40] The first of these words also carries a weight of evaluative valence in terms of class demarcation. So, while Coriolanus can speak of 'common chances common men could bear' to describe the commonplace misfortunes faced by all (*Coriolanus*, 4.1.5), Bertram can (falsely) accuse Diana of being 'a common gamester to the camp', meaning that she is promiscuous and vulgar (*All's Well That Ends Well*, 5.3.186). But 'common' can also be suggestive of enforced norms and legal process (e.g., common law);

think, for example, of Duke Vincentio's praise for Angelo in *Measure for Measure*'s opening scene:

> The nature of our people,
> And city's institutions and the terms
> For *common justice*, you're as pregnant in
> As art and practice hath enrichèd any
> That we remember.
> (1.1.10–14, my emphasis)

Shakespeare's yoking together of the 'nature' of people, city 'institutions', 'common justice', and the proleptic foreshadowing of 'pregnant' within these few lines, sets out what will be the play's central themes and fault-lines, not least the distinction between 'art and practice' in Angelo's subsequent application of the letter rather than the spirit of the law. 'Ordinary', though it also carries the additional meaning of judicial (and sometimes ecclesiastical) ruling, is more consistently used by Shakespeare (if much less frequently) to invoke the everyday, commonplace, and usual. For example, Caesar can speak of enflaming the 'blood of ordinary men' (*Julius Caesar*, 3.1.37).

But while no exact correspondence can be found for normal, there is a now-obsolete contemporary word for its opposite which derives from the same etymological root: 'enormous', meaning 'Deviating from ordinary rule or type; abnormal, unusual, extraordinary, unfettered by rules; hence, mostly in a bad sense, strikingly irregular, monstrous, shocking' (*OED* 1.a.*obs.*). (As Carla Mazzio notes in the Chapter 2, 'enormous' equates to 'out-of-norm'.) In the only two examples of this usage in Shakespeare's works, Lear speaks of 'this enormous state' (7.153), calling attention to England's abnormal state of affairs, while in *The Two Noble Kinsmen*, when praying to Mars, Arcite speaks of 'enormous times' to mean times of degenerate actions (5.1.62). ('Enormity' is the cognate term that is still current.) Shakespeare's plays also often reflect upon the mundanity (deriving from *mundanus* or 'worldliness') of human experience and the everyday passage of all from birth to death. From Jaques' seven ages to *Cymbeline*'s song about 'Golden lads and girls' becoming 'dust' (4.2.264–265), there is not simply a resigned contemplation about the inevitability of death but also a recognition, as expressed memorably by the Gravedigger in *Hamlet*, that everyone eventually shares the same fate.

The research in this volume builds upon studies of the 'everyday' in early modern England (another descriptor, incidentally, that Shakespeare never uses), and, in particular, studies of how everyday experience is represented mimetically in stage plays. The study of the former largely preceded and anticipated the study of the latter. In his statistics-driven *The World We Have Lost* (1965), Peter Laslett drew upon parish records of family life (e.g., records of marriage, baptism, death) to challenge old school Marxist-inflected readings of family and social structure in pre-industrial England. Employing statistical demography to produce (often controversial) broader sociological conclusions, Laslett characterized early modern English social relations as exploitative and oppressive for the majority of the population ('no paradise, no golden age of equality, tolerance or of loving kindness') and insisted upon a patriarchally-structured dynamic operating across familial and work relations.[41] Lawrence Stone's *The Family, Sex and Marriage in England 1500–1800* (1977), which attempted the sort of ambitious large-scale historical sweep rarely undertaken now, offered an unsettlingly bleak account of early modern English social dynamics. He argued for the rise of 'affective individualism' in the late seventeenth and the eighteenth centuries, which followed on, in a monodirectional sort of historical progressivism, from the cold, unloving, unsentimental society which preceded it.[42] Stone depicted a death-obsessed society where intimacy made little sense: 'high mortality rates made deep relationships very imprudent'.[43] This lack of intimacy permeated loveless marital relationships ('a low-keyed and undemanding institution') and parental responsibilities ('there was small reward from lavishing time and care on such ephemeral objects as small babies').[44] Reactionary accounts followed over the next decade, by cultural historians such as Keith Wrightson (1982) and Ralph Houlbrooke (1984), and by the social anthropologist Alan Macfarlane (1986), which each attested to the strength of affection and intimacy that existed in the England of Shakespeare's age, but Stone's evaluation of that society especially, rooted in economic determinism, remains influential. In ways, his was an avowedly old historicist account (and it is little surprise that Stone wholeheartedly rejected postmodernism in the forms of post-structuralism, cultural anthropology, and new historicism), asserting our historical distance from the norms and conventions of the past.[45] So, too, the vanguard of new historicism and cultural materialism insisted upon the connection between the text and historical context, but they also argued for the subjective and contingent nature of how and why certain ideologies might be present in extant writings and artefacts of the period, literary, and non-literary. Rather than identifying a 'spirit of the age', so to speak, which could offer to us a generalized account of what normal or everyday existence resembled in early modern England, they proposed a polyvocal and highly subjective shaping of history.

By the end of the twentieth century, literary critical attention began to turn in a sustained manner to the ordinary, everyday lives of early modern England, driven also by a new emphasis placed upon the role and status of women in the period, and, as ever, the writings of Shakespeare and other dramatists loomed large in the studies that followed. Criticism develops in stages and there first emerged a series of groundbreaking literary–historical studies, which often drew upon examples from stage plays, that discussed popular culture and social relations (e.g., Burke 1978; Kaplan 1984; Zimmerman and Weissman 1989; Cressy 1980, 1989, 1997; Archer 1991) and gave voice to the early modern female experience (e.g., Woodbridge 1984; Greene and Kahn 1985; Callaghan 1989). Developing from such research came original work, again often drama-focused, about the early modern domestic sphere, sexual politics, and subjectivity (e.g., Traub 1992; Dolan 1994; Traub et al. 1996). A breakthrough essay volume which responded to such critical trends and anticipated and helped encourage where the field was moving towards was Patricia Fumerton and Simon Hunt's *Renaissance Culture and the Everyday* (1999), which made the case for a 'new new historicism' that placed more focus upon the everyday:

> Foregrounded are the common person, the marginal, women, the domestic, and everyday speech as well as familiar things: mirrors, horses, books, foodstuffs, paintings, architecture, laundry baskets, embroidery, conduct manuals, money, graffiti. Included, though necessarily given "minor" representation, is the aristocracy in its own everyday practices – investing in dressage, holding to the homely accents of high English, and retreating as women into nunneries and other architectural spaces. In this expansive and variegated and sometimes even contradictory vision of everyday life – for we are nothing if not inconsistent in our day-to-day living – the strange [...] becomes not an alien other but a defining mark, however disfiguring, of everyday life.[46]

In the twenty years since this proposal was made, the fruits of such labour are everywhere to see in subject-specific studies of aspects of early modern everyday life. There have since been published (and the following is only representative of an expansive field but focuses upon studies of a literary critical bent) dedicated book-length studies of clothing (Jones and Stallybrass 2000), graffiti (Fleming 2001), gender and property (Erickson 2002; Korda 2002), household work (Wall 2002), privacy and domesticity (Abate 2003), alcohol (Smyth 2004), poor women (McNeill 2007), language use (Mazzio 2008), marriage and violence (Dolan 2008), women's work (Dowd 2009), everyday objects (Hamling and Richardson 2010), working subjects (Dowd and Korda 2011), inheritance (Dowd 2015), recipes and early modern cooking (Wall 2016) and, most recently, a study of *A Day at Home* for the middling classes in early modern England (Hamling and Richardson 2017). We are now in a position where we can say with greater accuracy what the normal everyday experience might have resembled for those living in early modern England.

Normality Staged

Despite such developments, no study has heretofore sought to bring together this range of new perspectives to freshly analyse and assess how, cumulatively, such qualitatively normal behaviours or things were depicted and deployed in early modern performance. In this short volume we could not hope to address that greater need, but, by drawing together a variety of critical approaches to explore staged normality, we hope to help to begin this holistically recuperative process. In the chapters included here, material aspects of performance, such as clothing and stage properties, fall within our purview. But we are less interested in the actual material or physical things or artefacts than with how they are being deployed in a recognizably normal way within performance (see, for example, Emily O'Brien's analysis of the spinning top in Chapter 11). Our focus throughout is rather on how what is recognized or understood as normal (again, always a subjective idea) forms part of, and contributes to, the performance. But normality remains a highly problematic idea, and especially in the context of the performance of an early modern play. As a sort of departure point, let us consider one possible example of staged normality in *Hamlet*, and the difficulties inherent in framing such a performance activity in this way.

Long after the slaying of Polonius, after the Ghost's appearance, after the Prince has spat out his disgust at the 'rank sweat' of the royal 'enseamèd bed\ Stewed in corruption' (11.90), after the Queen has sworn to uphold her son's demands to forego all sexual contact with his uncle, the scene seems to fall into a quiet lull. The excitement is over; those terrible thoughts previously repressed have been expressed. Then, switching topics entirely, Hamlet says 'I must to England' (11.196). His mother responds, 'Alack, I had forgot' (11.197). When I was first taught *Hamlet* as a teenager, my teacher made great play of this moment; here, he suggested, was a glimpse into the pre-existing relationship of mother and son, a revelation of mutual tenderness despite the horror, a snapshot of normality amidst the chaos. At the time, I thought it a brilliant insight—that son and mother, previously distant emotionally, recall together that they must now be distant physically—but it requires some further nuance. For tender though it may be, the exchange is also a bit absurd. How is it that Gertrude could forget that Hamlet, her only son, is to be packed off for England? How could she be so inattentive?

The abruptness of Hamlet's switch in topic is also, as any director of the play knows well, problematic in performance. This is exemplified by Gregory Doran's direction of this passage in his 2008 production. Penny Downie as Gertrude ended her speech declaring that she will abide by 'what [Hamlet] hast said to [her]' (11.196) by raising her finger to her lips, kissing it, and planting that finger on the lips of David Tennant's Hamlet. Tennant, on his knees, proceeded to embrace the seated Downie around the waist, while Downie holds him, rubs his back, and whispers 'shhh'. In the recorded version, these actions take up a full twenty-eight seconds of the performance. That is, roughly half a minute of unscripted action passes between Gertrude's oath and Hamlet's 'I must to England'. Formally, the play-text itself does not suggest that Shakespeare imagined such a temporal gap from one moment to the next: the shared line (11.196)—'What thou hast said to me'. 'I must to England'—means that the exchange was written to be performed continuously. Directors such as Doran must therefore work hard to create the illusion of normality that the text denies. The perceived normality of the exchange only functions in contrast to the extraordinary abnormality of what precedes it: a murder, a ghost sighting (or not), and a son's assault upon his mother's sexual liberty. Her forgetfulness only makes sense in the context of this particular scene, a scene that might, just possibly, rid all further thoughts from mind, and this particular character, a widow who with 'wicked speed' (2.156) proceeded from mourning remembrance to remarriage.

Earlier I lauded dramatists for their attentiveness in constructing a template of notional normality for their plays. But we see here, in this example from *Hamlet*, how actors must often work hard to tap into this notional normality that is at once present in, and absent from, the text. If anything, the demands placed upon playgoers are more severe. Most often described as a suspension of disbelief, a playgoer's experience seems much more exacting than that. Rather than simply suspending disbelief, a conscious mode of self-regulation, playgoers must also work hard imaginatively to create and supplement that which may be absent, aurally, visually, verbally, from the play-world offered and experienced. The Chorus in *Henry V* leaves us in no doubt about the significance of playgoer imagination: 'Piece out our imperfections with your thoughts' (Pro.23); plays, even plays as powerful as Shakespeare's great English histories, require the creative engagement of playgoers to fill in their missing backdrops. This process is happening constantly as we experience plays, and any critical interpretation of the work relies upon it. It has the effect of normalizing what is staged; that the characters enacted exist outside of what the performed text permits, that their motivations, words, and actions, have an un-textualized prehistory. But, of course, this is only what playgoers themselves imagine; it is only their way of creating a semblative normality to lend context to what happens on the stage.

Dramatists play their part, though, and little details can go a long way. Recall, for example, Falstaff quaffing wine at the Boar's Head, or the board game in *Arden of Faversham*. These are recognizable, familiar actions in recognizable, familiar situations. Hal's teasing of Francis the drawer, who becomes the butt of a more powerful person's joke, is also a somewhat universal experience. Settings play an important part, and again and again contributors to this volume focus on scenes of staged domesticity. (Indeed, the subgenre of domestic tragedy has tended to dominate discussions of staged normality—see Stephen Guy-Bray's Chapter 12 for how the parameters of this subgenre can be redefined.) Stage properties, costume, and linguistic register can also showcase the everyday, the recognizable. For example, the localized activities and rich vocabulary of the city comedies of Jonson and Middleton may offer glimpses into everyday life in Jacobean London. The staging of normality—or what we as playgoers are to perceive as the ordinary, everyday fictional world of the onstage characters—can provide the requisite scene-setting for the more demanding passages of high drama that follow. Not unlike the background sky in a painted portrait, it supplies context, lends shading and meaning, and supports the revelation of the extraordinary.

But, as dramatists must have known and as the chapters in this volume each attest, the staging of normality does this and much more. What is normal can be staged to be appreciated and cherished, at once establishing and endorsing the norms of everyday existence. Or what is normal can be staged in such a way as to be critiqued and undermined, offering a radical sociopolitical message. In either case, the normal is thereby foregrounded as a valid object of attention, thus forcing us to reconsider its relationship to the abnormal. While the staging of what is perceived of as normal may rarely command the attention of a playgoer or reader of early modern drama, perhaps it now should, returning once more to the idea of turning our attention to that which has slipped the span of our accumulated attentiveness. With such a shift in our foci, we might begin by asking simply what exactly it is that *we* perceive to be normal about what we see or read in early modern plays, and why?

Staged Normality

The volume is divided into three sections, the first of which, 'Discourses of Normality', begins with a series of essays about rules and habitual practices, analysing how normality is codified and communicated through the medium of performance. In the opening chapter, Carla Mazzio, taking as her departure point the etymology of 'enormous', meaning 'out-of-square', and Antony's description of his actions in Egypt with Cleopatra as having 'not kept [his] square', moves on to consider how the geometric figure of the square 'often stands as a kind of iconographic encapsulation of the constraints of normativity' (Chapter 2). Noting how straight lines have been historically associated with a kind of heteronormative masculinity, Mazzio argues that the square, as a figure of early modern masculinity, offered a 'definitive, elaborate, and shapely form or norm' (Chapter 2) that crossed moral, philosophical, architectural, and military discourses. Mazzio's essay then focuses on the ideological dimensions of a range of early modern philosophical and creative engagements with the idea of the square and squaring, before returning to a close reading of how Antony's out-of-squareness can be understood with relation to how Rome and Egypt are distinguished in the play, and how Antony's immoderate actions operate outside the norms and ideals of Roman masculinity. The essay pivots on the tensional relationships between the geometric square and the circle as competing models for thought, action, and being, and on Egypt's paradoxical dominance in the arts of measurement in *Antony and Cleopatra* that, Mazzio argues, grounds and surpasses the otherwise definitive model of the Roman 'norm'.

Concerned also with definitions and acts of defining, Elizabeth Hanson first considers the emergence of 'normal' as a form of classification before turning to methods and means of 'normalization'. Hanson reflects upon the early modern grammar school as a norming institution, looking at the way in which the course of study undertaken in the English classroom, with its disciplinary practices, instituted a set of expectations, conformities, and norms about the relationship between the individual and authority. Looking in particular at the Latin lesson scene in *The Merry Wives of Windsor*, Hanson argues that this scene and the play at large 'affords a structure of feeling that defends against the authority of institutions, such as the grammar school, to shape social experience' (Chapter 3).

Kristine Johanson's chapter takes a questionable pre-modern concept—that time is individual, and therefore can be self-regulated—and investigates how early modern dramatic writing might circulate and thereby normalize this idea. Offering an array of examples from Shakespeare's works, Johanson establishes that good time management was thought of as an essential individual and social responsibility related to self-governance (as opposed to idleness, waste, etc.). In readings drawn from *Hamlet*, *The Taming of the Shrew*, *3 Henry VI*, and *Richard II*, Johanson argues that 'Shakespeare's drama participates in constructing those temporal norms it investigates and interrogates', thereby resisting the 'totalizing individuality of time' (Chapter 4).

Julie Sanders then invites the reader into the groundling space of the Rose Theatre, detailing the sorts of sights, sounds, and smells to be experienced. In particular, Sanders describes the pungent smell of the heavily tanned leather jerkins worn by men in the period, made in the tanneries and other leather-making sites clustered close to the theatres in Southwark (as well as those close to other sites of performance in Shoreditch). Sanders proceeds to discuss the communities and practices which 'shaped and formed the contexts' for the dramatic writings of Shakespeare and others, producing case studies of the use of site, space, and locality in plays by Heywood and Dekker (Chapter 5).

The volume's second section, 'Negotiating Normality in Performance', offers a series of case studies that analyse how 'normality' is performed and made conventional, and that consider both its practical and far-reaching functionality. Brett Gamboa discusses some familiar conventions of stage drama deployed in Shakespeare's plays, noting how the dramatist often foregrounds the artifice of the play production itself. He first considers scenes involving ghosts, a stage convention used frequently in the period. Offering examples drawn from *Hamlet*, *Macbeth*, *Richard III*, and *Cymbeline*, Gamboa analyses the ways in which Shakespeare's plays challenge playgoers to question the reality of what they see and to reflect upon the dramatic set-up which establishes that reality. In the same vein, Gamboa moves on to scenes of stage deaths, discussing how the yet-still-living scenes in *King Lear* (Cordelia) and *1 Henry IV* (Falstaff) rely for effect upon the playgoers' familiarity with certain stage conventions surrounding the moment of a character's 'death'. Throughout Gamboa seeks to alert the reader to the tension between 'the spectators and the play itself' (Chapter 6).

Exploring extreme events and unfamiliar situations—an anti-immigrant riot, the operations of the Privy Council—as well as the everyday and mundane—citizenry, servants, family interactions, medical complaints—in *The Book of Sir Thomas More*, Edel Semple finds that normality can be transgressive and transgression can be normal. In staging these seeming contradictions, the play foregrounds the 'low' as worthy of attention and it infuses the ordinary with the power to question orthodoxies and voice alternative views. Moreover, Semple argues, in presenting its eponymous protagonist as both an everyman and an exceptional hero, *Sir Thomas More* ultimately exposes the inconsistencies in and hazards of state power to the individual (Chapter 7).

Michelle M. Dowd turns our attention to the legal norm of primogeniture, and to the staging of contraventions of patrilineal inheritance. Noting that exceptions to the 'legal ideal' were common in the period, Dowd considers one familiar family situation that posed a challenge to the patrilineal economy: families with daughters but without sons. Looking at how this scenario is staged in *The Winter's Tale* and *Cymbeline*, Dowd observes that Shakespeare introduces the dramatic convention of the 'lost-child plot' to help resolve the problem posed by a female heiress. In doing so, Dowd argues that Shakespeare's plays shed a light on the 'mechanisms' of the patrilineal economy, encouraging playgoers and readers 'to question the stability of early modern legal "norms"' (Chapter 8).

Brinda Charry looks at staged normality through the lens of gender and gender performativity, while also giving consideration to issues related to race, identity, 'otherness', and familiarity. Discussing the idea of the eunuch servant in the early modern imagination, and, in particular, how that figure might be partially identified in *Twelfth Night* (Viola as 'Cesario') and *The Tempest* (Ariel), Charry observes that the eunuch was at once familiar and alien, 'the same and simultaneously not the same' (Chapter 9). Charry argues that Shakespeare seeks to 'effectively erase or rewrite the eunuch', in various ways, to fulfil his ambitions with these comedies but that this has significant implications for our understanding of the role servitude plays in both works (Chapter 9).

The volume's third and final section, 'Staged Normality and Domestic Space', analyses how the home figures in the early modern imagination and how it is represented in stage performances. Emma Whipday considers the connection between the domestic home space and female virtue. Whipday first looks at conduct literature from the period wherein such a connection is made explicit, before considering the stage representation of the domestic space and the use of domestic objects in performance. Situating then a series of plays with scenes with domestic settings, including *Arden of Faversham* and *A Woman Killed with Kindness*, in dialogue with plays with scenes of 'tragic domesticity', *Macbeth* and *Othello*, Whipday investigates how the domestic sphere is elevated to the 'dramatic reach of tragedy' (Chapter 10).

Next, Emily O'Brien, discussing scenes of 'a familiar, recognizable, everyday world in which things go terribly wrong' in domestic tragedies, focuses upon the dramatists' use of child characters. Despite their relatively minor roles, O'Brien argues, these characters are significant for establishing 'domestic normality' (Chapter 11). With readings from *Arden of Faversham*, *A Warning for Fair Women*, and *A Yorkshire Tragedy*, O'Brien traces the use and function of such child characters in performance, arguing that they work to 'animate' the plays' central themes, and that normality is essential for the moral messages of each play.

Finally, Stephen Guy-Bray's chapter is concerned with how the 'normal' household space features and figures in early modern drama; in particular, he analyses the 'association between female transgression' and the domestic space that is 'often conceived of as a safe and female space'. Looking at domestic scenes in *Arden of Faversham* and *The Duchess of*

Malfi, Guy-Bray discusses such concepts as household authority, and domestic bliss, as well as societal norms about marriage. Comparing Alice and the Duchess, he sees the former as a transgressive product of an adaptive society, while identifying a sort of conventional domesticity in Webster's creation (Chapter 12).

Frances E. Dolan, in her Afterword, first points to foundational work in studies of the 'early modern that proceeded with greater confidence about what "normal" meant', before drawing together some of the key areas of focus from the volume (Chapter 13). In doing so, Dolan notes how material studies of culture have come to the fore, as well as studies of race and ethnicity, while observing that several of the studies turn to the site of domestic activity for readings of early modern normality. Dolan continues by reflecting upon how the staging of normality can have significant knock-on cultural effects for what is to be understood as normal.

Notes

1. Anonymous (1999: III.xxii.35–36).
2. Wittgenstein (2009: para. 129).
3. Anonymous (1999: III.xxii.35–36).
4. In his introduction to *The Elusiveness of the Ordinary*, Rosen sets out a chicken-and-egg situation that might be of interest here. He notes that the everyday received little attention from classic philosophers but later they realized that understanding the ordinary is what drives us to, and is the foundation for, understanding the extraordinary and wonderful, and that then philosophers moved to 'illuminate the ordinary' and guide everymen to key questions and truths (2002: 3–5).
5. Heraclitus's writings survive only in fragments (Fragment DK B72). This is quoted in Marcus Aurelius's *Meditations*, IV, 46.
6. Epstein (2016: 5).
7. Epstein (2016: 5).
8. See Aristotle's discussion of 'dran' in *Poetics*.
9. Early audiences, including censors, did object to *Waiting for Godot*, not quite knowing what to do with a drama that was so insistently undramatic. As reported in *The Guardian* (Alison Flood, 11 September 2017): 'It was subsequently viewed by examiner C. W. Heriot, who in his report to the Lord Chamberlain said that he had "endured two hours of angry boredom" for "a piece quite without drama and with very little meaning"'.

10. Ginzburg (1980).
11. Indeed, Wittgenstein was famously disparaging of what he perceived as the 'unrealistic' nature of Shakespeare's plays: 'It seems to me that his plays are like enormous sketches, not paintings; they are dashed off by one who could, so to speak, permit himself everything. And I understand how one can admire this and call it the highest art, but I don't like it' Wittgenstein (1980: 89, 98). For a fine analysis of Wittgenstein's commentary on Shakespeare, see Lewis (2005).
12. All subsequent references to the works of Shakespeare are taken from individual editions within *The New Oxford Shakespeare: Modern Critical Edition* and appear as in-text citations.
13. It was Ibsen who led the charge (in London at least) with his 'naturalist' drama. *Ghosts* was decried by critics as 'an open sewer' although it did nothing more disturbing than *Oedipus Rex* or *Hamlet*. What was disturbing was the presence of the ordinary in it. It was the mixture of the traditionally dramatic drama with natural normal that made it cut too close to the bone.
14. For an inexhaustive (but at least somewhat representative) of works of this kind, see my Introduction to *Staged Transgression in Shakespeare's England*, esp. 11–16. Much exciting work continues to emerge in this vein. See, for example, recent work about early modern sexual cultures (Traub 2016) and sex and language (Masten 2016), or revisionist analyses of early modern race (Erickson and Hall 2016; Kaufmann 2017) and gender (Loomba and Sanchez 2016).
15. Paradoxically, there was something very normal about the act of attending performances. With *c.* 15,000 attending the playhouses per week *c.* 1600, dramatists wrote plays for experienced audiences who were accustomed to drama's rules and conventions. (See Brett Gamboa's chapter for further discussion about these.)
16. Stubbes (1583: STC# 23376), sig. L7^{r-v}.
17. Prynne (1633; STC# 20464a), sig. I3^v.
18. Laura Levine notes that anti-theatricalists portrayed the relationship between spectator and actor as a somewhat mysterious, coercive process, even a dangerous one, where watching plays could lead to 'compulsive imitation' of what was taking place on stage or even worse 'to taking on the identity of the person watched' (1994: 13).
19. Modern film-makers understand this point well: think of any summer action blockbuster and how scenes of backstory, comic interlude, domestic interaction, etc., break up explosive scenes of high drama. This extends to filmed adaptations of early modern plays. See Hindle's *Studying Shakespeare on Film* which analyses Kenneth Branagh's film of *Much Ado About Nothing* and includes a graph of the dull/quiet

moments and the heightened/tense moments; Hindle proposes that you need the calm to appreciate and have respite from the stormy parts. Branagh, he argues, understands this and thus edits and moves scenes accordingly (2007: 245–247).
20. Shakespeare is the most likely author of this scene, but more research is required to determine this. See Taylor and Loughnane (2017: 503–506).
21. The *OED* first records the word as implied in the use of 'normallye' in A. M.'s 1598 translation of Guillemeau's *French Chirurg*. The earliest exact usage I could find is in Joseph Carlyle's *An Exposition* (1653; Wing C777): 'The Word is the Judge, that is the rule of Judgement. As here, God was the personal Judge of this, so his Word must ever be the Normal Judge of all controversies' (sig. D1^r). Here the word usage is clearly related to conforming to a 'rule'.
22. There has been much renewed interest in Canguilheim's work since the turn of the millennium. See Geroulanos' fine summary of work up until 2009 where he makes the case for the author 'entering the pantheon of French thought' (2009: 289).
23. Canguilheim (1991: 237).
24. Rabinow (1996: 84).
25. Canguilhem (1991: 239–240).
26. Croce and Salvatore (2017: 276).
27. Canguilhem (1991: 304).
28. Foucault focusing on the idea of the universality of sexual deviance, discussed three recurrent figures of abnormality: the human monster, the individual needing correction, and a masturbator. These lectures are available in translation, see Foucault (2003).
29. Heidegger (2001: *passim* and esp. 37–38, 42, 422).
30. Heidegger (2001: 422).
31. Lefebvre expanded upon his analysis of the quotidian across three published volumes. These are: *Critique de la vie quotidienne* (1947), *Fondements d'une sociologie de la quotidienneté* (1962), and *De la modernité au modernisme (Pour une métaphilosophie du quotidian)* (1982). I have drawn from John Moore's translation of the first volume, *Critique of Everday Life* (1991).
32. For a detailed analysis of Lefebvre's theory, see Chris Butler's excellent *Henri Lefebvre: Spatial Politics, Everyday Life and the Right to the City* (esp. 25–26).
33. Michel Trebitsch's Preface in Lefebvre (1991: xxiv).
34. Cavell (1984: 193).
35. Gould (1998: xiii).
36. Gould (1998: xiv).

37. Gould (1998: xiv). Two relatively recent studies have illuminated the cultural capital of the idea of the 'ordinary': for its political agency, viewed especially in connection to the pursuit of the American Dream, see Drumm (1999); for a detailed history of 'ordinariness' and its application in contemporary philosophy, see Rosen (2002).
38. Austin (1964: 3).
39. Rosen (2002: 2).
40. While Shakespeare and his grammar school-educated contemporaries may or may not have used the term 'normal' in English, they would have known the original word from the Latin.
41. Laslett (1965: 3).
42. Stone (1977: 22).
43. Stone (1977: 88).
44. Stone (1977: 60, 81).
45. See Stone (1991).
46. Fumerton (1999: 3, 6).

Works Cited

Abate, Corinne S. 2003. *Privacy, Domesticity, and Women in Early Modern England*. Farnham: Ashgate.

Anonymous. 1999. *Rhetorica ad Herennium*, trans. and ed. H. Caplan. Cambridge, MA and London: Harvard University Press.

Archer, Ian. 1991. *The Pursuit of Stability: Social Relations in Elizabethan London*. New York: Cambridge University Press.

Austin, J.L. 1964. *Sense and Sensibilia, Reconstructed from the Manuscript Notes by G.J. Warnock*. London, Oxford, and New York: Oxford University Press.

Burke, Peter. 1978. *Popular Culture in Early Modern Europe*. Aldershot: Wildwood House.

Callaghan, Dympna. 1989. *Women and Gender in Renaissance Tragedy: A Study of King Lear, Othello, the Duchess of Malfi, and the White Devil*. Atlantic Highlands, NJ: Humanities Press International.

Canguilhem, Georges. 1991. *The Normal and the Pathological*, trans. Carolyn R. Fawcett in collaboration with Robert S. Cohen. New York: Zone Books (First published in 1943 reprinted and expanded 1963–1966).

Carlyle, Joseph. 1653. *An Exposition*. London.

Cavell, Stanley. 1984. The Ordinary as the Uneventful: A Note on the *Annales* Historians. In *Themes Out of School: Effects and Causes*, 184–194. San Francisco: North Point Press.

Cressy, David. 1980. *Literacy and the Social Order: Reading and Writing in Tudor and Stuart England*. New York: Cambridge University Press.

Cressy, David. 1989. *Bonfires and Bells: National Memory and the Protestant Calendar in Elizabethan and Stuart England*. Berkeley, CA: University of California Press.
Cressy, David. 1997. *Birth, Marriage and Death: Ritual, Religion and the Life Cycle in Tudor and Stuart England*. New York: Oxford University Press.
Croce, Mariano, and Andrea Salvatore. 2017. Normality as Social Semantics: Schmitt, Bourdieu and the Politics of the Normal. *European Journal of Social Theory* 20 (2): 275–291.
Dolan, Frances E. 1994. *Dangerous Familiars: Representations of Domestic Crime in England, 1550–1700*. Ithaca, NY: Cornell University Press.
Dolan, Frances E. 2008. *Marriage and Violence: The Early Modern Legacy*. Philadelphia: University of Pennsylvania Press.
Dowd, Michelle M. 2009. *Women's Work in Early Modern English Literature and Culture*. Basingstoke: Palgrave Macmillan.
Dowd, Michelle M. 2015. *The Dynamics of Inheritance on the Shakespearean Stage*. Cambridge: Cambridge University Press.
Dowd, Michelle M., and Natasha Korda (eds.). 2011. *Working Subjects in Early Modern English Drama*. Farnham: Ashgate.
Drumm, Thomas L. 1999. *A Politics of the Ordinary*. New York: New York University Press.
Epstein, Andrew. 2016. *Attention Equals Life: The Pursuit of the Everyday in Contemporary Poetry and Culture*. Oxford: Oxford University Press.
Erickson, Amy Louise. 2002. *Women and Property in Early Modern England*. London: Routledge.
Erickson, Peter, and Kim F. Hall. 2016. A New Scholarly Song: Rereading Early Modern Race. *Shakespeare Quarterly* 67 (1): 1–13.
Fleming, Juliet. 2001. *Graffiti and the Writing Arts of Early Modern England*. London: Reaktion.
Flood, Alison. 2017. "Angry Boredom": Early Responses to Waiting for Godot Showcased Online. *The Guardian*, September 11.
Foucault, Michel. 1991. *Discipline and Punish*, trans. Alan Sheridan. New York: Penguin.
Foucault, Michel. 2003. *Abnormal: The College de France 1974–1975*, trans. Graham Burchell. London and New York: Verso.
Fumerton, Patricia. 1999. Introduction: A New New Historicism. In *Renaissance Culture and the Everyday*, ed. Patricia Fumerton and Simon Hunt. Philadelphia: University of Pennsylvania Press.
Geroulanos, Stefanos. 2009. Recent Literature on Georges Canguilheim. *Gesnerus* 66 (2): 288–306.
Ginzburg, Carlo. 1980. Morelli, Freud and Sherlock Holmes: Clues and Scientific Method. *History Workshop Journal* 9 (1): 5–36.

Gould, Timothy. 1998. *Hearing Things: Voice and Method in the Writings of Stanley Cavell.* Chicago and London: University of Chicago Press.

Greene, Gayle, and Coppelia Kahn. 1985. *Making a Difference: Feminist Literary Criticism.* London: Methuen.

Hamling, Tara, and Catherine Richardson (eds.). 2010. *Everyday Objects: Medieval and Early Modern Material Culture and Its Meanings.* Farnham: Ashgate.

Hamling, Tara, and Catherine Richardson. 2017. *A Day at Home in Early Modern England.* New Haven: Yale University Press.

Heidegger, Martin. 2001. *Being and Time*, trans. John Macquarrie and Edward Robinson. Oxford, UK and Cambridge, USA: Blackwell.

Hindle, Maurice. 2007. *Studying Shakespeare on Film.* Basingstoke, NY: Palgrave Macmillan.

Houlbrooke, Ralph. 1984. *The English Family 1450–1700.* London: Longman.

Jones, Ann Rosalind, and Peter Stallybrass. 2000. *Renaissance Clothing and the Materials of Memory.* New York: Cambridge University Press.

Kaplan, Steven (ed.). 1984. *Understanding Popular Culture: Europe from the Middle Ages to the Nineteenth Century.* Berlin: Mouton.

Kaufmann, Miranda. 2017. *Black Tudors: The Untold Story.* London: Oneworld.

Korda, Natasha. 2002. *Shakespeare's Domestic Economies: Gender and Property in Early Modern England.* Philadelphia: University of Pennsylvania Press.

Laslett, Peter. 1965. *The World We Have Lost: Further Explored.* London: Methuen.

Lefebvre, Henri. 1991. *Critique of Everyday Life*, trans. John Moore. London and New York: Verso.

Levine, Laura. 1994. *Men in Women's Clothing: Anti-theatricality and Effeminization, 1579–1642.* Cambridge: Cambridge University Press.

Lewis, Peter B. 2005. Wittgenstein, Tolstoy, and Shakespeare. *Philosophy and Literature* 29 (2): 241–255.

Loomba, Ania, and Melissa E. Sanchez (eds.). 2016. *Rethinking Feminism in Early Modern Studies: Gender, Race, and Sexuality.* New York: Routledge.

Macfarlane, Alan. 1986. *Marriage and Love in England: Modes of Reproduction, 1300–1840.* New York: Basil Blackwell.

Masten, Jeffrey. 2016. *Queer Philologies: Sex, Language, and Affect in Shakespeare's Time.* Philadelphia: University of Pennsylvania Press.

McNeill, Fiona. 2007. *Poor Women in Shakespeare.* Cambridge: Cambridge University Press.

Prynne, William. 1633. *Histrio-Mastix.* London: Edward Allde, Augustine Mathewes, Thomas Cotes, and William Jones for Michael Sparke.

Rabinow, Paul. 1996. *Essays on the Anthropology of Reason.* Princeton, NJ: Princeton University Press.

Rosen, Stanley. 2002. *The Elusiveness of the Ordinary: Studies in the Possibility of Philosophy.* New Haven: Yale University Press.

Shakespeare, William. 2016. *The New Oxford Shakespeare: Modern Critical Edition*, ed. Gary Taylor, et al. Oxford: Oxford University Press.
Smyth, Adam (ed.). 2004. *A Pleasing Sinne: Drink and Conviviality in Seventeenth-Century England*. Cambridge: D.S. Brewer.
Stone, Lawrence. 1977. *Family, Sex and Marriage in England, 1500–1800*. London: Weidenfeld & Nicolson.
Stone, Lawrence. 1991. History and Post-Modernism. *Past and Present* 131: 217–218.
Stubbes, Philip. 1583. *The Anatomie of Abuses*. London: W. Pickering.
Taylor, Gary, and Rory Loughnane. 2017. The Canon and Chronology of Shakespeare's Works. In *The New Oxford Shakespeare: Authorship Companion*, ed. Gary Taylor and Gabriel Egan, 417–602. Oxford: Oxford University Press.
Traub, Valerie. 1992. *Desire and Anxiety: Circulations of Sexuality in Shakespearean Drama*. London: Routledge.
Traub, Valerie. 2016. *Thinking Sex with the Early Moderns*. Philadelphia: University of Pennsylvania Press.
Traub, Valerie, M. Lindsay Kaplan, and Dympna Callaghan (eds.). 1996. *Feminist Readings of Early Modern Culture: Emerging Subjects*. Cambridge: Cambridge University Press.
Wall, Wendy. 2002. *Staging Domesticity: Household Work and English Identity in Early Modern Drama*. Cambridge: Cambridge University Press.
Wall, Wendy. 2016. *Recipes for Thought: Knowledge and Taste in the Early Modern Kitchen*. Philadelphia: University of Pennsylvania Press.
Wittgenstein, Ludwig. 1980. *Culture and Value/Vermischte Bermerkungen*, ed. G.H. von Wright and Heikki Nyman, trans. Peter Winch. Oxford: Blackwell.
Wittgenstein, Ludwig. 2009. *Philosophical Investigations* (Philosophische Untersuchungen), ed. P.M.S. Hacker and Joachim Schulte, trans. G.E.M. Anscombe, P.M.S. Hacker, and Joachim Schulte, Rev. 4th ed. Hoboken, NJ: Wiley-Blackwell.
Woodbridge, Linda. 1984. *Women and the English Renaissance: Literature and the Nature of Womankind, 1540–1620*. Urbana: University of Illinois Press.
Wrightson, Keith. 1982. *English Society 1580–1680*. New Brunswick, NJ: Rutgers University Press.
Zimmerman, Susan, and Ronald F.E. Weissman (eds.). 1989. *Urban Life in the Renaissance*. Newark, DE: University of Delaware Press.

PART I

Discourses of Normality

CHAPTER 2

Circling the Square: Geometry, Masculinity, and the Norms of *Antony and Cleopatra*

Carla Mazzio

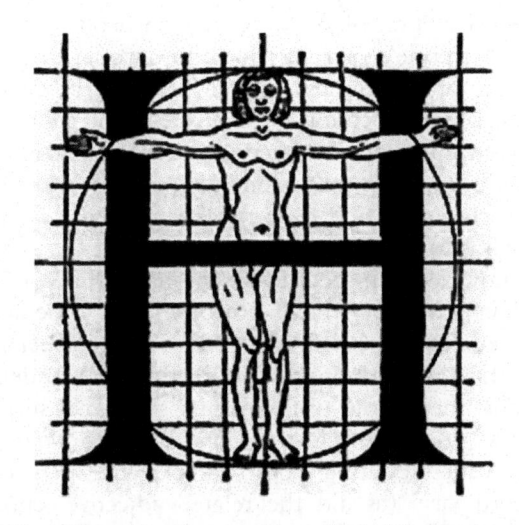

Fig. 2.1 Geoffroy Tory, The Roman letter "H", *Champ fleury* (Paris, 1529). The Huntington Library, San Marino, CA

C. Mazzio (✉)
Department of English, University at Buffalo,
State University of New York, Buffalo, NY, USA
e-mail: cjmazzio@buffalo.edu

> How does thought detach itself from the squares it inhabited before?
> —Michel Foucault, *The Order of Things*

QUEER PHILOLOGY: THE SQUARED, THE ENORMOUS, THE NORMAL

When Antony, alluding to his behavior in Egypt with Cleopatra, says to his new wife Octavia in Shakespeare's *Antony and Cleopatra*, 'I have not kept my square, but that to come / Shall all be done by th'rule,' he is, in the simplest of terms, saying that he has behaved badly in the past but will be well-governed in the future.[1] His words, however, draw upon geometrically demarcated conceptions of the 'norm,' derived from classical antiquity, in which the square as well as the straight line played a surprisingly central part. If 'kept my square' meant, as Ania Loomba suggests in her recent edition of the play, 'remained on a straight course,' the metaphor of 'th'rule' (or ruler) to follow would then simply reinforce the rhetoric of straightness aligned with the process of keeping oneself, in a still familiar locution, 'in line.'[2] But the geometric line and the square offered different, if related, models for imagining modes of personhood and behavior in early modernity, and the square as an index of moral and social ideals and expectations was more familiar in early modernity than it is today.

One might now, as then, be said to 'cross the line' or be 'twisted,' 'crooked,' or 'awkward,' but one is not often said to be acting 'out of square.'[3] And yet, Robert Cawdrey's 1604 *Table Alphabetical of Hard Usual English Words* uses the phrase 'out of square' to define an early English word that meant 'out of the norm,' somewhat surprisingly, the word 'enormous.'[4] According to the *Oxford English Dictionary*, 'enormous' in fact meant 'deviating from ordinary rule or type; abnormal, unusual, extraordinary' (as did the related adjective 'enorm') in the early sixteenth century shortly before it also acquired the now more common meaning of excessively large in scale.[5] 'Enormous' comes from the Latin terms for 'out' ($\bar{e}$) and 'the mason's square' or 'pattern' (*norma*), an etymology that can help us approach the logic of the once commonplace but now obsolete idioms for deviations from the norm: 'out of square' and 'enormous.'[6] Both senses of 'enormous' (the 'out of square' and the disproportionately huge) point to a structural relationship between 'norms' and geometric logic that would have been quite explicit to early modern humanists given the prominence of Latin. Indeed, the 'square' that Antony has not 'kept' would have signaled, in the most technical of terms, at once the geometric square, marked by four right angles and four equal sides, and the builder's tool or 'square,' long used to create and test the accuracy of right angles themselves. In metaphorical terms, the fact that the classical Latin *norma* long meant both the builder's square *and* a 'standard or pattern of practice or behavior,' and that *normālis* for 'right-angled' came to mean 'conforming to or governed by a rule' at least as early the fourth century AD, certainly suggests longstanding cultural and philological links between the literally 'right-angled' and a range of standards, patterns, and rules against which to measure forms of thought and behavior.[7]

But importantly, the even-sidedness along with the right-angled structure of the square was linked with predominantly masculine forms of strength, stability, and virtue in a number of classical and early modern texts. When Plutarch, for example, called upon the distinctly geometric figure of the square as a formal incarnation of the ideal man, stressing that 'a man should be four square, perfect,'[8] Simonides, Plato and Aristotle had already evoked the concept of the 'foursquare man' against which an individual, or a dramatic character such as Shakespeare's Antony, might imagine measuring himself.[9] Although a seemingly humble symbolic figure, the geometric square frequently stood as a formal incarnation of 'normal' masculinity that encoded both an ideal of masculine perfection *and* a potentially replicable standard through which masculinity might be regularized. By stressing the burdens that 'vnsquard' sons place upon parents in the 1602 additions to Thomas Kyd's *The Spanish Tragedy*, for example, Hieronimo implicitly underscores the value of the squared 'sonne,' his own recently deceased Horatio: 'The more he growes in stature and in yeeres / The more vnsquard, vnbeuelled he appeares, / Reccons his parents among the rancke of fooles, / Strikes care vpon their heads with his mad ryots.'[10] Being square here amounts to being controllable by others (such as parents) as well as maintaining self-control in the transition from boyhood to manhood. Indeed, if 'there is an originally prescriptive character of the norm,' as Michel Foucault once observed, the geometric square could not better embody those prescriptive dimensions of masculinity involving consistency, rectitude and regularity and a number of other attributes that were synonymous with ideal manhood in several early cultural and historical contexts.[11]

The 'foursquare man' in Aristotle's *Nichomachean Ethics*, meaning the man stable and upright enough to withstand the vicissitudes of fortune in order to maintain a consistent degree of happiness, is worth reconsidering in this respect. 'The person who will always or as far as possible act and think in a way consonant with virtue and suffer the mishaps of fortune as well as can possibly be done, in an absolutely consonant manner,' Aristotle observes, 'will be the person who is truly good, a foursquare man, free from all that can be faulted.'[12] The definition of such a man of course borders on the perfect and the imperfect, the ideal and the actual man, who can escape fault 'as well as can possibly be done.' And yet the metaphor of the geometric square granted a more abstract and in some sense more 'perfect' conception of human fortitude and balance than similar or analogous idealized quartets such as the balance of the four humors or qualities in medicine or even the four cardinal virtues in ethics. Although Aristotle discussed the constant flux of the four physical qualities (hot, cold, dry, and wet), creating what Mary-Floyd Wilson calls 'an ecology that undermines' conceptions of 'a solid, static, or contained self,'[13] of the geometric square itself he writes that 'the good man and the square are perfect.'[14] The square, perfect in the classical sense of 'whole and complete,' offered a model of consistent, self-contained masculinity, with entry and exit restricted, that could easily offset concerns about the dependent, fluid, permeable or changeable aspects of selfhood. The powerful appeal of this 'squared' model of manhood can (and shall soon) be gleaned by attending to early modern commentaries on relationships between squares, cubes, and men.

But if the metaphor of the 'foursquare man' was in some sense more 'perfect' than other models of strength and health, it was also, *as* a metaphor, less than perfect, or in rhetorical terms potentially dull, lackluster, and inert. Aristotle himself pointed this out in *On Rhetoric*, observing that although the description of a good man as 'foursquare' is philosophically apt it is also rhetorically ineffectual, since the metaphor is itself static. The square 'does not suggest activity,' he observed, and thus lacks the 'liveliness,' motion and vividness so characteristic of Homer who gave such 'metaphorical life to lifeless things.'[15] Aristotle's rhetorical demotion of the 'foursquare man' as a particularly static, passive, and non-vivid metaphor might well be situated alongside his ethical promotion of the 'foursquare man' in order to suggest the limits as well as potential of the square as a model of manly virtue.[16] Indeed, when we look carefully into the rhetoric of the 'square man,' we find a model of manhood often constituted by (rather than simply than constitutive of) a potentially static standard of measure aligned with geometric perfection. We find, that is, the man who must measure himself and others according to a model of regularity in which 'liveliness' is deeply compromised if not altogether repressed.[17] In this symbolic economy of geometric form, such vitality or 'liveliness' (as we shall eventually see) is often placed instead onto the curvilinear, the round, and the conspicuously 'out of square.'[18]

Recent critical approaches to the emergence of early modern 'norms' of gender, sexuality, and the body—by Valerie Traub, Jeffrey Masten, and Tom Conley—have in fact drawn upon the distinctly spatial, geometric figures of the square, which often stands as a kind of iconographic encapsulation of the constraints of normativity. The square that stands as, and/or in for, a space of normativity in Masten's *Queer Philologies*, for example, is grounded in the material and ideological conditions of writing and print. The capital letter 'Q,' he notes, when historically situated in terms of debates about language and writing, can stand as a veritable 'emblem' of 'queer philology,' not least because it was understood as a 'letter that does not maintain good order and moves beyond the square.'[19] Masten alludes here to the squares enclosing and also shaping each other letter of the alphabet in Geoffroy Tory's influential text on typography, *Champ fleury* (1529), where Q is the singular exception with a tail that exceeds the coordinates of the square. Tory overlaid some of his geometrically proportioned Roman capital letters onto the idealized figure of 'Vitruvian man' in an attempt to rationalize font and to elevate typography to a kind of microcosmic sphere that could reflect the geometric proportion of the cosmos and thus the glory of the creator (Figs. 2.1 and 2.2).

Just as importantly, however, the very idea that 'a man can fit in the square area,' writes Tom Conley in *The Self-Made Map*, 'suggests that a subject can be serialized according to Euclidean terms, hence regulated or replicated as an autonomous and infinitely reproducible form.'[20] This subjection of the human to spatialized models of standardization is similarly integral to what Valerie Traub has called the early modern 'conceptual logic of the grid,' literalized in cartographic contexts as a nexus of loosely quadrangular spaces into which representative persons or couples were placed on maps, instantiating for Traub an early conceptual syntax

Fig. 2.2 Geoffroy Tory, The letter "O", *Champ fleury* (Paris, 1529). The Huntington Library, San Marino, CA

of racial hierarchy intersecting with a monogamous, global heterosexuality.[21] The combination of Conley's allusion to a squared space that might enable the replication of standard human subjects and Traub's incipiently normativizing 'logic of the grid' makes it all too clear why Masten should close his Introduction with a moving desire to urge his readers, in and through the practice of queer philology, to move, in various ways, 'beyond the square.'

When Foucault asks, in *The Order of Things*, 'How does thought detach itself from the squares it inhabited before,' he raises a series of questions about how epistemology might function as a kind of 'normative' mode of thought articulated in and through the figure of the square.[22] If for Foucault, thought once 'inhabited' squares before managing to 'detach' itself, to find its way out, the presumption is of course that squares not only emblematize but lodge and structure thought itself. Without going so far as to suggest (à la Derrida) that there is nothing outside of the square, this essay aims, first, to trace the extent of the square's symbolic status as an icon of externally regulated and gendered forms of thought and behavior in early modern England. Second, it aims to demonstrate the paradoxically generative potential and constitutive status of the square for a range of 'deviant' dramatic subjectivities in plays including *Antony and Cleopatra* in which geometry and historically specific ideas of norms and normativity operate in ways that scholars have not fully recognized. By tracing relationships between squares and masculinity in early modern texts and contexts, we can consider the ideological dimensions of geometric form, reflect more deeply on the concept of *homo quadratus* in *Antony and Cleopatra*, and attend to broader questions of the geometry, gender and geography as well as the geometric history of 'norms.' Finally, by exploring the representation of Egyptian geometry in classical and early modern thought as well as in the play, I will argue that *Antony and Cleopatra* presents Shakespeare's most defiant critique of the logic of the square.

Squaring (with) Masculinity

In *Lines: A Brief History* (2016), the anthropologist Tim Ingold writes of the gendering and norming of rectilinearity in modern Western thought: 'The relentless dichotomizing dialectic of modern thought has, at one time or another, associated straightness with mind against matter, with rational thought as against sensory perception, with intellect as against intuition, with science as against traditional knowledge, with male against female.'[23] The longstanding epistemological analogies that have aligned the rectilinear not only with reason and intellect but with masculinity in particular are worth reconsidering from a number of different angles. For Ingold, Western distinctions between genders, cultures, and human 'kinds' have often been configured in terms of the rectilinear and the curvilinear, where 'straightness becomes an unambiguous index of masculinity, as curvature indexes femininity.'[24] Although Ingold does not use the word 'normal' in any critical or reflective way, his anthropology of lines may well recall, for literary and cultural critics, the rectilinear geometry of cultural norms that has fascinated scholars such as Sara Ahmed, whose 2006 *Queer Phenomenology: Orientations, Objects, Others* elaborated on the hegemony of the straight line in the establishment of various forms of sexual, gender, and cultural difference.[25] The vernacular concept of people who are straight rather than gay derives from this tradition.

But well before Ingold and Ahmed, the French philosopher and physician Georges Canguilhem—whose influential *The Normal and the Pathological* was first published in 1943—alluded not only to the line but to the perpendicular line and the T-square as part and parcel of an as-yet-unwritten prehistory of norms:

> When we know that *norma* is the Latin word for T-square and that *normalis* means perpendicular, we know almost all that must be known about the area in which the meaning of the terms 'norm' and 'normal' originated. [...] A norm, or rule, is what can be used to right, to square, to straighten. To set a norm (*normer*), to normalize, is to impose a requirement on existence.[26]

Expanding upon Ingold's connection between rectilinearity and masculinity in Western thought and Canguilhem's insights about the origin of the discourse and meaning of 'norms' in both the straight and the squared, I argue that the figure of the geometric square provided a more constraining form or norm of early modern masculinity than the straight, the upright, and the ruled might otherwise suggest.

For the list of oppositions noted by Ingold as features of modern thought might well be traced back to the Pythagorean oppositions, discussed in Aristotle's *Metaphysics*, which include not simply (and analogously) the male and the female, the straight and the curved, but *the square and the oblong*.[27] The square's potential as an icon of regularity, evenness, equality, and 'rightness' is certainly evident in early modern philosophical, theological, and broadly humanist traditions of thought as well, with masculinities often clearly indexed through the symbolism of the square rather than the straight line alone. When, for example, the preacher Edward Reynolds observed in *A Treatise of the Passions and Faculties of the Soule of Man* (1640) that 'all Goodnesse is necessarily adjoyned with Rectitude and Streightnesse (in that it is a Rule to direct our Life),' he was, of course, drawing on scripture.[28] But when he turns immediately from the line to the square, he borrows directly from Aristotle's more gendered discourse in the *Ethics*: 'and therefore a Good man, is called an Vpright man; one that is every where Even and Strait.

To which Aristotle perhaps had one Eye, when hee called his Happyman, a Foure-square man, which is every where smooth, stable, and like himself' (549). If the language of being 'like oneself' suggests a form of happiness that depends upon a constant imitation of oneself, such happiness can be, as Reynolds himself acknowledges, extremely 'uncomfortable' (350). To be 'like' oneself or 'every where Even and Strait,' that is, implies a constraining if morally regulated and philosophically authorized conception of selfhood that Reynolds calls 'uncomfortable' given 'mans Nature in this Estate of Corruption' which is 'Distorted' and 'Crooked.' Hence 'so many men are impatient of the close and narrow passage of honesty. For crooked and reeling Movers necessarily require more Liberty of way, more broad courses to exercise themselves in: [...] as we see in natural Bodies, a crooked thing will not bee held within so narrow bounds' (350). Such geometric metaphors of selfhood suggest that the process of being 'every where Even and Strait' is perhaps no less difficult than fitting a round peg in a square hole, and that the 'foursquare' man is aligned (to recall Aristotle's *Rhetoric*) with restricted mobility.

While Aristotle's 'square man' evoked for some early commentators the necessity of the four cardinal virtues ('cardinal' from *cardo* or 'hinge') of prudence (wisdom), temperance (moderation), justice (rectitude), and courage (fortitude) for the consistently happy man, the attention to the abstractly quadrangular and symmetrical dimensions of this masculinized norm were integral to numerous commentaries and translations.[29] Of the adage '*quadratus homo*,' for example, Erasmus cites Aristotle's *Ethics* and proceeds to observe, 'Now a square remains a square, whichever side it falls on. In the same way, the wise man remains unchanged in his essential self, however events fall out.' While glossing the aptness of the metaphor, Erasmus emphasizes the logic of self-same, firm, durable integrity, but goes further to suggest the appropriateness of the square as a fitting emblem for the mind and not simply (as he suggests that Aristotle had it) for the moral and behavioral constancy of the temperate, moderate, or 'wise' man: 'It will be even neater to apply the term 'four-square' to the actual mind of the wise man, which remains unshaken in the face of fortunes blows.'[30]

Erasmus's emphasis on the unshakably balanced and right-thinking *mind* is due, in part, to his understanding of classically and biblically structured relationships between the square and the principle of order itself: 'Anything appropriate and fitting is said to "square,"' he writes in a gloss on the classical adage '*in quadrum redigere*' ('to square up' or 'to put in order'). 'The metaphor is derived from stonemasons,' he adds, evoking the work of ancient builders and the biblical notion of God as a stonemason (Peter 2.5–2.9), which linked the practical and the divine in the foundational logic of the ideal pattern. The architectural and artisanal dimensions of the 'unshakable' square that could provide a strong, stable, solid foundation linked a physics of strength and stability with the good man. Erasmus in fact opens his gloss on *'in quadrum redigere'* with a reminder of the 'unalterable spirit' of Aristotle's *'quadratus homo,'* indirectly linking all that is 'appropriate and the fitting' with masculine stability and durability. As he observes elsewhere in a three-dimensional variant of the Aristotelian square man, 'The wise man is like a cube, always fixed and unmovable.'[31]

For Erasmus and many others, the 'square' functioned as a figure of discursive as well as personal (or moral, mental, spiritual and/or physical) structure and strength. Cicero used the phrase 'to square up,' observes Erasmus, 'in a metaphorical way in the *Orator*, when he was speaking of well-arranged, rhythmical diction.'[32] Much later, the nineteenth-century English physician Robert Bland, following Erasmus's gloss on *'in quadrum redigere,'* notes not only that when 'the parts of any object, or of any speech or composition, agree [...] they are said to be quadrate,' but adds that 'the man whose conduct is consistent and right, is said *to act upon the square.*'[33] The square thus offers a foundational material, lexical, and symbolic arena for exploring the early structure of 'norms' and the 'normal,' of acting, as it were, 'upon the square' as both an ideal *and* as a predictable and replicable form of masculine conduct.

In his *Arte of English Poesie* (1589), George Puttenham draws together Plato's alignment of the cube with the element of earth in his cosmology of creation, the *Timaeus*, and Aristotle's concept of the 'square man' or *'hominem quadratum'* as the man not easily bothered, in order to discuss the significance of the literalized geometric square as possible space within which to situate a poem. Personifying and masculinizing said *'quadrangle equilater,'* Puttenham writes:

> The square is of all other accompted the figure of most solliditie and stedfastnesse, and for his owne stay and firmitie requireth none other base then himselfe, and therefore ... is the square for his inconcussable [unshakeable] steadinesse likened to the earth. ... Into this figure [of Aristotle's square man] may ye reduce your ditties by vsing no moe verses then your verse is of sillables, which will make him fall out [of] square, if ye go aboue it.[34]

This 'square man,' self-reliant and strong, needing only his own 'base' for support, and aligned more with the earth than the heavens, may well convey the graphic conditions of reproducible masculinity in the guise of autonomy that, according to Conley, marked the geometrically uniform bodies in Tory's *Champ fleury*. While Puttenham's particular square provides a formal condition for artistic experimentation, it is presented in a way that prioritizes the geometric shape over the metrics of verse, the shape over the sound, since even an additional syllable in this shape poem would 'make him fall out [of] square' and since, in contrast to the other shape poems presented by Puttenham, there is no example provided of an actual square poem. The metaphysically supercharged language of geometric form, moreover, contrasts with the witty if comparatively trivial 'ditty' to be inserted. Here we *might* begin to see an instance of the 'logic of the grid' that in some sense counteracts, even as it informs, a newly 'rationalized' form of writing.

One of the common adjectival senses of 'square' in early modern England referred to a predominantly masculinized form of physical strength (a strong, solid frame), a usage likely rooted in earlier philosophical alignments between squares, earthly forms of embodiment and structural stability (*OED*, s.v. 'square, adj.'). Puttenham of course appeals to a classical rhetoric of proportion as a key to aesthetics while also conjuring the architectural vocabulary of foundational strength. The square as an icon of moral rectitude and humoral balance could, at times, operate across genders, as could the iconography of the squared human and the divine circle.[35] And yet symbolic geometry under a female sovereign led to a common alignment of the circle's perfection with both God and Queen. While Puttenham observes in traditional terms that spheres have no 'angle' to 'stay or entangle' motion (implying unimpeded agency and movement) and no beginning or end which suggested 'eternitie,' for example, he aligns the perfect, god-like curvilinear form with Queen Elizabeth, not simply as the sovereign exception aligned with both the curved and the straight, but as the dominant female 'ruler' who marks or measures the difference between sovereign and subject.[36] Whereas Puttenham uses the square to index the 'square man,' he uses the 'Roundel or Spheare' to make a tribute to Elizabeth, who, as exemplary 'beame' (meaning 'radius'), 'circle,' and 'center' makes it all too clear just how, as Puttenham emphasizes, 'eche subject […] is bound' (81–82).

Importantly, given the frequency with which the square came to instantiate a normative conception of regular masculinity, it is interesting to note that when put in explicit relationship to the circle or sphere, the square was also put in tension within competing hierarchies of perfection, potentially in its 'place' in socio-political as well as metaphysical terms. For even if the square is, as Aristotle put it, 'perfect,' the circle is, of course, *more* perfect. Aristotle himself followed Plato in understanding the circle (and its three-dimensional variant, the sphere) as the most perfect of shapes.[37] So too, Puttenham elevates circular over quadrangular and other forms, the sphere 'most voluble and apt to turne, and to continue motion, which is the author of life' (91).

Thus when the squared regularization or 'norming' of masculinity was set in relationship to the circle, the sphere, and related properties, uncomfortable conditions of inhabiting a norm could come into view, including specters of subjection, incommensurability, finitude or mortality, limited mobility, and fictions of autonomy. Tory's Roman capital letter 'O,' pictured above, may offer a hint of such discomfort. There the squared man may also be perfectly encircled, but his body is stretched to its physical limit. The potential discomfort of the square in relationship to the circle can be gleaned more directly, however, in an anonymous English academic allegorical drama set in contemporary Rome, *Blame Not Our Author* (c. 1633), in which all the characters are geometric shapes or instruments and the central character is 'Quadro' (the Italian for 'square' from the Latin *quadrus*).[38] The play in fact opens with Quadro lamenting his foursquare abjection in the cosmic order of things, momentarily wishing the world itself might be burnt and new-created, making 'a quadro of this circled universe' (37). Realizing the folly of such a conceit, he decides, despite the challenge of his own 'essential nature,' to 'change my forme' (40, 41). He then proceeds to attempt, through a variety of medical means and physical contortions (include being bound in two hoops) to become 'all orbicular' so that he might partake of the Nature's rounded form, and in fact be as morphologically 'vnbounded' as his 'passions' are at the start of the play (29–31). A twenty-first century production of this play might well stage it as a kind of geometrically imagined transgender fantasy, but the play ultimately dramatizes the limits of a masculinized norm configured as a square.

In this play of spatial hierarchy, the fact that Line is subordinate to Quadro mirrors the classical order of geometrical and cognitive progression (understood to move from point to line to plane to solid), but also speaks, again, to the centrality of the square in the structural history of 'norms.' Line's extensive praise of Quadro expands upon and beyond the tropes of the 'foursquare man' that we have seen thus far, making Antony's appeal to the normalizing function of the square legible in more ways than one. That Quadro, 'being stable and immouable on euery side' (368), as Line puts it, is 'compard to wisdome itselfe' (365–366) is no surprise. But Line elaborates on the foundational dimensions of the square for the establishment of Roman identity, alluding first to the *Roma Quadrata* of the legendary Romulus, observing that 'the very citty of Rome was in auncient time built in Quadro' (269–270), and then noting that, in architectural terms, the square stands firm as the 'basis of all the most potent and eminent pillars' of Rome (1025–1029). We might hear echoes here of Antony's invocation of the square, not least given his compromised status as a military defender of Rome, where he once fought, as he puts it, in the 'brave squares of war' (3.11.40). The squared foundation of 'the most potent and eminent pillars' of Rome also calls to mind the vivid image of the 'triple pillar of the world [now] transform'd' by Antony's passion for Cleopatra (1.1.12).

Quadro, in some ways a comic, two-dimensional variant of Shakespeare's Antony, finds the conditions of being 'four cornered' constraining and yet, in attempting to become round with the help of others, suddenly imagines himself all too close to death by realizing his transformation would itself be a form of assisted suicide ('I perish in my metamorphosis. Help! help!' [218]). Quadro's various states of emotional excess—melancholy, madness, and extremes of 'passion' which, as he puts it, 'draws me from myself' (308)—are aligned, in part, with his frustrating incommensurability with the circle. It is not that Quadro is anything less than 'square,' it is that he is nothing more: the constraints of inhabiting such a structurally 'ordinary' 'norm' are what gives rise to his equal and opposite condition acting, as it were, 'out of square.'[39] Here the square finds its space of abjection: Quadro remains a 'corner creeper,' giving a rather graphic sense of what 'being cornered' might look or feel like. When Line observes that any man who exceeds the Vitruvian anatomical ideal of squared proportion would be considered 'of extraordinary size' (that is to say, enormous), we hear a kind of double-edged compliment since the 'extraordinary' is precisely what our Quadro wants to be. From the opening moments of the play when he observes his 'passions' range 'vnbounded,' he is grappling with the constraints of being all too normal.

Such faultlines of normativity could become evident when geometry was set to stage, when at times familiar distinctions between the square and the circle were aligned not simply with finite and infinite (as in *Blame Not*) but with male and female. It is perhaps no surprise that at various moments in early modern drama, it is often a female figure who is understood as leading the male figure 'out of square.'[40] *Antony and Cleopatra* is a case in point, since the measured symbolism of the 'square' as an index of norm and deviance at once is used by Antony as an expression of his loss of composure (not to mention his reputation as military hero) under the influence of Cleopatra, whose 'strong Egyptian fetters' (chains) he 'must break' (1.2.105). The stakes of what it meant for Antony to be out of square are emphasized, it is important to note, in terms of a distinctly militarized conception of the square. This is made spatially and theatrically evident in Act Four as the soldiers '*place themselves in every corner of the stage*' (4.3). The square as a strong but also defensive formation in military contexts is signaled here, since the soldiers are, at this point, on watch. But if at this moment the square space of the stage becomes 'occupied,' militarized, masculinized, that space also becomes the platform upon which 'acting upon the square' becomes linked with a form of performativity subject to scrutiny.

The combination of qualities aligned with the square that included, as we have seen thus far, steadfastness, stability, moderation, reliability, self-reliance, honesty, and manifest physical strength were conceptually compatible with masculinities represented in military manuals which flourished in England in the sixteenth and early seventeenth centuries. The term 'squadron,' itself, which entered into English in the 1560s from the Italian *squadrone* for battalion and *squadra* for square, aligned the very existence of military groups with the geometrical formation of bodies at war. The etymological connection was not lost on Shakespeare's contemporaries. According to Henry Cockeram's 1623 *English Dictionarie: Or, An Interpreter of Hard English Words*, for example, the word 'squadron' is defined in full as 'a square forme in a battel,' so that we have here a striking conflation of the military formation of the 'square' with the military group itself.[41] Patricia Cahill has persuasively argued that the military manuals of sixteenth-century England worked, through geometric figurations as well as 'mustering' standards, to constitute and disseminate a new 'norm' of the 'common' soldier and refined ideas of masculinity in the process: '[p]erhaps the most succinct expression of this aggregate social body may be found in the diagrams of troop formations that turn up frequently in the pages of the Elizabethan military treatises.'[42]

Although Cahill observes that troop formations of course consisted of configurations beyond the 'straightforward square,' the square (the infantry or hollow square) was commonly discussed in classical historiographies of war and was often understood as a defensive formation, a way to minimize the impact of a sudden assault.[43] The word 'square' itself was all the more dynamic in the early modern period as it could imply both persons situated within an ordered military formation and persons engaged in an act of 'squaring' or fighting.[44] When Antony speaks nostalgically of his experience in the 'brave squares of war' (3.2.40), he evokes 'squares' as noun and verb, troop formation and courageous military action at once. If the military square was aligned with virtues of strength, reliability, and steadfastness, the vulnerability and violence subtending this spatially configured norm is, to a modern ear or eye, perhaps all too evident. When we hear, in *Henry V* of 'our superfluous lackeys and our peasants, / Who in unnecessary action swarm / About our squares of battle' (4.2.25–27), Shakespeare conjures a distinctly classed, male social body aggregated in the image of the swarm and military 'square' at once.

In Antony's avowed deviation from his 'square,' then, we have not only a rhetorical performance of moral and masculine norming demarcated in the language of geometric rectitude, self-sameness, and containment, but subtle attention to the square as a familiar military term. Antony's departure from the square as a military fighter and leader thus constitutes a double allusion to Aristotle's *quadratus homo*, as Aristotle in fact invoked the ideal 'military general' as one of just two specific examples of his 'foursquare man,' remaining consistent in action and temperament at once: 'For the man who is truly good and wise, we think, bears all the chances of life becomingly and always makes the best of circumstances, as a good general makes the best military use of the army at his command.'[45] Even when Antony attempts to 'make the best of circumstances' in the play, he is still often patently out of square.

Given the initial founding of Rome as a 'square,' discussed in Plutarch's 'Life of Romulus,' mentioned in *Blame Not*, and potentially indexed in the occupation of the four corners of the stage in *Antony and Cleopatra*, the square offers a kind of ground zero for a distinctly Roman variant of the 'foursquare' man. It is striking in this respect that in *Blame Not* (itself a veritable compendium of symbolic geometry), the circle is a kind of ground zero for Egyptian power and identity, said to have older historical and mythological roots than the square in the Egyptian figure of the Ouroboros, the serpent eating its own tail as a sign of eternal return. This very figure, central to the regeneration myth of Isis, as Barbara J. Bono has observed, also becomes aligned with Cleopatra late in *Antony and Cleopatra*, at Cydnus, where the phallic serpent takes a distinctly ecstatic circular turn, not least given Cleopatra's identification with, and death by, the serpent or 'asp.'[46] The sovereign Queen aligned with the straight and the circular, as we saw in Puttenham's tribute to Queen Elizabeth, is in many ways characteristic of the exceptionality of Cleopatra, who offers more capacious and kinetic geometries of identity and identification than the masculinized square.[47] Before further complicating distinctions between forms of geometry and gender in Shakespeare's play, however, I want to ask a more fundamental question about geometric form on stage.

What does or can drama 'do' with and to the 'foursquare man,' or the form of the square itself as indexed through character names, rhetorical terms, spatial coordinates, and the space of the stage itself? Given the two-dimensionality and inflexibility of the geometric square alone, it is perhaps no surprise to see that comedy often ensues, as in the case of Quadro unable to escape his bounds, and who is ultimately subject, in the final lines of the play, to both Ruler and Compass. In more nuanced terms, we might recall the character *Quadratus* (Latin for 'square' as well as a Roman cognomen) in John Marston's *What You Will* (1601). This ironically named Quadratus, anything but Vitruvian man or Aristotelian 'square man,' is fat, he overflows the measure in both corpulence and rhetoric, vacillates between joviality and melancholia, stoicism and epicureanism, undermining the geometrical logic of his name, to the audience's delight. If Aristotle's 'square man,' as Erasmus reiterates, is antithetical to the man of emotional extremes who 'appears as a kind of chameleon, being sometimes happy, sometimes unhappy, according as his circumstances change, just as the chameleon changes color,'[48] Marston's Quadratus is his own anti-type, a kind of Falstaff exceeding the bounds of masculine as well as military virtue. The particular alignment of the concept of geometric rectitude and consistency with a person's name, 'Quadratus,' was of course historical, as was the relationship between the square and ideals of moderation. But the very idea of *staging* 'quadratus' renders the ideal of spatial-behavioral rectitude not simply excessively idealistic, fictional and, in a way, absurd, but also rife for comic inversion.

Another striking instance in which the norm of squared masculinity is both challenged and potentially reified through comic inversion emerges in *The Lady of May*, Sir Philip Sidney's earlier (and only) dramatic entertainment, commissioned by his uncle Robert Dudley for Queen Elizabeth, which took place at Dudley's estate in Wanstead. Sidney's drama involved the monarch as the judge between two male competitors for a young woman's hand and featured a hilariously pedantic Latin teacher named 'Rombus.' Rombus, although most well known as the prototype for Shakespeare's Holofernes in *Love's Labour's Lost*, presents contortions of language and action clearly linked to the spatial structure of his name. For if the geometric 'rhombus' is, as Puttenham put it, 'in his kind a kind of quadrangle in reverse,' it is no surprise to find Sidney's 'Rombus' lacking 'squared' self-composure at every step. 'As a rhomboid lacks right angles,' Robert Stillman observed, Sidney's 'Rombus lacks rightness in his reasoning.'[49] The fact that Rombus' language is comically 'out of square' is especially ironic given his own emphasis on his use of 'geometricall proportion' in the training and disciplining of youths. His opening speech at the outset of the play should suffice to conjure his character:

> *Then came forward Maister Rombus, and with many speciall graces made this learned oration*:
>
> Now the thunder-thumping Ioue transfund his dotes into your excellent formosity which haue with your resplendent beames thus segregated the enmitie of these rurall animals I am *Potentissima Domina*, a schoole maister, that is to say, a Pedagogue, one not a little versed in the disciplinating of the iuuentall frie wherein (to my laud I say it) I vse such geometricall proportion, as neither wanted mansuetude nor correction, for so it is described.

This pedant who takes 'geometricall proportion' as his guide to the correct cultivation of discipline and docility ('*man*suetude')[50] in his students clearly undermines, with his inkhornisms, neologisms and mangled 'formosity,' the alignment between good rhetorical, behavioral and geometric form that he claims to stands for. The fact that Sidney has engaged Queen Elizabeth as judge raises, again, the specter of vulnerable geometries of masculinity in the face of a sovereign woman or *Potentissima Domina* ('most powerful woman').

While Sidney was clearly appealing to Dudley's special interests in geometry,[51] the fact that Dudley had vied unsuccessfully for Elizabeth's hand for many years leading up to *The Lady of May* suggests that the symbolic relationship between the square, the rhombus, and the sovereign would have been especially significant. Given the exceptional status of the sovereign who transcends strict definitions of gender, genre, and in this case, moral form, it is notable that Queen Elizabeth is positioned in the prefatory poem of the play as having characteristics of the best of both genders combined. Rombus offsets anxieties of masculinity by inhabiting, to an absurd degree, everything that might go wrong with an attempt to 'square' one's language and self in the 'geometricall proportion' while inhabiting a drama of political and theatrical subjection. The drama is set up of course to appeal to the Queen's power to judge, to decide which kind of 'man' (the poetic shepherd or the vitally active forester in this case) is preferable. The fact that the Queen chooses the shepherd, despite the rhetorical advantage that Sidney gives to the more active forester, would have created an uncomfortable situation for Sidney if not, as Stephen Orgel has suggested, an utter 'fiasco.'[52] But at the same time, the fact that Rhombus mangles the angles of ideal proportion in temperament, decorum and language alike work to generate a brilliantly entertaining comic figure that could appeal to sovereign and subject alike. Given Sidney's own emphasis in his *Apology for Poetry* on the importance of 'measured quantity' in language, entailing 'number, measure, order and proportion,'[53] moreover, Rombus in a sense reifies humanist ideals of measure and wisdom through the performance of error.[54]

The performance of particular norms in dramatic contexts could of course subject them to scrutiny and/or reify or reconstitute them. Characters such as 'Quadro,' 'Quadratus,' and 'Rombus' certainly do a combination of both—but they also open up further consideration of the etymological, spatial, symbolic and cultural grounds and paradoxes of normality as such.

CIRCLING THE SQUARE: GEOMETRY'S ORIGIN, ANTONY'S END

Tensions between the squared and the curved, as I have begun to suggest, inform just one strain of imagery in *Antony and Cleopatra* that pertains to the history of 'norms.' Given that the square is predominantly aligned with Rome rather than Egypt, it may well seem that

Shakespeare is adding the kind of 'European imaginative geometry' that polarizes East and West to the Pythagorean table of male and female, light and dark, square and oblong, straight and curved.[55] Recent criticism has shown the play to be more complex in its fleshed out engagement with social geometries,[56] but in criticism informed, variously, by deconstruction, feminism, queer theory and postcolonial studies, almost every binary in the play seems to have been examined and consequently undone—but for the opposition between a *literally* 'measured' Rome and an 'unmeasured' Egypt. It is that binary that I want to complicate in this final section as we work toward the more dynamic aspects of squaring and circling in the play itself.[57]

It is a commonplace of criticism on *Antony and Cleopatra* that Rome and Egypt are distinct in terms of ideologies and practices of 'measure' with which the play begins. 'The Roman world is a world of rigid ranks and boundaries, but from the very beginning this architectural order is threatened with dissolution by Egypt's "space",' writes a recent critic in an familiar formulation that is often upheld even by those who proceed to deconstruct a range of other binaries in the play.[58] This is certainly understandable given Antony's own confession of being out of 'square' while in Egypt, a comment anticipated by the opening words of the play, which of course aligns him with the Nile itself in a passion that 'o'erflows the measure' (or 'exceeds suitable bounds')[59] in Egypt as he neglects his military duties in Rome.

> *Philo*: Nay, but this dotage of our general's
> O'erflows the measure: those his goodly eyes,
> That o'er the files and musters of the war
> Have glow'd like plated Mars, now bend, now turn
> The office and devotion of their view
> Upon a tawny front.
>
> (1.1.1–6)

Not only does Antony 'o'erflow' the measure while in Egypt but also neglects the 'files and musters' of his military troops, or aggregated men, in the name of the singular Cleopatra.

But what is overlooked in the dichotomy between 'measured' Rome and a boundless or excessive Egypt is the play's attention to the specific practices of measurement and calculation alongside the more dramatic forms of prognostication *in Egypt*. Although I have largely focused on Antony's conflicted relationship with the ever symbolic 'square,' it is, curiously, Cleopatra who invokes a rhetoric of measure and geometry in the face of Antony's hyperbolic excess in the opening scene, and who returns to geometry in the final act of the play.

> *Cleopatra*: If it be love indeed, tell me how much.
> *Mark Antony*: There's beggary in the love that can be reckon'd.
> *Cleopatra*: I'll set a bourn how far to be beloved.
> *Mark Antony*: Then must thou needs find out new heaven, new earth
> (1.1.14–17)

The contrast between an Egyptian Queen setting a 'bourn' or geometric boundary and the Roman lover's rhetoric of immeasurability generates a playfully charged exchange. Yet the contrast itself, positioned at the outset of the play, might encourage us to remember that, in classical and early modern historiography, the science of measuring the earth (including land and water) was understood to have originated in Egypt. The Egyptian origin of geometry was recounted by Herodotus and Aristotle, followed by Proclus, Strabo and others, as was the further development and formalization of geometry by Euclid in Alexandria in particular under the reign of the Ptolomies.[60] If geometry informs a predominantly Western conception of 'norms,' Shakespeare sets the history of the Western norm in relationship with its Egyptian forebear in ways that can help us see the extent to which the play attends to the structural and cultural history of the 'normal' as an aspect of gender.

The origin of geometry in Egypt, and in relationship to the Nile in particular, was recounted in a number of Renaissance English texts, including those on the arts of measurement which flourished in the vernacular in the sixteenth-century, continuing a tradition of historiography of geometry that exists in textbooks today. 'Geometry,' as Thomas Paynell put it in the preface to Richard Benese's (1547) *The boke of measurying of lande*, was founded 'vpon the excursions and ouerflowing of the floud Nilus whose insidacions and surges were suche that they confounded and so troubled the lymytes and bondes of the land of Egypt, that they knew not theyr owne Lande from other mēnes.'[61] To be sure, poets such as Spenser, Drayton, and Shakespeare offered vivid associations of the Nile with distinctly troubled limits or bounds.[62] But it was the overflowing Nile, that dominant source of imagery in *Antony and Cleopatra*, that gave rise to the art of geometry, which included not only the setting of 'limits and bounds,' as Paynell puts it, but the measurement of water as well as land,[63] and the development of skills and tools for the arts of building, of war, and, suggestively for the play's trajectory, the lifting of heavy weights:

> Of this toke Geometrye hys Oryginall begynnyng the which includeth the *measuring both of lande & water, the vse of weyghtes and knowledge of the vniuersall ordre of the bodyes aboue,* ... Artyficers doe vse Geometrye, by the which all maner of ingynes and craftye ordynaunces of warre, and other apperteynynge vnto theyr arte doe depend as hangynge roofes, and Galaryes, wal|les, shyppes, Gallayes, Brydges, Milles Cartes, and wheeles, *with the whyche, thynges of great weyght, are verye easlye drawen and hoysed vp.* (italics added, sig. A4$^{r\text{-}v}$)

Recalling the much ado about Antony, himself 'of great weyght' who is 'drawen and hoysed vp' to Cleopatra in Act 4, may also prompt us to explore the play's engagement with 'geometric' language and problems at work in Egypt, even as the language of military 'rule' and moderation operates, to a certain degree, in Rome. In Act 5 it is Cleopatra's familiarity with geometry that stands out, particularly the geometric practice transported from Egypt to Rome where, she imagines, 'rules, and hammers' of Roman '[m]echanic slaves' working to 'Uplift us to the view' (5.2. 205, 207). More important than an Egyptian Queen versed in the language and work of geometry (itself a facet of historiography) is a Queen whose rhetoric challenges the opposition of 'Western' uses of geometry with those of the 'East,' not least as she resists a future in which Roman soldiers 'hoist me up,' preferring death upon the Pyramids: 'Rather make / My country's high pyramides my gibbet [gallows] / And hang me up in chains!' (5.2.59–61).

This contest of Egyptian and Roman geometric languages and practices comes earlier in the play. Antony, in conversation with Caesar in Act 2 while aboard Pompey's galley, for example, offers a gloss on the feats of measurement particular to Egypt:

> Thus do they, sir: they take the flow o' the Nile
> By certain scales i' the pyramid; they know,
> By the height, the lowness, or the mean, if dearth
> Or foison follow: the higher Nilus swells,
> The more it promises: as it ebbs, the seedsman
> Upon the slime and ooze scatters his grain,
> And shortly comes to harvest.
> (2.7.17–23)

Lepidus soon interjects, drunkenly, 'I have heard the Ptolemies' pyramises are very goodly things; without contradiction, I have heard that,' further connecting the legacy of the Ptolomies in Cleopatra's family line with the power of Egyptian and Alexandrian measurement.

The plainness of Antony's testament to the power of measurement in Egypt calls attention to a power that in many senses *exceeds* coordinates of Roman 'measure' alluded to in the opening line of the play. It is not simply the awe-inspiring construction of the Pyramids that is singled out, but again the capacity to measure water precisely and forecast agricultural conditions, even as that water may have seemed, in other contexts, to 'o'erflow the measure.' Pliny's *Natural History* (c. 77–79 AD), and Leo Africanus' *A Geographical Historie of Africa* (1550), translated into English in 1601 and 1600, respectively, included sections on Egyptian geometry and on techniques of measuring the 'flow' of water in particular.[64] Pliny, naval commander under the Roman Empire, observed the extent to which Egyptians were able to 'taketh good keep and reckoning' of the Nile: 'How high it riseth is knowne by certain markes and measures taken of certain pits,' with fluctuating heights calculated in cubits, the 'mean' or 'ordinary height' being 'sixteen cubits.'[65] The 'pit' is described more technically by Leo Africanus as a 'fouresquare cestern or chanell of eighteene cubits deepe, whereinto the water of Nilus is conueied by a certaine sluce vnder the ground. And in the midst of the cestern there is erected a certaine piller, which is marked and diuided into so many cubits as the cesterne it selfe containeth in depth' (1601: 312). The particular 'foursquare' device described is, as Africanus observes, located in 'Michias, that is to say, *The isle of measure*' where 'they haue a kinde of deuise inuented by the ancient Egyptians, whereby they most certainly foresee the plentie or scarcitie of the yeere following throughout all the land of Egypt' (312, italics added). The mobilization of the 'foursquare,' the 'cubit,' and the 'pillar' in 'the isle of measure' thus enabled Egyptians to rationalize agricultural forecasting and planning alike. Such testaments to the powers of measure and engineering in Egypt provide a striking contrast to the limits of Roman models of 'measure' (be it through 'files' 'squares' or lofty 'pillars') in *Antony and Cleopatra*. Indeed, Antony's distance from such power of applied geometry is perhaps allegorically indexed by his failures to win his battles at sea, not to mention his comic description of the crocodile that invokes a language of geometry and yet communicates absolutely nothing: 'It is shaped, sir, like itself, and it is as broad as it hath breadth. It is just so high as it is, and moves with its own organs' (2.7.40–42). The echo of the rhetoric of the geometric 'square' here, always 'shaped … like itself,' 'as broad as it hath breadth,' may suggest yet another being who cannot or does not fit within the logic of the square.

If, then, Antony fails to keep 'square' in the sense of the classical code of manly, military, and moral measure, such 'deviance' might be seen as a feature of the limits of Roman measurements and 'norms' in the face of a more capacious Egyptian history of, and approaches to, measurement. (Even the Egyptian soothsayer trumps, as Antony observes, the logic of fate or fortune incarnated in that cube, the die, upon which fates could so often be cast.) Given that Antony also incarnates the antithesis of the Roman norm of the emotionally moderate, steadfast, honest man (even turning from the orchestration of military troops in 'squares of war' on land to fruitless fight by water), it is as if he is, in more ways than one, stretching toward a more dynamic model of measurement that also leads to his tragic demise.

Indeed, recalling the logic of masculinity encoded in the classically based language of measurement discussed earlier in this essay, let us now return to Cleopatra's facility with the language of the 'mean' or moderate 'square man' of Aristotle's *Ethics*: 'What, was he sad or merry,' she asks of Antony during his time in Rome at the end of the opening act:

> *Alexas*:   Like to the time o' the year between the extremes
> Of hot and cold, he was nor sad nor merry.
> *Cleopatra*: O well-divided disposition! Note him,
> Note him good Charmian, 'tis the man; but note him:
> He was not sad, for he would shine on those
> That make their looks by his; he was not merry,
> Which seem'd to tell them his remembrance lay
> In Egypt with his joy; but between both:
> O heavenly mingle!
>   (1.5.50–58)

Cleopatra here lauds her Antony for inhabiting the very disposition described by Aristotle as the moderation of the 'foursquare man.' The masculine ideal of moderation is combined here with ideal of humoural balance, a pairing which worked, according to Alexandra Shepherd, to help shore up vulnerable ideologies of masculinity in early modern England.[66] Yet such a 'norm' is swiftly coded as fully performative and unnecessarily limiting by Cleopatra, as she continues, 'Be'st thou sad or

merry, / The violence of either thee becomes, / So does it no man else.'
(5.1.59–60)

Antony thus stands, for Cleopatra, apart from the ideal of masculinity. He is rather a singular 'man' whose extremes, excesses, or immoderation of temperament 'becomes' him *as* a man, in fact an enormous man. This singular masculinization of the passionate man, out of square, does more than counter the denigration of Antony by the Romans from the opening moments of the play.[67] If it is Egypt that offers an escape from the masculine norm, it is not because 'Egypt' is less inclined to measure, but because it is more capacious in doing so. Indeed, over the course of the play, in Cleopatra's imagination, Antony comes to stands a god-like figure in a world marked by imagery of circles, spheres, curves, and elemental fluidity:

> His face was as the heav'ns, and therein stuck
> A sun and moon, which kept their course and lighted
> The little O, the earth [...]
> His legs bestrid the ocean, his reared arm
> Crested the world. His voice was propertied
> As all the tuned spheres, and that to friends;
> But when he meant to quail and shake the orb,
> He was as rattling thunder. For his bounty,
> There was no winter in't; an autumn 'twas
> That grew the more by reaping. His delights
> Were dolphin-like, they showed his back above
> The element they lived in. In his livery
> Walked crowns and crownets. Realms and islands were
> As plates dropped from his pocket.
> (5.2. 79–90)

There is nothing angular, rectangular, or moderate about this extraordinary set of images. In Egypt, Antony has far exceeded the quadratic measure of man, has encountered the circles, the spheres and orbs, and liquid curves and become more not less, a man. The geography of land, of 'realms and islands,' is itself circular, like 'plates' (or 'silver coins') so distinct from the *Roma quadrata*. Rather than making 'the circle square,' as John Donne put it vividly of so much religious verse, which only 'thrust into straight corners of poor wit / Thee, who art cornerless and infinite,'[68] Cleopatra circles the square. Antony's enormity is different, here, from earlier celebrations of his singularity as, say, 'the greatest soldier in the world,' or as an Atlas bearing the globe on his powerfully squared shoulders, or even as that man so singularly out of square. This new Antony does not hold the world up but 'crests' or crowns and embraces it, rounds his reared arm about the globe as a body at once shaped for and by it. If the description combines the sacred imagery of divine perfection, be it the Ouroboros of Isis or the 'cornerless' eternality of Christianity, with an enormity (in both senses of the word) of gender, this brings us to the potential of sacred logic not simply to insist on the square or the straight, but also to aspire to a model of enormity that challenged even as it also helped to constitute the shape of the masculine norm.[69]

The word 'bourn' meant at once a spatial or geometric 'boundary' and a body of moving water, a 'small stream' (*OED* s.v. 'bourn, n.'). Having playfully promised to 'set a bourn' to measure love at the outset of the play, we might now recognize that Cleopatra has indeed set a 'bourn' for her love that, in a way, stretches toward a 'new heaven, new earth' by deconstructing the boundary between land and water, here and there, stasis and flow—in a way that perfectly suits historiographic accounts of Egypt as a land of precisely measured O'erflow and awe-inspiring geometric innovation.

Caesar's final call for a return to 'High order' in Rome thus not only recalls the limited and measured models of masculinity based upon a predominantly linear and squared model of order—the 'brave squares of war,' the mobilization of 'files' or lines of troop formations, and restraint in the expression of self—but proves second best to that higher order indexed by Cleopatra. At the same time, if Antony in fact is, as he is imagined by Caesar, the 'abstract of all faults / That *all men follow*' (1.4.9–10, emphasis added), he embodies the faultlines of normativity that Shakespeare transforms from deviance to dramatically partial (and thus tragic) potential.

Acknowledgements Enormous thanks to Rory Loughnane and Edel Semple for inviting me to contribute to this volume and pushing me well beyond my earlier work on the geometric figures and conceptions of the norm in early modern drama (Mazzio 2004). Deepest thanks go to Sujata Iyengar for asking me to collaborate on an essay on the topic of squares and *Antony and Cleopatra* for this volume. Our schedules made collaboration impossible, but she inspired this essay, pushed me in the direction of military discourse, and offered perspectives on Spenser and moral treatises that I hope to incorporate in a later incarnation of this essay. Tremendous thanks to William Fisher, Jeffrey Masten and Valerie

Traub for their generous comments on this essay, and to Catherine Bates, Heidi Brayman, Jen Jahner and Heather James for offering crucial insights on an early draft. Finally, I am grateful to Huntington Library, where I conducted the research for this essay.

Notes

1. Shakespeare (2011), gloss to 2.3.6–7. Unless otherwise noted, all citations to *Antony and Cleopatra* will be from Ania Loomba's edition. All other citations to Shakespeare's works are from the *Arden Shakespeare Complete Works* (2001).
2. Ibid.: 36, n. 6.
3. Georges Canguilhem long ago observed the social logic of the rectilinear, the straight and the right, as integral to the logic of the 'normal': 'The concept of right, depending on whether it is a matter of geometry, morality, or technology, *qualifies what offers resistance* to its application as twisted, crooked, or awkward' (1978: 146).
4. Cawdrey (1604), s.v. 'enormious.'
5. Ibid.: sv 'enormous, adj' and 'enorm, adj.'
6. *The Oxford English Dictionary*, 2nd edn., sv 'enormous, adj.'
7. Ibid.: s.v. 'norma, n,' and 'normal, adj,' 'enormous' and 'enorm.'
8. Plutarch (1924: 163).
9. On Vitruvius and the square as model for 'man,' the stage, and the architectonics of memory in the early modern period, see Yates's classic work (1966).
10. See Thomas Kyd, *The Spanish Tragedy*, 3rd Addition to 1602 Q4, scene XI (21–25) in Boas (1851: 59). I am indebted to Rory Loughnane for this particular citation.
11. Foucault (2007: 57). On manhood in early modern England in particular, see Alexandra Shepherd (2006) and Hutson (1994).
12. *Aristotle, Nichomachean Ethics, 1.10, translated in Erasmus's Adages* (1982: 378). See also Plato's *Protagoras* (esp. 339b3). For a discussion of Aristotle's figure in terms of the shifting status of the mean in early modernity, see especially Pender (2005: 363–400).
13. Floyd-Wilson (2004: 134).
14. Aristotle (2006: 127).
15. Ibid.: 127.
16. Aristotle's tetragonal figure in fact derives from Simonides's allusion to the 'good man' as 'four square,' discussed in Plato's *Protagoras*, the very text often linked with the transmission of the concept of 'man as the measure of all things.' On the transmission of this concept into the Renaissance and Shakespearean poetry and drama, see Blank (2006).

17. It is no coincidence in this respect, that Hieronimo evokes the model of the 'squared' Horatio after his death.
18. The 1526 English translation of Erasmus's *De immense dei misercordia* defines the word 'confounded' as 'troubled or all out of square and order.' Erasmus (1526: sig. 49^r).
19. Masten (2016: 21).
20. Conley (2011: 79). On the many manuals attentive to the art and science of Roman capital lettering before Tory, see especially Bowen (1979).
21. See especially, Traub (2009: 42–81, 2015a, b). Traub's scholarship on the biopolitical and cartographic prehistory of norms (in the modern sense of 'norm' as 'average' rather than ideal), early English uses of 'normal' and 'abnormal,' and, in particular, on the 'logic of the grid' central to racial and sexual taxonomies are crucial for developing scholarship on norms and normativity in early modernity. Whereas my essay stresses the early modern logic(s) of geometric selfhood in relationship to social expectations and ideals and Traub's focuses on incipient 'norms' in relationship to the later concept of 'averages,' 'populations,' and the biopolitics of governmental and institutional control, I am grateful to her and to the scholarship of Patricia Cahill for pushing me to think further about the way in which the classical/early modern logic of the 'square' presents a model of 'normality' that is still, in many ways, still with us today.
22. Foucault (2001: 235). Foucault famously argued for an epistemic break between the classical and the modern age, in which 'at the beginning of the seventeenth-century […] the great circular forms in which similitude was enclosed ere dislocated and opened so that the table of identities could be revealed.' The new taxonomies symbolized and constituted by charts, tables, and various 'quadrilateral' forms and grids in arenas of 'general grammar, natural history [and] wealth,' he suggested, were already giving way in his own historical time period of the 1960s (235). The book was published in the 1960s when the contemporary idiomatic expression of 'being a square' was well underway as part of a series of countercultural forces. It was also published just before the 'thinking outside the box' entered the English language, a phrase derived in large part from the idea of data management as a model for human programming. The *OED* cites Michael R. Notaro's (1971) definition of 'think[ing] outside the box' (published in *Data Management* no less), as one of the earliest uses of this phrase: 'If you have kept your thinking process operating inside the lines and boxes [of organization charts], you are normal and average, for that is the way your thinking has been programmed' (s.v. 'box n.2'). See also Kalas (2007) for a treatment of early modern 'frames' and a reading of this particular moment in Foucault (2007: 17).

Although Foucault's later historicized the normal, normalization, and normativity as distinctively modern phenomena, figured through discipline and biopolitics, it is the earlier work on structure and epistemology that remains most relevant to this essay.
23. Ingold (2016: 156).
24. Ingold (2016: 157). Such distinctions become evident in a range of spheres marked by a 'rich repertoire of circumambulatory metaphors for talking about [...] errant ways' which came to include 'the twisted mind of the pervert, the crooked mind of the criminal, the devious mind of the swindler and the wandering mind of the idiot' (2016: 159).
25. Ahmed (2006). See also Miller (1992: 28–29).
26. Canguilhem (1978: 146). It is worth noting that Canguilhem also aligns the etymology of 'normal' with the 'norm' as an unbending form, not too left, not too right, but in fact right in the middle (69)—a concept of moderation that is more explicitly articulated in and through the iconography of the geometric figure of the square.
27. Aristotle (1999: 1.5.986a 22–25). The square and the oblong may connote, to a modern ear, the straight and the round or 'oval,' but the 'square number' as 1, 4, 9 and so on, were represented graphically by dots that constituted perfect geometric squares. The 'oblong number' was, again rendered graphically through dots, often understood to be rectangular but not square.
28. Reynolds (1640: 529).
29. On the square man and the cardinal virtues, see Tracey (2008: 55–76, 57). In later contexts, for English rhetoricians such as John Rainolds absorbing and expanding Aristotle's formulation for the happy man, as Stephen Pender has observed, 'Happiness is not only the contemplation and execution of excellence, it is also self-governance, constancy, appropriateness, and moderation' (2005: 373). See also commentaries on Aristotle's Ethics 1.10 by Aspasius, for example, who emphasizes the perfectly squared stone that can land 'upright' no matter where fortune tosses him, or Peter Martyr Vermigli, who speculates on the 'four square' man in terms of square numbers as well as cubes.
30. Erasmus (1982: 378).
31. Ibid.: 7, s.v. '*Volvitur dolium*'.
32. Cicero indeed discusses the extent to which the Latin periodic style consisted of "'squaring up' practically every sentence and giving it rhythmical shape.' Cicero, *De Oratore*, 61.208, cited by Erasmus (1982), "*in quadrum redigere*," 623.
33. Bland (1814: 217). To 'act upon the square' situates the metaphorical square as ground or foundation on which to act rather than simply a structure in which to act.
34. Puttenham (1590: 87).

35. In Fletcher and Shakespeare's *Two Noble Kinsman*, for example, the Jailor's Daughter is described as utterly mad and 'out of square': The Doctor proposes a wild treatment hoping to turn 'what's now out of square in her into their former law and regiment' (4.3.94–95). When geometry *was* gendered, moreover, it was not always consistent. We might recall the masculinized divine circle in the House of Alma in Spenser's *Faerie Queene* or note the masculinization of all geometric shapes in Puttenham's *Arte of English Poesie*. Such gendering may well be related to the gendering of the Latin *circulus* or *quadratus* as well as the default gendering of God, represented by that perfect circle. Such variations existed alongside the longstanding binaries that oppose square and male against circle and female.
36. Looking forward to the exceptional status of the 'queen' in *Antony and Cleopatra*, it is notable that Puttenham notes the 'resemblance' of Queen Elizabeth to the 'pyramis' and 'pillar' as well as the 'sphaere' but not to the square.
37. On the circle and sphere as the most perfect of geometric figures, see especially Plato's *Timeus* and Aristotle's *De caelo*. On the theology of squaring the circle, with Christ as the solution, see especially Nicholas of Cusa's *On Learned Ignorance*, Book III.
38. Anonymous (1983: 85–132). Quotations from *Blame Not Our Author* will be referenced by line number. See Mazzio (2004).
39. Curiously, whereas the square is aligned in *Blame Not* in familiar terms with the foundation of Rome and Roman masculinities more generally, the circle's superior status is attributed, first, to the Egyptians ('memphian sages') who linked the circle to 'vnbound eternity,' and then to the Greeks and Romans. It is as if Egypt in this play somehow lacks angles, a topic to which we shall return.
40. On humoural temperance as one of the central models for manhood, see Shepherd (2006). As she puts it of the departure of men from the ideal of masculinity: 'Conduct manuals frequently deflected attention from men by blaming women for many of the dangers posed to patriarchal manhood by marriage' (2006: 78).
41. Cockeram (1930: 174), s.v. 'squadron'.
42. Cahill (2004: 172). See also Cahill (2008). Thanks to Sujata Iyengar and Valerie Traub for calling my attention to Cahill's book.
43. On the square formation in classical contexts, see Sabin et al. (2007, esp. 159, 192, and 422). The 'square battle' formation was, according to a number of military manuals, particularly ideal as a defensive posture, a way to minimize the impact of a sudden attack or assault. See, for example, Clayton (1591, esp. 44–45).
44. While to 'square' could be to make even, to put into order and agreement, moreover, it could also suggest resistance to a pattern or model

for behavior (OED, s.v. square, v.). Such linguistic tensions and contradiction may express the power of the square to index its opposite or disavowed 'other.' If, as Enobarbus says in the play, 'Mine honesty and I begin to square' (or to 'conflict'), Antony might well have said as much upon avowing to keep to his square after marrying Octavia, as he tells us moments later, 'will to Egypt: / And though I make this marriage for my peace, / I' the east my pleasure lies.' (3.13.41, 2.3.29).
45. Aristotle (2011: 17).
46. Bono (1984).
47. The language and action of the play, including circular forms as well as the four 'corners' hailed in the script of *Antony and Cleopatra* and occupied onstage, would have rendered the default structure of the theater all the more visible. The Globe featured a square thrust stage surrounded by a vertically impressive and seemingly curved outer wall, 'round,' or, as we hear in the Prologue to *Henry V*, 'wooden O.' Shakespeareans are by now deeply familiar with the supercharged symbolism of that circular 'wooden O' of *Henry V* (Rotman 1987; Jaffee 1999; Williams 2012) as well as the possible alignment of the quadrangular stage 'plot' with surveying practices of the period (Bruckner and Poole 2002; Turner 2006). It is the iconography of a square within a round, however, that comes into view in a play such as *Antony and Cleopatra*.
48. Erasmus (1982: 378).
49. Hagar (1984: 23–38). But from another perspective, as Alan Hagar has argued, 'Rombus alone suggests the possibility of geometric order in Wanstead Garden and its environs' (1990: 489).
50. The *OED* defines the term as 'gentleness, meekness, docility' (*sv* 'mansuetude,' n.): I opt for the more charged sense of 'docility' in context of schoolroom 'discipline' in Rombus's speech and also italicize *man*—given the relevance of the speech to questions of male servitude, docility, and tameness in the face of the Queen.
51. Dudley was tutored by John Dee and chastised by the famed humanist Roger Ascham for his fascination with geometry. As Ascham wrote, 'I think you did yourself injury in changing TULLY's wisdom with EUCLID's pricks and lines' that compromised his interest in Cicero's 'wisdom' (1864: II, 103).
52. Orgel (1963: 198).
53. Sidney (1595: sig. G3^r).
54. Sidney's use of the term 'right,' which infiltrates his conception of generic decorum as well as 'reason' in his *apology* (see especially the famous passage on 'mingling Kinges and Clownes'), is particularly suggestive in this respect.
55. Ania Loomba, citing Edward Said, in 'The Imperial Romance of *Antony and Cleopatra*,' in *Antony and Cleopatra*, Norton Critical Edition, ed. Loomba, 261–280, 265.

56. An early study that influenced so much recent criticism was Janet Adelman's *The Common Liar* (1973).
57. The habitual alignment of Rome with 'measure' and Egypt with lack of 'measure' needs attention, less in terms of measured and unmeasured passions, which has been by now well addressed, but in terms of the language and status of geometry and measurement at work in the play more generally.
58. Sacerdoti (2014: 107). See also Crane (2014) who aligns Shakespeare's Egypt with older, Galenic and Aristotelian approaches to nature involving humors and direct, common sense approaches to nature and Rome with more abstract forms of measuring and controlling the environment.
59. Shakespeare (2011: 7, n. 2).
60. See especially McDonald (1950: 12). Cleopatra, aligned with both Isis and the Ptolomies, herself offers a potential symbolic bridge between Egyptian and Greek geometry.
61. Benese (1547: sig. A4r).
62. In *Titus Andronicus*, for example, 'My grief was at the height before thou cam'st, /And now like Nilus it disdaineth bounds' (3.1.71–72). See also Spenser's *Faerie Queene* and Michael Drayton's *Idea's Mirror* (1594) for similar imagery of the Nile. Thanks to Rory Loughnane for this note.
63. The fact that the very word 'bourn' in Cleopatra's opening lines could mean a geometric boundary but also a 'small stream' may be particularly significant in this respect.
64. Leo Africanus (1600) and Pliny (1601). Both texts are cited in brief in glosses to Antony's speech at 2.7.17–23 in Edmond Malone's edition of *Antony and Cleopatra* (1821).
65. Pliny (1601), cited in Shakespeare, *Antony and Cleopatra* (1821: 120, n. 6).
66. Shepherd (2006).
67. On Cleopatra's recuperation of Antony's heroic masculinity, see James (2007: 145) and on the alignment of Antony with forms of femininity, see Little (2001).
68. Donne (2014: 581).
69. Cleopatra's speech stands as a response to or revision of Philo's description of Antony's 'turn' in the opening lines of the play (cited above). There Antony's 'bend' or 'turn' is linguistically mirrored in overabundance of 'o's (19 in just 6 lines) that themselves enact a kind of 'O'erflowing' of the measure at the level of the letter. The speech, by juxtaposing those 'files' of ordered military men with the circular bend of Antony, sets the stage for a drama that pivots, in many ways, on the deeply charged set of symbolic relationships between the curved and the straight.

Works Cited

Adelman, Janet. 1973. *The Common Liar: An Essay on Antony and Cleopatra.* New Haven: Yale University Press.
Africanus, Leo. 1600. *A Geographical Historie of Africa: Written in Arabicke and Italian....,* Trans. and Collected by John Pory. London: G. Bishop.
Ahmed, Sara. 2006. *Queer Phenomenology: Orientations, Objects, Others.* Durham: Duke University Press.
Anonymous. 1983. *Blame Not Our Author,* ed. Suzanne Gossett. Malone Society Collections 11.
Aristotle. 1999. *Metaphysics,* 2nd ed., trans. Joe Sachs. Santa Fe: Green Lion Press.
Aristotle. 2006. *On Rhetoric: A Theory of Civic Discourse,* 2nd ed., ed. and trans. George A. Kennedy. Oxford: Oxford University Press.
Aristotle. 2011. *Nichomachean Ethics,* trans. David Ross. Oxford: Oxford University Press.
Ascham, Roger. 1864. *The Whole Works,* ed. A.J. Giles. London: J.R. Smith.
Benese, Richard. 1547. *The Boke of Measurying of Lande.* London.
Bland, Robert. 1814. *Proverbs, Chiefly Taken from the Adagia of Erasmus.* London: T. Edgerton.
Blank, Paula. 2006. *Shakespeare and the Renaissance Mismeasure of Man.* Ithaca: Cornell University Press.
Boas, Federick S. 1851. *The Works of Thomas Kyd.* Oxford: Clarendon Press.
Bono, Barbara J. 1984. *Literary Transvaluation: From Vergilian Epic to Shakespearean Tragicomedy.* Berkeley, Los Angeles, and London: University of California Press.
Bruckner, Martin, and Kristen Poole. 2002. The Plot Thickens: Surveying Manuals, Drama, and the Materiality of Narrative Form in Early Modern England. *English Literary History* 69 (3): 617–648.
Cahill, Patricia A. 2004. Killing by Computation: Military Mathematics, the Elizabethan Social Body and Marlowe's *Tamburlaine.* In *Arts of Calculation,* ed. D. Glimp and M. Warren. New York: Palgrave Macmillan.
Cahill, Patricia A. 2008. *Unto the Breach: Martial Formations, Historical Trauma, and the Early Modern Stage.* Oxford: Oxford University Press.
Canguilhem, Georges. 1978. *On the Normal and the Pathological,* trans. Carolyn R. Fawcett. Holland: D. Reidel.
Cawdrey, Robert. 1604. *Table Alphabetical of Hard Usual English Words.* London.
Clayton, Gyles. 1591. *The approoued order of martiall discipline with euery particuler offycer his offyce and dutie: With many other stratagemes adioyning.* London.

Cockeram, Henry. 1930. *The English Dictionarie of 1623/by Henry Cockeram; with a Prefatory Note by Chauncey Brewster Tinker.* New York: Huntington Press.
Conley, Tom. 2011. *The Self Made Map: Cartographic Writing in Early Modern France.* Minneapolis: University of Minnesota Press.
Crane, Mary Thomas. 2014. *Losing Touch with Nature: Literature and the New Science in 16th-Century England.* Baltimore: Johns Hopkins University Press.
Donne, John. 2014. Upon the Translation of the Psalms. In *The Complete Poems of John Donne*, ed. Robin Robbins. New York: Routledge.
Erasmus, Desiderius. 1526. *De immensa dei Misericordia.* London.
Erasmus, Desiderius. 1982. *Adages, Collected Works of Erasmus*, vol. 36, ed. and trans. John N. Grant and Betty I. Knott. Toronto: University of Toronto Press.
Fletcher, John, and William Shakespeare. 2015. *The Two Noble Kinsmen*, Rev. ed., ed. Lois Potter and Arden Shakespeare. London: Bloomsbury.
Floyd-Wilson, Mary. 2004. English Mettle. In *Reading the Early Modern Passions: Essays in the Cultural History of Emotion*, ed. Gail Kern Paster, Katherine Rowe, and Mary Floyd-Wilson. Philadelphia: University of Pennsylvania Press.
Foucault, Michel. 2001. *The Order of Things*, 2nd ed. Abingdon: Routledge.
Foucault, Michel. 2007. *Security, Territory, Population: Lectures at the Collège de France 1977–1978*, trans. Graham Burchell. New York: Palgrave.
Hager, Alan. 1990. Rhomboid Logic: Anti-idealism and a Cure for Recusancy in Sidney's *Lady of May. ELH* 57 (3): 485–502.
Hutson, Lorna. 1994. *The Usurer's Daughter: Male Friendship and Fictions of Women in Sixteenth-Century England.* London: Routledge.
Ingold, Tim. 2016. *Lines: A Brief History.* New York: Routledge.
Jaffee, Michele. 1999. *Story of O: Prostitutes and Other Good for Nothings in the Renaissance.* Cambridge: Harvard University Press.
James, Heather. 2007. To Earn a Place in the Story: Resisting the Aeneid in *Antony and Cleopatra.* In *Shakespeare's Troy: Drama, Politics, and the Translation of Empire*, 119–150. Cambridge: Cambridge University Press.
Kalas, Rayna. 2007. *Frame, Glass, Verse: The Technology of Poetic Invention in the English Renaissance.* Ithaca: Cornell University Press.
Little, Arthur L. 2001. *Shakespeare Jungle Fever: National-Imperial Re-visions of Race, Rape, and Sacrifice.* Stanford: Stanford University Press.
Loomba, Ania. 2011. The Imperial Romance of *Antony and Cleopatra.* In *Antony and Cleopatra*, ed. Norton Critical. New York: Norton.
Masten, Jeffrey. 2016. *Queer Philologies: Sex, Language and Affect in Shakespeare's Time.* Philadelphia: University of Pennsylvania Press.

Mazzio, Carla. 2004. The Three-Dimensional Self: Geometry, Melancholy, Drama. In *Arts of Calculation*, ed. David Glimp and Michelle R. Warren, 39–65. New York: Palgrave.

McDonald, C. 1950. Herodotus and Aristotle on Egyptian Geometry. *The Classical Review* 64: 12.

Miller, D.A. 1992. *Bringing Out Roland Barthes*. Berkeley: University of California Press.

Notaro, Michael R. Jr. 1971. Management of Personnel: Organization Patterns and Techniques. *Data Management* 9 (9).

Orgel, S.K. 1963. Sidney's Experiment in Pastoral: The Lady of May. *Journal of the Warburg and Courtauld Institutes* 26 (1/2): 198–203.

Pender, Stephen. 2005. The Open Use of Living: Prudence, Decorum and the Square Man. *Rhetorica* 24 (4): 363–400.

Plato. 2006. *Protagoras*, ed. Nicholas Denyer. Cambridge: Cambridge University Press.

Plutarch. 1924. *The Roman Questions of Plutarch: A New Translation, with Introductory Essays & a Running Commentary*, ed. and trans. Herbert Jennings Rose. New York: Biblo & Tannen Publishers.

Puttenham, George. 1590. *Art of English Poesie*. London.

Reynolds, Edward. 1640. *A Treatise of the Passions and Faculties of the Soule of Man*. London.

Rotman, Brian. 1987. *Signifying Nothing: The Semiotics of Zero*. Stanford: Stanford University Press.

Sabin, Philip, Hans van Wees, and Michael Whitby (eds.). 2007. *The Cambridge History of Greek and Roman Warfare*, vol. I. Cambridge: Cambridge University Press.

Sacerdoti, Gilberto. 2014. *Antony and Cleopatra* and the Overflowing of Roman Measure. In *Identity, Otherness and Empire in Shakespeare's Rome*, ed. Maria Del Sapio Garbero, 107–118. New York: Routledge.

Shakespeare, William. 1821. *Antony and Cleopatra*. In *The Plays and Poems of William Shakspeare: Julius Cæsar. Antony and Cleopatra*, ed. F.C. Edmond Malone and J. Rivington. London.

Shakespeare, William. 2001. *Arden Shakespeare Complete Works*, ed. David Scott Kastan, Richard Proudfoot, and Anne Thompson. New York: Bloomsbury.

Shakespeare, William. 2011. *Antony and Cleopatra*, ed. Ania Loomba. New York: Norton.

Shepherd, Alexandra. 2006. *Meanings of Manhood in Early Modern England Man's Estate*. Oxford: Clarendon Press.

Sidney, Philip. 1595. *An Apologie for Poetrie*. London.

Stillman, Robert. 1984. Justice and the 'Good Word' in Sidney's *The Lady of May. Studies in English Literature* 24: 23–38.

Turner, Henry. 2006. *The English Renaissance Stage: Geometry, Poetics and the Practical Spatial Arts*. Oxford: Oxford University Press.

Tracey, Martin J. 2008. *Virtus* in the Naples Commentary on the *Ethica Nova*. In *Virtue Ethics in the Middle Ages: Commentaries on Aristotle's Nicomachean Ethics 1200–1500*, ed. István Pieter Bejczy. Leiden: Brill.

Traub, Valerie. 2009. The Nature of Norms: Anatomy, Cartography, *King Lear*. In *Shakespeare & Science*, ed. Carla Mazzio, Special Double Issue of *South Central Review* 26 (1) (Winter and Spring): 26.2, 42–81.

Traub, Valerie. 2015a. History in the Present Tense: Feminist Theories, Spatialized Epistemologies, and Early Modern Embodiment. In *Mapping Gendered Routes and Spaces in the Early Modern World*, ed. Merry E. Wiesner-Hanks. Farnham: Ashgate.

Traub, Valerie. 2015b. Shakespeare and Global Cartography. In *The Cambridge Guide to the Worlds of Shakespeare, Vol. 1, Shakespeare's World, 1500–1660*, ed. Bruce Smith. Cambridge: Cambridge University Press.

Williams, Travis. 2012. The Story of O: Reading Letters in the Prologue to *Henry V*. In *Shakespeare Up Close*, ed. Travis D. Williams, Russ McDonald, and Nicholas D. Nace, 9–16. London: Arden Shakespeare.

Yates, Frances A. 1966. *The Art of Memory*. New York: Routledge.

CHAPTER 3

Normal School: *Merry Wives* and the Future of a Feeling

Elizabeth Hanson

In modern English, 'normal' and related words such as 'norm,' 'normalcy,' and 'normality,' possess a rich semantic range, most of which was unavailable to 'normal' in early modern English. Only the adjectival form appears to have been in use before the nineteenth century and the sole meanings the *Oxford English Dictionary* documents for 'normal' from the turn of the seventeenth century to the turn of the nineteenth are 'exact, according to rule,' and 'having the function of prescribing a course of action or way of living; prescriptive,' so that a 'normall patterne' is one that *should be* followed, not one that usually is.[1] The latter usage is obsolete. Nor does the word appear to have been frequently used. Then in the nineteenth century, use and usages proliferate in science, medicine, mathematics, and common speech. While the prescriptive meaning persists, the new meanings recognize quantitative ideas such as statistical frequency so that 'normal' also becomes descriptive, designating the most frequently occurring form of something, either within a population or in an organism, or the range that captures most

E. Hanson (✉)
Queen's University, Kingston, ON, Canada
e-mail: hansone@queensu.ca

© The Author(s) 2019
R. Loughnane and E. Semple (eds.), *Staged Normality in Shakespeare's England*, Palgrave Shakespeare Studies,
https://doi.org/10.1007/978-3-030-00892-5_3

individual instances of the phenomenon whose norm is being charted.[2] In modern usage, however, the older prescriptive meaning and the modern descriptive meanings are in fact not easily distinguished. The OED's first definition for 'normal'—(I.1.a.) 'constituting or conforming to a type or standard; regular, usual, typical; ordinary, conventional'— demonstrates that in modern usage the prescriptive and descriptive imply one another; the rule to which the 'regular' conforms now derives from statistical observation rather than moral doctrine but with the clear suggestion that the pressure could go both ways, so that moral rules might be reflected in and derive their authority from the statistical frequency with which they are observed. This possible conflation of the usual and the moral is especially evident in definition 1.4: 'heterosexual.'

The semantic complexity of our 'normal' is thus a symptom of our epistemic condition. In early modern England, while a *rule* could be 'normal,' it was not possible for any *person* save Jesus Christ to be so. Women and men knew that their sinful humanity meant that they could never truly 'conform [to the] way of living' prescribed them (OED A.2.*obs.*), nor be 'free from any disorder' (OED A.1.b). Thus, the Book of Common Prayer's order for daily morning prayer, 'normally,' that is, prescriptively, directed worshippers to cry: 'Correct us, O Lord;...] for there is no health in us.'[3] The modern 'normal' likewise harnesses the formal and the moral to ideas of sickness and health, but this hybrid is in turn linked to mathematics and metrics, and from there to social description, allowing for both affective and aesthetic dimensions. The normal can signify 'healthy,' 'statistically probable or modal,' 'conforming to a rule,' 'conventional,' 'boring,' 'banal,' or 'comfortable,' with each meaning drawing color from others depending on the situation, but in most cases with quantifying and scientific habits of thought inflecting moral and aesthetic judgments.[4]

In *The Normal and the Pathological* (1943), Georges Canguilhem offered a historical account of how the complex modern meaning of 'normal' arose as a result of the term's opposition to shifting understandings of the pathological. As 'health is life in the silence of the organs,' Canguilhem argues, 'the biologically normal [...] is revealed only through infractions of the norm.'[5] However, how that infraction was understood has shifted several times as modern medical thinking developed. Canguilhem characterizes early modern humoural accounts of disease, whereby '[n]ature (*physis*) within man as well as without, is harmony and equilibrium,' as inimical to an opposition between the pathological and the normal.[6] In this case, he argues, 'disease is not somewhere in man, it is everywhere [...and is] not simply disequilibrium or discordance; it is [...] an effort on the part of nature to effect a new equilibrium in man.'[7] Only later, when disease comes to be understood in 'ontological' terms, as the invasion of the body by a 'foreign substance,' does the pathological emerge as a term that can call forth the normal as its stable opposite.[8] However, this opposition shifts again, as the pathological is reconceived in 'physiological' rather than ontological terms, 'not so much by *a-* or *dys-* as by *hyper-* or *hypo*' or, as he puts it later, through a conceptual 'reduction of quality to quantity.'[9] Canguilhem's account of the shifting relationship between the pathological and the normal demonstrates the way that our conception of the normal, which conflates the optimal condition with the statistically frequent one, depends on scientific developments that post-date the early modern period.

As interesting, however, is the way Canguilhem's account suggests a reverse process, whereby biological science itself relied on more established concepts and analogies to articulate new ideas so that, for example, the long-established idea of a sovereign territory invaded by a foreign power can be recruited to understand the relation between the 'normal' healthy body and sickness, once the concept of the pathogen has emerged. The multidirectional borrowing among moral and social ideas and new scientific thinking, I would suggest, not only produces the polysemy and flexibility of our modern 'normal,' but also complicates the etymological narrative whereby we presume a meaning is not culturally available until all determining historical conditions have converged on the word in question. Like the proclamation of Lear's Fool, 'this prophecy Merlin shall make, for I live before his time' (3.2.95–96).[10] The modern normal portends itself in the process whereby concepts loan themselves to one another under the pressure of circumstances, producing feelings and associations which are namable only retrospectively. In this respect, Shakespearean comedy is a particularly sensitive and productive site for developing ideas and feelings that anticipate new versions of normal; its preoccupation with the loss and restoration of equilibrium within communities may invoke a humoural social body, but in its reliance on scapegoating expulsions it also imagines the ontological normal Canguilhem associates with the later discovery of pathogens.[11] And, in its restoration of social order, expressed in forms such as multiple marriages with varying degrees of promise, it often portends a more majoritarian than idealizing mode of authority. In this essay I argue that *The Merry Wives of Windsor* instances this proleptic condition, grafting a comedy of correction focused on but not limited to the 'normalizing' of Falstaff (who is also an aristocratic pathogen invading the social body of Windsor) to an apprehension of normalcy in a more modern, quantitatively informed sense. It is particularly the play's relation to the most modern, quantitative normal that interests me, a relation I attempt to grasp through attention to the famous Latin lesson scene. The presence of this apparently gratuitous scene, which does no plot work and is absent from the 1602 Quarto, suggests that the play world is imaginatively under pressure from an institution—the grammar school—that will begin to make available the methods and principles of the new quantitative normal by bringing boys up against the old prescriptive norm of the Latin curriculum, but in a manner that permitted comparison and numerical analysis.[12] However, while schooling is represented in the play, the full social regime it supports or, more accurately, will support, is not. Instead, the play affords a structure of feeling that defends against the authority of institutions, such as the grammar school, to shape social experience. Within this structure of feeling, the natural, the numerous, and the quotidian align against (among other unnatural objects including the lust of an old, fat knight), the rules of Latin grammar and the pedants who measure with them. *Merry Wives* suggests that the rich and dynamic semantic range of the modern normal may reveal not just an epistemically specific alignment of ideas, but a *ressentiment* that celebrates the average as 'normal' in proleptic defiance of the forces that make such a concept thinkable in the first place.

I

If the temporality of this formulation according to which a play responds to an order that has not yet arrived seems confused, I would observe that *Merry Wives* seems to invite anachronistic characterization. Numerous distinguished critics have been unable to resist referring to it as Shakespeare's 'middle class' play, using a term that Shakespeare would not have recognized and for which there was as yet no referent.[13] Rosemary Kegl, in an insightful 1994 essay provides a substantial list of critics who refer to the play this way.[14] Kegl's specific observation, it should be noted, is the apparent need of these critics to couple 'middle class' with 'bourgeois.' Absent this Boolean principle, the list of critics referring to the play as 'middle class' would have likely been longer, and critics in more recent years have continued to favor the term. For instance, Walter Cohen introduces the play in the *Norton Shakespeare*, by observing that, 'Certainly, this is Shakespeare's most middle-class play in its subject matter, setting, and outlook.'[15] Kegl's specific argument is that critics' double barreled labeling (calling the play both 'middle class' *and* 'bourgeois') registers an unacknowledged internal heterogeneity in the entity the critics strive to name; in particular, it conflates an urban property owning group with professionals and small service providers who do not exactly share the former group's interests. Kegl admits that there was in fact an Elizabethan term, the 'middling sort,' that embraces most of *Merry Wives*' *dramatis personae*, but argues that this merely spatial term similarly fails to capture the productive internal heterogeneity of the echelon the play's characters inhabit, the historically specific 'process of constructing alliances among groups characterized by their simultaneous participation in multiple structures of oppression,' a process that ultimately produces and continues to characterize the modern middle class.[16]

Kegl's point is well taken, and I will return to the fissures among the middling sort below, but it needs to be supplemented with another observation; like 'middle class,' 'middling sort' designates a position on a vertical axis, but it does so in relation to a society that was not only explicitly hierarchical but also pyramidal; the middling sort were a minority in a society in which less than twenty percent of the population dwelt in any kind of town, and the largest population group by far was the bottom one of artificers and agricultural laborers.[17] The modern 'middle class,' in contrast, names a group that is *modal* as well as middle. It enjoys a political importance in modern capitalist democracies, which has only been emphasized by the consequences of its hollowing out in the twenty-first century, because of its claim to embrace a majority of the population; its sociopolitical authority as well as its power to operate 'normally' in the old, prescriptive sense by imposing its own characteristics as universal virtues, relies on simple quantitative heft. Moreover, the expanse of the modal middle class derives not just from alliance building among those participating in different 'structures of oppression,' as Kegl would have it, but by the broad capture of people in modern democracies by certain *structures of participation* such as home ownership, voting, and consumption of goods and services. It is these structures of participation that also make social groups statistically intelligible, in effect normalizing, the modal middle.

Among the most powerful of these modern structures of participation is schooling. Not only does formal schooling dominate childhood in modern developed societies, but it determines the form of adult lives, including the disposition of individuals within those 'multiple structures of oppression,' through the uneven distribution of cultural capital which it effects. In fact, a plausible definition of 'middle class' might be 'that large segment of the society whose socio-economic position depends on their relative success in school.' If, as Canguilhem argues, the modern 'normal' involves the uneasy interaction of two different concepts, the statistical normal and a 'species normality' that shows a 'certain tendency toward variety,' then surely schooling, as much as the biological sciences, furnishes a context within which this 'normal' becomes thinkable.[18] The school aggregates children of a common age and compares them to prescriptive 'normall patterns.' It then sorts them according to the degree of their success, which permits the establishment of 'normal' progress as well as disclosing productive species variety as students display different aptitudes.

The schooling displayed in Shakespeare's 'most middle-class play' hardly resembles this modern apparatus. The special Latin exam which Parson Evans administers to young Will Page at Mistress Page's behest, with its single teacher and lone pupil, is 'normal' only in the old sense of offering a pattern to which Will struggles to conform. More importantly, the comic point of the scene is precisely the travesty of Lily's 'normall patterne' for grammar pupils wrought by Parson Evans' Welsh tongue and Mistress Quickly's unschooled female ears. While the scene is crucial to the play's famous staging of the *English* language as a normative force, it does so by defeating the school's own norming power by subjecting the *sermo patris* to the combined assault of Evans's Welsh inflections and Mistress Quickly's salacious mis-translation. Moreover, the scene is part of Shakespeare's detailed social description of a specifically early modern 'middling sort' Windsor, insofar as the town grammar school was a sign not of universal social practice but of the ambitions of well-to-do burghers. Sending a boy to school permitted him to acquire the Latinity that would mark him as a gentleman, prepare him for a career in the church or the law, or otherwise permit him to assume a role in the governance of city, county or realm. The Pages' schooling of Will, like their skirmishing over Anne's marital options, give them a particularly local (and temporal) habitation.

Yet the scene serves to locate the Pages diachronically as well as synchronically, presenting an early instance of a tension between parents and teachers as agents of social reproduction that will become a structuring principle of the modern middle class. Mistress Page initiates this special lesson on a day when the boys have 'leave to play,' observing: 'Sir Hugh, my husband says my son profits nothing in the world at his book. I pray you, ask him some questions in his accidence' (4.1.10, 12–14).[19] In other words, she prompts the examination of her son in order that the boy's parents can see into his schooling and assess his progress for themselves. In so doing, she echoes a concern that parents of grammar school boys in the period had begun to express as they delegated the nurture of their sons to men to whom they were not related, who were often not of their kind with respect to status, and whose efficacy was hard to judge if the parents themselves lacked the learning which they wished their children to possess. In fact, as we shall see, parents' anxiety about the opacity of the institution to which they had entrusted their sons' instruction incited at least one school to expand ad hoc examination, such as Evans provides, into systematic tracking of boys' progress, practices that would propel the prescriptive early modern 'normal' in its evolution toward a modern descriptive and modal one. If such practices arose in response to parental ambition and anxiety, however, they actually helped to reinforce the division between family and school that structures the experience of the modal middle class and contributes to the ambivalence of the modern normal. Pierre Bourdieu argues with respect to twentieth-century social order, that while academic achievement adds value to children, families also risk loss of status if their children do not fare well in the consecration and ordination the school performs. For this reason, Bourdieu asserts, 'the educational system tends increasingly to dispossess the domestic group of the monopoly of the transmission of power and privileges.'[20] In other words, the system that permits the aggregation of pupils, the comparison and quantitative analysis of their achievements, and thus their subjection to a modern conception of the normal, also diminishes the power of the family and the community as a mechanism for norming and sorting, even as it drives a division between the quantitative normal and the excellent.

Rivalry between parents and teachers features in the most famous texts of humanist propaganda, reminding us that it was humanist pedagogues themselves who presented the school as a challenge to the dominion of parents. 'Cockering mothers' who sought to shield their sons from the rigors of grammar training have received a good deal of recent critical attention but it is important to recall that fathers hardly fare better in these texts. Erasmus describes aristocratic fathers, 'intoxicated and uttering streams of profanity' before their impressionable sons, while Ascham recalls a gentle father and mother who laugh at the many 'ugly oaths' that their four-year-old had picked up from serving men.[21] Humanist ideology, we might say, assaulted the well-born family with the logic of the supplement, insisting on the paradox that without the additional service of school masters, or in other words, lower status men equipped with a peculiar expertise that could equally be imparted to poor boys, well-born youth could never actually possess the condition that they were born to. A predictable effect of inculcating such a sense of lack was to render the schoolmaster an object of suspicion and resentment. It is perhaps not surprising, however, that the richest demonstrations of such suspicion arise in the context not of great households but of urban and provincial grammar schools where the lesser status of the parents (merchants, well-to-do artisans, professionals, and lesser gentlemen) may have made the pedagogue's argument about parental deficiency more persuasive, just as the independence of the grammar school from the household gave schooling a more robust institutional life.

One particularly full expression of such parental suspicion is the probation (i.e., examination) practice that was adopted by the Merchant Taylor's School in 1607. The original statutes of the school made provision for annual examinations to determine both the progress of the pupils and the diligence of the teachers.[22] However, the minutes of a 'court of assistants, holden at Marchantailors hall, upon Wednesday the xiiii day of January, anno domini 1606-7,' observed that:

> it hath fallen out of late daies, that some persons (having had their children five of six yeres in our schoole) have complained that their sonnes have not risen in learnyng, to be worthely placed in the highest formes, as others have ben of lyke continuance, it is to be thought that such a complaint of the schoole-maister and ushers is noe novelty, or that it should, (as they report) proceeded commonly of the maisters default; but rather rise by faults in such parents as have not due regard in houlding their children to the schoole, or by want of capacity in such schollers, or by other defects, rather then by any negligence in their teachers. But, however it be, the company greatly disliketh any evill report of their schoole or teachers and doe rather wish and desire all good deservings and good reports, both of the maister and schoole.[23]

The response was the establishment of a thrice yearly examination of the pupils to be carefully recorded in a Register kept by the company. It is clear from the procedures of this regime, described in detail in the Register's prefatory matter, that the system was meant to scrutinize the teachers as closely as the pupils.[24] Thus, in addition to the examination of the pupils by the Headmaster and ushers, there was to be, twice yearly, a further examination of the pupils by 'two judicious men well learned both in Greek and Latin,' from outside the school, intended to verify that the boys really did possess the capacities the probations credited them with, and that those whom the headmaster had designated the 'best and forwardest boyes' in each form were in fact the best.[25] The regularization of the examination regime also entailed a recording system, the establishment of a 'probation register' that begins, self-reflexively, with a command that the Company maintain 'a booke called the Register of the Schooles probation conteyning 400 leaves of large paper in the forme of a brief table or callender.'[26] For each probation day, the Register sets out, by form, columns which record each boy's name, date of birth and admission to the school, the years, months, and days he has continued in the form, and then on the far right-hand side, the examination exercises set.[27] The Register does not record individual performances; nevertheless, it is possible to discern different levels of performance based on the length of time boys linger in a particular form, because there was evidently no such thing as social promotion.

Like modern grade books, the Register records minimal information about the pupils, stressing instead their equal subordination to common academic tasks. Nevertheless, it is richer than modern academic records, demonstrating that the reduction of children to comparable units is a slow historical achievement rather than a natural way of looking at them. Crucially however, the entries omit the status of the boys' fathers, information that is recorded in many other social contexts. In this manner, the Register demonstrates the dispossession of the family group which Bourdieu ascribes to the school, even as it purports to address parental concerns about the pupils' progress. Defensively answering parental anxiety about how boys are getting on and why one boy is progressing faster than another, the Register reduces the boys to units suitable for comparison and quantitative analysis. This is not to say that the Register performs such analysis; in fact, what it claims to demonstrate is the probity of school practices rather than outcomes they produce. Nor does the

Register calculate averages or medians; its commentary reveals instead an interest in outliers: which boys are 'absolutely the best' and 'simply the worst.'[28] Nevertheless, to a modern reader the Register seems to invite at least casually quantitative observations such as, it was 'normal' for most boys to have left the school before the fourth form or to spend longer than a year in a form, or that only five percent of the boys who were in the first form at the first probation went on to university, so that such an outcome was not the 'norm'. My point here is not simply that the Register prepares for quantitative analysis without actually instantiating it, but also that it does so to enforce the authority of the school and justify the 'dispossession' of the parents it effects. Twenty-five years earlier, Richard Mulcaster, the Merchant Tailors' School's most famous headmaster, fearing a glut of learned men, observed in his *Positions on the Training Up of Children* (1581) that 'Everie one desireth to have his childe learned [... b]ut though everie parent be thus affected toward his owen child, as nature leades him to wish his owne best, yet for all that everie parent must beare in memorie that he is more bound to his country than to his child.'[29] Mulcaster thus anticipates Bourdieu in his observation of the conflict between the natural impulses of parents to advance their children and his school's imperative to limit the consecration it bestows. The Register, which charts aggregate participation so that it may distinguish the best from the rest, is one tool the school devises for this struggle.

II

The school regime penetrates the 'middling sort' world of *Merry Wives* via the Latin examination that interrupts the progress of Mrs. Page to Mrs. Ford's house for the execution of the second prank in the wives' two-birds-with-one stone disciplining of lecherous Falstaff and jealous Ford. Despite the widely acknowledged extraneousness of the scene—the eighteenth-century adaptor John Bell referred to it as 'that ridiculous excrescence'—numerous critics have followed the lead of Arden editor Giorgio Melchiori in deeming it nevertheless 'pivotal [...] at the level of the ideological structures of the play.'[30] These 'ideological structures,' with some variation in each critical formulation, pertain to the English language and the play's display of the 'fright[ing] of [a personified] English out of his wits' (2.1.124–125) by a host of florid or incompetent speakers including not only Mrs. Quickly and Parson Evans, but also Pistol, Dr. Caius, Master Slender, and even Falstaff, establishing a normative English through these negative examples. The school scene's function is thus explicitly to thematize linguistic regulation, via the familiar drill derived from Lily's Latin grammar, at the same time that it undermines the authority of the *sermo patris* in favor of the merry vernacular. This two-step maneuver, the argument goes, serves the play's larger project of marginalizing foreign things, learned men, and deviant sexuality in favor of the well-managed English speech, households and marriage beds of the omni-competent Mistresses Page and Ford.[31]

One virtue of this reading, for our purposes, is its implicit recognition that the scene foregrounds norming as such, and the prescriptive normal in particular, by sizing up young Will against the measuring stick of Lily in the manner set for the boys in the first form at Merchant Taylors'. 'Hold up your head,' Evans instructs Will at the beginning of the lesson, which he then concludes with a garbled version of the standard pedant's threat, 'If you forget you *quis*, your *quaes*, and your *quods*, you must be preeches' (4.1.69–70). But this demonstration of norming is a hilarious failure as Mistress Quickly hears sexual invitations in instruction—a 'good root' (47) in the 'focative [which] is *caret*,' (46), and genitals in the genitive 'Vengeance of Jenny's case, fie on her!' (54)—and responds to this dirty talk with her own counter-norming: 'Never name her, child, if she be a whore' (54–55). While the prescriptive normal is hoist by its own petard in this scene, the plot as a whole nevertheless depends on it as the principle underlying the wives' correction of Falstaff. Indeed, Falstaff himself recognizes that he is in same position as Will, twice construing himself as a schoolboy. First, when the Host calls him 'clerkly,' he responds that a woman 'hath taught me more wit than ever I learnt before in my life and I paid nothing for it neither, but was paid for my learning.' (4.5.57–60). Then he confesses to 'Master Brook' that, 'Since I plucked geese, played truant and whipped top, I knew not what 'twas to be beaten till lately' (5.1.24–26). Given the wives' comparative pedagogical flair, one function of the Latin lesson scene is undoubtedly to pass the birch, as it were, from the incompetent Latin master to the competent English mistresses. But the early modern prescriptive normal is not the only version of normality implicated in the scene. David Landreth demonstrates that the inclusion-for-the-sake-of-exclusion strategy, which explains how the Latin lesson scene can be both pivotal and extraneous, also describes a more general pattern in the play. The plot turns on the wives' repeated drawing in and then defeating of Falstaff's monstrous lechery, while the language entertains Ovidian and other not very 'middling sort' erotic allusions, without ever allowing it to penetrate the action or affective atmosphere of the play.[32] In this manner, the play also entertains the ontological normal in Canguilhem's terms, imagining the social body of middling sort Windsor as an entity defending itself, albeit good-humouredly, from foreign penetration.

There is of course no conflict between prescriptive and ontological normal in this scene; Evans' defeat by Mistress Quickly's salacious misunderstandings only serves to emphasize the skill of the wives' defensive game, indicating that with an opponent such as this, the 'domestic group' might well win against the school's looming 'dispossess[ion]' of it. Certainly Wendy Wall's compelling reading of the play as envisioning 'a nation founded on a domestic labor that doesn't have to be disavowed in the name of gender maturation,' that is, one in which domesticity has effectively sidelined the male puberty rite of Latin learning, suggests as much.[33] Wall's argument depends, however, on the assumption that Latin pedagogy enters the play carrying primarily the somewhat old-fashioned baggage of masculine authority, gentlemanly aspiration, and possible pederasty. As we have seen, however, the school is also a harbinger of a future that includes a new quantitative normal. In that future, the middling sort will rise to become the middle class, not through the defeat of the school but by submission to a power-sharing agreement with it. To characterize the scene as a skirmish in the play's successful ideological campaign for English domestic supremacy does not do justice to the scene's prevarications, even the bad faith, that attends its effects as it negotiates such an arrangement.

Perhaps the most obvious prevarication is the one already discussed: the purposeless purposiveness of a scene that manages to qualify for critics as at once 'pivotal' and 'extraneous.' In fact, a tension between idleness and busyness is established dramatically at the outset of the scene. The encounter between Mistress Page and Parson Evans interrupts the urgent business of the play, the second act in the disciplining of Falstaff by the wives. There is some time pressure because Falstaff is already on his way to the Fords' house, and Mrs. Quickly tells Mrs. Page that 'Mistress Ford desires you to come suddenly' (4.1.5). Mrs. Page replies, 'I'll be with her by and by: I'll but bring my young man here to school,' (6–7), a comment that, like the handy presence of the buck basket, serves as a reminder that these middling sort women have actual work to do. Unlike the buck basket, however, which is introduced solely to be recruited for ludic purposes, this obligation seems momentarily like an obstacle to the wives' 'more tricks with Falstaff,' a project that Mistress Page represents as necessary ('His dissolute disease will scarce obey this medicine') but it is hard not to feel that it is undertaken because the first round was so much fun (3.3.176–177). Mrs. Page's maternal diligence is, however, met by schoolmasterly otium. 'Look where his master comes,' she immediately observes, ''tis a playing day, I see' (4.1.8). In short, this scene with no work to do in advancing the plot opens with a series of quick reversals and inversions between work and play, the wives' game competing with maternal duty, and specifically the work of negotiating between the 'domestic group' and the school. The scene will close with a similar reversal: William's confession that he has forgotten the 'declensions of [his] pronouns' that leads Evans to warn him 'If you forget your *quis*, your *quaes* and your *quods*, you must be preeches' implying of course, with inadvertent bawdy, that William has work to do, is followed immediately by 'Go your ways and play, go' (69–71).

It is a 'playing day' because Master Slender has asked that it be, presumably so that Evans can pursue Ann Page for him, a reminder that the real business of Shakespearean comedy is usually courtship with its objective the renewal of the social order. School's out to accommodate procreation, so it should be no surprise that in this lesson the 'genitive case' becomes 'Jenny's case,' that 'pulcher' turns to 'polecats' and, thanks to Evans' Welsh tongue, the 'focative' will become what does not need explaining. In Mistress Quickly's inadvertent bawdy takedown of Latin instruction, an opposition familiar from humanist propaganda, that between the vulgar (female) nursemaid and the humanist (male) pedagogue, is re-framed so that womanhood, English, sex, and food— 'hang-hog is Latin for bacon, I warrant you' (4.1.42)—align against a ludicrous combination of masculine authority, Latin grammar, and Welsh incompetence. While Evans registers this assault as chaos—'Oman art thou lunatics? Hast thou no understandings for thy cases, and the numbers of the genders?' (4.1.61–63)—the inescapable conclusion here is that vitality is on the side of the aptly named Mistress Quickly who knows very well the number of the genders and as a result has turned schoolwork to playing around.

While it would hardly be surprising in a comedy that a character who signifies work, such as a schoolmaster, would be defeated by sexual play, that is not exactly what happens in this scene. Rather, the scene's toggling between work and play, purposiveness and confusion, makes it difficult to tell the difference between these modes or to know exactly what success or failure might be for any of the participants in their respective aims. Mistress Page initiates the examination (flipping Will's 'playing day' to work) to address Master Page's fear that young William 'profits nothing in the world at his book,' as I have suggested, voicing the concern that led to the Merchant Tailors' cycle of regular, recorded probation. And she concludes the scene as though she has just efficiently ticked off an item on her to-do list, observing that Will 'is a better scholar than I thought he was,' before collecting herself and Mistress Quickly with 'Come, we stay too long' (4.1.72–73; 78). This conclusion is funny because Mistress Page's tone of brisk satisfaction seems at odds with the linguistic three-way crash she and the audience have just witnessed. What does she think she saw and heard?[34] To whom does she direct her injunction, 'Prithee, hold thy peace?' Is it to Mistress Quickly who is chastising Evans for 'teach[ing] the child such words,' or to Evans who is losing his temper, barking at Mistress Quickly and about to threaten William's 'preeches'? In other words, is she trying to support Evans' endeavors or correct his irascibility? And what has Will demonstrated in showing himself 'a better scholar than [his mother] thought he was' and earning Evans' exhortation 'Go your ways and play, go' (4.1.70–71)? He answers five out of nine questions correctly; his response of 'pebble' to 'What is "a stone"' is not exactly wrong, while he seemed to be on the right track in reciting the accusative form of 'hic' before Evans' interrupts him (29–30). Will is thus likely to be, in the terms of the Merchant Tailors' probation register, neither 'absolutely the best' nor 'simply the worst' in the Windsor grammar school. He is a modest success, or perhaps, a relative failure, an indifferent student, or as we might say, 'average.'

The Merchant Tailors' Company was confident that its probation regime would vindicate its schoolmasters' diligence and so answer the claims of parents, an outcome that would bolster the emerging bourgeois order that, as Bourdieu argues, requires some dispossession of the 'domestic group.' It imagines a dialectic encounter between the parent, who in Mulcaster's words 'as nature leads him wish[es] his owne best' and the school which will rigorously determine who really is best. In that encounter between two fierce purposes, a way of thinking about boys, and the social groups more generally, will emerge in which most children will, like William Page, turn out to be alright, but that's all. For Bourdieu and Mulcaster alike, this demonstration must spell disappointment for parents. The Latin examination in *Merry Wives* preserves this dialectic encounter in the brisk bustle of Mistress Page and the irritable perseverance of Evans, but denies it the capacity to construct a social order. Instead, the pedagogical regime is undermined by Mistress Quickly's insistent reminder of what really drives social reproduction and ends with all parties going their ways to play. To put the point another way, the scene layers the opposition between schools and parents, which in the historical long run will produce quantitative ideas such as 'average performance,' onto one between work and 'play,' an activity that embraces pretty much the entire social life of Windsor save Evans' pedagogical efforts. As a result, the finding of Will's mediocrity, that he is perfectly poised between, 'You must be preeches' and 'He is a good sprag memory,' issues not in parental disappointment but in the happy demonstration that he is 'normal'. Sadly, the same cannot be said for Evans who the play figures as belonging to a class that also includes the foreigner Dr. Caius and Shallow (whose son, it will be recalled was studying at Oxford in *2 Henry IV*), the learned professionals and gentlemen whose ranks historians argue swelled the ranks of both grammar schools and universities in the late sixteenth and early seventeenth centuries.[35] Shallow recognizes that they constitute a class when he proclaims, 'Though we are justices and doctors and churchmen, Master Page, we have some salt of our youth in us – we are sons of women, Master Page' (2.3.42–44). The form that this claim to normality takes—'we are sons of women'—serves in its ridiculousness precisely to deny the incipient bourgeois order, imaginatively segregating the family from the institutions that have produced such men as these, even as we see young William Page being guided by his parents toward their ranks.

In her compelling account of the role domesticity played on the early modern stage, Wendy Wall argues that *Merry Wives* offers an 'allegory' that 'anchors the social world to the ordinary yet authoritative worlds of women that, in fact, upholds the position of an eager "middling sort"— innkeepers, justices of the peace, householders, local businessmen.' This 'allegory' she notes, shows 'the limits of pedagogy for a practical middling-class citizenry,' because English is its tongue. She calls this allegory 'largely a middle-class fantasy.'[36] The slipperiness in Wall's terminology testifies to an attempt, which as we have seen the play seems to provoke even in the most penetrating modern critics, to posit a relation between the social world of the play and the modern middle class, an effort that seems inevitably to collapse into anachronism because the world of the play feels 'ordinary,' in a way the Shakespeare's play-worlds usually do not. Wall's description of the play as 'a middle-class fantasy,' in its ambiguity as to whether the middle class is the fantasizing subject, and therefore already in existence, or the thing fantasized, and therefore something the play brings into being, inadvertently captures the play's intrinsic anachronism.[37] But her choice of words to describe this entity—'eager,' 'practical,' 'ordinary,' also remind us that this conundrum presents itself in the play as a good feeling rather than as a historical problem. Only the 'excrescence' of the Latin lesson scene, reminds us that the normal is the middling sort dreaming its own consolation.

Notes

1. *Oxford English Dictionary Online*. Accessed January 2017.
2. See Canguilhem (1989: 261–267) for a discussion of the relationship between normality and statistical frequency.
3. 'An Order for Morning Prayer Daily Throughout the Year,' quoted from *The Book of Common Prayer*, 1559—see Booty (1976: 49–50). The first part of the quotation comes from 10 Jeremiah and is among the 'sentences of the Scriptures' the rubric provides for the minister to read.' The second part comes from the 'General Confession' with which the congregation responds to the minister.
4. This list excludes the numerous technical meanings of 'normal' in meteorology, mathematics statistics, formal logic, geometry, physics, biology, geology, and education.
5. Canguilhem (1989: 118).
6. Ibid.: 40.
7. Ibid.
8. Ibid.: 41.
9. Ibid.: 42, 109.
10. All citations to *King Lear* are to Kenneth Muir's edition: Shakespeare (1972).
11. At the same time as he advances a historical argument, Canguilhem also observes that this way of thinking about disease is 'as old as man himself' (1989: 40).
12. On the significant difference between the Quarto and Folio versions of *Merry Wives*, see Marcus (1996: 68–101).
13. In this respect, the play instances the anachronistic openness that Simon Palfrey has attributed to Shakespeare's plays generally. See Palfrey (2014: 147–159).

14. Kegl (1994: 254–257). The critics Kegl lists include Camille Wells Slights, Carol Thomas Neely, Jan Lawson Hinely, Peter Erickson, Anne Barton, Sandra Clark, Marvin Felheim and Philip Traci, Muriel Bradbrook and Marilyn French.
15. Citations drawn from *The Norton Shakespeare* (2007: 1255). Cohen's comment is especially remarkable because it seems to be an endorsement of a remark Engels made in a letter to Marx, that 'the first act of the *Merry Wives* alone contains more life and reality than all German literature.' This exchangeability of 'middle class' and 'life and reality' exemplifies the quantitatively informed idea of normal I am discussing.
16. Kegl (1994: 257).
17. For discussions of early modern demography in relation to status, see Sharpe (1997: esp. 205–211), Amussen (2011: 271–284), and Hoyle (2004: 311–329). Sharpe comments that the 'middling sort' designation, should be used 'as sparingly as possible,' though his objection seems to be akin to Kegl's objection to 'middle class,' that it is too internally heterogeneous (1997: 206).
18. Canguilhem (1989: 262).
19. Citations are to Melchiori's Arden edition of the play (2000) Shakespeare, hereafter cited parenthetically by act, scene, and line number.
20. Bourdieu (1986: 253–254).
21. Potter (2002: 244–279), Erasmus (1978: 308), and Ascham (1967: 46).
22. The original statutes are printed in Draper (1962). The specific statute is XXXV, at 248.
23. Cited in Wilson (1812: 158).
24. For a discussion of the Register which records the probation exercises, and what it suggests about the role of the grammar school in the lives of the pupils and the aspiration of their parents, see Hanson (2013).
25. "The Register of the School's Probation," MS 34282/1, The Guildhall Library, London (6^r).
26. Register of the School's Probation (2^v).
27. For the first probation, for example, the boys in the fourth form were to recite the rules of Latin grammar, some of Cicero's disquisition on fortitude from *De Officiis* and the first seventy-six verses from Ovid's *De Tristibus* and render an English letter as a Latin dialogue, letter and poem. Register of the School's Probation.
28. Register of the School's Probation (4^r).
29. Mulcaster (1994: 146).
30. From Odell (1963), quoted by Melchiori (2000: 89), and Melchiori, Introduction to *Merry Wives of Windsor* (2000: 7).

31. For versions of this argument see Landreth (2004), Wall (2002: 90–93; 112–126), and Outland (2011). For more general arguments about the play's investment in Englishness, see Marcus (1996: 68–101) and Helgerson (1999: 162–182).
32. Landreth (2004: 430–432).
33. Wall (2002: 93).
34. Pittenger, 'Dispatch Quickly' (397), asserts that Mistress Page is not paying attention and so is oblivious to the contest between pederastic and heteronormative erotics; Landreth (2004: 440) argues more persuasively that she ignores what needs to be ignored in order to advance domestic order.
35. Simon (1966).
36. Wall (2002: 92–93).
37. Warley (2014: 20), cites Wall's emphasis on domesticity as an example of the evasion of class as a category of analysis.

Works Cited

Amussen, Susan D. 2011. Social Hierarchies. In *The Elizabethan World*, ed. Susan Doran and Norman Jones, 271–284. London and New York: Routledge.

Ascham, Roger. 1967. *The Schoolmaster*, ed. Lawrence V. Ryan. Ithaca and New York: Cornell University Press for the Folger Shakespeare Library.

Booty, John E. (ed.). 1976. *The Book of Common Prayer* [1559]. Charlottesville: The University Press of Virginia for the Folger Shakespeare Library.

Bourdieu, Pierre. 1986. The Forms of Capital. In *Handbook of Theory and Research for the Sociology of Education*, ed. John G. Richardson, 253–254. New York and Westport, CT: Greenwood Press.

Canguilhem, Georges. 1989. *The Normal and the Pathological*, trans. Carolyn R. Fawcett. New York: Zone Books.

Draper, F.W.M. 1962. *Four Centuries of the Merchant Taylor's School, 1561–1961*. London: Oxford University Press.

Erasmus, Desiderius. 1978. A Declamation on the Subject of Early Liberal Education for Children [De pueris statim ac liberaliter instituendis declamation]. In *The Collected Works of Erasmus*, vol. 26, trans. Beert V. Verstraete, ed. J. K. Sowards. Toronto: University of Toronto Press.

Hanson, Elizabeth. 2013. The Register of the School's Probation, 1607, from the Merchant Taylors; School, London. *The Journal of the History of Childhood and Youth* 6: 411–427.

Helgerson, Richard. 1999. The Buck Basket, the Witch and the Queen of Fairies. In *Renaissance Culture and the Everyday*, ed. Patricia Fumerton and Simon Hunt, 162–182. Philadelphia: University of Pennsylvania Press.

Hoyle, R.H. 2004. Rural Economy and Society. In *A Companion to Tudor Britain*, ed. Robert Tittler and Norman Jones, 311–329. Oxford: Blackwell.
Kegl, Rosemary. 1994. "The Adoption of Abominable Terms": The Insults That Shape Windsor's Middle Class. *ELH* 61: 254–257.
Landreth, David. 2004. Once More into the Preech: The Merry Wives' English Pedagogy. *Shakespeare Quarterly* 55: 420–449.
Marcus, Leah. 1996. *Unediting the Renaissance: Shakespeare, Marlowe, Milton*. New York: Routledge.
Mulcaster, Richard. 1994. *Positions Concerning the Training Up of Children*, ed. William Barker. Toronto: University of Toronto Press.
Odell, George C. 1920. *Shakespeare from Betterton to Irving*, 2 vols. New York: Charles Scribner's Sons (reprinted in 1963).
Outland, Allison M. 2011. "Ridden with a Welsh Goat": Parson Evans' Correction of Windsor's English Condition. *English Literary Renaissance* 41: 301–331.
Palfrey, Simon. 2014. *Shakespeare's Possible Worlds*. Cambridge: Cambridge University Press.
Potter, Ursula. 2002. Cockering Mothers and Humanist Pedagogy in Two Tudor School Plays. In *Domestic Arrangements in Early Modern England*, ed. Kari Boyd McBride, 244–279. Pittsburgh: Duquesne University Press.
Shakespeare, William. 1972. *King Lear*, ed. Kenneth Muir. London and New York: Methuen.
Shakespeare, William. 2000. *The Merry Wives of Windsor*, ed. Giorgio Melchiori and Arden Shakespeare, 3rd Series. London: A & C Black Publishers.
Shakespeare, William. 2007. *The Norton Shakespeare*, 2nd ed., ed. Stephen Greenblatt, et al. New York and London: Norton.
Sharpe, J.A. 1997. *Early Modern England, a Social History 1550–1760*, 2nd ed. London and New York: Arnold.
Simon, Joan. 1966. *Education and Society in Tudor England*. Cambridge: Cambridge University Press.
'The Register of the School's Probation,' MS 34282/1, The Guildhall Library, London, 6r.
Wall, Wendy. 2002. *Staging Domesticity*. Cambridge: Cambridge University Press.
Warley, Christopher. 2014. *Reading Class Through Shakespeare, Donne, and Milton*. Cambridge: Cambridge University Press.
Wilson, Harry Bristow. 1812. *The History of the Merchant Taylor's School from Its Foundations to the Present Time*, vol. 1. London.

CHAPTER 4

Regulating Time and the Self in Shakespearean Drama

Kristine Johanson

> God has given you one pace and you make yourselves another.
> *Hamlet* (3.1.144–145)[1]

In the Folio's so-called 'nunnery scene', Hamlet rails against women's 'prattlings' before assaulting their inclination to create their own 'pace'. Distinct from Q1 and Q2's use of 'painting' and 'face' to repeat the commonplace insult of women's falseness and to reiterate Hamlet's disgust with beauty's power, the Folio's lines rely upon a different misogynistic critique, one that imagines women as both garrulous and self-fashioning; that is, as the opposite of the silent, obedient ideal of an early modern woman. These lines set up a passage that, in all three versions of *Hamlet*, obsesses about women's behavior: in the Folio they 'gidge' [jig], 'amble', and 'lisp', and Hamlet's response to such a lack of control is to determine Ophelia's movements himself: 'To a nunnery, go!' (3.1.150). We can see behind these lines a compositor's (mis)reading of 'p' for 'f', rather than an uncontested authorial change by Shakespeare. Yet the Folio's

---

K. Johanson (✉)
University of Amsterdam, Amsterdam, The Netherlands
e-mail: K.A.Johanson@uva.nl

© The Author(s) 2019
R. Loughnane and E. Semple (eds.), *Staged Normality in Shakespeare's England*, Palgrave Shakespeare Studies,
https://doi.org/10.1007/978-3-030-00892-5_4

setting articulates a coherent attack on women, and the lines suggest that the idea of an individual making her own pace is not a wholly implausible one. If we read the Folio lines as a corruption, then such a reading implies that the compositor accepted the possibility that humans make their own speeds—against God's best efforts at uniformity. Modern editors have relegated these lines to textual footnotes, but Hamlet's insults about 'prattling' and 'pace' remained in subsequent Folios and in Rowe's 1709 edition.[2] This inclusion suggests that the idea of personal, individual speed, 'pace', and one's ability to construct it was an established norm by 1623 and through the following century. To make your own pace depends upon the idea that time is artificial, subjective, and individual—that it belongs to a person and can be shaped by her or him.[3] But in early modern England, how normal is the idea that individuals can manage their time—the idea that time belongs exclusively to them? Does Shakespeare's drama stage and circulate this idea?

Recent critical and cultural turns highlight the importance of these questions, which in essence ask for a re-evaluation of our history of self-regulation. Research in early modern studies on time and emotion, on momentary time (*occasio/kairos*), and on queer temporalities demonstrates just one example of how questions concerning time and subjectivity are being framed and explored.[4] My interest in early modern temporal norms departs from an awareness of the role such norms play in contemporary western society. With the ubiquity of Time Management titles and the high visibility at universities of 'time management' and 'work/life balance' workshops for both staff and students, the possibility of managing time seems irrefutable now, even if our success with it appears quite uncertain.[5] This essay reflects on how time management is 'normal' for us by seeking out the origins of the self-regulating individual beyond their usual post-Cartesian, Enlightenment foundations. As has been widely acknowledged, early modernity proved a crucible for the dissemination of the idea of individual, controllable time. The Reformation, and technological, cultural, and economic developments, were complementary engines of a changing awareness of personal time, its subjectivity, its preciousness, and consequently its need to be organized and used well.[6] In early modernity, these ideas could be produced on a larger scale through the explosion of the book trade alongside public theater and civic pageantry. Almanacs, diaries, and the continued use of books of hours, as well as the increasing consumption of personal time-keeping devices through the end of the sixteenth and into the seventeenth century, all indicate that early modern individuals thought about tracking, and tracked, their use of time. Romeo can make the bittersweet jest that 'in a minute there are many days' (3.5.45); Titania can demand that her fairies leave 'for the third part of a minute' (2.2.2); Richard II cannot give lost minutes to John of Gaunt (1.3.220). Yet the minute hand, invented in 1577, only came into 'regular use' in the eighteenth century.[7] Howsoever a shared sense of subjective time might seem to bind early modernity with the twenty-first century, it would be anachronistic to think that early moderns 'managed' their time precisely as we do now. As I argue below, social norms consistently circumscribe the idea of wholly individual time.

As numerous scholars have shown, anxieties about wasting time and the deeply personal consequences of perceived idleness have deeper roots than late capitalism. Catholics, Protestants, and Jews urged strict time organization, although it has been argued that a particularly Calvinist insistence on punctuality and the pervasive suspicion of idleness and wasting time contributed to the attention to personal time use in early modernity.[8] In sixteenth-century England, idleness endangered your soul—it 'is Sathan's featherbed and pillowe' and 'the mother of all vice'.[9] In that nourishing vein, it is also 'the nourse of sin' in Spenser's *Faerie Queene* (1.4.6).[10] Montaigne writes about the dangerous fecundity of idleness, a paradox that echoes through Shakespeare's plays.[11] Reproofs against idleness and reminders of time's value went hand-in-hand, as emblem books addressing 'Time Wasters' to the figure of 'Occasion' demonstrate (see Fig. 4.1).[12] (The emblem's image of the ship, suggestive of both individual and society, also intimates the dual impact of idleness.) As these examples indicate, idleness was an individual problem with personal and social ramifications: the perpetrator lost salvation, and the society was further filled with vice, inching ever closer to God's wrath. Time-use was an individual responsibility with an individual solution that depended on—so Shakespeare's plays suggest—both social norms and personal factors, including emotional state, profession, and self-knowledge. That time is available to be wasted forms a crucial element of understanding time's use and management in Shakespeare's plays, because the awareness of time wasted encapsulates both the subjective experience of time as within the individual's control *and* as subject to social norms of how time should be employed.

Fig. 4.1 "To Time Wasters", in A Person of Quality, *Emblems divine, moral, natural, and historical expressed in sculpture, and applied to the several ages, occasions, and conditions of the life of many* (London, 1673; By permission of the Huntington Library, San Marino, CA)

In attending to both time's subjectivity and its dependence on larger social expectations, this essay departs from, and contests, recent conclusions about time's subjectivity in Shakespeare by examining the relationship between Shakespeare's keen interest in personal temporal experience and the social norms he associates with that experience. Tiffany Stern's recent work on time has argued that, given the ubiquity of differing clocks, 'it will have been impossible for [a group of people] to have an agreed sense of the hour, and so impossible for them to come up with a shared idea about the length of a play'—thus urging the individuality of time—and that, furthermore, Shakespeare relies on unreliable devices in imagining 'time'.[13] For Shakespeare, Stern persuasively claims, the experience of time is more 'fictional' than 'real': 'A keenness to write chronographically, combined with the obvious untrustworthiness of timepieces, made Shakespeare very alert to the fact that time is experienced subjectively—that "real" time is in this way more fictional than "experienced" time'.[14] Yet these conclusions suggest that for Shakespeare, temporal *experience*—in the examples we will look at, indivisible from temporal *use*—is set apart from social norms. But while Shakespeare is clearly interested in thinking with temporal devices, he considers them in human terms; thus he might be 'thinking in sundial terms',[15] but to think in those terms is actually to think anthropocentrically about time: time is often not like time, it is often like a human. And while David Houston Wood has importantly considered the 'volatility' within the pre-Cartesian unitary model of the self, and that self's negotiations within and with its 'environmental circumstances', Wood's focus excludes a consideration of how temporal subjectivity might be circumscribed by social expectation.[16]

By attending to social temporal norms in Shakespeare's drama, this essay problematizes recent thinking on subjective time in two ways. Firstly, by attending to the way Shakespeare's temporal thinkers rely on individuals in community for his parsing of time, I pressurize the common critical opposition of individual- and state-power over time.[17] Power and personal success in Shakespeare are dependent on committing to the social norm of good time use: what today we would call 'time-management'. But such use is not without critique in Shakespeare. As we know, many plays dramatize individuals' deep concerns with using their time: how to use it, how to know it, who manages it, and so forth. Secondly, following a consideration of how time-use is represented in Elizabethan plays that think explicitly about time-organization, and that recent temporal scholarship has used to argue for time's exclusive subjectivity, I focus on *Richard II* to attend to the questions of how 'normal' it is to believe that time is one's own.[18] I consider how there must be an idea of what 'normal' time looks like in order to judge that it is 'wasted', a recurring anxiety and accusation in *Richard II*. Shakespeare's plays participate in normalizing and questioning the possibility of personal temporal regulation and control, and thus the self-regulation that today seems so familiar.

SELF-GOVERNANCE THROUGH TIME: TEMPORAL SUBJECTIVITY AS TEMPORAL NORM?

Historians of time and time-use do not often employ literary examples for evidence of changing attitudes to, and ideas of, time.[19] However, as medieval and early modern literary critics have demonstrated, literary texts offer perspectives on the diverse systems of personal and public time-keeping that were used, and they represent how those systems were imagined in relationship to the self and society in pre-modernity. Sandglasses, water-clocks, hour-tracking candles, public clocks, church bells, and cock-crow all represent the multiplicity of time-keeping methods that persisted into the early modern period, as the Chorus of Henry V makes clear: 'The country cocks do crow, the clocks do toll / And the third hour of drowsy morning name' (4.0.15–16); for the English and French soldiers anxiously awaiting dawn there are various ways to chart time's progress through 'the foul womb of night' (4.0.4). The image of time-awareness in pre-modernity, as Chaucer critics have argued, is complicated by Chaucer's use of clock-time and 'idealized time schemes' and by *attemprance*, 'tempering one's time-telling to suit the occasion', which demonstrates how Anglo-French writers brought objective time into the realm of the personal and subjective experience.[20] Crucially for the early modern period, the literary and visual circulations of *attemprance* indicate how self-government was linked to telling time and temporal awareness. Pre-modern European culture was certainly familiar with exhortations against idleness and the 'right' use of time—these were biblical ideas.[21] The Ecclesiastical aphorism '*Omnia tempus habent*: "Everything has its time"' was 'one of the most widely cited proverbs in all medieval literature'.[22] The relationship of time-keeping to good (self-)rule was perpetuated through legends of kings. Christine de Pizan details Charles V's strict daily schedule in her 1404 biography of him, and according to one legend, King Alfred first divided a day into eight-hour blocks of time—exemplifying the "aspirational narrative of the day".[23] In these reports, the king becomes the ideal executor of time, demonstrating his own power through his power over time and, it is suggested, over himself and his own impulses as he controls exactly what he does and when he does it. As Bradbury and Collette remind us, '*Attemprance* as restraint is central both to a clock's steady movement and to the stability of a realm; power and energy must be harnessed and flow in predictable patterns'.[24]

This correlation between self-governance, time-awareness, and time-control is a critical foundation from which to view Shakespeare's depiction of the relationship between ruler and subject, between society and individual. From his earliest plays, Shakespeare associates self-governance with managing time. In *The Taming of the Shrew*, after Baptista decides to hire tutors for his daughters, he instructs his eldest that she 'may stay [behind], / For I have more to commune with Bianca', leaving Katherina alone onstage (1.1.100–101). Her retort is quick and bitter: 'Why, and I trust I may go too, may I not? What, / shall I be appointed hours, as though, belike, I knew / not what to take and what to leave? Ha' (1.1.102–104). This response highlights not only Katherina's 'wonderful forward'—that is, ungovernable—self but her resentment of the assumption that she needs instruction and control (1.1.69). 'Hours' signifies a timetable, as if Baptista, and not Katherina, manages her time. At this early moment of the play, for Katherina, and for the playgoers, the sign of self-governance is her personal control of time, acting when she will—going or staying, taking or leaving.[25]

3 Henry VI similarly illustrates Shakespeare's interest in exploring ideas of time-control as representative of good governance and an individual's possible control over time, ideas that he returns to in the second tetralogy and *Richard II* in particular. On the run from the Yorks at the battle of Towton, King Henry famously sits upon the ground to contemplate not sad stories of the deaths of kings, but rather how he would use and understand time if his lot was different, if he were 'a homely swain' and could

> [...] carve out dials quaintly, point by point,
> Thereby to see the minutes how they run:
> How many make the hour full complete,
> How many hours bring about the day,

> How many days will finish up the year,
> How many years a mortal man may live.
> When this is known, then to divide the times:
> So many hours must I tend my flock,
> So many hours must I take my rest,
> So many hours must I contemplate,
> So many hours must I sport myself [...]
> So minutes, hours, days, months, and years,
> Passed over to the end they were created,
> Would bring white hairs unto a quiet grave.
> (2.5.21, 22–40; a scene attributed to Shakespeare)[26]

Shakespeare's Henry, oblivious to kingly control of time, reveals his confidence that it is the lowliest of his subjects that in fact would best understand time and its control and in doing so confirms his own ineptness as king.[27] Implicitly opposing court and country, artifice and nature, he links the knowledge of time-use to the swain's imagined ability to craft time materially ('To carve out dials'), and consequently to manage it. And what does Henry imagine here if not a hypothetical pastoral agenda? Visualizing the available time leads to 'divid[ing] the times' into flock-tending, rest, contemplation, and 'sport', an addition uncharacteristic for Henry in all senses of that word. The ability to see 'the minutes how they run' and therefore to know, to know and therefore to organize time, results in Henry's assurance in the pleasure such time management would bring: 'Ah, what a life were this! How sweet! How lovely!', he concludes (2.5.41). In such a scheme, ordered individual activity reflects providential time and results in a peaceful end ('a quiet grave'). For Henry, achieving that union is impossible without time's visualization, without temporal instruments to guide the individual's use of time. Man alone is an insufficient time-keeper (and woman alone as timekeeper a threat to patriarchal dominance, as Ophelia and Katherina suggest). Through his imaginary solitary shepherd, Henry both fantasizes that time control exists outside of social norms and courtly artifice, and he intimates that society interrupts, and corrupts, the providential use of time. He imagines time as apart from the power of others. Yet 'must' is repeated as much as 'I' in the passage cited above, suggesting that individual temporal control is complicated by society's own command of that individual's time, and the attention to temporal subjectivity in these plays must always be checked by the social forces Shakespeare imagines acting upon such subjectivity.

Such a check is particularly pertinent now, as scholarship has increasingly insisted that time for the early moderns was normally abnormal—its lack of sameness, its consistent inconsistency, were recognizable. Shakespeare's metaphorical uses of time hinge on that normal-abnormality, on time's inherent subjectivity despite its outward show as objective phenomenon. That Shakespeare represents time's inherent subjectivity and unreliability reflects the material reality of experiencing time in the early modern period: through timepieces that were changeable, through the possibility of 'hour' having a multiplicity of meanings, in the large-scale absence of minutes.[28] In Shakespeare's drama, the experience of time is exclusive to the individual and their aspects of selfhood such as emotional state, place of origin, profession, or gender.[29] Rosalind and Orlando's banter about time in *As You Like It* is often persuasively enlisted as evidence of this subjectivity, as Rosalind argues that certain people function as well as clocks to tell the time; thus if there is 'no clock in the forest', as Orlando observes, there can be no lovers either (3.3.254–255). For 'time travels in divers paces with divers persons', trotting 'hard with a young maid between the contract of her marriage and the day it is solemnized', ambling 'with a priest that lacks Latin, and a rich man that hath not the gout', galloping 'with a thief to the gallows', and staying 'With lawyers in the vacation' (3.3.292–293, 299–300, 304–305, 309–310, 316, 320).[30] Rosalind reflects on someone akin to herself (the waiting, desirous maid), but then considers occupations (priest, thief, lawyer) rather than emotional states. In her witticisms, she imagines time as both objective and subjective: it 'ambles' and 'travels *with*', alongside and outside, the individual (my emphasis). Yet such movement is dependent on that individual's emotional state and occupation, which directly impact how a person experiences time and its effects. Furthermore, the individual's ability to control time lies beyond his/her power, as it is circumscribed by social norms—the maid must wait for her wedding day. However personal time may appear to the individual, it is in a constant state of negotiation with social circumstance. For King Henry, human time-control depends on artifice in nature, and he sees time as available for control in a state of nature—apart from society. Yet for Rosalind, time can only be told through a human instrument. Even though she never actually tells Orlando what time it is, her response suggests it does not actually matter anyway, since the idea of clock-time as divorced from subjective time is unedifying. According to Rosalind, Henry, and others in Shakespeare's works, clock-time cannot be experienced as objective, but that does not signify that it is wholly individual, either.[31]

Normal Time in *Richard II*

The idea of a 'norm' itself leads us to a puzzling situation with regard to subjective time. 'Subjective time' as I have used it indicates an individual, exclusive possession. But understanding what 'normal' or 'normality' signifies in a given situation is contingent upon an agreement between an individual and their community. What is read as 'normal' depends upon the relationship between that individual and that society. Using monarchical protagonists to pose questions such as—what is the duty a subject owes to a king? What is the duty a subject owes to a tyrant? What is the most effective strategy to secure loyalty and power? (Henry VI; Richard II; Henry IV and Henry V)—Shakespeare's history plays examine the individual-social bond, a key element of which is the individual's understanding and use of his time. In the second tetralogy in particular, Shakespeare investigates the relationship between good governance of time and good governance of England, as various scholars have considered.[32] Taking the plays together, on the surface there seems to be a clear message: wasting time results in poor leadership and usurpation (Richard II), and knowing when to act brings power (Henry IV), but the recognition of idleness and the correction of time-wasting leads to redemption and glory (Hal-Henry V). Yet Shakespeare rarely constructs such moralizing messages for his audience, and his thinking on time (historical and clock-time) and individuals' control over it is no different.[33] In the second tetralogy, Shakespeare probes time's subjective manifestations, interrogating how time might be managed individually and what the consequences are if it is, consequences which again urge the point that subjective time-use is circumscribed by social norms.

In *Richard II*, Shakespeare aggrandizes politically the power struggle centered on time that is exemplified above by Baptista and Katherina, where the daughter chafes at the father's control over her time. The history plays, and *Richard II* in particular, have consistently garnered the attention of critics writing on time, and they often turn to Richard's final soliloquy, where his famous confession—'I wasted time and now doth time waste me'—illustrates the tragic figure whose tardy self-recognition is bound to his temporal awakening that his time is no longer his own, but rather that he is now Bolingbroke's 'jack of the clock' (V.v.60). Yet to waste time is to manage time (poorly). What then does it mean to 'waste' time in *Richard II*, and what can that tells us about the play's temporal norms?

The idea of time-based *waste* suggests first and foremost that time is possessed by the individual wasting it; secondly, that time has an inherent value that is not dependent on the individual who possesses it; and finally that if time is determined to have been 'wasted', then there is a social agreement on what that value *is*. In the play, 'normal', acceptable values of time are time spent listening to good counsel and pursuing policies for the general good. *Richard II* asks its audience to accept John of Gaunt's, the rebels', and Richard's own judgement that the king has indeed wasted his time, through his seen and unseen actions. The play suggests that Richard has used his time inappropriately, badly—it expresses the sense of 'waste' as 'To spend, consume, employ uselessly or without adequate result' (*OED* 2016). Both 'uselessly' and 'without adequate result' stress the inherent value of productivity built into time, while 'adequate' alone implies the role of social norms in understanding 'waste'.

What cements the idea of time-use and time-waste as a social negotiation in *Richard II* is Shakespeare's use of the Gardener to affirm Richard's profligacy. In Act 3, the Gardener bookends his critical speech with ideas of waste that represent the spectrum of the word's use in *Richard II*. He explains that

> [...] Bolingbroke
> Hath seized the wasteful King. O, what pity is it
> That he had not so trimmed and dressed his land
> As we this garden! We at time of year
> Do wound the bark, the skin of our fruit trees,
> Lest being overproud in sap and blood
> With too much riches it confound itself.
> Had he done so to great and growing men
> They might have lived to bear, and he to taste
> Their fruits of duty. Superfluous branches
> We lop away that bearing boughs may live.
> Had he done so, himself had borne the crown
> Which waste of idle hours hath quite thrown down.
> (3.4.54–66)

This speech emphasizes the duality of 'waste' in *Richard II* as both destruction and inaction. Calling up its primary sense as destructive, the Gardener implies how 'the wasteful king' through inaction has permitted 'the bark', 'overproud in sap and blood', to 'confound itself'. Once again for Shakespeare, Richard's idleness produces a dangerous growth;

something comes from nothing. The Gardener's offer of himself as an example to Richard's neglectful self-tending activates the second sense in which he uses 'waste': as misspent time.[34] 'Had he done so' states not only opinion, but common political knowledge: the good prince rids his court of flattering sycophants. It is the recognition of this erroneous in/action that enables the Gardener to arrive at his reflection on Richard's use of time, his 'waste of idle hours'. The Gardener's reliance on what Richard has not done demonstrates the king's failure to understand time as incremental and opportunistic. That is, Richard is wasteful not merely because he pursues a policy of inaction; from a Ciceronian perspective his inaction might be viewed as *occasio*, 'a period of time offering a convenient opportunity for doing or not doing something'.[35] Indeed, the play offers two such occasional, or kairotic moments: Richard's throwing of the warder, and Bolingbroke's well-timed return from exile. Yet Northumberland and the other rebels urge this second act as a social good, while Richard's interruption of a legal trial shocks his and Shakespeare's audience. Richard's perception of time as belonging *only* to him establishes his sense of time as lacking social norms, as unable to be wasted by him because of his protected status as monarch (cf. 3.2.53–57).

Prior to the Gardener's arrival in 3.4, Shakespeare uses Queen Isabel to underline Richard's anti-normative attitude toward time.[36] As 3.1 begins, Shakespeare links the queen's emotional state with her use of time, and she asks her ladies: 'What sport shall we devise here in this garden / To drive away the heavy thought of care?' (3.4.1). Playing bowls, dancing, telling tales, singing, and finally weeping, all notably communal activities, are proffered in turn and in turn rejected. Her decision finally to eavesdrop on the gardeners—and her bet on what they will discuss—suggests her disinclination to virtuous time-use here. The queen's remarks about what to do in the meantime, and the gardeners' own subsequent reflections on how time has been used by the king and by themselves exemplify together the play's insistence on thinking about the norm of individual time-use and its relationship to the community at large.

Richard II's interrogation of the good of individual time control is represented not only in Richard's perceived idleness, but also in Bolingbroke's use of time. Unsurprisingly, his work ethic offers a foil to Richard's. Having secured his return through the nobles' support, Bolingbroke swiftly and illegally sentences Bushy and Green to death before turning to the Welsh threat, instructing his officers: 'Come, lords, away, / To fight with Glendower and his complices. / Awhile to work, and after, holiday' (3.1.42–44). Opposed to Richard's idleness, Bolingbroke's future planning of work and rest suggests a return to kingly-temporal control as a model for time-use. However, both Bolingbroke and the queen reinforce Peter Burke's argument that it is those in power who control when leisure or holiday are made, thus pressuring again the totality of individual time-control.[37] But to understand individual, subjective time it is not enough to say that it is subject to Foucauldian state-power dynamics. Bolingbroke's pursuit of 'justice' problematizes his time-use, as the patently illegitimate execution of Bushy and Green interrogates the ethics behind that central power's monopoly on norms of time-control and time-use.

As with Henry VI, it is ironically only in isolation, away from the society that constructs temporal norms, that Richard can understand his role in that construction and its relation to the time of the individual. He laments:

> How sour sweet music is
> When time is broke, and no proportion kept.
> So is it in the music of men's lives;
> And here have I the daintiness of ear
> To check time broke in a disordered string,
> But for the concord of my state and time,
> Had not an ear to hear my true time broke.
>   (V.v.43–48)

Richard suggests that time enables and preserves the sweet nature of music; the misuse of time sours that which was sweet—here, Richard himself. The individual's nature depends on time-use, and human nature itself is soured when 'no proportion' is kept. Significantly, it is not objective clock-time that first instructs Richard, but that time which is often associated with the ordered self and social harmony: musical time.[38] It is only outside of society that Richard can understand its temporal norms, and this placement suggests that reflection and isolation are essential for understanding personal time use. 'Proportion' is the crucial word for him here to signify his awareness of his actions in relationship to all others. Furthermore, half of the four uses of 'time' in this passage are personal. '[M]y state and time' and 'my true time' urge the image of dissonance between the demands and temporal norms of state and society and the pursuit of personal, subjective desires. Alternatively, Richard's 'true time' is providential, broken in pursuit of his 'idle hours', as the Gardener called them. The collapse of musical metaphor onto the image of state—evident in 'disordered string' and 'concord' (where we hear 'chord')—further fuses the temporal norms established by society with the image of harmonious subjectivity which the music metaphor offers.

Richard's persistent disinterest in time throughout the play makes his invocation of clock-time then all the more powerful when he invokes established medieval imagery to imagine his powerlessness.[39] 'I wasted time, and now doth time waste me' unifies how Shakespeare has been thinking about 'waste' throughout the play: as destruction and as idleness.

> For now hath time made me his numbring clock.
> My thoughts are minutes, and with sighs they jar
> Their watches on unto mine eyes, the outward watch,
> Whereto my finger, like a dial's point,
> Is pointing still in cleansing them from tears.
> Now, sir, the sound that tells what hour it is
> Are clamorous groans which strike upon my heart,
> Which is the bell. So sighs and tears and groans
> Show minutes, time, and hours; but my time
> Runs posting on in Bolingbroke's proud joy,
> While I stand fooling here, his jack o'th' clock.
> (5.5.50–60)

Richard is now his own timekeeper, the supreme image of Shakespeare's subjective time, as it is the usurped monarch's suffering 'which tells what hour it is'. Yet following on these images of temporal collapse—of music to state, of self to clock—Shakespeare crafts the image of divorce from time, of Richard apart from his own time and used to tell that of another. He is Bolingbroke's, and time's, 'jack of the clock'.[40] Where the possession of time dominated the first half of this speech, in 'my state and time' and 'my true time', through the poetic process that transforms Richard into a clock, time leaves him to 'run [...] posting on' with Bolingbroke. In this way, in his loss of individual time, Richard himself becomes the exemplar of the time-use norms which he flouted. His address to an off-stage 'sir' and his image of himself as a clown, 'fooling here', both highlight how Richard thinks of himself in this exemplary manner. He remains to tell time to us, the audience.

Conclusion

Instability and subjectivity have been located in clock-time, and as a result scholars have focused on the multiplicity of time itself, rather than on what that multiplicity signifies in terms of the relationship between the subject and their sense of control over, and use of, time. That the experience of time is individual and contingent upon each individual strongly implies that a subject *should* or *could* possess control over their time. Such implicit agency is essential to the notion of self-regulation, the notion that a person can manage his or her time. The subjectivity of clock-time, then, rather than its objectivity, becomes a critical building block in the larger history of our own time management norms.

Yet that focus on the individual inherent in the 'subjective' suggests that subjective time is not influenced and shaped by social temporal norms. By examining those texts so often attended to by Shakespearean critics of time, I have sought to problematize the critical inclinations to make time wholly individual and subjective through clock-time's accepted abnormality, and, further, to make subjective time the exclusive purview of the state. To do so, I have examined the way that dramatic social norms—which are not, in my view, synonymous with absolute state power however they may be informed by it—encroach upon and shape the norms of individual time use in Shakespeare's drama. For howsoever obvious it may seem to claim that our time is society's time, until now we have not fully interrogated how our inclination to structure and manage time responds to, and is shaped by, expectations of our time-use as individuals. As we have seen, time use and control in Shakespearean drama is imagined as bound to gender roles, affective states, and offices (Ophelia, Katherina, Rosalind; Henry VI and Richard II). We thus need to think further about these aspects in relationship to time in early modern drama. Shakespeare's drama participates in constructing those temporal norms it investigates and interrogates, and in doing so it resists the totalizing individuality of time implied in Quinones's identification of time as a 'force of consciousness'.[41] Time is indeed a Renaissance force of consciousness—but it is one not driven by the individual alone.

Notes

1. Thompson and Taylor (2006); all future citations to the *Norton Shakespeare* (2016).
2. Torczon (1967: 522). Alexander Pope includes the alternative readings in footnotes to his vol. 6 (402). Thompson and Taylor also note the inclusion of 'pace' in certain modern editions (2006: 262).
3. 'Make your own pace' as a phrase is not easily discoverable in early modern texts if we base such a search in EEBO-TCP. However, Shakespeare does repeat the sense of making one's own pace, and exploits the tension between willed-speed and controlled movement (as with a horse), in *All's Well That Ends Well*. The Countess says of the Clown Lavache that 'he has no / pace but runs where he will' (4.5.56–57).
4. Recent examples include Stern (2015), Wood (2009), Cohen (2014), Paul (2014), Harris (2009), Sipiora and Baumlin (2002), Goldberg and Menon (2005), and Freeman (2010).
5. My thanks to Edel Semple for noting that this ubiquity suggests our failure at managing time.
6. This idea has been documented by many scholars, but cf. Quinones (1972), Le Goff (1980), Dohrn-van Rossum (1996), and Glennie and Thrift (2009).
7. Stern (2015: 13).
8. Le Goff (1980: 50), Dohrn-van Rossum (1996: 253–259), and Engammare (2009).
9. Wilson (1970: 396). Wilson cites respectively proverb I 10, J. Northbrooke's *Treatise Against Dicing* (1577) and proverb I 13 citing James VI's *Basilikon Doron* (1599).
10. For this passage and further discussion of idleness (including Chaucer's use of it), see Engel, Loughnane, and Williams (2016: 283–287). My thanks to Rory Loughnane for reminding me of this moment in the poem.
11. 'Just as fallow lands, when rich and fertile, are seen to abound in hundreds and thousands of different kinds of useless weeds so that, if we would make them do their duty, we must subdue them and keep them busy with seeds specifically sown for our service; and just as women left alone may sometimes be seen to produce shapeless lumps of flesh but need to be kept busy by a semen other than her own in order to produce good natural offspring: so too with our minds', Montaigne's 'On Idleness' (2000: 31). And cf. Shakespeare, 'Ten thousand harms […] / My idleness doth hatch' (*Antony and Cleopatra*, 1.2.128–290); France's 'even mead' 'Conceives by idleness' (*Henry V*, 5.2.48, 51).
12. From the emblem of Occasion in A Person of Quality (1673: sig. C2^v).

13. Stern (2015: 20, 13).
14. Ibid.: 21.
15. Ibid.: 13.
16. Wood (2009: 18).
17. The idea that whoever controls time possesses social control is found in Le Goff (1980: 47–49), but, of course, it recalls Foucauldian ideas in *Discipline and Punish*; this idea of temporal domination equal to state domination is also used by Hyman (2013) and Sauter (2007).
18. cf. Cohen (2006), Hyman (2013), and Stern (2015).
19. A few recent examples include Sauter (2007), Dohrn-van Rossum (1996), and Glennie and Thrift (2009) (who do make use of letters and autobiography, however).
20. See, for example, Bolens and Taylor (2001: 287, 288, 291), Bradbury and Collette (2009: 352, 259), and Humphrey (2001: 108).
21. cf. Proverbs 19:15 and 31:27, and Ecclesiastes 10:18.
22. Bradbury and Collette (2009: 365). The popularity of Ecclesiastes remained throughout the sixteenth and into the seventeenth century (see Johanson 2017).
23. Dohrn-van Rossum (1996: 218ff), Humphrey (2001: 107).
24. Bradbury and Collette (2009: 261).
25. Katherina's time control is overturned by the play's end, when Petruccio makes the return to Padua conditional on Katherina's agreement with him that the sun is the moon (4.6.6–8). There is more to say on this issue, but that is beyond this essay's limits.
26. There is a growing scholarly consensus in attribution studies that *3 Henry VI* is co-authored. See Craig and Burrows (2012) and Taylor and Loughnane (2017, esp. 496–499).
27. As Quinones (1972), Cox and Rasmussen (2001), Stern (2015: 10–11), and Lake (2016), among many others, also argue.
28. See Stern (2015).
29. cf. Sarah Lewis's forthcoming monograph *Time and Gender in Early Modern England* (Cambridge University Press).
30. For the impatience of a maid, cf. Juliet, 'So tedious is this day / As is the night before some festival / To an impatient child that hath new robes / And may not wear them' (*Romeo and Juliet* 3.2.28–31). That time moves slowly for women absent from their lovers became, according to one view, conventional in the Renaissance (Glasser 1972: 134–136).
31. Salerio in *Merchant* details how he would experience time only in relation to thinking about his material future in his hypothetical ship of fortune: 'I should not see the sandy hour glass run / But I should think of shallows and of flats' (1.1.25–26).

32. See, for example, Kastan (1973), Quinones (1972), and Cox and Rasmussen (2001).
33. That message would only be available if a spectator thought about the plays together, back-to-back, which would only have been possible for the first time in 1599. Regrettably, there is no space in this essay to discuss Hal's dismissal of Falstaff's 'what time of day is it lad?' (1.2.1).
34. The Gardener's charge repeats Gaunt's earlier accusation at 2.1.100–103 in which, through a synecdochal conflation of Richard with his crown and his country, Richard 'wast[es]' England just as time wastes him. For recent critical arguments concerning the political implications of the garden scene, see Condren (2016) and Doty (2010, esp. 197–199).
35. Cicero (1949) I.xxvii.40. '*Occasio autem est pars temporis habens in se alicuius rei idoneam faciendi aut non faciendi opportunitatem*'.
36. Condren also argues that Shakespeare's use of the queen is representative of Richard's own faults: wryly noting that if the garden were Lipsian, 'it has not done her much conspicuous good', he sees in her 'tyranny-tainted outburst' a model of Richard's own tyranny (2016: 13).
37. See Burke (1995).
38. See Lindley (2006).
39. Cohen (2006: 138). Cohen cites Otto Mayr citing Christine de Pizan: 'because our human body is made up of many parts and should be regulated by reason, it may be represented as a clock in which there are several wheels and measures' ('L'Epitre d'Othea'). Chaucer and Froissart also provide evidence for this image; see Bradbury and Collette (2009) and Bolens and Taylor (2001).
40. cf. Hyman (2013) for a fuller discussion of the significance of 'jack' in Shakespeare's works. While Stern (2015), Hyman (2013), and others also observe Richard's loss of power here, my point is that in that loss Richard represents the tension between belief that time is personal and society's ability to determine and to check that individual temporality.
41. Quinones (1972: 1).

Works Cited

A Person of Quality. 1673. *Emblems Divine, Moral, Natural and Historical Expressed in Sculpture, and Applied to the Several Ages, Occasions, and Conditions of the Life of Many*. London.

Birth, Kevin. 2011. The Regular Sound of the Cock: Context Dependent Time Reckoning in the Middle Ages. *KronoScope* 11 (1–2): 125–144.

Bolens, Guillemette, and Paul Beckman Taylor. 2001. Chess, Clocks, and Counsellors in Chaucer's "Book of the Duchess". *The Chaucer Review* 35 (3): 281–293.

Bradbury, Nancy Mason, and Carolyn P. Collette. 2009. Changing Times: The Mechanical Clock in Late Medieval Literature. *The Chaucer Review, Time, Measure, and Value in Chaucer's Art and Chaucer's World* 43 (4): 351–375.

Burke, Peter. 1995. The Invention of Leisure in Early Modern Europe. *Past & Present.* 146: 136–150.

Cicero, Quintus Tullius. 1949. *De Inventione*, trans. H.M. Hubbell. London: William Heinemann Ltd.; Cambridge, MA: Harvard University Press.

Cohen, Adam Max. 2006. *Shakespeare and Technology: Dramatising Early Modern Technological Revolutions.* London: Palgrave.

Cohen, Simona. 2014. *Transformations of Time and Temporality in Medieval and Renaissance Art.* Leiden: Brill.

Condren, Conal. 2016. Skepticism and Political Constancy: *Richard II* and the Garden Scene as a Model of State. *The Review of Politics* 78: 1–19.

Craig, Hugh, and John Burrows. 2012. A Collaboration About a Collaboration: Authorship of *King Henry VI, Part Three*. In *Collaborative Research in the Digital Humanities*, ed. Willard McCarty and Marilyn Deegan, 27–66. London: Routledge.

Dohrn-van Rossum, Gerhard. 1996. *History of the Hour: Clocks and Modern Temporal Orders*, trans. Thomas Dunlap. Chicago and London: University of Chicago Press.

Doty, Jeff S. 2010. Shakespeare's *Richard II*, "Popularity", and the Early Modern Public Sphere. *Shakespeare Quarterly* 61 (2): 183–205.

Engel, William E., Rory Loughnane, and Grant Williams (eds.). 2016. *The Memory Arts in Renaissance England: A Critical Anthology.* Cambridge: Cambridge University Press.

Freeman, Elizabeth. 2010. *Time Binds: Queer Temporalities, Queer Histories.* Durham, NC: Duke University Press.

Glasser, Richard. 1972. *Time in French Life and Thought*, trans. C.G. Pearson. Manchester: Manchester University Press.

Glennie, Paul, and Nigel Thrift. 2009. *Shaping the Day: A History of Timekeeping in England and Wales, 1300–1800.* Oxford: Oxford University Press.

Goldberg, Jonathan, and Madhavi Menon. 2005. Queering History. *PMLA* 120 (5): 1608–1617.

Harris, Jonathan Gil. 2009. *Untimely Matter in the Time of Shakespeare.* Philadelphia: University of Pennsylvania Press.

Humphrey, Chris. 2001. Time and Urban Culture in Late Medieval England. In *Time in the Medieval World*, ed. Chris Humphrey and W.M. Ormrod, 105–117. Woodbridge: York Medieval Press.

Hyman, Wendy Beth. 2013. "For Now Hath Time Made Me His Numbering Clock": Shakespeare's Jacquemarts. *Early Theatre* 15: 143–156. http://dx.doi.org/10.12745/et.16.2.7.

Johanson, Kristine. 2017. "Our brains beguiled": Ecclesiastes and Sonnet 59's Poetics of Temporal Instability. In *The Sonnets: The State of Play*, ed. Hannah Crawforth, Elizabeth Scott-Baumann, and Clare Whitehead, 55–76. London: Arden Bloomsbury.

Kastan, David Scott. 1973. The Shape of Time: Form and Value in the Shakespearean History Play. *Comparative Drama* 7: 259–277.

Le Goff, Jacques. 1980. *Time, Work, & Culture in the Middle Ages*, trans. Arthur Goldhammer. Chicago: University of Chicago Press.

Lindley, David. 2006. *Shakespeare and Music*. London: Thompson Learning.

Montaigne, Michel de. 2000. *Essays*, trans. and ed. M.A. Screech. London: Penguin.

Paul, Joanne. 2014. The Use of *Kairos* in Renaissance Political Philosophy. *Renaissance Quarterly* 67 (1): 43–78.

Quinones, Ricardo. 1972. *The Renaissance Discovery of Time*. Cambridge, MA: Harvard University Press.

Sauter, Michael J. 2007. Clockwatchers and Stargazers: Time Discipline in Early Modern Berlin. *The American Historical Review* 112: 685–709.

Shakespeare, William. 2001. *3 Henry VI*, ed. John D. Cox and Eric Rasmussen. London: Arden Shakespeare.

Shakespeare, William. 2006. *Hamlet: The Texts of 1603 and 1623*, ed. Ann Thompson and Neil Taylor. London: Arden Shakespeare.

Shakespeare, William. 2016. *The Norton Shakespeare*, ed. Stephen Greenblatt, et al. New York and London: Norton.

Sipiora, Phillip, and James S. Baumlin (eds.). 2002. *Rhetoric and Kairos: Essays in History, Theory, and Praxis*. Albany, NY: State University of New York Press.

Stern, Tiffany. 2015. Time for Shakespeare: Hourglasses, Sundials, Clocks, and Early Modern Theatre. *Journal of the British Academy* 3: 1–33. https://doi.org/10.85871/jba/003.001.

Taylor, Gary, and Rory Loughnane. 2017. The Canon and Chronology of Shakespeare's Works. In *The New Oxford Shakespeare: Authorship Companion*, ed. Gary Taylor and Gabriel Egan, 417–603. Oxford: Oxford University Press.

Torczon, Vern. 1967. Paperback Editions of *Hamlet*: The Limits of Editorial Eclecticism. *College English* 28: 519–524.

Wilson, F.P. (ed.). 1970. *The Oxford Dictionary of English Proverbs, Compiled by William George Smith*, 3rd ed. Oxford: Oxford University Press.

Wood, David Houston. 2009. *Time, Narrative, and Emotion in Early Modern England*. Aldershot: Ashgate.

Under the Skin: A Neighbourhood Ethnography of Leather and Early Modern Drama

Julie Sanders

It is afternoon on a midsummer day in London in the 1590s. You, along with several other hundred people, have decided to come to see a play at one of London's commercial playhouses. The play is about to start and so the press of standing spectators in the pit or groundling area of the Rose Theatre in Southwark—for this is where you are—has become a little more intense, crowded indeed, as people jostle for a good position. You are now pressed so close to your fellow audience members that you can quite literally sense, feel, touch, hear, smell them. It is warm and humid in London this midsummer and that heightens some of the aural, haptic and indeed olfactory sensations you are experiencing. Among other smells that arrest your nose you can detect the foodstuffs that are either on sale or being consumed at the theatre this afternoon—fruit, beer, nuts—you can even hear the shells of the latter being crunched underfoot as the crowd jockeys for position and elbow room. The wet

---

J. Sanders (✉)
Newcastle University, Newcastle upon Tyne, UK
e-mail: Julie.Sanders@newcastle.ac.uk

© The Author(s) 2019
R. Loughnane and E. Semple (eds.), *Staged Normality in Shakespeare's England*, Palgrave Shakespeare Studies,
https://doi.org/10.1007/978-3-030-00892-5_5

straw that is strewn beneath your feet also releases its own slightly pungent odour in the heat. Body odour and sweat are undoubtedly in the mix; perhaps wafting from the seated galleries is the slightly more refined though no less heady perfume of 'civeted' individuals—those wearing the fashionable musky civet-based perfumes of the day. In the groundling space, people's clothing also emits a scent and that scent acts as a marker of identity, perhaps of rank, or of consumer patterns, and even more readily perhaps of occupation.

Right by your nose, for example, is the shoulder of a man wearing a leather jerkin, the smell of its heavily tanned leather hitting your nostrils with a particular intensity.[1] A leather jerkin might in itself signify that you are stood behind a working man, a notion further underscored by his presence today as a groundling, a standing member of the theatre audience. But in a moment of involuntary association, a whole series of other thoughts are conjured up. Your mind travels to the tanneries and leatherworking communities that are clustered close by around the site of the Rose Theatre and which, in addition to the parish of St Saviour Southwark, characterise other enclaves and parts of the growing urban space of London: Bermondsey and Shoreditch. You think perhaps of some of the recent arguments around the commodity of leather and the practice of tanning; maybe you look, voluntarily or involuntarily, down at your shoes and are reminded of the Clerkenwell workshops where they were made, the clouted patchwork leather used by your shoemaker, the related sights, smells, and sounds of that trade, its particularised nails and forms, and its intimate workshop rooms abutting the shared family home of the owner.

Ah, but your mind must be brought back into the present moment, for the play is about to begin. Concentrate … I am distracting you with my stories.

Narrative, Neighbourhood, and Everyday Experience

A number of scholars have been working of late to look at the component parts of the cultural and social map of London, and to offer a thick description of its neighbourhoods and parishes.[2] As a literary scholar I am interested in thinking from the playhouse outwards; to consider what is proximate to the playhouse and how in turn that influences both what is staged and how what is staged at specific venues in turn has agency in the surrounding parish. I want in the process to invoke Bertrand Westphal's points about geocriticism, and his argument that as an approach it often commences from the vantage point of a specific neighbourhood or region and that it should involve a form of immersive practice, not just journeying to a place, then, but starting from it, a kind of 'locality criticism'.[3] The parish is a helpful unit to think with, one which returns us with fresh eyes to important earlier scholarship on neighbourhood and society.[4] The fieldwork for this essay predominantly takes place in St Saviour's Southwark, and that district of London is viewed in particular through the lens of its leatherworking practices and trades. I aim to get 'under the skin' quite literally of a series of overlapping communities and practices–labour-based, social, religious, mercantile, and normal–and as well as exploring specific sites and places related to these normalised activities and cultural practices, to consider how that everyday experience was rendered back to both familiar and unfamiliar audiences through staged drama. Plays by Thomas Heywood and Thomas Dekker will form the case study close readings of this form of 'staged normality' in the essay.[5]

GETTING UNDER THE SKIN: LEATHERWORK AND CUTWORK IN SOUTHWARK

Getting back to the specific theme of leather, though, I want to think through the prism of the first part of Thomas Heywood's two-part dramatic history, *Edward IV*. Written in the 1590s, this play was probably performed in at least three key venues of the time over the next decade or so: the Boar's Head in Shoreditch, the Rose in Southwark's Bankside and the Red Bull in Clerkenwell.[6] There is, of course, a version of this essay that could look at the influence of those theatre spaces on the construction and content of the play and that could think of these as a version of site-specific performance.[7] The Revels editor Richard Rowland, for example, suggests that the extensive use of an '*above*' space in *1 Edward IV* is the residual trace of the Rose and Red Bull theatre performances that took place between 1602 and 1605.[8] But in thinking about the everyday or normal geographies of early modern London, I prefer to 'follow the things' and to think through a particular artefact and material culture.[9] Building on Robin Bernstein's work on twentieth-century American constructions of race, I want to work with the concept of 'scriptive things', things that are as she says, 'citational in that they arrange and propel bodies in recognisable ways' and the ways in which this plays into early modern dramatic representation.[10]

In its multiple and variant forms and in its presence, implied or explicit, leather in early modern drama is undoubtedly a 'scriptive thing'. It tells us stories about making and use, and by extension about the working day, but also about status and rank. Different grades and provenance of leather—kid, calf, or pigskin, for example—would have signified the wealth, and by extension the social access, of the wearer and this would have been understood through haptic engagement with the leather—softness and suppleness to the touch indicating more expensive varieties— and through something as visceral as the smell of that leather jerkin in the Rose Theatre. Many of the essays in this collection are in their different ways attending to what Patricia Fumerton has previously referred to as 'the new historicism of the everyday'.[11] In her analysis, Fumerton recognises that 'The sense of the everyday is very much caught up in sensuality or physicality' and the leatherwork of this essay is very much to be understood through sensory as well as parochial geographies.[12]

Heywood's *1 Edward IV* in generic terms is part of the wider English chronicle movement in drama at this time though it is also in significant ways resistant to that tradition. It is also a play replete with 'scriptive things', encouraged by the predominance of craftsmen as characters. In both its parts, *Edward IV* is aware of the differences and distinctiveness of metropolitan and provincial identities, especially as it maps the journey of Falconbridge and his southern county rebels through the counties abutting London and through the suburbs up to the physical threshold of the city walls and gates and in the stand-alone scenes that involve an encounter between John Hobs, the tanner of Tamworth, and a disguised monarch (itself a very literal reworking of a specific folk ballad tradition).

The rebels imagine themselves taking over the physical workshops of London, the craft neighbourhoods of use and making of which the Southwark tanneries and leatherworking communities were one important component part:

> *Falconbridge*: We will be masters of the Mint ourselves,
> And set our own stamp on the golden coin.
> We'll shoe our neighing coursers with no worse
> Than the purest silver that is sold in Cheap.
> At Leadenhall we'll sell pearls by the peck,
> As now the mealmen use to sell their meal.
> (Scene 2 ll. 49–54)[13]

It is fascinating to register the mercantile idiom here—of measurement, sale, and expenditure—but also the mention of specific sites such as Cheapside, famous for its gold and silversmiths, and memorialised in other early modern plays such as Thomas Middleton's *A Chaste Maid in Cheapside*. In their discourse of hostile takeover, the rebels also draw attention to the mercers and silk workers of that neighbourhood:

> *Spicing* You know Cheapside? There are the mercers' shops,
> Where we will measure velvet by our pikes
> And silks and satins by the street's whole breadth!
> (Scene 2, ll. 66–68)

We have here in action a version of spatial occupation. The rebels imagine themselves appropriating the different neighbourhood geographies, the wards and the parishes, of the capital. Interestingly, these geographies in their craft-defined hands and mouths are largely defined by trade. Delineating the craft occupations of London in this way is a means of mapping and understanding, of knowledge making. The rebels imagine unfettered access to the city's resources: to its bakers, brewers, mercers, and vintners, as well as physically to its streets and houses. As it is, as the play proceeds, a mobilised citizenry beats the rebels back and their fantasies of takeover remain just that.

But provincial identity is not only figured through the rebels' linguistic and physical movements in *1 Edward IV*, but even more significantly perhaps through the singular figure of Hobs, a tanner from Tamworth in Warwickshire. We first encounter Hobs on his way back from Coleshill market near Coventry where he has just purchased a number of cowhides for the purpose of his trade (Scene 11, ll. 125–127). His opening lines, addressing his offstage serving-man Dudgeon, provide a series of deictic markers for the benefit of the audience, enabling them to imagine the leather hides if not to actually see them as properties onstage:

> Dudgeon! Dost this hear? Look well to Brock, my mare; drive Dun and her fair and softly down the hill, and take heed the thorns tear not the horns of my cowhides as thou goest near the hedges. Ha? What says thou, knave? Is the bull's hide down? Why, lay it up again; what care I? I'll meet thee at the stile, and help to set it all straight. And yet, God help, it's a crooked world, and an unthrifty, for some that have ne'er a shoe had rather

go barefoot than buy clout-leather to mend the old, when they can buy no new, for they have time enough to mend all, they sit so long between the cup and the wall.

(Scene 11, ll. 1–11)

At this point in the action, Hobs takes out his leather pouch (another meaning-making object on the stage and yet another example of leatherwork) and carefully works out his spending at market, 'A dicker of cowhides cost me—' (ll. 18–19). As well as conjuring a vivid imaginative picture, this little scene tells us much about the contemporary politics and economics of trade and making. The scene highlights the everyday activities and their attendant sensory geographies that were highly pertinent to various groups of Southwark parishioners who might well have assembled as an audience for this play in its Rose Theatre performances. Hobs draws our attention here not only to the fairing and marketing activities that provided the rhythm of travel and barter to a tradesman's life, but also to the acts of buying and repair that determined local economies.

The 'clout' leather that Hobs refers to was specifically used for patching shoes, and the general resistance to its use would have been readily understood by contemporary audiences as part of a general decline in the good reputation and standing of the leather trades at this time. William Harrison's *Description Of England*, a compendium text first published in 1577 alongside Raphael Holinshed's *Chronicles*, treats directly with graziers who are grown 'so cunning that if they do but see an ox or bullock, and come to the feeling of him, they will give a guess at his weight, and how many score or stone of flesh and tallow he beareth'.[14] Since he soon after reports some of those same graziers riding out in velvet coats, the implication of a trade growing fat on its business is inescapable. He also mentions that many farmers are abandoning their main trade to enrich themselves as tanners, woodmen, and the like.

There was, then, a perception of general corruption in the leather-related industries in the late sixteenth century and indeed the 1563 'Acte Touching Tanners, Couriers, Shooemakers and Other Artyffices occupyeing the cutting of lether' (5.Eliz.I.c.8) was designed to address this issue. The act forbade the tanning of certain hides, including the bull's hide that Hobs is transporting in this scene.[15] All of this detail would seem to position audiences to categorise Hobs as a stereotypically corrupt tanner but, as we will see, in reality, the steady empathy that the play strives to build between him and watching spectators has quite the opposite effect.

Rowland notes astutely the '[u]nremitting specificity of the play's handling of the tanner, both his industry and his habitat', and it is this specificity that appears to create a potential for empathy between audiences and the onstage artisanal character. Between Hobs's first encounter with the monarch in disguise and his closing exchange with a widow reluctantly primed by the King to marry Hobs—and presumably enable for him the kind of social mobility and financial security that his occupation could never provide—spectators are party to a rich seam of dialogue and exchange with the monarch in disguise. Edward IV could be seen to be gathering intelligence about his subjects in a performative manner akin to Hal's Eastcheap sojourns in Shakespeare's *Henry IV* plays. We witness in operation the basic generosity and kindness of the tanner and his open-mindedness as he welcomes 'Ned the King's butler' (Edward IV's assumed persona) into his home. Hobs expresses a clear preference in the play for his regional homespace rather than the court—'I ha' nothing to do at court. I'll home with my cowhides, and if the King will come to me, he shall be welcome' (Scene 13, ll. 69–71).

In the domestic scene involving the disguised monarch that ensues, Hobs makes mention of the investment he has made in the education of his daughter at a forward-thinking Lichfield school (Scene 14, ll. 9–11). The tanner will demonstrate similar generosity of spirit when, even far from the King's presence, or at least so he assumes, he readily contributes to fund-raising for the King's campaign against the rebels and makes considerable efforts to persuade his more reluctant neighbours to do the same. There is a performance of a regional neighbourliness here and a momentary glimpse into the everyday, tangible lives of workmen. Such a scene can be usefully read alongside something like the press-ganging scene in the Gloucestershire orchards in Shakespeare's *2 Henry IV*. These examples suggest that the genre of the English history play, with its sometime interest in the motivations and actions of mustered soldiers (compare *2 Henry VI*, *Henry V*), offers a rich repository of staged normality.

Interestingly, thrillingly, Hobs is so taken with Ned the butler's company that he even imagines marrying his daughter Nell to him but only if Ned will take up a worthy trade like tanning, since a courtly profession is in Hobs's view a less than reputable occupation:

> And I like thee so well, Ned, that hadst thou an occupation – for 'service is no heritage'; 'a young courtier, an old beggar' – I could find in my heart to cast her away upon thee. And, if thou wilt forsake the court, and turn

tanner, or bind thyself to a shoemaker in Lichfield, I'll give thee twenty nobles ready money, with my Nell, and trust thee with a dicker of leather, to set up thy trade.

(Scene 14, ll. 59–65)

We might read into this attention to the life of a tanner and the time the monarch happily spends in Hobs's company a stamp of approval of sorts from the king. The normal, regional, and the everyday is by extension elevated and deemed worthy of such attention. In the process, Edward IV experiences albeit momentarily, and again in a manner akin to Shakespeare's Hal/Henry, a 'normal' life, gaining a valuable alternative perspective on the court in the process. Via the 'Ned the butler' scenes, then, audiences too might have viewed their own normal existences through a new lens.

Later in the play, Hobs falls into a swoon when he realises he is conversing with the actual king. He not unreasonably assumes that he will be thrown into jail and face hanging, a fate akin to that of Hobs's own son who has been arrested for petty thieving. Instead, his case is taken up by the King and both father and son are offered a generous pardon. A watching audience might be taken back to the initial surprise of Edward IV (as Ned) that this provincial tanner is not going to self-servingly grab his moment to petition the monarch for personal gain; Hobs confirms yet again that he is his own man, faithfully plying his trade.

It is the specific onstage and offstage resonance of the leather hides in the Hobs scenes that I wish to focus on a moment longer. As Rowland notes:

> In *Edward IV* [...] Hobs's participation in the leather industry permeates the (sometimes obscure) language he uses and, by extension, governs the rapport between himself and the audience [...][16]

He suggests that '[e]very member of that audience would have had some acquaintance with the leather trade, if only as a consumer' and that '[m]any spectators [were] likely to have had direct involvement with one of the many manufacturing outlets of the industry'.[17] Historical research indicates that there were as many as 3000 shoemakers in the capital at this time with as many again working in the light leather trades.[18] These workers tended to cluster geographically, especially in the neighbourhoods of Shoreditch, site of the Boar's Head where *1 Edward IV* was most likely first performed, and in Southwark, site of the Rose, its subsequent performance venue. By the late sixteenth century, there were 80 tanneries in Southwark alone. Parish and practice can then be seen to shape and inform both repertoire and reception in significant ways. If we return to the idea of proximity as a maker of relationship and meaning, a partial definition perhaps of 'neighbourhood', then these would have been the sights, sounds and, often noxious, smells that playgoers would have crossed through both *en route* to and on the way back from a performance of *1 Edward IV* and in this way the affordances of the local environment, its 'scriptive things', physical and visceral as much as theological, would inform the ways in which that play made meaning in the world.[19]

As Hobs's anxieties about expenditure and market share in *1 Edward IV* reveal, leatherworking and tanning was a precarious trade prone both to the acquisitive attention of monopolists and to drawing the opposition of London communities who objected to the attendant smells and water pollution that were a regular industrial offshoot of the enterprise. Maps from the time indicate that tanneries, and therefore the homesteads of their owners and operators, were deliberately placed on the margins of the city for this reason, a performance of the kind of social marginalisation witnessed in the reaction of the widow at the end of *1 Edward IV* to the King's proposition that she should marry Hobs.[20] Her explicit scorn for the hobnailed boots the artisan worker wears is indicative of an even deeper social disregard: "Clubs and clouted shoes! There's none enamoured here" (Scene 23, ll. 147–148).

Fortunately, Hobs seems even less keen than the widow on the monarch's matchmaking efforts:

> 'S' nails, twenty pound for a kiss? Had she as many twenty pound bags as I have knobs of bark in my tan-fat, she might kiss them away in a quarter of a year. I'll no St Katherine's widows, if kisses be so dear.
> (Scene 23, ll. 143–146)

The tanner's idiom once again locates him among the objects and practices of leatherworking trades and in particular the tanneries in which he has spent his working life. He invokes here the bark used in the tanning process and this places him directly in the context of his Tamworth community which simultaneously works to locate Southwark parishioner-spectators in theirs, surrounded as they were by the practical realities of the leatherworking trade.[21]

But this rootedness in a community of practice also makes Hobs the object of the widow's social scorn. As a group, tanners lacked the standing of those dignified by guilds and companies. Their presence remained geographically and symbolically on the margins of the city, as compared to the Cordwainers, Shipmakers, Goldsmiths, et al. They had no formal livery company so they lacked representation (the Bermondsey tanners did not even gain a charter until the early eighteenth century). In this way, the parochial themes of the play would have had resonance for certain groups of spectators. Heywood's play can and has been read as a propaganda exercise to win respect for the tannery trade in a manner akin to Thomas Dekker's *The Shoemaker's Holiday*. Both playwrights are often understood as being interested in artisanal practice and in part an advocate for these trade communities. Certainly, *Edward IV* provides insight into the way in which the communities and neighbourhoods of trade are brought onto the early modern stage and how parish politics might figure in the production of meaning at a given performance.[22] More specifically, Hobs's good deeds and good nature automatically test the cultural stereotype of the corrupt tanner and enables those spectators associated with the trade to feel pride in their own occupation while simultaneously testing the unconscious bias of others.

The limited availability of leather to leather workers and tanners caused real hardships out in the everyday communities and neighbourhoods of London and the provinces. A 1554 document spoke of:

> Many poore Artficers [...] Now being very poore Men and not able to buyer two or three Hides or Backes of Leather at one tyme, nor to paye ready moneye for the same, arre enforced to gyve upp their Occupations in greate number [...] (I Mary st.3.c.7)[23]

This high level of unemployment would have had a very visible impact in St Saviour's Southwark. The problem had only begun to ease in the early 1600s when we know Heywood's play was being performed at the Rose. Thus, agency is multidirectional in this reading. We can see the Southwark parish, a heartland of leatherworking industries as well as open air theatres at this time, much like Blackfriars or St Paul's precincts in other recent studies, proving 'crucial in shaping the multiple sensibilities—religious, civic, social, economic' of its inhabitants and indeed its visitors, the audiences for the plays at the Rose like Heywood's *1 Edward IV*.[24] But, equally, drama has a profound effect on its spectators. What merits further analysis are the ways in which the story of Hobs the Tanner or the appropriating rebels could have mobilised an audience on any given day to think not only about historical but also very local, very current, very topical, and indeed topographical, conditions. The dramatic architecture of plays performed in the open air playhouses like the Rose, where act breaks were not yet the norm or absolute standard that they would become in the candlelit indoor playhouses, often relied on the particular meaning-making of juxtaposition.[25] We might apply the same concept of juxtaposition to understand the importance to the playhouse or indeed the parish of everyday experience of proximate spaces and activities.

Handwork and Footwork

We have thus far concentrated on the suggestive presence of leather in its early stages of manufacture in early modern drama: as hides for sale and as objects for tanning. But, for the remainder of this essay, I want to turn our attention to the specific artefacts fashioned from leather that themselves performed, in Bernstein's suggestive terms, as citational 'scriptive things' on the early modern stage, and specifically, to shoes.

Other leather artefacts that would warrant similar attention would include gloves, saddles, and bellows; each tells its own socio-spatial history on the stage. Gloves, of course, were made of variable raw materials, from silk and wool to leather, but the deployment of leather gloves onstage often signified specific activities such as falconry or archery and featured heavily in the masculine worlds of the Shakespearean history play. Shakespeare's own father John was in the glove-making trade and his plays evidence a good understanding of the craft involved from accurate references to specific tools of the trade in *The Merry Wives of Windsor*, where Mistress Quickly declares at one point: 'Does he not wear a great round beard, like a glover's paring-knife?' (1.4.18–19) to Mercutio's witty evocation of easily stretched kidskin leather in *Romeo and Juliet* ('Oh, here's a wit of cheveril, that stretches from an inch narrow to an ell broad!', 2.4.83–84).[26]

Shakespeare's father and by extension his son would have been familiar with all kinds of animal hides and their texture, scent, and appearance as well as their sociocultural associations. During the reign of Queen Elizabeth I, heavily embroidered kid leather gloves became a highly fashionable accoutrement and status symbol for elite women and so regularly signified both aspiration and conspicuous consumption in city comedies. In Jonson's *Epicene*, for example, the character Haughty exclaims:

> We see no ensigns of a wedding here, no character of a bridal: where be our scarves and our gloves? (3.6.70–71)[27]

Saddlework in turn featured in many plays engaged with themes of domestic travel and mobility such as Jonson's *The New Inn* (1629), with its extensive scenes that take place in the inn stables, site of various nefarious activities intended to hoodwink the paying customers. The playwright's earlier scam-based play, *The Alchemist* (1610–1611), where there are numerous references to the bellows that fan the alchemist's fires in the Blackfriars household of that play, ensures that this particular leather artefact would have been the focus of extensive comic stage business.

Shoes have already been invoked in Heywood's *1 Edward IV* with the mention of Hobs's clouted or hob-nailed boots as a visual, and indeed aural, marker of his artisanal trade and by extension his social status.[28] Another 1590s play, already cited as having a parallel interest in the trades of making of early modern London, *The Shoemaker's Holiday* by Thomas Dekker (c. 1599, published 1600), focusses especially on the making space of the shoemaker's workshop to tell its story of civic duty and aspiration. There is a quasi-propagandistic element to the arc and narrative of Dekker's play, which charts the rise of a London shoemaker, Simon Eyre, to the position of Lord Mayor. *The Shoemaker's Holiday* is also a site-specific play in a number of interesting ways— the play closes with extended discussion about Eyre's plans for a new building in the capital: Leaden Hall (so-called because of the lead discovered in the digging of its foundations and used as a roofing material) or Leadenhall Market, which was gifted a special royal charter controlling the sale and purchase of leather (and presumably therefore protecting the rights of consumers as well as the concerns of honest tradesmen like Heywood's Hobs the tanner). *The Shoemaker's Holiday* is a play deeply invested in handicraft and the sites of making, bringing the workshop space actively onto the stage from the opening scenes. In the course of the play, we spend extended time both in the cobblers' workshop of Eyre and his journeymen and the seamstress's shop in which Ralph's wife Jane will of necessity ply her trade when her husband is absent fighting as a conscripted soldier.

It is interesting to pause and consider how *The Shoemaker's Holiday*'s leatherworking workshop could have been staged. Scene 13 of play opens with '*Hodge at his shop board*'. A 'shopboard' was usually either a hinged counter that covered a window at night and which could be let down during the day to form a shelf, or a stall from which to sell goods, although sometimes it was simply a moveable worktable. It was frequently a key prop on the early modern stage, telling the story of buying and selling as well as making in city comedies and even figuring in a murder scene in *Arden of Faversham*. Reading out from specific references elsewhere in the text of *The Shoemaker's Holiday*, it appears to be the first example of a shopboard that Dekker imagined for this particular play. Sharing a respect for artisanal culture with Heywood, the workshop scenarios of *The Shoemaker's Holiday* proffer an extremely positive presentation of the shoemaking trade. This time our focus as an audience is less on a specific individual life, such as that of Hobs the tanner, but rather of a working community. We are introduced in turn to its tools and activities, its customs, its idioms and expectations and indeed its aspirations. We see the native and migrant workers who make up the working community of the cobblers' workshop (one plotline concerns the arrival of a supposedly Dutch cobbler which would have been a very real possibility in the shoemaking communities of London at this time) and in the process explore the tensions of the fast-growing metropolis, with its increasing demand for resources and things, and indeed for the makers of those things. Another obvious stage property, also highly visible to the audience, are the shoes being worked on as lasts and finished artefacts by the journeymen. How the stage might have realised the sensory geographies of the contemporary capital and its occupational spaces merits further reflection. Could the audience for Dekker's play (first performed by the Admiral's Men at the Rose in 1599) smell the leather as it was worked? Could they perhaps even have heard the nails as they were driven into the clogs and working boots? To what extent was real work taking place on the stage or just mimetic representation of the same and would that have fundamentally altered audience responses?

Certainly, shoes form a significant prop in the plotline of *The Shoemaker's Holiday* as well as a resonant stage presence. On leaving his new wife for the life of soldiery, Ralph's parting gift is tellingly not the traditional scarf or ring of parting lovers (compare for example Shakespeare's *Troilus and Cressida* or the Belmont gift of Bassanio to Portia in *The Merchant of Venice*) but instead a pair of lovingly handcrafted leather shoes. These are a collaborative product of the workshop that we as audience have already witnessed as a performance of neighbourhood:

> Now, gentle wife, my loving, lovely Jane,
> Rich men at parting give their wives rich gifts,
> Jewels, and rings to grace their lily hands.
> Thou know'st our trade makes rings for women's heels.
> Here, take this pair of shoes cut out by Hodge,
> Stitched by my fellow, Firk, seamed by myself,
> Made up and pinked with letters for thy name.
> Wear them, my dear Jane, for thy husband's sake
> And every morning, when thou pull'st them on,
> Remember me, and pray for my return.
> Make much of them, for I have made them so
> That I can know them from a thousand moe.
> (1.235–246)[29]

I am interested in what contemporary spectators in 1599 in the Rose would have made of this detailed description, with its mention, for example, of pinking or 'gimping' which is itself a form of cutwork decoration and embellishment. The physical presence of and attention focussed on this leather object on the stage would cast fresh eyes on artefacts that would also have been part of spectators' everyday attentions. Their own shoes might have been as carefully stitched and valued in the making, wearing and mending as those carried, worked and referred to by the characters on stage. There is a much larger story to tell here of how writers like Dekker and Heywood, and indeed Jonson and Nashe, engaged with the world of craft societies and artisanal neighbourhoods, and not least with the world of the shoemaker, but for now it is enough to consider the multi-sited imaginaries—and imaginative geographies—that this one pair of shoes, or one yet to be processed leather hide, on the stage would and could mobilise. We are asking what the effect of staging the normal could have been. Did spectators recognise their everyday experiences, and their attendant sights, smells, and emotions, onstage and if so did this recognition add value to their sense of self-worth or did it in any way challenge their perception of themselves and their everyday contexts? In the kinds of props and actions that this essay has been describing did spectators see something recognisably normal, tangible, understandable? And if so what did those associations with their own lives encourage or foster?

Coda

But I have been distracting you from the task at hand; we are still in Southwark, still at the Rose, awaiting the staging of a play. It's quite warm and sticky now. The noises of the proximate working river of the Thames drift in and out of our ken. Think carefully and you might even hear some of the activities of the nearby workshops and tanneries carrying on while we yield ourselves up to the moment of performance. That man with his leather jerkin is annoyingly close, however, his shoulder pressing against your nose (he is much taller!) such that you may have to shove him slightly to get a better, less impeded, view of the stage.

Ssshhh though, settle, concentrate ... I think King Edward IV and his Duchess are about to enter ...

Notes

1. For related work on masculinity and trade at this time, see Arab (2011) and her edited collection with Dowd and Zucker on *Historical Affects* (2015). On labour-related geographies and taskscapes, see Korda and Dowd (2011) and Sanders (2011).
2. I would cite in particular the work of Harkness (2007); and two essays recently published in Smuts (2016) by Highley (2016) and Hentschell (2016). Highley advocates there for an 'attention to topographical specificity and local contingency' (617). Particular thanks to Chris Highley for the sharing of ideas and work on this theme during the development of the essay and to contributors to the 'Early Modern Literary Geographies' conference at the Huntington Library, California in October 2016 for related discussions.
3. Westphal's position is usefully summarised in Tally (2013); on 'locality criticism', see Huang (2009: 27).
4. See pioneering work by Wrightson (2002) and also Boulton (2008).
5. Many of Shakespeare's non-London locations have, of course, been read as analogues for the capital and its everyday spaces and practices, not least the careful delineations of urban and suburban practices in the 'Vienna' of *Measure for Measure*. Some of the London content of *Arden of Faversham* has also previously been attributed to Shakespeare not least in the wake of digital analysis of linguistic occurrences (see, for example, Kinney 2009); but it is notable that in a recent book on *Shakespeare in London* by Crawforth, Dustagheer and Young (2015), *Arden* does not feature in the discussion of mainstream Shakespearean drama.

6. For further discussion of the performance history of the play, see Richard Rowland's introduction to the Revels edition of the play: Heywood (2005).
7. Cf. Bennett and Polito (2014).
8. Rowland's Introduction to Heywood (2005: 6).
9. Appadurai (2011: 5).
10. Bernstein (2009: 67, 69). My thanks to Ayanna Thompson for this reference.
11. Patricia Fumerton's 'Introduction: A New New Historicism' in Fumerton and Hunt (1998), loc. 46–47, loc. 127.
12. On sensory geographies, see Pink (2015).
13. *1 Edward IV* in Heywood (2005). All subsequent references to this edition are in parentheses in the essay.
14. Harrison (2001: 1577), Book III, Chapter 8; 1587, Book III, Chapter I.
15. Details courtesy of Rowland's introduction to Heywood (2005: 28–29).
16. Ibid.: 29.
17. Ibid.
18. L. A. Clarkson, cited by Rowland in Heywood (2005: 29, n. 85).
19. On neighbourhood and proximity, see Sanders (2015).
20. See maps and details reproduced in *Bankside (the parishes of St Saviour and Christchurch Southwark)*, Vol. 22 of the *Survey of London* (London: London County Council, 1950) and see also the Southwark parish as delineated in the Agas map with the aid of the Map of Early Modern London site: https://mapoflondon.uvic.ca/.
21. Cf. McGavin and Walker (2016).
22. From this vantage point, Shakespeare's *Coriolanus* might be another play of a very different genre to consider as part of a cluster of trade-related drama at this time. I am indebted to Chris Foley's paper at a 2015 Shakespeare Association of America seminar (co-convened with Garrett A. Sullivan, Jr.) on 'Landscape, Space and Place' which examined grain mills in Southwark and their direct spatial and socioeconomic signification for *Coriolanus*.
23. Rowland in Heywood (2005: 35).
24. Hentschell (2016: 635).
25. For a fuller discussion of act-division in the early modern commercial theatre, see Taylor (1993).
26. Citations from Melchiori's and Weis's Arden editions: respectively, Shakespeare (2000) and (2012).
27. Citations from Dutton's Revels edition: Jonson (2003).
28. Eleanor Lowe rightly notes that shoes are a frequently 'overlooked participant in the Renaissance soundscape' indicating how "the sound of hobnail boots is quite different to new (squeaking) shoes or even heeled shoes […]" and how therefore someone's footfall (in life but also on

the stage where after all auditory attention is heightened) could identify social status (2010: 335).
29. Citations from Smallwood and Wells' Revels edition: Dekker (1979).

Works Cited

Appadurai, Arjun (ed.). 1988. *The Social Life of Things: Commodities in Cultural Perspective*. Cambridge University Press (reprinted in 2011).
Arab, Ronda. 2011. *Manly Mechanicals in Early Modern English Stage*. Selinsgrove: Susquehanna University Press.
Arab, Rona, Michelle M. Dowd, and Adam Zucker (eds). 2015. *Historical Affects and Early Modern Theater*. London: Routledge.
Bankside (the parishes of St Saviour and Christchurch Southwark). 1950. Vol. 22 of the *Survey of London*. London: London County Council.
Bennett, Susan, and Mary Polito (eds.). 2014. *Performing Environments: Site-Specificity in Medieval and Early Modern Drama*. Basingstoke: Palgrave.
Bernstein, Robin. 2009. Dances with Things: Material Culture and the Performance of Race. *Social Text* 27 (4): 67–94.
Boulton, Jeremy. 2008. *Neighbourhood and Society: A London Suburb in the Seventeenth Century*. Cambridge: Cambridge University Press.
Crawforth, Hannah, Sarah Dustagheer, and Jennifer Young. 2015. *Shakespeare in London*. London: Arden Bloomsbury.
Dekker, Thomas. 1979. *The Shoemaker's Holiday*, ed. R. L. Smallwood and Stanley Wells. Manchester: Manchester University Press.
Dowd, Michelle M., and Natasha Korda (eds.). 2011. *Working Subjects in Early Modern English Drama*. London and Burlington, VT: Ashgate.
Fumerton, Patricia, and Simon Hunt (eds.). 1998. *Renaissance Culture and the Everyday*. Philadelphia: Pennsylvania University Press.
Harkness, Deborah. 2007. *The Jewel House: Elizabethan London and Scientific Revolution*. New Haven: Yale University Press.
Harrison, William. 1909–1914. *The Description of England* (1577, Book III, Chapter 8; 1587, Book III, Chapter I). Chapter XII: Of Cattle Kept for Profit. In *The Harvard Classics*. New York: Bartleby (reprinted in 2001; Online edition).
Hentschell, Roze. 2016. The Cultural Geography of St Paul's Precinct. In *The Oxford Handbook to the Age of Shakespeare*, ed. Malcolm Smuts, 633–649. Oxford: Oxford University Press.
Heywood, Thomas. 2005. *The Two Parts of Thomas Heywood's Edward IV*, ed. Richard Rowland. Manchester: Manchester University Press.
Highley, Christopher. 2016. Theatre, Church and Neighbourhood in the Early Modern Blackfriars. In *The Oxford Handbook to the Age of Shakespeare*, ed. Malcolm Smuts, 616–632. Oxford: Oxford University Press.

Huang, Alex C.Y. 2009. *Chinese Shakespeares: Two Centuries of Cultural Exchange*. New York: Columbia University Press.

Jonson, Ben. 2003. *Epicene*, ed. Richard Dutton. Manchester: Manchester University Press.

Kinney, Arthur. 2009. Authoring *Arden of Faversham*. In *Shakespeare, Computers and the Mystery of Authorship*, ed. Hugh Craig and Arthur Kinney, 78–99. Cambridge: Cambridge University Press.

Lowe, Eleanor. 2010. Clothing. In *Ben Jonson in Context*, ed. Julie Sanders, 330–337. Cambridge: Cambridge University Press.

McGavin, John J., and Greg Walker. 2016. *Imagining Spectatorship: From the Mysteries to the Shakespearean Stage*. Oxford: Oxford University Press.

Pink, Sarah. 2015. *Doing Sensory Ethnography*, 2nd ed. London: Sage.

Sanders, Julie. 2011. *The Cultural Geography of Early Modern Drama, 1620–1650*. Cambridge: Cambridge University Press.

Sanders, Julie. 2015. "In the Friars": The Spatial and Cultural Geography of an Indoor Playhouse. *Cahiers Élisabéthains* 88: 17–31.

Shakespeare, William. 2000. *The Merry Wives of Windsor*, ed. Giorgio Melchiori. London: Arden Shakespeare and Bloomsbury.

Shakespeare, William. 2012. *Romeo and Juliet*, ed. Rene Weis. London: Arden Shakespeare and Bloomsbury.

Smuts, Malcolm (ed.). 2016. *The Oxford Handbook to the Age of Shakespeare*. Oxford: Oxford University Press.

Tally, Robert. 2013. *Spatiality*. London: Routledge.

Taylor, Gary. 1993. The Structure of Performance Act-Intervals in the London Theatres, 1576–1664. In *Shakespeare Re-shaped, 1606–1623*, ed. Gary Taylor and John Jowett, 3–50. Oxford: Oxford University Press.

Wrightson, Keith. 2002. *English Society, 1580–1680*, 2nd ed. London: Routledge.

PART II

Negotiating Normality in Performance

CHAPTER 6

Shakespeare's Strange Conventionality

Brett Gamboa

In an important sense, nothing that happens on a stage is normal.[1] Each utterance, step, or gesture is understood by spectators to indicate the speech, presence, or motion of a metaphysical entity that is not really present, and even the bodies and other material objects appearing onstage are ontologically uncertain, because they pertain simultaneously to two concurrent but distinct realms of coherence. Of course, the paradox occasioned when a realm of fictional coherences temporarily supersedes the real identities of actors, and their actual situations and setting, is a primary source of theatrical attraction. That paradox is especially vitalizing because the artifice is borne of natural elements, each voice and body continuously asserting its authenticity even as it helps to establish and uphold an illusion, providing spectators with ongoing opportunities to harmonize truth and fiction.

As noted in the volume's introduction, any instance of 'normality' on stage, because it is staged, can only be notional—a product of the audience's imaginative acts of complicity with fiction—so that theatre can never entirely escape its own artifice and abnormality, as its Puritan objectors frequently argued. But in presenting its artificial version of normality, theater cannot avoid transmitting the narrative through

---

B. Gamboa (✉)
Dartmouth College, Hanover, NH, USA

© The Author(s) 2019
R. Loughnane and E. Semple (eds.), *Staged Normality in Shakespeare's England*, Palgrave Shakespeare Studies,
https://doi.org/10.1007/978-3-030-00892-5_6

conventions that, because of their simplicity and familiarity, can mask their power over the audience and allow playwrights to exploit them to advantage. Shakespeare's plays are distinguished by their pursuit of ways to complicate and enhance basic theatrical paradoxes, often allowing those already seeing double to see three or four in one. Ordinary bodies and voices are made extraordinary through mimesis, but Shakespeare frequently augments the effect by having stage figures cross-dress, disguise themselves, double roles, or exchange one fictional identity for another by becoming actors in plays (within plays).[2] It is well-known, for example, how characters like Rosalind amplify interest and pleasure by multiplying the actor's capacity to signify, how Cordelia can seem to haunt Lear and intensify his regret when productions return the same actor to his side as the Fool, or how Starveling can heighten awareness of the fragility of *A Midsummer Night's Dream* when his performance as Moonshine is impugned by the onstage audience. In each case, the play exploits mimetic convention—the 'normal' stage practice of having one actor represent one character—to intensify the paradox of acting. In the case of cross-dressing or doubling, the way to transcend convention becomes a convention in itself.

Of course, Shakespeare is not exceptional for using stage conventions to advantage, as the proliferation of disguise plays and meta-theatrical devices in the period attests. But he stands apart for how persistently, subtly, and variously he enforces or augments them to enrich theatrical paradoxes. This essay explores how Shakespeare's plays facilitate engagement by exploiting our reliance on stage conventions and our awareness of what is normal.[3] Like mimesis, conventions pertaining to genre, the representative capacity of the stage, or the ontological status of the players can be manipulated to productive ends. Many plays feature characters in extraordinary states of being—as ghosts, 'dead' bodies, and figments of dreams, as sleeping, sightless, or invisible subjects—achieving the representations through conventions that can be undercut or recreated to generate surprise, disorientation, curiosity, or suspense. Some plays rely on the spectator's willingness to imagine settings established by the dialogue, then use his or her awareness of the physical stage and its limitations to intrude upon or override what is imagined. And nearly all Shakespeare's plays complicate the genres implied in their expositions, creating further opportunities for tension and engagement. In some cases, the ordinary, non-theatrical identities of a production's constituent parts reassert themselves and confront spectators with problems that mirror those encountered by the fictional characters. At other points, the plays restrict their elements' capacities to function mimetically, the spectator's resulting awareness of the 'real' ontologies and uses of bodies, props, or the stage, then momentarily disrupting the illusion in ways that can simultaneously enrich it. In short, the plays rely on our awareness of what is normal—both in and out of the theatre—then use eruptions of the anti-mimetic aspects of the play's components to create secondary dramas for spectators, each generating opportunities to harmonize truth and fiction, and complementing theatrical paradoxes and the themes of the plays thereby.

Ghosts

A notable way in which Shakespeare complicates the ontological status of the players is to cast them in non-human roles—ghosts, fairies, spirits, and gods. While conventions of representation allow actors to portray absent metaphysical entities, those entities are typically human and so logically correlated to the human actors. When such entities are (fictionally) ethereal, audience reception is more complex because the usual synchronization of truth and fiction at the site of the actor (i.e., actor and character) is extended to the real and the ethereal.[4] It was and is conventional for 'real' people to play ghosts, but the interest here is not the act of representing non-humans so much as Shakespeare's willingness to undermine his own strategies and conventions for doing so.

For example, the rules by which such creatures can be seen by human characters are rarely clear or consistent. When the fairies first enter *A Midsummer Night's Dream* all signs suggest that they are visible to the characters in the fiction, as they are to the spectators offstage. Oberon and Titania's jealous sparring over their respective affairs with Hippolyta and Theseus, along with their dispute over the 'changeling boy', provide casual notice that the fairies interact with and so are perceptible by human beings. But when Demetrius and Helena enter 2.1, Oberon provides new information about the status of the fairies: 'But who comes here? I am invisible, / And I will overhear their conference' (2.1.186–187).[5] The news is not hard to process, though it presents spectators with the complex and pleasurable task of imagining that a stage figure currently under their observation is not—indeed, has not all this while been—observable.[6] Part of the pleasure comes about because invisibility is established by convention about a character that is so clearly visible. The result is a secondary paradox at the site of the actor, but also a welcome instance of dramatic irony, since, as Chloe Porter points out, Oberon's invisibility engages spectators 'in the construction of an imagined visual plain to which only they and the invisible character have access' (159). At such a moment the audience sees from its own point of view, largely in common with Oberon's but also encompassing him, while at the same time seeing the play from the point of view of the lovers, whose field of vision does and does not include Oberon. Porter notes that the play does not invite spectators 'to imagine that they cannot see Oberon; instead they are encouraged to imagine that the lovers cannot see the fairy king that they can see' (159). For the spectators, the last instance of 'they' in this sentence applies as well to the lovers as to the spectators, whose pleasure is significantly enhanced by watching Demetrius and Helena pretend not to see (within the fiction) what they must see and account for in their movements (as actors). In such moments, the spectator becomes more than usually aware of the playing of the play, engaged not only by the dramatic action but also by how the actors manage its progress. Further interest is created because the conventional way to represent an invisible character is precisely the way to represent a visible one, so that spectators perceive ontological differences and hierarchies of authenticity that are essentially unrepresented in production.

Later in the play, when Bottom becomes the object of Titania's affection, the play overlooks any potential difficulty about Bottom seeing Titania or the other fairies. The result suggests that Oberon's statement 'I am invisible' was a description of a temporary state or even a speech act that brought about the invisibility, though this is far from clear at the time unless the actor indicates it. Instead, the play seems to deploy or dispense with the idea of invisibility when it suits the plot, thereby complicating the role and perception of the spectators. The effect is extended when Puck leads Lysander and Demetrius 'up and down' after having 'o'ercast the night' at Oberon's command. In this case, Puck beckons each man to a fight while ventriloquizing his rival, using the darkness to conceal the impersonations. Of course, Puck need not conceal anything if he is invisible, or if he can shift his shape, as he tells the First Fairy he can in 2.1. Here, however, the play generates interest not by making the character 'invisible' but by changing the convention by which invisibility is brought about. In this case, the darkness that Puck ushers in is yet another opportunity for imagination. There was no credible darkness during Shakespeare's daytime performances, nor is there in any modern production that wants its characters to remain visible to the audience. Darkness is achieved by convention, creating invisibility without obscuring anyone, both a reprise and a reversal of Oberon's disappearing act. Employing separate and related conventions of invisibility is valuable to spectators thereby enabled to see from multiple perspectives, while remaining aware that the stage figures see as they do (and also do not). But for spectators experiencing this play—one in which the characters' affections result from a kind of blindness and second sight due to Oberon's botanical interventions—the conventions allow them to experience the world of the play more like the characters themselves do.

A famous example of a similar phenomenon occurs when Hamlet's Ghost enters the 'closet scene' (3.4). At that point, the Ghost is visible to Hamlet and the audience but not to Gertrude, despite it having been visible to Horatio and the watchmen in Act one. Theatrical interest is heightened because spectators are given opportunity to watch the Gertrude actor's willful delusion, and because the play suggests that the three bodies onstage are at once so alike and so different in their experiences and ontologies. But when Gertrude asks, 'Alas, how is't with you / That you do bend your eye on vacancy / And with th'incorporal air do hold discourse?', spectators cannot but sense the alteration to the play's representational conventions (3.4.115–117). Has the Ghost gained the capacity to become selectively perceptible (a possibility the play has not indicated), or has Hamlet gone mad indeed? The answer to the either/or question is almost inevitably 'yes'—that is, the Ghost is clearly perceptible (by sight and sound), yet the audience has seen evidentiary grounds for Gertrude's conclusion both in Hamlet's interview with Ophelia (3.1) and at the performance of 'The Murder of Gonzago' (3.2). Spectators can imagine a ghost that is either universally or selectively perceptible, but this one fits both descriptions without explanation, and so raises questions about the integrity of the play or the consistency of its internal logic. As a result, spectators momentarily become a locus of dramatic action, forced to harmonize logical premises that are, or at least ought to be, mutually exclusive. The result is more significant than a simple change of definition or shift in convention to which spectators must adapt; rather, the play uses the alterations to intensify doubts about its own integrity and that of its protagonist, doubts that are attractively suited to tragedy, a genre that thrives by instilling feelings of inconclusiveness, doubt, and disorientation.[7] Again, the conventions are ripe for exploitation because they are so readily adopted and relied upon, their impact greater for being concealed by their familiarity. Spectators understand that a ghost can 'appear' in the form of a human actor, and even that such a ghost can be 'invisible' to the human characters onstage. But Shakespeare's play uses those conventions against the spectators, piling up familiar cues to understanding that, individually, inform our sense of what is normal, but that, in concert, cannot function normally.

When the ghost of King Hamlet is not generating doubts about its existence, its ontological status remains much in question. For one thing, it conspicuously wears armor. It is difficult to imagine a more persuasive suggestion of the Ghost's physical vulnerability than by having him armed 'from head to foot' (1.2.227).[8] While his armor and helmet seem useful in creating a sense of physical intimidation and mystery, and may tacitly comment on the tense situation between Fortinbras and Denmark, they seem especially inconvenient for one expected to flit about like a sprite or shadow and then vanish in an instant: "Tis here. 'Tis here. / 'Tis gone' (1.1.140–141). However, the armor also seems necessary considering that Horatio advises Marcellus to attack the Ghost with his 'partisan' if it will not stay. After the Ghost vanishes, Marcellus reports on the attempt:

> We do it wrong, being so majestical,
> To offer it the show of violence,
> For it is as the air, invulnerable,
> And our vain blows malicious mockery.
>
> (1.1.142–145)

Again the play insists on having things both ways. Audiences are prepared for a ghost that, by convention, is unassailable by material beings. But *Hamlet* relies on that conventional awareness only after it has worked to establish the materiality and vulnerability of this ghost. If Marcellus hits this ghost with a stick, his blow will not be in vain. The weapon will strike a real body (or at least the real armor protecting that body). When the line is preserved in productions, directors tend to put Marcellus in a position where he cannot reach the Ghost, lest the scene turn comic. But his line ('our vain blows') can create a moment of disruption in performance because it either describes blows that were not struck, or comments on a performance of invulnerability that did not happen, and could not possibly have happened—just as the actors have not seen the Ghost flit about the stage as the dialogue suggests it does. In such moments, a play that has taken a fork in the road seems suddenly to be traveling on the neglected path, and spectators are forced to contemplate a ghost that is flesh and spirit, vulnerable and invulnerable, walking as they do and yet flashing here and there like a sprite. The conventions are both upheld and undermined, the result adding to the spectator's awareness of the playing of the play, and of the shortcomings of the player in representing what is laid out for him.

Such incidental disruptions to the dramatic frame and the credibility of the drama complement a play that seems eager to create doubts about such things as the protagonist's sanity, Ophelia's suicide, Claudius's penitence, and many others. The Ghost itself figures in several bewildering cruxes, such as when Hamlet vacillates before the prospect of suicide because death is an 'undiscovered country from whose bourn / No traveler returns' (3.1.78–79), despite so recently having met a traveler newly returned from thence. And if the actor playing the Ghost doubles as Claudius—a possibility created by the dramaturgy and invited by insistent comparisons of the two figures throughout the play—the contradictory conventions employed to establish the Ghost will tacitly comment on the actor who begins the play portraying a dead king (who lives) and ends it playing a living king (who dies). Indeed, *Hamlet* and its conventions seem designed to make it more difficult for the audience to tell hawks from handsaws.

Critics have long noticed that Shakespeare's ghosts are not especially ghostly. Anne Rosalind Jones and Peter Stallybrass (2000) noted the 'gross materiality' that characterizes Renaissance ghosts, suggesting that its material clothing partly explains why ridicule has been a more consistent response to Hamlet's ghost than fear (246, 248). Banquo's ghost has also attracted attention, and it, too, has been characterized by nothing so much as its physicality. At his reappearance after the ambush, Banquo seems more zombie than ghost, as Macbeth indicates at first sight, 'Never shake / Thy gory locks at me!' (3.4.51–52). Each time the 'blood-boltered' Banquo appears, the play emphasizes his physical appearance and gestures, even while suggesting his ethereality by making him undetectable to all but Macbeth. When he complains of 'juggling fiends [...] / That palter with us in a double sense' (5.7.49–50), Macbeth also hints at how the play works upon its audience when a ghost like this one appears onstage. After all, though Macbeth seems to be going mad, he is the lone character who sees as we do.

The play presents sufficient grounds to conclude that Banquo's appearance at the banquet does or does not occur, though audiences on and offstage have starkly different reasons to reach the same doubts or conclusions. Lady Macbeth and the lords see someone tormented by his misdeeds and in the midst of a hallucination; the spectators see a character on the verge of madness but who alone perceives the world (one that includes the dramatic action but is not limited to it) as it is, in a sense making him the only other sane person in our purview.[9] The variation on the convention allows spectators to understand why the sane people behave as though they were insane and why the madman is not mad. It allows them to know that the ghost is real, to know why nobody but Macbeth believes it is, *and* to know that the ghost may not be genuine in the context of the fiction despite the physical presence of the actor portraying it.

Again, ghosts are not normal, but they attain a notional normality based on the conventions employed in their representation and reception by the human characters. By relying upon those conventions to continue tracking the plot, spectators find their position as spectators undermined when the conventions are disrupted, creating a tension that is not possible but for their reliance on norms of representation. In addition, because the spectators have good reason to believe their own eyes, and to believe that Macbeth sees something that the sane characters do not, they become somewhat implicated in Macbeth's madness, and they are aligned yet further with a protagonist-turned-villain from whom the play, by genre, should want us to defect. Whereas in *Hamlet* a change in convention raises questions about the protagonist's sanity, *Macbeth* works to suggest that the ghost is both a reanimation of the ostentatiously human Banquo just murdered (because of the bloodstains) and a hallucination. Spectators harmonize the diverging possibilities, but without a clear indication about which convincing yet contradicting piece of evidence should trump the others. As a result, the play becomes a 'juggling fiend' that simultaneously leads and misleads the audience, as the witches do Macbeth.

The two largest 'ghost' scenes in Shakespeare occur near the beginning and the end of his career, in *Richard III* and *Cymbeline* respectively. In 5.3 of *Richard III* eleven ghosts visit Bosworth Field on the eve of battle, infiltrating the dreams of Richard and Richmond to deliver messages of despair and hope, while in 5.4 of *Cymbeline* Posthumus's dead family of four visits him in prison. Again, the ontological status of these ghosts and their reception by the audience is multi-layered. First, the ghosts are present onstage as real people: as real actors, of course, and as characters who foretell fates and may also potentially act to enforce them. But these ghost-characters participate in dreams, suggesting that their obvious presence may not be a fact of the plot so much as a sign of their existence within the thoughts of the 'real' characters whose dreams they enter.[10] In *Macbeth* the spectators see as Macbeth sees. In *Richard III* and *Cymbeline*, however, the spectators see characters that 'sleep', and that are therefore unable to see the figments of their dreams as we do. As a result, we seem to see, but do not see, what they do in their dreams; the ghosts present a kind of dumbshow for something that ultimately cannot be presented. In addition, these ghosts appear in such numbers that they cannot but be portrayed by actors who have played these or similar roles already in the production (much like Banquo and his line of kings), and who will imminently play further roles in resolving the plot. In the former case, the ghosts that curse Richard and encourage Richmond are ghosts of characters who have already suffered at Richard's hands and cursed him throughout the plot, and the actors portraying them will go on to enforce both sets of prophecies as members of the army that triumphs over Richard at play's end. The play thus establishes their earthliness alongside their ethereality, and seems to highlight their roles in the past, present, and future—all at once. Meanwhile, in *Cymbeline* the outcome the ghosts seek is one they will bring to pass if the two ghostly brothers become Posthumus's prospective brothers-in-law, Guiderius and Arviragus, and the warlike yet kindly father is realized in Cymbeline himself. Both plays can thus work to establish the ghosts' presence, to question whether they are actually present, and to allow them to regress to physical agents of the fates they foretell. Each of the actors involved in these scenes is merely representing a ghost, but the result for Shakespeare's plays when rules of representation are altered or transcended is more extensive and impactful than such representations would otherwise allow.

STAGE DEATH

Much as Shakespeare's plays complicate conventional representations of ghosts and fairies to augment tensions conducive to engagement, so they often exploit conventions involved in presenting 'dead' characters to heighten theatrical interest. Shakespeare's plays are even better stocked with dead bodies than they are with ghosts, again suggesting Shakespeare's interest in creating opportunities for spectators to harmonize fiction and reality at the site of the actor, this time by invoking a paradox wherein the same figure is both living and 'dead'. The conventional representation of dead characters by live actors is theatrically vitalizing in its own right, but, as we may expect, Shakespeare's dead bodies prove a means to use audience awareness of convention to advantage. Frequently, the plays establish and then undermine the deaths to create doubt about a given character's status and add suspense to the play. Romeo, Othello, Lear, Hal, Pericles, Polydore and Cadwal, and even Pyramus hover over dead bodies that are actually alive (in as well as out of the fiction). In some cases, their speeches call attention to special powers of discernment (e.g. Lear's 'I know when one is dead and when one lives; / She's dead as earth', 5.3.256–257) or else soundly confirm the finality of the death (e.g. Othello's 'I think she stirs again! No.' 5.2.94).[11] But while spectators may at least suspect that Juliet or Imogen remains alive, and that the dimly perceptible but aggressively monitored vital signs of the actors portraying them are congruent with the characters' actual health status, most of the 'dead' characters die according to stage convention, so that their rising abdomens or twitching faces, however perceptible, do not indicate any reason for continued hope that the characters will recover. But Desdemona, Cordelia, Thaisa, and others do recover, at least temporarily, and so our incidental perceptions of the actors' vital signs, and their light intrusions into the experience of fiction, turn out to be better cues to each character's ontological status than the fiction itself. And by having characters like Othello and Lear scrutinize the dead for signs of life, the plays augment our awareness of evidence that contradicts what we believe to be the actual status of the body (within the fiction), when the actual status is more evident in the actor's life than in the character's supposed death. For instance, when Lear proposes to test whether Cordelia lives based on whether 'her breath will mist or stain the stone' or cause a feather to stir, the spectators can be sure of the result before the test is administered (5.3.236). Of course, the feather will stir and prove the vitality of the actor, if not of Cordelia. The tests make it momentarily more likely that the actor's health is an indicator of the character's prospects, thus creating hope for the characters and the play as a whole, even after the tragic end seems assured. Just as *The Winter's Tale* attains a better end than the one seemingly promised by its first four acts, so the tragedies attain more disastrous ends than initially seem imaginable, because they exploit the convention of stage death to bait spectators into false hopes.

Based on the play's genre and performance history, Falstaff's 'death' in *1 Henry IV* may appear a less fruitful example. But while it has become conventional in performance for Falstaff to conspicuously fake his death to avoid being killed by Douglas, the text does not dictate this choice. Instead, both Q1 and the Folio indicate only that Falstaff fights with Douglas and then falls '*as if he were dead*' (5.4.75). Having Falstaff make a show of playing dead is viable in part because the character is known more for resourcefulness than valor, and because the comedy and cowardice of the act can take the edge off Hal's otherwise callous jokes at discovering his friend's corpse. But the text allows for what spectators would understand to be Falstaff's actual death, a tragic moment that realizes the separation of the two friends that Hal had predicted, and which occurs to the seeming sadness of all but Hal in Part II, while laying foundations for a greater comic resolution in the present play. This outcome is possible because the playwright can rely on spectators that see the heaving belly of Falstaff and do their duty to discount it as a predictor of the character's actual status. In this case, when Falstaff does rise up, truth turns out to be a more reliable key to the fiction than convention, and the spectators become uncertain as to whether reality or fiction is the best guide for interpreting onstage events. In seeming to rise from death, Falstaff somewhat validates his own worries that Hotspur might rise up again too, thus creating suspense for an audience where it otherwise could not exist. Whereas in *King Lear* the potential for comic resolution is emphasized and perpetuated to deepen the effect of tragedy, here, because we potentially see Falstaff's 'corpse' as Hal does, the tragedy of Falstaff's death and Hal's relative calm concerning it makes the comic end more welcome while leaving doubts about the friendship that complement audience awareness that the future Henry V must eventually dispense with such friends.

Shakespeare exploits conventional awareness of the stage to similar ends. The stage in Shakespeare's plays is whatever the players say it is: 'Well, this is the forest of Arden' (*As You Like It*, 2.4.11); 'Unto Southampton do we shift our scene' (*Henry V*, 2.0.42). A mostly bare stage fluidly adapts to the needs of the present scene, so a play like *1 Henry IV* can move between a tavern, a Welsh castle, and the English court simply by alternating their inhabitants (2.4–3.2). But an audience's dependence on dialogue to indicate changes of setting can also be used to confuse or disorient that audience. In *King Lear*, for example, Edgar leads Gloucester up what he—and we, initially—think is a seaside cliff:

> *Gloucester:* When shall I come to th' top of that same hill?
> *Edgar:* You do climb up it now. Look how we labor.
> *Gloucester:* Methinks the ground is even.
> *Edgar:* Horrible steep.
> Hark, do you hear the sea?
> *Gloucester:* No, truly.
> *Edgar:* Why, then, your other senses grow imperfect
> By your eyes' anguish.
>
> (4.6.1–6)

The spectators may be as blind as Gloucester in this instance, since—in the theatre—watching two actors walk across a flat stage does not mean that they are not climbing to a great height. The news that the characters do not hear or smell the sea likewise does not mean that there is no sea gaping beneath them. Gloucester's sense that 'the ground is even' is true, of course, and a source of meta-theatrical pleasure for spectators who know that he is correct about the experience of the actor, but likely incorrect about that of the characters.

Like one playing Falstaff, the Edgar actor can signal to the audience that he is deceiving his father, but the text suggests that spectators will piece out the cliff with their thoughts, reconciling flat stage and mountain, much as they do the live actor and the dead Falstaff. Jan Kott suggests that the moment shows 'the paradox of pure theatre', brought about because the limitations of the stage are both transcended and invoked (146).[12] But as with stage deaths, the reality of the production's physical components—in this case the stage itself—can prove a better guide to understanding the fiction than the fiction. Once Edgar places Gloucester at 'th'extreme verge' Gloucester 'leaps' to a prone position on that same stage, proving that the imagined cliff was *actually* imaginary. Watching a man leap from a ledge, only to find himself lying on the very ground upon which he has been standing is ridiculous, and it would seem to reveal the absence of a cliff and the impossibility of any jump from height. This should be most apparent to the jumper. And yet Shakespeare immediately calls the cliff's status back into question by having Gloucester ask whether he has fallen, then by having Edgar (impersonating a new bystander) pretend to have seen him fall.[13] The paradox is intensified because the cliff that was imagined to be present has suddenly vanished from imagination despite having functioned as the setting for the scene, and despite the characters proceeding to behave as though it looms above them. Edgar's continued presence confirms that Gloucester has remained just where he was. But this realization dawns only after Gloucester's initial 'fall' makes us question whether the fall is real, since the play may simply have reached a representational limit in trying to present a 'real' fall so that Gloucester's poor excuse for one stands in for a real fall just as a human actor stands in for Hamlet's ghost. Still, if Edgar deposits the blinded actor at the edge of a raised stage, like the Globe of Shakespeare's time (or ours), it may be that the platform itself presents a real danger to the actor. This would create anxiety for spectators that complements and likely exceeds their concern for Gloucester. As a result, Gloucester can appear both safer and yet more vulnerable than the armor-clad Ghost.[14] In the end, the conventional use of the stage is exploited to create suspense, as well as to create doubts for the audience about the role of reality in fiction. We readily adopt the definitions provided in the dialogue—they establish a notional normality for the spectators—only to find our dependence on those definitions a source of personal dramatic involvement and interest.

Genre

Genre is among the greatest arbiters of what we experience as normal in the theatre. Like mimesis, genre is such a conventional aspect of theatrical experience that spectators are extremely susceptible to its manipulations. Generic cues combine to offer a roadmap to each play that is seductive because we need not consciously employ it; as a result, we can be led into moral or existential quandaries when the plays reach predictable destinations by unpredicted routes. Shakespeare's plays are known for resisting generic categorization.[15] Though Polonius is often seen as a fool when listing the categories in which the 'tragedians of the city' particularly excel ('The best actors in the world, either for tragedy, comedy, history, pastoral, pastoral-comical, historical- pastoral, tragical-historical, tragical-comical-historical-pastoral' [2.2.324–326]), he may more accurately describe Shakespeare's generic categories than the compilers of the First Folio. And while it is well known that Shakespeare blended genres throughout his career, we may overlook how consistently the plays supply the conventional endings they anticipate, and miss how the appropriateness of those endings can be a source of psychic dissonance or defection for spectators.

The most prominent examples occur in so-called 'problem' plays.[16] The endings of *The Merchant of Venice* and *Measure for Measure*, for instance, are often discussed in terms of their perverseness. *The Merchant of Venice* closes with the Christians celebrating their good fortune amid news that Shylock's fortune is available to subsidize Lorenzo's profligacy, a disturbing reminder of the tragedy that erupted in Act Four. The last act concludes several of the plot's comic premises, but it does so only after most spectators have lost their appetites for comedy, having watched a trial in which Shylock is welcomely frustrated in his pursuit of Antonio's flesh, but then punished beyond any imaginable justice—forced under threat of death to convert from Judaism and to enrich the man who ran off with his daughter—by a fraudulent doctor of law who had spent much of the scene promoting mercy.[17] Meanwhile, in *Measure for Measure* it seems morally reprehensible for the Duke to propose marriage to Isabella, after needlessly prolonging her suffering in order to style himself the more magnanimous savior. The fact that she is a prospective nun and he spends most of the play posing as a Friar only makes his actions more unsavory. These endings typically incite frustration and anxiety in spectators, as evidenced by productions that frequently project that anxiety by having Isabella end one play by rejecting the Duke, or Jessica end the other singing Hebrew hymns that seem to acknowledge Shylock's plight.[18]

But the audience's discomfort results because each play asserts the generically appropriate ending—the Prince-like figure's proposal to the ingénue and the triumph of young lovers over the tyrannous father who would hinder them—while casually overlooking the fact that it has transcended its generic boundaries across the middle acts, creating a sense among spectators that the plays lose track of what transpired to invalidate those endings. As a result, our moral sympathies are set at odds with our generic interests, and a natural desire to see the action fulfill its implicit contract is frustrated because the outcome initially desired no longer seems desirable. Completing the comedies as comedies is natural and even necessary given the outlines of the plots and the genre, but it is unnatural for the plays as actually delivered, and the spectators are forced (or allowed) once again to harmonize contrarieties at one point of perception, as they do with actors.

Shakespeare's plays often generate dramatic energy by dividing the audience's generic from its moral investments. Such it is that Richmond or Malcolm seems disappointing by design, or that Prospero, like

Duke Vincentio, can appear the chief instigator of problems that he, as the protagonist, works to set right. Again, it is worth considering that the endings suited to the genres do not fit because the plots supersede the premises upon which they are built. But the ill-fitting endings are so because they assert and uphold each play's *normality*. It is the insistence on a correct generic conclusion that provides some of the most affecting moments in Shakespeare. In *Measure for Measure* this is the ending; in *Macbeth* it is the sense of irresolution that haunts the ending, in large part brought about because Malcolm is the Hamlet-like son of a dear father murdered, but the plot has never allowed him to take the audience for his own as Hamlet does. Consequently, the audience cannot defect from Macbeth and finds itself asked to support a character who is greatly overshadowed by both the tyrant and the more esteemed avenger, Macduff. As in many foregoing examples, the imposition of what should be normal and expected (e.g. Malcolm's triumph at the fulfillment of the revenge plot) becomes a site of resolution and rupture for spectators, proving responsible for both their engagement and detachment. The detachment, though, paradoxically tends to facilitate interest in the plays, if we can consider the spectators' anxieties, frustrations, or desires to see plays behave differently than they do the signs of that interest. Our sense that the plays should behave differently, along with the prospect that their perversions (brought on by insistence on generic completion and correctness) are orchestrated to frustrate us, is theatrically vitalizing, analogous in effect to the interest we take in Hamlet's Ghost or Gloucester's health because of the actors' physical vulnerabilities.

Ordinary and Extraordinary Acts

In closing I want to consider one other way in which Shakespeare's plays exploit what is normal or conventional to theatrical advantage. In short, the plays routinely have actors do ordinary or mundane things—drink, dance, belch, read, sing, tend animals or babies—any of which invites and possibly constrains spectators to consider whether the action occurs in truth, fiction, or both, much like Gloucester's leap from Dover cliff. For instance, when Toby Belch appears onstage with a 'stoup of wine' there likely never has been a playgoer that does not silently monitor whether there is liquid in the bottle (2.3.13). If there is liquid, spectators might silently affirm to themselves that it is unlikely to be alcohol—a result that makes 'drinking' seem simultaneously to occur and not occur—while continuing to try to discern whether the actor actually imbibes or merely pretends to do so. At work are a series of possible conventions—that an empty bottle may stand in for a full one, that a pretended drink may stand for a real one, that a real drink of water may stand for one of wine, that multiple drinks will sanction an affected drunkenness. Meanwhile, if the actor does drink this is itself seems to undermine mimesis, since one who drinks is in some sense no longer pretending, and the spectators can give conscious consideration to the actor's charge to drink and whether, for instance, the drink could disrupt or assist his effort to deliver speeches.

Reading onstage creates similar internal dialogues and drama for audiences. It is therefore little wonder that Shakespeare's plays are so extensively populated with readers.[19] *Much Ado About Nothing* famously begins with the reading of a letter; Lady Macbeth's most famous soliloquy succeeds the reading of Macbeth's letter; the pronouncement of the Oracle is the crux of Hermione's trial. Letters abound and become prominent subjects of the fiction in such plays as *Love's Labour's Lost*, *Julius Caesar*, and *Twelfth Night*. Each letter read aloud onstage, the audience cannot but know, may be a script, and so may give the actor a momentary advantage in fulfilling his role. Audiences are rarely alive to anything so much as what, if anything, appears on the pages in an actor's hands. They wonder about and try to spot whether the letter is typed or handwritten, the degree of the actor's reliance on it, the size of the letters, the indications of rehearsal or spontaneity in the reading, etc. Reading a letter or book is another natural act, one that potentially is happening, even as the concomitant act seems to occur in the fictional world. In short, when the actor reads or drinks, or performs one of the other aforementioned actions, the audience grows more than usually mindful of artifice, of the playing of the play. As the role of the actor attains a kind of co-primacy in the actual experience of fiction, the fiction itself is energized by the exposures of artifice. It is as though the fiction is imperiled by the obtrusion of the actor and his performance of actions that cannot exclusively be considered mimetic. In short, stage reading and drinking and the like become mimetic conventions for the fictional versions of these same behaviors, but audiences reading them as mimetic cannot set aside their awareness of their potential authenticity. In other words, a simple drink from a bottle or a brief reading of a letter can temporarily suspend mimesis, highlighting the comparative artificiality of nearly all other actions onstage, thus drawing more scrutiny to the acts of performance. Other components of the fiction, like prop babies, or sharp swords, or dogs that the director cannot control, remind us of nothing so much as their independent uses outside the bounds of the plot, and the potential danger they present to the play and its participants. Swords and dogs are conventional markers, but markers that always present a latent threat to the performance, or at least threaten to create unforeseen obstacles to the performance's completion.[20]

Conversely, there are instances where the plays ask actors to do something that spectators do not believe can be happening, such as when Lady Macbeth sleepwalks or Ophelia raves. It should not be surprising that even poor performances in these two roles tend to attract acclaim for these particular scenes, when we consider that film actors are routinely honored for playing drunk characters or those who suffer from mental illness. The scenes of sleepwalking and madness foreground mimetic convention and remind audiences of the artifice involved in producing the play. We know, indeed we are never so mindful of the fact that the actors are not sleeping, and are sane, and so the drama that matters is one of acting, animated by awareness of the actor's inability to convince us that he or she is sleeping or suddenly insane. At such moments, the play advertises the inevitable and ongoing failure of mimesis, without which mimesis would cease to matter. But Shakespeare invites the actor's failure as the best means to her success. He foregrounds the conventionality of acting by drawing attention to the fact that it cannot convince us. But this failure is key to convincing ourselves that we are convinced. Again, it is the simple fact of the actor, her normal and anti-virtuosic qualities that leak through and make the convention legible. And, as with ghosts, stage deaths, genre, props, and the like, it is often the assertion of what is conventional, the disruption of artifice by the ordinary components that bring it about, that significantly enhance our experience of theatre. Though perhaps all normality onstage is only notional—is already problematized by its status as performance—its role in guiding the transmission of narrative makes it seem unusually familiar and dependable. As a result, changes and disruptions to the tools for transmission are a potent source of drama for spectators, who have no option but to rely on the conventions established.

When an armor-clad ghost is admired for his ethereality, when Falstaff's rise from the dead makes Hotspur's ontological state momentarily less certain, when Gloucester behaves as though Dover cliff is a real site in the fiction even after the play reveals it as fake, and when *The Merchant of Venice* attains a comic close that is perfectly appropriate and inappropriate for the play, Shakespeare shows himself willing to use conventions to create suspense and rupture, willing to assert or uphold conventions even after his plays seem to have abandoned or transcended them. Normality on Shakespeare's stage, then, while often considered a means to enhance extraordinary moments and events by way of contrast, can be a site of excitement and engagement in its own right, some plays creating interest by embracing rather than abandoning what is ordinary and familiar, persisting according to established premises and conventions even after they no longer seem reasonable or appropriate. As we have seen, the results of adhering to conventions, or affirming them alongside what threatens them, can create tensions between the spectators and the plays themselves, initiating dramas in which the spectators become protagonists, their situations resembling those of the actual protagonists onstage.

Notes

1. In the introduction, Rory Loughnane describes the problems posed for philosophers and critics trying to define what is 'normal' in the early modern period, as well as the additional challenge involved for modern thinkers given their temporal distance from the period. Throughout this essay, concerned principally with how Shakespeare exploits the audience's awareness of and reliance on stage conventions to create theatrical interest, I use the word 'normal' with reference to aspects of theater and theatricality whose simplicity and familiarity (in Wittgenstein's terms) help to conceal their potential impact on the play and the spectators.
2. Shakespeare's cross-dressed heroines (e.g. Rosalind, Viola), disguised characters (e.g. Duke Vincentio, Edgar), and plays within plays are so well known as not to warrant explanation. Doubling roles may have been a still greater (because near-constant) means to augment the actor's duplicity, particularly when one considers that plays like *Henry V*, *Coriolanus*, and *Pericles* contain nearly 50 roles, though each was structured so as to be playable by a cast of twelve or fewer. My book, *Shakespeare's Double Plays* (2018), takes up the subject of doubling in considerable detail; here I note merely that unless one supposes Shakespeare's company regularly cast three-dozen or more actors, doubling must have been a consistent and prominent factor in the performance and reception of its plays.
3. The examples I discuss in this essay most urgently concern theater audiences, though they also tend to complicate, undermine, or enhance the reader's relationship to the text and its characters.

4. In saying such entities are 'fictionally' ethereal, I mean only that they are ghostly or invisible within the plot or context of the fiction. Thus, spectators harmonize not only the real identity of the actor with the fictional one of the character, but also the real body of that actor with the character's imagined ethereality. Of course, the notion of a ghost or spirit's 'fictionality' would not have been taken for granted in early modern culture. The majority of playgoers in Shakespeare's time likely accepted the possibility that souls could return after death, as David Cressy (1997) and Stephen Greenblatt (2001) have pointed out.
5. All citations are from *The Norton Shakespeare* (2016).
6. Oberon's line occurs in a speech full of voluble commentary, about his plot to get the changeling boy and the arrival of Demetrius and Helena. Though there are no strong textual cues for the choice, some actors use the line 'I am invisible' to help indicate a shift from visibility to invisibility. This choice does not obviate the complex visual dynamics I describe in the paragraph, but it can help resolve what I think a worthwhile dissonance. Without the choice, audiences likely understand Oberon to seem to affirm a convention in which non-human spirits and fairies can see each other but humans cannot see them, despite the fact that the fairies clearly have been visible to human characters in the past, and despite Bottom having no trouble seeing and talking with them in Titania's bower. Further suggesting that Oberon's line is a statement of reality—though that reality is in conflict with other examples—is the fact that Puck has no comparable moment in which to indicate a transition to invisibility before he interacts with the mortals.
7. Doubts could also arise concerning Gertrude, whose selective blindness might be explained as resulting from either her guilt or her innocence of the murder. But while it is possible to read Gertrude's failure to perceive the Ghost in this way, the plot works more extensively to create doubts about Hamlet's sanity, making it a topic of the fiction and repeatedly creating starkly untenable inconsistencies of character (e.g. 'I did love you once […] I loved you not' 3.1.113–117).
8. Because the armor is the 'very armor' King Hamlet wore when he fought the 'sledded Polacks', it has been explained as a comment on the tense military situation between Fortinbras and Denmark. See for example Foakes (2005) and Zimmerman (2005). However we explain it, though, the audience is confronted with the mere fact that a physically invulnerable ghost wears what can only reasonably protect physically vulnerable people. It may help the soldiers recognize King Hamlet, and it suggests a military threat (or helps to blur the military and supernatural threats to Denmark), but it jars with what we think we know of ghosts and, worse, what is voiced clearly about this one.

9. Of course, judgments of Macbeth are further complicated because he's indirectly guilty of Banquo's murder, and that guilt—which seems to manifest as a kind of madness in following scenes—may indicate to spectators that Banquo's ghost is a hallucination. But unless the production omits the ghost the audience will see it as Macbeth does, so the scene thus simultaneously asserts that Macbeth may be imagining the figure clearly present before him and that he sees precisely what is there. Marvin Rosenberg describes approaches to the scene and their effects in *The Masks of Macbeth* (439–451). Also, see Kott (95).
10. Compare Antigonus's account of Hermione visiting him in a dream to tell him where to leave Perdita (*The Winter's Tale*, 3.3.15–45). Though this visit is reported and not staged, Hermione's presence in the dream works to assure Antigonus (and the audience) of her death—and thus her absence from the plot that remains.
11. T. W. Craik discusses both deaths (1979).
12. On the flat 'cliff' at Dover in *King Lear*, 4.6, also see Matchett (1979) and Dessen (1975).
13. In addition to aforementioned discussions, R. A. Foakes discusses the problem of the cliff in his Arden edition of *King Lear* (1997: 47, 62–63).
14. Arthur's appearance on the rooftop in *King John* can make similar use of the stage, the potential danger to an actor who climbs out of the gallery above Shakespeare's stage, or hovers at the edge of a scaffold, creating perhaps more suspense and concern for that actor than the play can do otherwise for the character.
15. Judging from the title pages on the early quarto editions, disagreements over categorizing Shakespeare's plays appear to have been ongoing since they were written. For more recent inquiries into how the plays reflect and resist generic categories, see Danson (2000) and Drakakis (2013).
16. F. S. Boas first used the term to describe plays that 'preclude a completely satisfactory outcome' (1908: 345). By this definition, it is worth considering that from at least one character's point of view nearly every play by Shakespeare qualifies as a 'problem play'. *The Merchant of Venice*, though not traditionally classified with the problem plays, is discussed as one here because of the notorious difficulties associated with the ending, particularly the seeming marginalization of Antonio and his initial sadness, and the universal disregard by the characters onstage for Shylock.
17. I discuss the appropriateness and inappropriateness of the ending in 'Letting Unpleasantness Lie' (2012).
18. Trevor Nunn's 1999 production of *The Merchant of Venice* was probably the first major production to end the play focused on Jessica's nostalgia and seeming regret. The production exerted such an influence that the ending has become almost a convention in itself. The open silence after

the Duke's proposal in *Measure for Measure* has long presented an opportunity for directors to reject or at least hedge against a gleeful acceptance that is suited to the genre but not the play. Edward L. Rocklin (2000) traces the long history of the moment onstage, and, particularly since the 1970s, productions have as often undermined the engagement as they have celebrated it.

19. Based on the work of Alan C. Dessen and Leslie Thompson (1999), Heidi Brayman Hackel (2005) notes that Tudor-Stuart stage directions mention more than 400 letters and more than 130 books (19). Jonas Barish (1991) observes that every play by Shakespeare except *The Two Noble Kinsmen* calls for books, letters, or other paper documents onstage at one or more points. For more on letters and small hand properties, see Gil Harris and Korda (2002), especially Douglas Bruster's chapter, 'The Dramatic Life of Objects in the Early Modern Theatre' (67–96).

20. Spectators tend to be intensely mindful of the choreography involved in theatrical swordplay, and they know that the training and rehearsal undergone for stage combat is not only to create shows of skill and daring but to accommodate the threat of real swords. Stage combat, I suggest, is animated more by the potential for failure (someone actually getting struck or stabbed) than it is by any potential virtuosity. In a similar way, dogs attract such intense interest primarily because—regardless of their training—audiences know that they might imminently do something the actors or director would not wish them to do. The ongoing doubt about whether they will continue to comply with their fellow actors' hopes heightens suspense for audiences. I discuss dogs and other comparatively ungovernable phenomena onstage in '"Is't real that I see"' (2013).

WORKS CITED

Barish, Jonas. 1991. "Soft, Here Follows Prose": Shakespeare's Stage Documents. In *The Arts of Performance in Elizabethan and Early Stuart Drama*, ed. Murray Biggs, et al. Edinburgh: Edinburgh University Press.

Boas, F.S. 1908. *Shakespeare and His Predecessors*. New York: Charles Scribner's Sons.

Craik, T.W. 1979. 'I Know When One Is Dead and When One Lives'. Annual Shakespeare Lecture 1979. In *The Proceedings of the British Academy*, vol. lxv. London: Oxford University Press.

Cressy, David. 1997. *Birth, Marriage and Death: Ritual, Religion and Life Cycle in Tudor and Stuart England*. Oxford: Oxford University Press.

Danson, Lawrence. 2000. *Shakespeare's Dramatic Genres*. Princeton: Princeton University Press.

Dessen, Alan C. 1975. Two Falls and a Trap. *English Literary Renaissance* 5: 291–307.

Dessen, Alan C., and Leslie Thompson. 1999. *A Dictionary of Stage Directions in English Drama, 1580–1642.* Cambridge: Cambridge University Press.

Drakakis, John. 2013. Shakespeare Against Genre. *Pólemos* 7 (1): 83–97.

Foakes, R.A. 2005. "Armed at Point Exactly": The Ghost in *Hamlet*. *Shakespeare Survey* 58: 34–47.

Gamboa, Brett. 2012. Letting Unpleasantness Lie: Counter-Intuition and Character in *The Merchant of Venice*. In *Shakespeare's Sense of Character—On the Page and From the Stage*, ed. Yu Jin Ko and Michael Shurgot. Aldershot: Ashgate.

Gamboa, Brett. 2013. "Is't Real That I See?": Staged Realism and the Paradox of Shakespeare's Audience. *Shakespeare Bulletin* 31 (4): 669–688.

Gamboa, Brett. 2018. *Shakespeare's Double Plays: Dramatic Economy on the Early Modern Stage*. Cambridge: Cambridge University Press.

Greenblatt, Stephen. 2001. *Hamlet in Purgatory*. Princeton: Princeton University Press.

Hackel, Heidi Brayman. 2005. *Reading Material in Early Modern England: Print, Gender, and Literacy*. Cambridge: Cambridge University Press.

Harris, Jonathan Gil, and Natasha Korda. 2002. *Staged Properties in Early Modern Drama*. Cambridge: Cambridge University Press.

Jones, Rosalind, and Peter Stallbrass. 2000. *Renaissance Clothing and the Materials of Memory*. Cambridge: Cambridge University Press.

Kott, Jan. 1964. *Shakespeare Our Contemporary*. Garden City: Doubleday.

Matchett, William. 1979. Some Dramatic Techniques in *King Lear*. In *Shakespeare and the Theatrical Dimension*, ed. Philip C. McGuire and David A. Samuelson. New York: AMS Press.

Porter, Chloe. 2014. *Making and Unmaking in Early Modern English Drama: Spectators, Aesthetics, and Incompletion*. Manchester: Manchester University Press.

Rocklin, Edward L. 2000. Measured Endings: How Productions from 1720 to 1929 Close Shakespeare's Open Silences in *Measure for Measure*. *Shakespeare Survey* 53: 213–232.

Rosenberg, Marvin. 1978. *The Masks of Macbeth*. Berkeley: University of California Press.

Shakespeare, William. 1997. *King Lear*, Arden Third Series, ed. R.A. Foakes. London: Bloomsbury.

Shakespeare, William. 2016. *The Norton Shakespeare*, 3rd ed., ed. Stephen Greenblatt, et al. New York: Norton.

Zimmerman, Susan. 2005. *The Early Modern Corpse and Shakespeare's Theatre*. Edinburgh: Edinburgh University Press.

CHAPTER 7

Transgressive Normality and Normal Transgression in *Sir Thomas More*

Edel Semple

Conversing with a wily thief in a courtroom, the wise and witty Sir Thomas More declares that 'I am true subject to my king' (2.68).[1] By the conclusion of the play that bears his name, however, More's head lies on the executioner's chopping block for his decision to let his 'conscience […] parley with our laws' (10.73). Charting the rise and fall of this (in)famous English statesman, the fortunes of an urban rebellion, the operations of civic and royal authority, and a household in crisis, *Sir Thomas More* is a topical play replete with episodes of social disorder and political transgression. Although the play is set in London's Henrician past, the events and tensions it presents and the problems it debates were all too familiar to a late Elizabethan audience. Rebellion, disobedience, and deviancy were not as aberrant as the early modern authorities—the play's civic leaders, Privy Council, and unseen monarch, and even Edmund Tilney the Master of the Revels and censor of the play—would like and are staged as part of the normal fabric of society and indeed human life itself. Friction and outright conflict between

E. Semple (✉)
School of English, University College Cork, Cork, Ireland
e-mail: e.semple@ucc.ie

© The Author(s) 2019
R. Loughnane and E. Semple (eds.), *Staged Normality in Shakespeare's England*, Palgrave Shakespeare Studies,
https://doi.org/10.1007/978-3-030-00892-5_7

individuals and between groups are presented as inevitable and commonplace. While a xenophobic revolt and More's martyrdom are central to the play's action, juxtaposed with these episodes are moments of normal life: More's routine work as a sheriff, his everyday interactions with his family and servants, his entertainment of guests at work (Erasmus) or in his home (the Lord Mayor), and, even on his way to his death, his dealings with his captors have an air of the pedestrian. This chapter seeks to direct attention to these quieter, less historically momentous passages, and analyses the function of their inclusion in the overall play.

While critics have often focused on issues related to the authorship and censorship of *Sir Thomas More*, I attend to the play's staging of normality as a heretofore neglected, but significant, matter.[2] Specifically, I argue that in *Sir Thomas More* normality is a troublesome force, and that the 'normalising' of transgressions (that vary in quality and seriousness) contributes to the play's questioning of authority and its power to engage its audience. In several key moments, *Sir Thomas More* presents transgression as an everyday occurrence. Through such repetition, the play implies that disorder and rebellion are unavoidable corollaries of inhabiting a world where inequality and injustice are a familiar experience. Throughout, the play invests the normal—which I use here to indicate the ordinary, typical, familiar, and unremarkable, essentially the everyday that would be familiar (in part or totality) to the play's intended audience, including common people such as servants, domestic items, everyday concerns, and habitual actions—with the ability to critique the 'high' and to foreground the 'low' as worthy of consideration, widening the scope and impact of the narrative. Crucially, as I will show, the depiction of the familiar and the banal forms part of a key conflict that is central to the play's critique of power structures. More is frequently singled out as unique—only he can quell the riot and in his disobedience to the King he is near exceptional—but the recognisable and relatable aspects of his life and work are used to make him an everyman figure, a subject for the audience's empathy, a home-grown city hero worthy of admiration, and finally an ordinary man who falls victim to the vagaries of the state. More, then, brings together the everyday, state politics, and high tragedy. As such a figure, More is made relatable to the audience, his fate made all the more compelling, and he is ideally positioned to expose the inconsistencies in and perils of state power to the individual.

***

The opening third of *Sir Thomas More* centres on the growing racial tensions in London, the Ill May Day riot of 1517, and the fallout for the rioters and the peacemaker More.[3] Several scholars have noted the topicality of these scenes for a late Elizabethan audience. While the composition date of the original text of *Sir Thomas More* is oft-discussed—critics have suggested c.1593–1595 as well as the late 1590s as possibilities[4]— it is certain that events early in the play would have resonated with an audience who could recall the civic unrest and anti-alien hostility that permeated London in the early 1590s. Commenting on the detailed picture of London's social and topographical makeup in the play, Tracey Hill observes that 'through enacting the infamous local events of 1517 the specificity of the play's locations cannot help but bring the current moment [the early 1590s] to mind'.[5] The play's detailed depiction of London and its citizens not only makes them recognisable to the audience but, as Jean Howard notes of city comedy, the '[c]artographic exactitude creates and intensifies identification with the city and marks it, while nominally the king's, in actuality the familiar territory of its citizens'.[6] While Lloyd Edward Kermode remarks that '*Sir Thomas More*, for all it is nominally set seventy-five years in the past, interferes too much with the stability of the present—in particular, stability associated with a young, theatre- and game-oriented demographic' who might be incited to imitate the staged disorder.[7] Thus, through its specificity and topicality, *Sir Thomas More* contracts the distance between Henrician London and Elizabethan London and renders its characters recognisable, strengthening the spectator's identification with them. The audience can lay claim to the play's events both as part of their own history and own experience. More's city is the audience's city and its people, their livelihoods, and way of life, are under threat.

The first scene establishes that a new norm is emerging in the city and the native citizens are resistant to it. This nascent status quo, Doll Williamson indignantly observes, sees 'free-born / Englishmen, having beaten strangers within their own / bounds, [being] braved and abused by them at / home' (1.80–83). In the first interaction between native and foreigner, the Lombard de Barde has attempted to abduct Doll, and the second interaction stages a theft of a different variety as Caveler, a Lombard or Frenchman, has stolen the doves bought by Doll's husband. Williamson and Sherwin's protest to Caveler establishes that both Englishmen know and abide by the city's laws and customs:

> *Williamson*: I bought them [the pair of doves] in Cheapside, and paid my money for them.
> *Sherwin*: He did, sir, indeed, and you offer him wrong, both to take them from him and not restore his money neither.
> *Caveler*: If he paid for them, let it suffice that I possess them. Beefs and brewis may serve such hinds. Are pigeons meat for a coarse carpenter?
>
> (1.18–25)

Caveler and de Barde run roughshod over the city's norms, even mocking the citizens' powerlessness. As the onlooker George Betts speaks of revenge, de Barde warns that the civic authorities will take his side. Williamson worries that this is likely as there is precedent for such bias: 'Indeed, my Lord Mayor on the / Ambassador's complaint sent me to Newgate one day / because, against my will, I took the wall of a stranger' (1.45–47). Williamson is careful to note that he knows the correct way to behave and he conforms; it is polite custom to let a stranger pass on the inside and he failed in this only 'against [his] will'. The opening scene thus jingoistically presents Londoners as the guardians of not only civic but national identity. They are the embodiment of English law and customs whereas the foreigners encroach on the native norms and seek to institute a new order. To Lincoln, who has for a 'long time' overlooked the outrages committed by the foreigners, the situation seems almost irreparable: 'Will this gear never be otherwise? Must these / wrongs be thus endured?' (1.91, 37–38). Even Henry's courtiers are aware that the abuses committed by the aliens have become habitual, 'daily wrongs' (3.68), and they imagine that popular revolt is a foregone conclusion (3.57–63, 78–80). The play implies that with injustice an everyday experience and with the authorities passive or prejudiced, social conflict and outright violence—whether in the Henrician London of the play or by extension the Elizabethan London of the play's audience—are an inevitable, normal feature of urban life. It is no wonder then that Tilney marked much of the discussion of civic unrest in scene 3 for deletion.

More arrives to the Ill May Day riot hoping, along with the Lord Mayor, Surrey, and Shrewsbury, that his persuasive oration, rather than civic or royal might, will 'appease [...] this flux of discontent' (5.38–39). His speech in defence of the immigrants, which uses the Gospel ethic of 'do unto others', succeeds in pacifying the rioters. Drawing on Stephen Greenblatt's work, Simon Hunt notes how 'victory is accomplished not by royal or noble forces but, through the vehicle of a privileged commoner'.[8] This is certainly the case as the rioters, including Doll and Lincoln, the Mayor, and the courtiers acknowledge that it was the words of Shrieve More that saved the city.[9] Indeed, More was called to intervene in the insurrection due to his remarkable qualities—wisdom, learnedness, and 'especial favour with the people' (3.87). Critics have also noted how the play as a whole 'focuses consistently upon [More's] unique features […] which set him apart from ordinary men'.[10] More's exceptionality and proximity to civic power seems to exclude him from the category of the everyday individual, as described by Patricia Fumerton: 'the everyday tends to place up front particular kinds of subjects: the common person, the marginalized, women'.[11] However, in staging the everyday—in the localised setting, characters (primarily commoners) and their trivial concerns, the ordinariness of much of More's work and interactions, the familiarity of More's *De casibus* story to the audience, amongst other things—the play lays claim to More and pluralises his story, broadening it to encompass ordinary people and underscore how their lives are enmeshed in larger discourses and histories of power.

The play's second scene serves to introduce More's character within a familiar setting—the civil law court.[12] An arras is drawn to reveal the mayor, justices, recorder, sheriffs including More, plaintiff, and accused assemble '*as in sessions*' in the City Guildhall (2.0. SD). With 'weightier business' concluded, the officials turn their attention to 'petty felonies' (2.1–2) and specifically the case of the career criminal Lifter. In this scene, More is established as a seasoned sheriff; he advises the mayor, receives orders, and knows the city's habitual offenders. As their exchange demonstrates, More and Lifter are familiar with one another and More's wisdom and mercy are renowned even amongst the criminal class (2.51–67). Unlike the naïve justices in Greene's *A Notable Discovery of Cozenage* who need canting language explained to them, More is *au fait* with the lexicon of cony-catching.[13] He volunteers to be Lifter's 'setter' (2.80) and orchestrates the robbery to teach a lesson to Suresby, the self-righteous justice. More eventually returns the justice's purse and his good-natured lecture to Suresby—which cannily repeats Suresby's own warning to not 'tempt necessity' but 'lock your money up at home' (2.183)—offers a moral lesson to both the on- and offstage audience.

Placed against the backdrop of the banalities of a court at work, the gulling of Suresby and salvation of Lifter underscores More's exceptional intellect and integrity. He is shown to be, as Melchiori observes, 'the very incarnation of the marriage of Wit and Wisdom'.[14] This episode, then, presents More in a dual light: he is an ordinary city official capably executing his duties, but he is also remarkable as he dispenses justice regardless of status (judge or cutpurse) but with due regard for Christian benevolence and prudence.

More's tricking of Suresby, like his practical joke on Erasmus and his performance in the players' comedy (scenes 2 and 8), demonstrates his sense of humour. In his interaction with the ruffian Falconer however, More embodies order and good sense. Falconer is brought to More for judgement as an instigator of an organised riot held at Paternoster Row.[15] Although Melchiori views the addition of 'yet another riot in the play' as a 'miscalculation' on Munday's part,[16] the riot is something of a side issue. Rather, the target of More's ire and focus of the scene is Falconer's 'foul head' (8.129).[17] Here a servant, a common figure on the Elizabethan stage and common occupation in the period, is shown in an act of defiance.[18] The ruffian's beloved shag-hair operates as a kind of low-level resistance to social norms. As More notes, Falconer falls short of the ideal retainer; he does not act like or resemble an ecclesiastical secretary's servant as he should (8.85–86). Falconer's infraction of tonsorial custom is compounded by his contrariness; he swears repeatedly, he contradicts the Sheriff's report, and, like a poor man's Aaron or Iago, his only regret is that the brawl was half-over before he 'had a lick at it' (8.70). For all of his bluster, however, the ruffian stands as a figure of only mild disorder. Falconer is a rebel without a cause—he seems unable even to explain his stubborn opposition to cleanliness beyond a vague claim to an arbitrary vow—and his rebellion is speedily quashed. Faced with a lengthy prison sentence, Falconer consents to have his 'odious' mane cut and we next see him with his 'face [...] like an honest man's' (8.121, 237). Falconer resists conformity, but ultimately submits ('to the mercy of the barber') and bears the mark of authority's judgement on his head, emerging 'a new man' (8.228, 232).[19] If Falconer subverts order but is ultimately contained by it, it is a containment not without its difficulties. As Alan Sinfield argues, even if a dominant discourse endeavours 'to contain a subordinate perspective [it] must first bring it into visibility [... and] once that has happened, there can be no guarantee that the subordinate will stay safely in its prescribed place'.[20] Falconer's resistance to authority seems typical for such a hot-headed man. In fact, it appears to be outright trivial to More, who has weightier business in hand. Falconer's changeability and his tears to his master further undercut the seriousness of any threat or validity of any views he propounds (8.250–291). And yet, while the audience is encouraged to read More in this scene as a benevolent patriarch, and although Falconer regains his freedom through submission—order wins out and normality is restored—he remains an angry young man resentful of his treatment at the hands of authority (8.250–267, 286–291). There is closure here, then, but like Falconer the audience does not have to respect it.[21] In the end, Falconer is a figure that is betwixt and between; we may read him as both a serious and a clownish model of discontent.

The play presents More not only as an important statesman, but also as a proud Londoner and family man.[22] In his family's first appearance, the play underscores More's self-confessed gregariousness—his 'merry heart [which] lives by good company' (9.18)—and his active social life. The Mayor, his wife, with attendants and city officials are to visit More and the household busies itself with preparations.[23] The multiple authorial hands in and additions to the play may help produce inconsistencies in the scene. Within a mere forty-two lines the guests are described as on the way to the house and then as having dined, during which time More has not left the stage, and yet when the visitors enter at line 91 he welcomes them 'again' (9.92). Such inconsistencies aside, the scene succeeds in conveying More's hospitality. He is concerned first of all that his guests enjoy a good meal and that the household therefore upholds tradition: 'be careful [...] [that] Our diet be made dainty for the taste. / For, of all people that the earth affords, / The Londoners fare richest at their boards' (9.19–22). The English love of food was renowned in the period: 'a cultural fixation with eating, cooking and hospitality gained the English a reputation both at home and abroad in the sixteenth and seventeenth centuries'.[24] Holinshed recorded that English 'tables are oftentimes more plentifullie garnished than those of other nations' and even the rioter Lincoln acknowledges 'Our country is a great eating country' (6.7).[25] If the play was first written in the 1590s, More's pride in London's bounty would surely have struck a chord with the urban audience who were enduring a European-wide period of scarcity.[26] Even in the prosaic duties of hosting then, the play offers commentary upon the contemporary state of affairs; indeed, More's words might be read by the audience as a nostalgic allusion to better days or resentment at the present decline in English fortunes.

The visit of the Mayor to More's home is somewhat of a special occasion as is evinced by the music of hautboys, the visitors' ceremonial costume (*'in scarlet'*), and the large size of the group which includes *'so many Aldermen as may'* (9.91. SD). The mundanities of the convivial gathering are apparent nonetheless as More and his family organise the meal, the stools and seating arrangements (9.26–32, 111–125), the lighting of torches (9.37–38), the supper for the visiting players (9.80–81), and the entertainment of the guests through conversation, music, and theatre (9.40–44, 55–58, 83–84). While More is the Lord Chancellor of England (since scene 7), he is shown to be at ease in the domestic space and takes care to work with his family and please his guests. The everyday activity normalises More who is celebrated as a local boy done good. The scene shows More as a remarkable but recognisable everyman whose achievements and virtues are not beyond the realm of possibility for the ordinary citizen. While at first glance it could appear that More's character lacks interiority (he has, for example, just one soliloquy), he dominates the stage with 'one of the longest roles in Elizabethan drama' and he is 'situated at the center of the audience's narrative desire'.[27] Focusing on Catholicism in the play, Gillian Woods suggests that the play engineers an 'ethically important [...] theatrical engagement' that 'produces a relationship between the audience and More'.[28] I would extend this analysis further to suggest that the audience's investment in More, their familiarly with him established through the everyday in his private and public life, casts a critical light on his treatment at the hands of the state. The audience's intimate knowledge of More, built up in scenes like that of the Mayor's visit, underscores the state's unfamiliarity with domestic More and, more broadly, its distance from its people in the world of the play.[29] Consequently in the subsequent scene, the downfall of the city's hero appears to come at the hands of an unseen exterior force with ambiguous motives.

The meeting of the Privy Council in Westminster sees More and his colleagues gather to discuss matters of state. If the previous scene was one of civic community and merriment, this scene reveals the 'toil and careful watching' of the King's councillors to ensure the 'health and preservation of the land' (10.15, 18). With various lords and the Clerk in the background, Shrewsbury, Surrey, the Bishop of Rochester, and More commence a back-and-forth debate on the possibility of employing the emperor of Germany in the English campaign against France. While the Council deals with such 'matters / Of high importance' (10.7–8), the meeting is routine and, for the audience, the war and military alliances serve as examples of the Council's typical concerns. The scene's opening makes the ensuing business with the articles all the more abnormal. Palmer enters abruptly and, in just four lines he presents the articles '*With great reverence*'—carefully highlighted both in his own words and specified in the scene direction (10.7. SD.)—and then responds to each individual as Henry commanded. (The King clearly has the upper hand, having prepared an answer for every kind of response.) Tilney marked the succeeding lines, from 80 to 104—Rochester's departure, More's resignation, and Surrey and Shrewsbury's signing—for alteration.[30] Although the articles are not named and their content goes undescribed, 'Tilney realised that if on the one hand this caution prevented the play from becoming an apology for the Roman Church, on the other it made it politically more dangerous as a questioning of the arbitrary use of royal power against personal conscience'.[31] The challenge to royal authority presented by Rochester and More is highlighted by the deviation from the norm. The setup of the scene makes the articles stand out as a jarring aberration in the orderly running of the realm.[32] Further, Palmer's interruption implies that the problem does not originate with the religious and noble figures whom we have just seen in service of the state, but with the state itself. The King implicitly demands blind allegiance, but More forestalls this, noting 'Our conscience first shall parley with our laws' (10.73). Having surveyed the articles, the Bishop of Rochester refuses to sign: 'My heart will check my hand whilst I do write. / Subscribing so, I were an hypocrite' (10.77–78). His caution might seem sensible, especially to an audience that recalled Marlowe's Doctor Faustus, another learned man who, in failing to heed the warnings of his own flesh, signed away his soul. Rochester's refusal leads to a charge of 'capital contempt' (10.82), but More's response is more circumspect as he begs time to consider 'this task' and pre-emptively resigns the Chancellorship (10.86). With Rochester and More's downfalls before them, the consequences of offending the state are clear to Surrey and Shrewsbury. The pair hastily sign the documents:

> *Palmer.* Will you subscribe, my lords?
> *Surrey.*   Instantly, good Sir Thomas.
>   We'll bring the writing unto our sovereign.
>
>   (10.98–99)

The lords' swift agreement could be staged as the certitude of loyal subjects or as comical self-preservation, but in valorising More and presenting him as a tragic hero deserving of empathy, the play encourages the audience to look askance on those who differ from him. Surrey and Shrewsbury's acquiescence marks them as faithful, but also as unquestioning and perhaps fearful subjects. To the state which acts as an indifferent *deus ex machina*, these would be appealing figures, but they would be less so for an audience engaged by More.

More's family become more prominent as his end approaches, appearing in scenes 11, 13, and 16. What makes these scenes compelling is the clash of the familiar and strange; an ordinary family is placed in an extraordinary situation as they face the impending death of their patriarch for treason to the state and loyalty to his religion and conscience. In scene 11, the family stroll in the garden of their house in Chelsea and discuss their collective foreboding dreams. The discussion gives the audience an insight into the dynamics and habits of the family. Roper does not wish to trouble his mother-in-law, and so he shares his worries only with his wife: 'Our dreams all meet in one conclusion, / Fatal, I fear' (11.42–43). According to Lady More, this is not the first time that she has been side-lined by her family: 'This is your fashion still: I must know nothing' (11.46). Later, she shows impatience with her condemned husband as he makes light of the situation. Munday uses More's characteristic wit to obscure the details of his treason, but More's levity infuriates his wife.[33] Like the comically suffering wives of Candido in *The Patient Man and the Honest Whore* and Old Merryweather in *Knight of the Burning Pestle*, Lady More is exasperated—for the umpteenth time we imagine—by her husband: 'Lord, that your honour ne'er will leave these jests! / In faith, it ill becomes ye' (11.63–64). Through incidental interactions like these the audience comes to know the family and can empathise with their situation and impending loss. Whereas Roper only remarks that he has 'been troubled' with dreams of More (11.35), Lady More and Mistress Roper recount their dreams in detail. Lady More dreamt of boating on the Thames with the King, but the boats were separated due to the 'violence of the stream' and she drowned with her husband in a whirlpool by the Tower (11.8–26). Mistress Roper imagined her father dying a bloody death in Chelsea church, anachronistically 'defaced' by Reformation iconoclasm (11.36–41). The dreams express some of the 'political and religious details [that] have been repressed in the text' and show these themes 'as having a fatal effect on one political subject that also traumatizes numerous ontological subjects'.[34] Roper and the three women are minor figures in the play; More's Second Daughter has only 7 lines, for example, most of which she shares with her sister. However, these secondary characters form a visible presence that registers the personal effect of More's downfall. Throughout scenes 11, 13, and 16, family bonds and roles are emphasised as the characters repeatedly refer to More as 'husband' or 'father' and he refers to his family members as 'daughter', 'wife', and 'son'. The state may view him as an obstinate subject deserving of strict judgment (13.146–149), but More's family experience and register his punishment as a private tragedy; they are deprived of a father, husband, and role model.

As Rory Loughnane notes in this volume's Introduction, characterisation is one means by which the everyday is staged. In addition to sundry servingmen, *Sir Thomas More*'s dramatis personae lists seven servants in More's employ and many, like Randall the manservant and Ned Butler, are individualised by name and position.[35] In scene 15, with the family at court, More's butler, brewer, porter, horsekeeper, secretary, and steward gather to discuss their shared concern: the fate of their master. While this domestic scene is included in order to avoid staging a more contentious one—More's trial—its very ordinariness nonetheless encompasses the subversive. In late Elizabethan London, More was popular for his capability and fairness as a civil servant and was often 'remembered with real affection'.[36] This familiar sentimental view of the statesman is evident in his servants' interaction. Drawing on their personal experience, and willing even to go on record ('if I / might speak my mind'; 'I'll put that in upon my own knowledge' [15.12–13, 16]), they deem him to be uniquely benevolent. Like the servingmen in *Timon of Athens*, More's servants are minor characters that offer a perspective on the play's main action. But, more than this they are—by virtue of their position as workers and as part of More's family—casualties of that tragic action. Suddenly masterless, Timon's Third Servant summarises the situation for his colleagues: 'We are fellows still, / Serving alike in sorrow. Leaked is our barque, / And we, poor mates, stand on the dying deck' (4.2.18–20). More's steward Catesby similarly highlights the dependency of servants: 'Thus the fair-spreading oak falls not alone, / But all the neighbour plants and under-trees / Are crushed down with his weight' (15.56–58). Catesby's final words underscore this point but also reveal the fellowship found in suffering: 'go / Fellow-like hence, co-partners of one woe' (15.59–60). Even as their ties are sundered, the servants are united by their experience and, rather than denounce their master whom the state has deemed a traitor, they share in More's woe. As Jyotsna Singh observes, tragedy typically focuses on the fall of a great man but the interventions of secondary characters can do much to expose the workings and cost of political power.[37] Here, More's servants highlight the ripple effect of the individual's fall; with their views in the spotlight, the calamity is pluralised. More is still valorised then, but so too are his loyal servants.

By the scene's close, More's servants are unemployed—a situation familiar to some in the audience—but they take comfort in being proved right in their judgement.[38] As they attested and as his naming of each servant and philanthropic bequest of 20 nobles to his 140 dependents proves (15.46–52), More is indeed a good master. Nevertheless, while More may be the wisest, merriest, most honourable, 'harmless gentleman' in the world, as the Butler and Brewer declare (15.14–15), he remains the King's subject. Dissident opinions then are placed in the mouth of the lowly servant class and the validity of their grievance may be compromised by their status. The servingmen remain a powerless group; their testimonials cannot affect the outcome of the court case, and so More goes to the scaffold. For the audience however, the servants might proffer a subversive endorsement of a view of More that does not accord with the state's position either in the play (More is a misguided shirker of his duty to the King and God [10.105–109, 13.146, 17.126]) or in Elizabethan London (More was an obstinate Papist traitor).[39] As Rory Loughnane notes of secondary characters in *Henry VIII*, 'their position as observers at the court's periphery connects them to the viewing playhouse audience' and enables them to fulfil a choric function, guiding the audience's interpretation.[40] Subaltern disapproval may go unrecorded in official accounts of state events, but it may be imagined and voiced on stage as it is here in *Sir Thomas More*. This short scene in More's house works then to recuperate marginalised voices from the past to speak to a new, and perhaps more attentive, audience.

In the play's final scenes, the Londoners again imagine More as both ordinary and extraordinary. When More is taken to the Tower, three warders await him at the gate. Their exchange has an air of the quotidian as they discuss from where More travels, the burgeoning crowd of spectators, and More's favour with the poor. The First Warder remarks, 'be it spoken without offence to any, / A wiser or more virtuous gentleman / Was never bred in England' (14.9–11), while the Second observes that he is 'bewailed of everyone' (14.14). As Patricia Fumerton notes, 'transgressive behavior often found expression *within and through* everyday practices and representations'.[41] The First Warder's pointed lines indicate the difficulties the play's subject presents to the dramatists and, within the narrative, the difficulties More's situation presents to the common man. The playwrights must engage an audience with More's *De casibus* story but omit the reason for his fall, an avoidance that makes a 'felt absence' in the play.[42] For the warders, they must do their duty but engage with a popular home-grown hero whose crime is obscure. The First Warder's opening words are defensive, even wishful, and bespeak an anxiety about public speech and esteem for More; surely it can be no offence to declare the well-known fact of More's virtue, but in a world where the worthiest wise man has fallen victim to the vagaries of the state, who knows? The capriciousness and mysterious inner workings of power are here articulated and exposed for the audience's consideration.[43] Moreover, as in scene 15, the disparity between the views of the people and the court is again foregrounded. According to Melchiori, 'the play as a whole had been plotted with a precise intention: that of showing the abuses perpetrated under cover of the absolute power of the king'.[44] The warders' discussion illustrates how even the most ordinary of situations (chitchat at work) can expose not just tensions between the rulers and the ruled, but how these tensions are commonplace.

As the warders await More's arrival, a poor woman presses her way to the front of the (offstage) crowd. Interrogated by the warders, the petitioner reveals that she has a case in the Court of Chancery and More possesses her evidentiary documents. When More disembarks, she makes a heartfelt plea for the return of these papers, without which she is 'utterly undone' (14.26). This episode, which appears in both Holinshed and Harpsfield's accounts of More's life, supports the warders' claims about More's popularity amongst the poor. Further, it foregrounds the everyday as it presents the impending execution of a mighty man as the backdrop for the predicament of a poor woman. The petitioner's needs, seemingly inconsequential to the authorities, are shown as meaningful and she takes centre stage for a brief moment. The petitioner's dependency on More shows too the burdens on the former statesman. More is elevated—he is in demand despite being deposed—but he is also an everyman whose work pursues him even to the edge of doom.[45] His punning joke to the petitioner—'Thou must bear with me' (14.42)—further reminds the audience that he is not the only one to suffer from his fall. Although the poor woman is familiar with the former Lord Chancellor (14.36) and despite the theatrical interactions of monarchs and citizens in plays like *Edward IV* and *Henry V*, the possibility of suing to the King, as More waggishly suggests, is surely impossible for the ordinary person (14.41). The petitioner speaks for all the indigent when she says 'Farewell, the best friend that the poor e'er had' (14.44). With More's death, the play implies that London's poor will lose their only advocate.

In contrast to its sources and to texts by 'contemporary Protestant and Catholic martyrologists', the play uses martyrological conventions—such as wit and gallows humour—to conceal rather than reveal More's beliefs.[46] Additionally, with his execution imminent, More's good humour displays his *contemptus mundi* and the '[t]heatrical divestment [by More of his clothes, beard, purse etc.] becomes a Christian metaphor for relinquishing the mortal body'.[47] However, More's jokes about ordinary things—his urine in scene 16, bloodletting and his beard in scene 17—also undercut the power of the state spectacle of punishment. In his cell in the Tower, More examines his urine to make an incisive joke, the thrust of which is aimed at Henry as the agent of More's downfall.[48] Playing the role of physician, More tells his Servant that the patient would likely 'live long enough, / So pleased the King' (16.26–27). More caustically concludes that he will cheat the doctor of a fee as, thanks to the King's prescription of a death sentence, he now has a permanent cure for his kidney stones (16.19–21). This joke is sandwiched between more serious matter: More's ascertainment that he will be executed in the morning and that the Bishop of Rochester has already been executed. Thus, More's jest and urinary ailment punctures the formality and gravity of the state's authority. Moreover, the joking about More's maladies and mortality brings the unstaged King back into the frame. Here, the joke has the effect of deprecatingly placing the 'high' (the monarch, law, religion) alongside the 'low' (the common man, bodily infirmities, urine) and of elevating the 'low' to a matter of dramatic, historical, and indeed national interest. The boundaries between 'high' and 'low' are exposed as permeable, the hierarchy of values mocked as unstable and meaningless.

The play's finale protracts More's ascent to the scaffold as the sheriffs of London collect him from the warders, the Lieutenant bids a tearful farewell to his captive, and he meets the hangman, watched over by Surrey and Shrewsbury. In his final moments, More is again presented as both exceptional and familiar. He frequently engages in badinage with the agents of authority, including the hangman, but in his dealings with the sheriffs he calls to mind his connection to London's traditions and its citizens, both on and off stage. More thanks the sheriffs for meeting him, joking that it is a courtesy: 'I see by this you have not quite forgot / That I was in times past as you are now, A sheriff of London' (17.30–32). More is an everyman here; he once worked in and for the city, but he is now an object, rather than an instrument, of civic and state power. Although the First Sheriff is all business—'Sir, then you know our duty doth require it'—More underscores his familiarity with the men and their responsibilities: 'I know it well, sir [...] Ah, Master Sheriff / You and I have been of old acquaintance' (17.34, 36–37). The significance of the city and its people to More is marked as he reminds the Second Sheriff that he once attended More's lecture at St. Lawrence's Church and was represented by More '[when he] studied the law in Lincoln's Inn' (17.38–47). As several scholars have noted, 'the text foregrounds the various roles More played in his city' to present him as 'a legendary citizen'.[49] While the play offers no clear moral or unambiguous judgement of More as a Catholic martyr,[50] the final scene emphasises More's identity as a Londoner and his familiarity to the audience so that he stands as a *memento mori*. More is both 'one of us' and 'the best of us' and his fate—his rise and fall, his treatment at the hands of the state, his death, whether the audience mourns or celebrates it—could be ours.

***

A xenophobic riot, More's martyrdom, and a complex textual history have made *Sir Thomas More* the subject of much critical debate, but as I have argued the play's staging of normality, although often overlooked, is no less important than these conspicuous issues. While the scenes of urban unrest and More's treason caught the censor's eye, the play stages transgression, disaffection, and discontent in nearly all levels of society, in groups and individuals of different professions and genders. Transgression is not unusual then but normal in *Sir Thomas More*, and the play implies that it is an inevitable consequence of inhabiting a world where inequalities are common. Dissent, competition, and conflict are natural and to be expected when there are 'haves' and 'have nots' and when the individual's will meets state power. The common, in terms of class and everydayness, is also used in the play to critique and deflate the 'high'. Servants, haircuts, family dynamics, medical complaints, and other ordinary things are imbued with the power to voice alternative or dissenting opinions, and they bring the 'low' centre-stage as a valid object of attention, broadening the scope and impact of the drama.

Throughout *Sir Thomas More*, the staging of normality works to claim and situate its protagonist as both exceptional and everyday, unique and ordinary. With More as such a figure and with the audience distanced from state power—there are no court scenes, Henry never appears on stage, and Surrey and Shrewsbury play limited roles—the connection between More, the Londoners, and the audience is strengthened. Using this figure who is not-unlike-us, the play brings politics home to the audience with efficient immediacy. Just as there is no redress for the rioting citizens' legitimate grievances,[51] it becomes clear that there is no reconciliation to be had between the state and More's conscience. Having been a 'state-pleader', More is made to become 'a stage / player' in a 'tragedy' written by his erstwhile benefactor and friend, King Henry (17.75–77). For the audience who has followed More's rise and fall—the everyday work, daily interactions, habitual actions, and quotidian concerns which the play strives to foreground—when he mounts the scaffold, it is not as a monstrous or strange aberration, but as an all too familiar victim of political exigencies. At the close of the play, then, More stands as a cautionary exemplum on the dangers of state power to the individual, and the audience is keenly aware that his tragedy could easily be theirs.

Notes

1. I am indebted to Goran Stanivukovic, Ema Vyroubalová, and Darragh Greene for their insightful and helpful comments on this essay. All quotations are from the Arden edition of *Sir Thomas More* (2011).
2. The censorship, composition, and manuscript history of *Sir Thomas More* has been the focus of several articles on and editions of the play, as well as Howard-Hill's 1989 collection on the play and Shakespeare.
3. With such a focus, these scenes were of particular concern to Tilney, the Master of the Revels. Indeed, the play's opening is 'the most heavily censored' scene with Tilney ordering significant changes including the omission of the insurrection and its causes (Jowett 2011: 356).
4. In the most recent comprehensive study of the chronology, Taylor and Loughnane's 'best guess' for the revised version of the play (to which Shakespeare contributed) is 1604, but they offer a date range of 1600–May 1606. Their date range for the original version is 1590–1600, but

they propose that the play was most likely composed at the end of the range (2017: 548–553). For an account of the latest thinking on the division of authorship, see Taylor and Loughnane, as well as Jowett's edition of the play.
5. Hill (2005: para. 5).
6. Howard (2003: 307).
7. Kermode (2009: 79).
8. Hunt (1999: 306).
9. For example, Doll states that More 'hast done more with [his] / good words than all they could with their weapons' (6.184–185). Earlier in the play, More, Palmer, and Surrey expressed their hope that speech would prove more effective than might (3.88–90; 5.38–41, 50–51).
10. Forker and Candido (1980: 86).
11. Fumerton (1999: 5).
12. Mukherji notes that 'one does not have to look far to see the ubiquity of the law in the products of the [early modern] literary imagination' (2009: 706).
13. Greene (1930: 132).
14. Melchiori (1989: 77).
15. The scene with Falconer is an anecdote borrowed from the life of Sir Thomas Cromwell in John Foxe's *Book of Martyrs*.
16. Melchiori (1989: 80).
17. In Munday's original text, More and Surrey give instructions to the Sheriff to maintain order amongst the warring factions of servants, but More's exchange with Falconer still focuses on his displeasing appearance. For the original text, see OT2b in Appendix 1 in Jowett's edition.
18. Burnett notes that 'servants were to be found in 29 percent of all households during the period, and a substantial proportion of young people of both sexes could expect to be servants at some stage in their lives' (1997: 1). See also Neill (2000).
19. In contrast to Falconer, More will keep his personal vow but nonetheless 'send [the King] for [his] trespass a reverent head' (5.4.75). Brietz Monta discusses More and Falconer's varying approaches to vows (2005: 169).
20. Sinfield (1992: 48).
21. Ibid.
22. See Hill (2005) for a discussion of More and the city, and Woods (2011) for a discussion of More's treatment of and importance to his family.
23. Revisions to the play present the Mayor's visit as unexpected, but the original dramatist imagined that More had extended an invitation.
24. Meads (2001: 1).

25. Holinshed (1587: 165). For more on food in the play, see Kermode (2009: 81–82) and Fitzpatrick (2007: 83–93).
26. For more on food and diet in the period, see Withington, who notes that for the poor of English society 'not only hunger but famine was a real concern' (2014: 150).
27. McMillin (1987: 61), Gabrieli and Melchiori (1990: 32), and Woods (2011: 17).
28. Woods (2011: 25).
29. Earlier in the play, the state and its agents were imagined to be impotent against (1.1.40–44, 69–70) or ignorant of the inequalities between the citizens and foreigners (1.3.64–70). The late arrival of the pardon for the hanged rioter Lincoln (2.4.133–144), as Woods remarks, further undermines the state's power (2011: 27). Hill sees a '"division between ruler and ruled"' in these scenes (2005: paras. 11 and 15).
30. For a discussion of Tilney's hand in the manuscript, see Jowett's edition (2011: 26–27, 356–362).
31. Gabrieli and Melchiori (1990: 18).
32. In scene 9, an Addition by Heywood sees More urgently summoned to the Council: 'What's the business now / That all so late his highness sends for me?' (9.332–333).
33. For a discussion of More's silence and his silencing of his wife, see Woods (2011: 19–20).
34. Ibid. (23).
35. For details on casting possibilities, see Jowett's Doubling Chart (2011: 487–488). From the chart, it is clear that the play makes serious demands upon the cast in terms of doubling and that servants have a significant stage presence in the play.
36. Gabrieli and Melchiori (1990: 10) and Woods (2011: 4).
37. Singh (2003: 416–427).
38. Servants were not uncommon theatregoers. See Gurr (2004: 63, 69, 78–79, 149) and Whitney (1999). Unemployment, fears over 'masterless men', and tensions around work and wages were high in the 1590s. For details see Archer (1991), Neill (2000), Netzloff (2014), and Rappaport (2002).
39. For more on the Elizabethan and Jacobean reception of the historical Thomas More, see Woods (2011) and Questier (2002). For more on Tilney's censorship, see Howard-Hill (1989), and the Introduction to Jowett's and to Gabrieli and Melchiori's edition of the play. Tilney was mostly concerned with avoiding references to civic disorder, but he ordered all of 4.1, the scene of the Bishop of Rochester's impeachment and More's resignation of the Chancellorship, to be altered.
40. Loughnane (2013: 110).

41. Fumerton (1999: 12).
42. Woods (2011: 5).
43. I draw here on Singh and her observation that focusing on minor characters in tragic drama can illuminate or at least lead us to ruminate on modern politics where often 'decisions about war and its political realignments are far removed from those who are its victims' (2003: 420).
44. Melchiori (1989: 77).
45. Levine insightfully observes that 'the proximity of More's disobedience and the May Day rising also registers a common bond between the Lord Chancellor and the ordinary men and women of the opening scenes' (2007: 39).
46. Brietz Monta (2005: 160).
47. Jowett (2011: 89).
48. For more on urine and uroscopy in the period, see Paster (1993) and Stolberg (2015).
49. Hill (2005: para. 2) and Manley (1995: 35).
50. Woods (2011: 26–27).
51. Jowett (2011: 46).

Works Cited

Archer, Ian. 1991. *The Pursuit of Stability: Social Relations in Elizabethan London*. Cambridge: Cambridge University Press.
Brietz Monta, Susannah. 2005. *Martyrdom and Literature in Early Modern England*. Cambridge: Cambridge University Press.
Burnett, Mark Thornton. 1997. *Masters and Servants in English Renaissance Drama and Culture: Authority and Obedience*. London: Macmillan.
Fitzpatrick, Joan. 2007. *Food in Shakespeare: Early Modern Dietaries and the Plays*. Aldershot: Ashgate.
Forker, Charles R., and Joseph Candido. 1980. Wit, Wisdom and Theatricality. In *The Book of Sir Thomas More*. Shakespeare Studies 13: 85–104.
Fumerton, Patricia. 1999. Introduction: A New New Historicism. In *Renaissance Culture and the Everyday*, ed. Patricia Fumerton and Simon Hunt. Philadelphia: University of Pennsylvania Press.
Gabrieli, Vittorio, and Giorgio Melchiori (eds.). 1990. Introduction. In *Sir Thomas More*. Manchester: Manchester University Press.
Greene, Robert. 1930. A Notable Discovery of Cozenage. In *The Elizabethan Underworld*, ed. A.V. Judges. London: Routledge and Sons.
Gurr, Andrew. 2004. *Playgoing in Shakespeare's London*. Cambridge: Cambridge University Press.
Hill, Tracey. 2001. "Since Forged Invention Former Time Defaced": Representing Tudor History in the 1590s. In *The Anatomy of Tudor Literature*, ed. Mike Pincombe. Aldershot: Ashgate.

Hill, Tracey. 2005. "The Cittie Is in an Uproar": Staging London. In *The Booke of Sir Thomas More*. *Early Modern Literary Studies* 11 (1): 2.1–19.

Holinshed, Raphael, et al. 1587. Book 2 Chapter 6: Of the Food and Diet of the English. In *The First and Second Volumes of Chronicles*. London: John Harrison.

Howard, Jean E. 2003. Shakespeare, Geography, and the Work of Genre on the Early Modern Stage. *Modern Language Quarterly* 64 (3): 299–322.

Howard-Hill, T.H. (ed.). 1989. *Shakespeare and Sir Thomas More: Essays on the Play and Its Shakespearian Interest*. Cambridge: Cambridge University Press.

Hunt, Simon. 1999. "Leaving Out the Insurrection": Carnival Rebellion, English History Plays, and a Hermeneutics of Advocacy. In *Renaissance Culture and the Everyday*, ed. Patricia Fumerton and Simon Hunt. Philadelphia: University of Pennsylvania Press.

Jowett, John. 2011. Introduction. In *Sir Thomas More*. London: Bloomsbury Arden Shakespeare.

Judges, A.V. 1930. *The Elizabethan Underworld*. London: Routledge and Sons.

Kermode, Lloyd Edward. 2009. *Aliens and Englishness in Elizabethan Drama*. Cambridge: Cambridge University Press.

Levine, Nina. 2007. Citizens' Games: Differentiating Collaboration and *Sir Thomas More*. *Shakespeare Quarterly* 58 (1): 31–64.

Loughnane, Rory. 2013. Semi-choric Devices and the Framework for Playgoer Response in *King Henry VIII*. In *Late Shakespeare, 1608–1613*, ed. Andrew J. Power and Rory Loughnane. Cambridge: Cambridge University Press.

Manley, Lawrence. 1995. *Literature and Culture in Early Modern London*. Cambridge: Cambridge University Press.

McMillin, Scott. 1987. *The Elizabethan Theatre and the Book of Sir Thomas More*. London: Cornell University Press.

McShane, Angela, and Garthine Walker. 2010. Introduction. In *The Extraordinary and the Everyday in Early Modern England: Essays in Celebration of the Work of Bernard Capp*, ed. Angela McShane and Garthine Walker. Basingstoke: Palgrave Macmillan.

Meads, Chris. 2001. *Banquets Set Forth: Banqueting in English Renaissance Drama*. Manchester: Manchester University Press.

Melchiori, Giorgio. 1989. *The Booke of Sir Thomas More*: Dramatic Unity. In *Shakespeare and Sir Thomas More: Essays on the Play and Its Shakespearian Interest*, ed. T.H. Howard-Hill. Cambridge: Cambridge University Press.

Mukherji, Subha. 2009. "Understood Relations": Law and Literature in Early Modern Studies. *Literature Compass* 6: 706–725.

Munday, Anthony, et al. 2011. *Sir Thomas More*, ed. John Jowett. London: Bloomsbury Arden Shakespeare.

Neill, Michael. 2000. Servant Obedience and Master Sins: Shakespeare and the Bonds of Service. In *Putting History to the Question: Power, Politics, and Society in English Renaissance Drama*. New York: Columbia University Press.

Netzloff, Mark. 2014. Work. In *The Ashgate Research Companion to Popular Culture*, ed. Andrew Hadfield, Matthew Dimmock, and Abigail Shinn. Surrey: Ashgate.

Paster, Gail Kern. 1993. *The Body Embarrassed: Drama and Disciplines of Shame in Early Modern Europe*. New York: Cornell University Press.

Questier, Michael. 2002. Catholicism, Kinship and the Public Memory of *Sir Thomas More*. *The Journal of Ecclesiastical History* 53 (3): 476–509.

Rappaport, Steve. 2002. *Worlds Within Worlds: Structures of Life in Sixteenth-Century London*. Cambridge: Cambridge University Press.

Shakespeare, William. 1994. Timon of Athens. In *William Shakespeare: The Complete Works*, ed. Gary Taylor and Stanley Wells. Oxford: Clarendon.

Sinfield, Alan. 1992. *Faultlines: Cultural Materialism and the Politics of Dissident Reading*. Oxford: Oxford University Press.

Singh, Jyotsna G. 2003. The Politics of Empathy in *Antony and Cleopatra*: A View from Below. In *A Companion to Shakespeare's Works: The Tragedies*, ed. Richard Dutton and Jean E. Howard. Oxford: Blackwell.

Stolberg, Michael. 2015. *Uroscopy in Early Modern Europe*. Oxford: Routledge.

Taylor, Gary, and Rory Loughnane. 2017. The Canon and Chronology of Shakespeare's Works. In *The New Oxford Shakespeare: Authorship Companion*, ed. Gary Taylor and Gabriel Egan. Oxford: Oxford University Press.

Whitney, Charles. 1999. "Usually in the Werking Daies": Playgoing Journeymen, Apprentices, and Servants in Guild Records, 1582–92. *Shakespeare Quarterly* 50 (4): 433–458.

Withington, Phil. 2014. Food and Drink. In *The Ashgate Research Companion to Popular Culture*, ed. Andrew Hadfield, Matthew Dimmock, and Abigail Shinn. Surrey: Ashgate.

Woods, Gillian. 2011. "Strange Discourse": The Controversial Subject of *Sir Thomas More*. *Renaissance Drama* 39: 3–35.

CHAPTER 8

'So like an old tale': Staging Inheritance and the Lost Child in Shakespeare's Romances

Michelle M. Dowd

At the height of Leontes's jealous rage against Hermione in *The Winter's Tale*, when his counselors are desperately attempting to calm his thoughts, Antigonus defends Hermione's virtue in a remarkably odd speech. In response to Leontes's claims that Hermione is 'honor-flawed,' Antigonus exclaims:

> I have three daughters – the eldest is eleven;
> The second and the third, nine and some five –
> If this prove true, they'll pay for't. By mine honor,
> I'll geld 'em all; fourteen they shall not see
> To bring false generations. They are co-heirs,
> And I had rather glib myself than they
> Should not produce fair issue.
> (2.1.145–151)[1]

M. M. Dowd (✉)
Hudson Strode Program in Renaissance Studies, University of Alabama, Tuscaloosa, AL, USA
e-mail: mmdowd1@ua.edu

© The Author(s) 2019
R. Loughnane and E. Semple (eds.), *Staged Normality in Shakespeare's England,* Palgrave Shakespeare Studies, https://doi.org/10.1007/978-3-030-00892-5_8

Antigonus responds to Leontes's anger with some verbal violence of his own; he swears that he will geld his own daughters if Hermione proves to be unchaste. The speech is certainly extreme, suggesting both the security of Antigonus's faith in Hermione and the misogynistic logic that subtends anxieties about female chastity in the period and justifies certain forms of violence against women. But although Antigonus's rhetoric is excessive, the socioeconomic situation to which he refers—the difficulties that ensue in a patrilineal society when the succession falls on female heirs—was actually quite commonplace in early modern England. Antigonus's family drama replicates in miniature one of the central problems of the second half of *The Winter's Tale* (following Mamillius's real and Hermione's apparent death): namely, how to restore patrilineal order when family lineage depends upon a (lost) daughter. Antigonus's unusual outburst is thus in many ways not unusual at all, as it gestures toward a central problematic within both the play and the system of patrilineage in Shakespeare's England.

The common-law doctrine of primogeniture, which stipulated that the eldest son inherited the entirety of his father's estate and title, was one of the most influential forces shaping social and economic order in early modern England, affecting not only wealth and property transfer but also interpersonal and familial relationships. Primogeniture, as Lawrence Stone puts it, was 'the prime factor affecting all families which owned property' in the period, and Amy Louise Erickson describes it as 'the most familiar aspect of inheritance prior to the twentieth century' in England.[2] Indeed, primogeniture was such a dominant feature of early modern inheritance law that we have come to take it for granted as a normal, perhaps even unremarkable, component of premodern English culture. However, while primogeniture constituted a legal norm in the period, a range of socioeconomic and demographic factors meant that exceptions to the practice were common; the contingencies of everyday life often necessitated variations on the legal ideal. The status quo, in other words, was not as static or as clearly delineated as we might initially suppose. This seems to me a particularly important point for considering how and when inheritance gets evoked on the early modern stage. As the essays in the current volume remind us, scholars of early modern drama have often tended to focus on transgression and disorder at the expense of the everyday or the ordinary. It might be tempting, for instance, to read patrilineal inheritance as a norm to which the drama presents exceptions, alternatives, and even subversive counternarratives. But this would be to assume two things that closer historical and literary examinations prove to be untrue: (1) that patrilineal inheritance was in fact a well-defined, normative process; and (2) that the drama functions primarily to subvert that process. Instead, I suggest that we need both to think critically about what constitutes the legal 'norm' of primogeniture (as many historians have done in recent years) and investigate how the drama helps to manage, sustain, and actively promote a kind of legal normality during a period of acute socioeconomic pressures. This is certainly not to deny the transgressive potential of the drama. Rather, by analyzing the dramatic mechanisms by which the patrilineal economy could be creatively upheld, we can uncover some of the important cultural work those dramatic narratives were performing in Shakespeare's England. And part of that work is an exposition of the multivocality of the patrilineal 'norm,' a process that at once upholds a conservative narrative of patriarchal right and provocatively suggests the instability of that position.

In what follows, I consider how Shakespeare staged one common eventuality within the patrilineal economy: families with daughters but without sons. Looking specifically at Shakespeare's late romances, especially *The Winter's Tale* and *Cymbeline*, I explore how these plays animate and interrogate the familiar socioeconomic problem of the heiress by turning to another kind of 'norm'—the lost-child plot, a feature of Roman new comedy that was frequently revived in late sixteenth- and early seventeenth-century drama. In the romances, I argue, this dramatic convention enables Shakespeare to stage a comforting resolution to the problem posed by the female heir, as the lost-child plot performatively mitigates the flexibility and wandering represented by the heiress, thereby assuaging cultural concerns about loss of lineage through formal, dramaturgical means. In showcasing the productive polysemy of the normative, Shakespeare's romances are ultimately less interested in dramatizing how legal norms might be overturned than they are in staging how those norms are creatively enabled, sustained, and redefined.

The Everyday Heiress in Shakespeare's England

As ideally imagined, the common law doctrine of primogeniture supported an unbroken line of male succession and the direct transfer of land, goods, and titles through succeeding male generations. And certainly, this theoretical formulation of legal practice was extremely powerful in the period, in both material and ideological registers. At its most basic level, the preference for patrilineal descent in the common law led to a desire among fathers at all levels of society to 'bequeath their property to the heirs of their bodies and blood,' with a clear preference for sons.[3] Primogeniture thus preserved male privilege while also establishing a model for social order that had broad and long-lasting implications for both the economic and the interpersonal lives of early modern families.[4]

At the same time, however, primogeniture was not a universal practice in early modern England, nor was it an internally consistent legal doctrine. Modifications on primogeniture were quite common, leading to a variety of practices that were often contradictory. For instance, the common law was only one of five legal systems governing property rights and inheritance in the period.[5] Other systems, such as equity law, frequently provided explicit alternatives to the more rigorous mandates of the common law. Furthermore, the gap between legal theory and actual practice was often quite wide, and this was especially true where women's legal rights were concerned. Evidence from wills, probate records, and marriage settlements document the multiplicity of practices built into the legal framework of England's patrilineal system.[6] And the uncertainties that arose from demographic anomalies, uncertain marital arrangements, and the everyday whims of affect and personality meant that however powerful patrilineage remained as a cultural and ideological force in the period, its precise applications were always heterogeneous and mutable. Put another way: variations on the legal norm of primogeniture were so common in Shakespeare's England that those variations effectively became the norm.

One of the most common contingencies within England's patrilineal culture was a family's lack of a male heir. An obvious complication to the legal ideal of patrilineage, the heiress necessarily brought a degree of flexibility and movement into patterns of succession because families had to look outside their immediate line of descent to ensure continuity through marriage. The situation was particularly acute in the early modern period; as Lawrence Stone has calculated, due to a combination of factors including high infant mortality rates and low marital fertility, a full 19% of 'all first marriages among the nobility between 1540 and 1660 were childless' and 29% produced no male children.[7] One factor that distinguished English common law from that of other European countries in the period was its preference for lineal heirs of either gender to collateral heirs. For this reason, Englishwomen did inherit with some frequency. Nevertheless, as Eileen Spring has argued, '[t]he succession of females meant that land wandered from name and title—in landowners' eyes, "went out of the family"'.[8] The figure of the heiress in early modern England thus represented a complex set of socioeconomic realities for elite families, as she signified that possibility of loss, alienation—the 'wandering' of name and title—even as she also helped secure a form of lineal descent. While in its ideal form, patrilineage grants privilege to the unbroken and the direct, the heiress suggests movement away from the patrilineal bloodline, an issuing forth that raises the specter of exogamy and even familial dissolution. The female heir was thus a richly evocative conundrum in Shakespeare's England, as she both posed a challenge to the normal functioning of patrilineage (as theoretically conceived) at the same time as she was a remarkably common figure—an everyday example of both the mandates and the limits of primogeniture.[9]

Shakespeare's romances are particularly rich texts for investigating the problem of the heiress in the period, as they frequently exacerbate the socioeconomic tensions posed by the female heir in order to stage different scenarios by which patrilineal order can be reestablished or maintained. In *Pericles*, *The Winter's Tale*, *Cymbeline*, and *The Tempest*, (in addition to the late tragedy *King Lear*), aristocratic inheritance depends upon—or initially seems to depend upon—daughters. Dynastic continuity is thus fundamentally linked in these plays to the uncertain position of heiresses within England's system of patrilineage. Furthermore, by staging the temporary loss or physical displacement of the female heir, these plays amplify the heiress's uncertain position by introducing additional spatial and familial dislocation. In part, the narrative dilation and tropes of loss we see in these plays are indebted to the genre of romance itself.[10] As Patricia Parker has demonstrated, early modern romance narratives display a tension between 'the formal movement towards an ending' and endless deferral or exile.[11] Plays such as *Pericles* and *Cymbeline* thus deploy the narrative structures of romance to emphasize risk, mobility, and potential loss.

But I am particularly interested here in exploring how Shakespeare borrows from and adapts another literary 'norm' that was readily available to him: the lost-child plot from Roman new comedy. As Robert Miola has discussed, the Roman comedies of Plautus and Terence 'bequeathed to posterity the essential genetic make-up' of early modern dramatic comedy.[12] Plautus and, especially, Terence featured prominently in the English grammar school curriculum in Shakespeare's day, with students and, later, playwrights encouraged to refigure the classical models to suit new theatrical purposes. Renaissance playwrights thus mixed the components of Roman comedy with those from other dramatic traditions, resulting in what Miola calls a creative 'polyphony' and 'interplay of voice' between dramatists such as Shakespeare and their classical sources.[13] One common structural device of new comedy, which also became a recurring theme in the plays, was that of the lost child who is ultimately recovered. In Roman comedy, the 'miraculously-preserved child' who is often 'restored to its parents after a lapse of years' is usually female, and the process of restoration enables a resolution of the plot that is favorable to the comedy's young male protagonist.[14] Disguise, mistaken identity, and the 'climactic use of *pistis*, or proof of identity' frequently accompany the lost-child plot and its eventual resolution. Classical commentators Evanthius and Donatus categorized these and other similar comic devices as *errores*, that is, 'mistakes of identity resolved through recognition.' Derived from the Latin *errare*, meaning 'to wander,' the errors of Roman comedy typically involve mistakes and accidents (rather than outright deceits).[15] But they also imply movement, both in the form of physical wandering and in the sense of familial dislocation. On the early modern stage, the lost heiress, borrowed and adapted from Roman comedy, thus becomes a particularly resonant touchstone of contemporary concerns about inheritance and succession.

This was especially true of early modern stage romances, as New Comedy played a particularly prominent role in their formal development. While on the Renaissance stage, some of the Roman comic themes of loss and recovery get Christianized in distinct ways, the basic archetype of the lost child who is ultimately reunited to her parents (most frequently a father) is an underlying feature of most Shakespearean romances.[16] Through this formal structure, I argue, Shakespeare is able to stage and check the wayward movement of the heiress, dramatizing both the possibility of familial dissolution and proffering a literary, and specifically dramatic, solution to the heiress's threat to patrilineal security. Considering *The Winter's Tale* and *Cymbeline* in particular, I analyze the dramaturgical means by which Shakespeare transforms the historical problem of the heiress into a dramatic performance that both engages and actively works to resolve that socioeconomic problematic.

'Poor Thing, Condemned to Loss:'
Restoring the Heiress in *The Winter's Tale*

The opening scene of *The Winter's Tale* (first recorded performance in May 1611) brings the plot of the lost child into the audience's awareness long before such loss is actually felt in the play. Speaking in praise of Mamillius, heir to Leontes's throne, Camillo and Archidamus remark on his extraordinary 'promise' and his restorative ability to heal the body politic (he 'physics the subject') (1.1.31, 33). But Archidamus's final lines presage both loss and the possibility of eventual restoration. He tells Camillo: 'If the King had no son, they [the King's subjects] would desire to live on crutches till he had one' (39–40). This soon-to-be-true hypothetical begins to prepare the audience for the loss of issue that is central to this play. But the death of Mamillius sets up yet another loss by shifting the burden of dynastic succession to the heiress, who herself will be 'lost' in due course. Indeed, when we first learn of Perdita's birth, the onstage dialogue replicates the inexact substitution of daughter for male heir:

> *Emilia*: She is something before her time delivered.
> *Paulina*: A boy?
> *Emilia*:   A daughter and a goodly babe,
> Lusty and like to live.
>   (2.2.26–28)

Inheritance and rightful succession hang in the balance at the caesura following Paulina's deceptively simple question. And of course the oracle soon makes explicit the conjunction of lost child and lost succession. Leontes tells Hermione of Perdita's fate: 'Thy brat hath been cast out, like to itself, / No father owning it' (3.2.85–86). But shortly thereafter, the oracle proclaims that 'the King shall live without an heir if that which is lost be not found' (132–133). As is true of the riddle in *Pericles*, the oracle of *The Winter's Tale* offers up genealogy and rightful succession as puzzles to be solved, not foregone conclusions. The structural device of the lost child formalizes this patrilineal conundrum, transforming genealogical uncertainty into the vehicle of dramatic action.

Mamillius's death triggers one kind of dynastic crisis that is further exacerbated by Perdita's displacement from Sicilia. Of course, Perdita from the beginning stands for loss itself (her name means 'lost one' in Latin, and Antigonus refers to her as a '[p]oor thing, condemned to loss' [2.3.191]), and it is her dramaturgical trajectory that shapes the second half of the play's plot. But Perdita's physical loss in the play is also directly tied to lineage and its fragility, signaled in part through the reiterated use of the word 'issue.' When Leontes initially commands that Perdita be 'instantly consumed with fire,' for instance, a Lord pleads with him to 'change this purpose, / Which being so horrible, so bloody, must / Lead on to some foul issue' (2.3.133, 150–152). As Valerie Forman has noted in her analysis of the play, *The Winter's Tale* puns on 'issue' frequently 'to refer simultaneously to offspring, profit, expenditure, and even an exit from the stage'.[17] I am particularly interested in the ways in which the word 'issue' suggests both progeny and outward movement (*OED*, 'issue,' n. def. 1, 2 and 3), a conjunction of meanings that, I argue, is particularly vital to *The Winter's Tale*. The Lord's plea to Leontes certainly affirms that killing Perdita would have terrible consequences, but it also reminds us that those consequences are genealogical in nature while simultaneously foreshadowing the issuing forth that will ultimately be Perdita's fate.

In a patrilineal culture such as early modern England, the heiress represents a kind of normative deviance—a break from the strict process of primogeniture that was nonetheless a common cultural occurrence. She also embodies a movement away from the direct patriline, a spatial process that dovetails nicely with the dramatic plot of the lost child. In *The Winter's Tale*, Shakespeare makes the consequences of the loss of issue explicit, especially in the later acts of the play. Polixenes laments with Camillo about the 'loss of his [Leontes's] most precious queen and children,' and, after inquiring about his own son, concludes: 'Kings are no less unhappy, their issue not being gracious, than they are in losing them when they have approved their virtues' (4.2.22–26). Even more pointedly, Leontes himself recognizes that his errors of judgment have 'heirless [...] made my kingdom'; sin, he claims, has left him 'issueless' (5.1.10, 173). The urgency of this point is confirmed during the discussion of Leontes's possible remarriage. Dion warns, for instance, of the 'dangers by his highness' fail of issue / May drop upon his kingdom' and urges Leontes to remarry (5.1.27–28). The word 'issue' rhetorically emblematizes the wandering of the heiress enacted through the lost-child plot, infusing that specific dramatic structure with distinct early modern concerns about daughters, loss, and inheritance.

Furthermore, the loss of the heiress is directly linked to the problem of female chastity and its perceived vulnerability. If we return to

Antigonus's odd speech about gelding his daughters with which I began this essay, we see that it is the slipperiness of female chastity—the ability of women to breed 'false generations'—that threatens the alienation of the family name and line. In Antigonus's hypothetic formulation, Hermione's chastity becomes the litmus test for much broader conclusions about female honor and the genealogical certainty such honor upholds. And in fact, Antigonus does seem to question Hermione's honor, an error of judgment that is directly linked in the plot to Perdita's loss in Bohemia. He asserts that the child is 'indeed the issue/ Of King Polixenes' and therefore concludes that it is proper for her to be 'laid, / Either for life or death, upon the earth / Of its right father' (3.3.42–45). The choice of Bohemia, the physical placement that inaugurates the lost-child plot for Perdita, thus depends on a misreading of lineage, one based on the assumption of female infidelity. For 'thy mother's fault,' he tells the child, 'art thus exposed / To loss and what may follow' (49–50). Antigonus's speech activates a triple pun on 'issue' (as problem, lineage, and outward movement) and, in the process, it invokes the *errores* of Roman new comedy: the mistakes of discernment and identity that can only be resolved via familial and spatial displacement.

Such displacement directly affects the play's formal structure, yielding travel to far-flung locales and the famous temporal gap between acts three and four, both features typical of much early modern romance. At the same time, in turning to the plot of the lost-child in the second half of the play, Shakespeare deploys a formal mechanism that simultaneously addresses the play's inheritance problem and the vagaries introduced by the romance mode. In *Pericles*, the choric figure of Gower provides a paternal marker of narrative stability that guides the audience through that play's episodic plot. He frequently instructs the audience as to the specific locations of scenes ('Imagine Pericles arrived at Tyre' [4.0.1]) or explains away the rapid passage of time ('Thus time we waste, and long leagues make short [...] / Making to take our imagination / From bourn to bourn, region to region' [4.4.1–4]).[18] Similarly, the character of Time in *The Winter's Tale* offers playgoers an authoritative voice of narrative coherence in the face of temporal flux. Asking the theatrical audience to forgive his 'swift passage' over the 'wide gap' of sixteen years in the plot, Time notes that it is in his power to 'o'erthrow law' and 'plant and o'erwhelm' custom' (4.1.5–9). This 'wide gap,' of course, is occasioned by Perdita's loss and coming of age. It is, in other words, a dramaturgical problem determined in large part by the normal disorders that attend the heiress within a patrilineal system. In *The Winter's Tale*, Time's measured intervention in the play's action begins the process of restoration necessary for both dramaturgical and patrilineal resolution. As he tells us at the end of his soliloquy, the ensuing action, which will focus on Perdita as 'a shepherd's daughter / And what to her adheres,' is explicitly 'th'argument of Time' (27–29). Time thus initiates the process of restoring patrilineal patterns of descent through structural, dramaturgical means. By helping us to trace the heiress who has been lost, Time offers up the promise of a familiar narrative teleology to prefigure the play's ultimate return to proper genealogical ordering. In doing so, Time dramaturgically reinforces the supposed norms of patrilineage by charting a course back to those norms.

The resolution of the lost-child plot in the last two acts of *The Winter's Tale* takes the form of a conservative narrative of restoration that resituates the heiress within patrilineal lines of descent. We can trace the path to this eventual conclusion through Perdita herself, who in Act 4 displays her insuppressible nobility of manners, speech, and virtue, a scenario common to the lost-child plot of Roman new comedy. Not only does her adopted father the Shepherd chide her for behaving like 'a feasted one' rather than the hostess of the festival, but her famous exchange with Polixenes about grafting establishes her as a champion of traditional patrilineal values (4.4.63). As she tells him:

> the fairest flowers o'th' season
> Are our carnations and streaked gillyvors,
> Which some call nature's bastards; of that kind
> Our rustic garden's barren, and I care not
> To get slips of them.
> (4.4.81–85)

Perdita rejects flowers produced through crossbreeding, resisting Polixenes's arguments to the contrary (which of course soon become bitterly ironic when he violently rejects Florizel's proposed union with Perdita-as-shepherdess). Her insistence here on a conservative narrative of bloodline helps counteract the fact of her loss, assuring playgoers that her wandering away from home, family, and title is a physical and temporal, but not a moral or ideological displacement. As is true of Marina in *Pericles*, who maintains her chastity throughout the brothel scenes in Mytilene, Perdita's virtuous behavior helps guide the play's trajectory leading toward rightful aristocratic marriage and dynastic continuity.

However, there is one more plot twist in the play that threatens Perdita's return and the resolution of the inheritance dilemma she represents. Following Polixenes's rage over the discovery of Florizel's romantic connection with Perdita, the two young lovers are set to embark on yet another series of travels, another set of spatial and dramaturgical displacements. As Florizel tells Camillo, 'I am put to sea / With her who here I cannot hold on shore,' adding that he will not disclose to him '[w]hat course I mean to hold' (4.4.489–490, 493). Several lines later, he admits that his plan is something they undertake 'wildly,' calling himself and Perdita the 'slaves of chance' (531–532). Florizel's proposed journey promises only further disjunction, separation, and physical as well as familial 'loss.' But much in the same way that Time's earlier intervention begins to direct a dramaturgical course toward familial restoration, here it is Camillo who proffers narrative orders as a means of obtaining patrilineal closure. As he instructs Florizel in clear, orderly syntax:

> Then list to me.
> This follows, if you will not change your purpose
> But undergo this flight: make for Sicilia,
> And there present yourself and your fair princess,
> For so I see she must be, fore Leontes;
> She shall be habited as it becomes
> The partner of your bed. Methinks I see
> Leontes opening his free arms and weeping
> His welcomes forth; asks thee there, "Son, forgiveness,"
> As 'twere i'th' father's person [...]
>
> (4.4.534–542)

Camillo's narrative plotting unintentionally anticipates the familial restoration that will close the play, making Florizel Leontes's son in both genealogical and affective terms. Crucially, Camillo's advice necessitates a curtailment of the heiress's wandering. In giving their wild voyage a distinct trajectory ('make for Sicilia'), Camillo enables a spatial counter-narrative that works to correct the *errores* of both plot and rightful inheritance represented by her loss. Indeed, he explicitly offers his plan up as a 'course more promising / Than a wild dedication of yourselves / To unpathed waters, undreamed shores, most certain / To miseries enough' (557–560). Camillo, in effect, saves Florizel and Perdita from another play, another sequence of tragicomic loss; his advice (and its ensuing application) directs the plot both spatially and ideologically away from wandering and instead toward patrilineal restoration. As a figure of patriarchal authority, Camillo (like Time) ensures that the heiress eventually returns home.

Camillo's words and actions are particularly significant given that the play declines to stage the father–daughter recognition scene (a hallmark of much Roman new comedy) in favor of the scene of husband–wife reunion. When Florizel and Perdita arrive in Sicilia, Leontes's response to their proposed marriage mirrors precisely the central dilemma of the lost-child plot from Roman comedies. As he tells Florizel, he is 'sorry / Your choice is not so rich in worth as beauty, / That you might well enjoy her' (5.1.212–214). The noble son, in other words, cannot marry until it is revealed that the bride too is of noble birth.[19] This revelation, however, famously occurs offstage. The narrative reporting of this unseen reunion emphasizes both its extraordinary and unexpected character and its indebtedness to literary tradition. On the one hand, as the Second Gentleman reports the conclusion to Perdita's lost-child plot, he describes it as an unlikely, even unbelievable event: 'The oracle is fulfilled; the King's daughter is found. Such a deal of wonder is broken out within this hour that ballad-makers cannot be able to express it' (5.2.21–24). On the other hand, he quickly connects Perdita's 'discovery' to older narratives: 'This news which is called true is so like an old tale that the verity of it is in strong suspicion. Has the King found his heir?' (26–28). The repetition of plot embedded in Perdita's story of loss and return throws the veracity of her narrative into doubt, at least until the Third Gentlemen quickly confirms that the news is '[m]ost true' (29). But this citation of the lost-child plot also situates Perdita within a literary and theatrical tradition that effectively assuages the concerns about the wandering heiress and the threat to patrilineal stability she represents. In electing to have the climactic father–daughter reunion narrated instead of staged, Shakespeare draws attention to the formal, dramaturgical methods—his reliance on old tales and comedic plotlines—that offer a resolution to the common problems posed by the heiress within England's patrilineal system of inheritance. Through its deployment of the lost-child plot, *The Winter's Tale* thus demonstrates the efforts needed to counteract familial dissolution and restore proper lines of descent. The old tales of Roman comedy provide a theatrical, performative medium through which the presumed norms and stability of patrilineage can be creatively upheld and reimagined.

Finding the Heiress and Losing a Kingdom in *Cymbeline*

In *Cymbeline*, we find another variation on the lost-child plot, one in which the ideal workings of patrilineal inheritance are put to the test through the structural repetition of the loss of issue. Whereas *The Winter's Tale* intensifies the importance of the heiress by staging Mamillius's actual death, the plot of *Cymbeline* is organized around two separate narratives of temporary loss. And unlike *Pericles*, which stages multiple scenes that involve different families with sole daughters who are in turn lost or destroyed, *Cymbeline* doubles its plot by staging a pair of lost sons and a lost daughter, a dramaturgical choice that both amplifies the dynastic problem at the heart of the play and, as I'll argue, offers playgoers a fanciful resolution to the sociohistorical dilemma of the heiress by ultimately taking her out of the equation entirely. *Cymbeline*, that is, puts on display to theatergoers another possible route to patrilineal restoration, one in which the heiress is not merely reclaimed but negated.

As is true of the opening scene of *The Winter's Tale*, the opening dialogue of *Cymbeline* emphasizes the problems presented by the sole daughter and suggests the spatial dislocations attendant on her marriage. We learn that Imogen is the heir of Cymbeline's Britain, but due to her marriage to the 'poor but worthy' Posthumus Leonatus (7), she has been imprisoned and her husband banished. In this instance, Imogen's status as sole heiress occasions additional forms of displacement, the symbolic and actual wandering away from courtly life signified by the acts of imprisonment and banishing. But we also learn in this opening scene that Imogen is only Cymbeline's heir by unhappy accident. When asked by the Second Gentlemen 'Is she sole child to th'King,' the First Gentleman responds:

> His only child.
> He had two sons – if this be worth your hearing,
> Mark it – the eldest of them at three years old,
> I'th' swathing clothes the other, from their nursery
> Were stol'n, and to this hour, no guess in knowledge
> Which way they went.
>
> (1.1.56–61)

When the Second Gentleman in turn wonders at the strangeness of this story, the other assures his that 'Howso'er 'tis strange […] Yet is it true, sir' (65–67). In a direct borrowing from new comic plotting, *Cymbeline* opens by drawing attention to the machinations, the narrative workings that underlie the path to familial restoration. At the same time, the voiced disbelief about the story of Cymbeline's lost sons perhaps ironically highlights not the unusualness of this narrative but rather its deep familiarity to early modern playgoers.

As is the case with the recurrent pun on 'issue' in *The Winter's Tale*, the repeated pun on 'air' and 'heir' in *Cymbeline* similarly highlights the conjunction of lineage and physical movement. In her opening exchange with Posthumus, Imogen begs him not to take his leave from her too quickly, noting: 'Were you but riding forth to air yourself / Such parting were too petty' (111–112). She immediately gives him her mother's diamond ring and asks that he keep it until he woos 'another wife, / When Imogen is dead' (113–114). Here, the movement forced by Posthumus's banishment combined with Imogen's immediate turn to the language of marriage and inheritable property, activates the connection between 'air,' 'heir,' and the wayward movement of 'riding forth.' As Sujata Iyengar has argued, the pun also suggests the threat posed to Cymbeline's kingdom through 'the ability of the heir/air to communicate disease as well as health and peace',[20] a point made explicit when Cymbeline calls Posthumus a 'poison to my blood' (1.1.128). But the pun's connection to the succession is further reinforced later in the play, when we are introduced to Cymbeline's lost sons, Guiderius and Arviragus, living in a remote cave in the woods. Guiderius, bristling against his adopted father Belarius's self-imposed life of retreat and solitude, exclaims: 'We, poor unfledged, / Have never winged from view o'th' nest, nor know not / What air's from home' (3.3.27–29). The heir/air is clearly indeed 'from home,' Belarius having stolen the boys as infants explicitly to 'bar thee [Cymbeline] of succession' (102) in retaliation against his own unjust banishment. Once again the loss of lineage prompts not only a crisis of succession but also physical displacement. As in *The Winter's Tale*, this spatial break in patrilineal order in *Cymbeline* requires a formal, narrative resolution.

But first, the play doubles down on the lost child plot by dramatizing and exacerbating Imogen's own precarious dynastic position as the apparent sole heir to Cymbeline's kingdom. In a sense, Shakespeare stages a variation on the plight of Marina in *Pericles*, who is first 'lost' when she is stolen away by pirates and then subject to repeated threats on her chastity in the Mytilene brothel. In *Cymbeline*, Shakespeare reverses this order by first dramatizing the assault on Imogen's chastity in the wager and bedroom scenes with Giacomo. These scenes effectively combine the common socioeconomic problem of the heiress in early modern England with the equally common patriarchal anxiety about female chastity to produce a worst-case scenario of female circulation within patrilineage. Posthumus' famously misogynistic diatribe upon learning of Imogen's supposed adultery crystalizes the patriarchal ideology that upholds patrilineal succession. As he asks the audience incredulously: 'Is there no way for men to be, but women / Must be half-workers?' (2.5.1–2). Posthumus's fantasy of androgenesis highlights the uncertainty at the heart of patrilineal succession, a fairly normative anxiety in the period despite the excessiveness of Posthumus' rhetoric. When the succession depends upon daughters, *Cymbeline* suggests, there is always a strong possibility of *errores*, of wandering away from name, title, honor, and even one's literal homeland.

Imogen, like Marina, maintains her chastity in the face of assault, but the false attack on her honor prompts in turn her literal departure from England, inaugurating the second lost-child narrative in the play. With Pisanio's aid, Imogen flees to Milford Haven, a journey marked in the text by an awareness of the temporal disjunction such a flight will precipitate. Imogen asks Pisanio to explain how they will be able to excuse the 'gap / That we shall make in time from our hence-going / And our return' (3.2.62–64). Although far less pronounced than the gap in time narrated by Gower in *Pericles* or by Time in *The Winter's Tale*, the temporal lapse that Imogen is anxious to explain points to a break in the narrative structure of this romance that correlates directly with her departure from the court and, in the mind of Cymbeline and the other courtiers, from the direct line of familial succession.[21] Indeed, after her departure, there is frequent reference to her as being missed, lost, or forgotten. Pisanio tells her directly: 'You shall be missed at court' and instructs that she 'must forget to be a woman' (3.4.126, 154). At court, Cymbeline asks a messenger in consternation 'Where is she, sir' (3.5.41), and later in the play, laments that both Imogen and Cloten are 'gone' and cannot be recovered (4.3.5–7). In the play's push to final resolution, the multiplied lost-child plot maps genealogical instability onto dramatic form, offering a familiar theatrical plot by which to guide audience response in the face of *Cymbeline*'s wide-ranging and episodic romance narrative. When Pisanio muses to himself: 'O Imogen, / Safe mayst thou wander, safe return again!' (3.5.104–105), he makes explicit the progressive, reassuring pattern that the lost-child plot superimposes onto the socioeconomic uncertainties posed by the heiress: if the heiress introduces greater instability into patrilineage that is in turn compounded by her loss and wandering, the promise of safe return navigates a path to rightful succession and familial resolution.

In the end, Shakespeare resolves the problem of the heiress in *Cymbeline* in a doubled sense, by both demonstrating her preserved chastity and returning her to the court and by rendering her ultimately irrelevant to the succession narrative. Imogen herself anticipates the second part of this narrative teleology upon first meeting Guiderius and Arviragus, who welcome her as a brother: she wishes that they were indeed her father's sons so that her own 'price' had 'been less,' making her of 'more equal ballasting' to Posthumus (3.6.74–75). And of course this is exactly what is revealed in the play's final scene, when Belarius uncovers the truth of the boys' identity to Cymbeline '[t]hey are the issue of your loins, my liege, / And blood of your begetting' (5.5.329–330). Cymbeline's response neatly captures the logic of inheritance and generation that has been accommodated through the play's lost-child plot:

> O, what am I?
> A mother to the birth of three? Ne'er mother
> Rejoiced deliverance more. Blest pray you be,
> That, after this strange starting from your orbs,
> You may reign in them now! O Imogen,
> Thou hast lost by this a kingdom.
> (5.5.367–372)

The astrological image identifies the brothers' 'strange starting' as a physical displacement from rightful succession, while Cymbeline's self-identification as delivering mother brings full circle Posthumus' dream of androgenesis. Imogen's return corresponds with yet another loss, but one that cleverly resolves the socioeconomic instability that she has represented throughout the play. And in the final explication of Jupiter's riddle, the pun on 'air' returns to underscore powerfully Imogen's dispossession. Posthumus has found 'without seeking' a 'piece of tender air' (5.4.109–110), which the Soothsayer interprets for both the onstage and theatrical audiences as Cymbeline's 'virtuous daughter' (5.5.444). No longer an heir, Imogen as 'tender air' is free to marry Posthumus. Indeed, the finale also endeavors to gloss over the heiress's potential aggrievement by presenting Imogen as happy with her new circumstances; as she tells her father, she has not lost a kingdom but instead has gained two brothers: 'I have got two worlds by't' (373). By multiplying and expanding the reach of the lost-child narrative in this play, Shakespeare offers in the end a more conservative and fanciful narrative of familial restoration and rightful inheritance than that found in either *Pericles* or *The Winter's Tale*. The normative patrilineal disorder signaled by the heiress provides the foundation of the play's dramatic plotting, but the dilemma that she poses to patrilineage is finally resolved by removing her (in this case willingly) from a position of significance within her own story.

In his late romances, Shakespeare transforms an everyday occurrence within England's patrilineal economy—the prevalence of families with only daughters to inherit—into the basis for dramatic tension. Through the well-worn new comic device of the lost-child plot, he in turn materializes the instabilities that accompany the heiress, deploying tropes of wandering, movement, and loss, in order to stage genealogical uncertainties for a theatrical audience. In terms of patrilineage, then, the 'normal' is clearly a matter of perspective; loss, wandering, and dislocation may be remarkable events for the dramatic characters who experience them, but for early modern theatergoers knowledgeable of both comic form and the multivocality of the everyday patrilineal economy, such events would be familiar and even expected. Ultimately, the new comic story of loss and return provides a comforting, conservative narrative that compels a kind of new normality into existence. That is, these plays offer dramaturgical solutions to historical and economic concerns, assuaging parental anxieties about child loss, inheritance, and the potential dissolution of familial property heralded by the heiress within primogeniture. As is particularly clear in the case of *Cymbeline*, this process reactivates paternal control over and against the heiress's own desires or freedom of movement. Dramatic form (the convention of the lost-child plot) thus enables Shakespeare to shore up patrilineal inheritance by providing a theatrical solution not readily available in the culture at large. Certainly, the romances also display the extensive effort needed to bring about this resolution, highlighting in the process the other paths and directions (both literal and figurative) that could result from the wandering heiress, the loss that may or may not be restored in the end. The return to, or, perhaps more accurately, the creative construction of patrilineal norms in these plays can be staged as a process of struggle in part because it is also presented formally as a foregone conclusion: the lost child will eventually be found, the plot will indeed resemble an 'old tale.' In other words, Shakespeare's romances do not so much undermine or challenge patrilineage but rather expose its hidden workings, showcasing for theatergoers the mechanisms by which the patrilineal economy sustained itself under pressure. In doing so, these plays both encourage us to question the stability of early modern legal 'norms' and to interrogate more fully the ways in which the theater was actively engaged in producing and maintaining those norms.

Acknowledgements I would like to thank Rory Loughnane and Edel Semple for their very helpful feedback on this essay.

Notes

1. All citations of Shakespeare's plays are from *The Norton Shakespeare* (2016).
2. Stone (1977: 87–88) and Erickson (2011: 93).
3. Crawford (2004: 214).
4. On this point, see Murray (2004: 128).
5. The other four were: equity, ecclesiastical law, manorial (or borough) law, and parliamentary statutes. See Erickson (1993: 5), Stretton (1998: 25–33), and Zaller (2007: 267–274).
6. Bonfield (1983, 2012), Davis (2004), Erickson (1993), Prior (1990), and Stretton (1998).
7. Stone (1967: 76–79), Hollingsworth (1964), and McLaren (1985).
8. Spring (1993: 182–183).
9. I have written elsewhere in more detail about inheritance practices in early modern England and the many exceptions to the common law ideal. See Dowd (2015).
10. It should be noted that all of these plays are hybrid forms that elude strict generic classification. I share the position taken by Helen Cooper and others that "romance" is itself more about a set of "romance motifs" or characteristics rather than fixed generic categories. See Cooper (2004) and Fuchs (2004).
11. Parker (1979: 63).
12. Miola (1994: 2).
13. Miola (1994: 9).
14. Nelson (1985: 202) and Barber (1979: 62).
15. Miola (1994: 18, 19, 21).
16. Miola (1994: 140–169) and Nelson (1985: 202).
17. Forman (2008: 108). On the connection between generation and narrative structure that the word 'issue' often implies in early modern romance, see Hackett (2000: 154).

18. For a more extensive discussion of Gower's function in *Pericles* as a means of narrative and patrilineal control, see Dowd (2015: 180–186). See also Hiscock (2012) and Loughnane (2012).
19. Barber (1979: 62).
20. Iyengar (2015: 188).
21. Imogen refers to inheritance in this speech as well, although obliquely, asking Pisanio: 'how Wales was made so happy as / T'inherit such a haven' (60–61). The application of the logic of inheritance to physical geography rather than human relationships perhaps prefigures Imogen's own eventual loss of inheritance in the play; the transferal at work in Imogen's anthropomorphic image will be replicated in the later transferal of her own inheritance to her older brothers.

WORKS CITED

Barber, Lester E. 1979. Introduction. In *Misogonus*. New York: Garland.
Bonfield, Lloyd. 1983. *Marriage Settlements, 1601–1740: The Adoption of the Strict Settlement*. Cambridge: Cambridge University Press.
Bonfield, Lloyd. 2012. *Devising, Dying and Dispute: Probate Litigation in Early Modern England*. Farnham: Ashgate.
Cooper, Helen. 2004. *The English Romance in Time: Transforming Motifs from Geoffrey of Monmouth to the Death of Shakespeare*. Oxford: Oxford University Press.
Crawford, Patricia. 2004. *Blood, Bodies and Families in Early Modern England*. Harlow: Pearson Longman.
Davis, Lloyd. 2004. Women's Wills in Early Modern England. In *Women, Property, and the Letters of the Law in Early Modern England*, ed. Nancy E. Wright, Margaret W. Ferguson, and A.R. Buck. Toronto: University of Toronto Press.
Dowd, Michelle M. 2015. *The Dynamics of Inheritance on the Shakespearean Stage*. Cambridge: Cambridge University Press.
Erickson, Amy Louise. 1993. *Women and Property in Early Modern England*. New York: Routledge.
Erickson, Amy Louise. 2011. Family, Household, and Community. In *The Oxford Illustrated History of Tudor and Stuart Britain*, ed. John Morrill. Oxford: Oxford University Press.
Forman, Valerie. 2008. *Tragicomic Redemptions: Global Economics and the Early Modern English Stage*. Philadelphia: University of Pennsylvania Press.
Fuchs, Barbara. 2004. *Romance*. New York: Routledge.
Hackett, Helen. 2000. *Women and Romance Fiction in the English Renaissance*. Cambridge: Cambridge University Press.

Hiscock, Andrew. 2012. *Pericles, Prince of Tyre*: Pericles, Prince of Tyre and the Appetite for Narrative. In *Late Shakespeare, 1608–1613*, ed. Andrew J. Power and Rory Loughnane. Cambridge: Cambridge University Press.

Hollingsworth, T.H. 1964. The Demography of the British Peerage. *Population Studies.* Suppl. 18: 3–107.

Iyengar, Sujata. 2015. Shakespeare's Embodied Ontology of Gender, Air, and Health. In *Disability, Health, and Happiness in the Shakespearean Body*, ed. Sujata Iyengar. New York: Routledge.

Loughnane, Rory. 2012. *King Henry VIII (All Is True)*: Semi-choric Devices and the Framework for Playgoer Response in *King Henry VIII*. In *Late Shakespeare, 1608–1613*, ed. Andrew J. Power and Rory Loughnane. Cambridge: Cambridge University Press.

McLaren, Dorothy. 1985. Marital Fertility and Lactation 1570–1720. In *Women in English Society, 1500–1800*, ed. Mary Prior. London: Methuen.

Miola, Robert S. 1994. *Shakespeare and Classical Comedy: The Influence of Plautus and Terence.* Oxford: Clarendon Press.

Murray, Mary. 2004. Primogeniture, Patrilineage, and the Displacement of Women. In *Women, Property, and the Letters of the Law in Early Modern England*, ed. Nancy E. Wright, Margaret W. Ferguson, and A.R. Buck. Toronto: University of Toronto Press.

Nelson, T.G.A. 1985. "Bad Commodity' or 'Fair Posterity"?: The Ambivalence of Issue in English Renaissance Comedy. *English Literary Renaissance* 15 (2): 195–224.

Parker, Patricia. 1979. *Inescapable Romance: Studies in the Poetics of a Mode.* Princeton, NJ: Princeton University Press.

Prior, Mary. 1990. Wives and Wills, 1558–1700. In *English Rural Society, 1500–1800: Essays in Honour of Joan Thirsk*, ed. John Chartres and David Hey. Cambridge: Cambridge University Press.

Shakespeare, William. 2016. *The Norton Shakespeare*, 3rd ed., ed. Stephen Greenblatt, et al. New York: Norton.

Spring, Eileen. 1993. *Law, Land, and Family: Aristocratic Inheritance in England, 1300–1800.* Chapel Hill: University of North Carolina Press.

Stone, Lawrence. 1967. *The Crisis of the Aristocracy, 1558–1641*, Abr ed. Oxford: Oxford University Press.

Stone, Lawrence. 1977. *The Family, Sex, and Marriage in England, 1500–1800.* New York: Harper & Row.

Stretton, Tim. 1998. *Women Waging Law in Elizabethan England.* Cambridge: Cambridge University Press.

Zaller, Robert. 2007. *The Discourse of Legitimacy in Early Modern England.* Stanford, CA: Stanford University Press.

CHAPTER 9

'Proper' Men and 'Tricksy' Spirits: The Eunuch in Disguise in *Twelfth Night* and *The Tempest*

Brinda Charry

English trader John Hawkins's journey to good fortune began when he was told that 'Negroes were very good marchandise in Hispaniola'. Having got into his possession some three hundred Africans 'partly by the sword, and partly by other meanes', Hawkins set sail to the West Indies and after making several good deals returned to England 'with prosperous successe and much gaine to himselfe [...]'.[1] Hawkins's business trip is part of the early phase of the long history of trans-Atlantic slavery. It was an enterprise approved by the Aristotelian notion of natural slavery, an idea revived in the Middle Ages and one that 'achieved considerable intellectual respectability' during the Renaissance.[2]

Hawkins's compatriot William Biddulph describes another slave market, an even older one: 'There is also a usual market in Constantinople', he writes, 'wherein they sell men and women of all ages as ordinarily as we doe cattle in England, which are for the most part Christians'.[3]

B. Charry (✉)
Keene State College, Keene, NH, USA
e-mail: bcharry@keene.edu

© The Author(s) 2019
R. Loughnane and E. Semple (eds.), *Staged Normality in Shakespeare's England*, Palgrave Shakespeare Studies, https://doi.org/10.1007/978-3-030-00892-5_9

Yet another English writer, Henry Blount, also describes Ottoman slave markets, but appears to be less disturbed by slavery itself than by 'the confidence' with which the Turks 'catch or buy up for slave any Christian they find in their countrey'. This, writes Blount, was 'the onely beastly piece of injustice I found among the Turks'.[4] The sale of Christians was a novel and troubling sight; they did not confirm to the European notion of 'natural slaves,' and trade in them was yet another indication of Ottoman brutality and arrogance.

Among those slaves imported into Ottoman territory were thousands of castrated men. The custom of enslaving eunuchs was one that the Ottomans partly inherited from Byzantium and partly from other Muslim cultures. Even the Muslim theologians and jurists who managed to justify other forms of enslavement were hard put to justify the breaking of the *hadith* of the Prophet that states, 'he is not of my people who makes another a eunuch or becomes so himself' (*The Quran* 4:118). But the hold of centuries-old custom was stronger than religious edict and the *ulema* (Islamic theologians) found consolation in the fact that there was no canonical text forbidding the purchase of slaves emasculated by infidels. Not only were most eunuchs from foreign lands (black eunuchs mainly from Darfur, Egypt, Ethiopia, and Sudan and white eunuchs generally from areas around the Black Sea, usually Hungary, Georgia, Armenia, and Slovenia), the surgical procedure was required by law to be performed outside Ottoman territory.[5]

'Normal' implies 'physically and mentally sound, free from any disorder, healthy' (OED); the mutilated body of the eunuch is irregular, aberrant, *not normal*. Yet the eunuch was part of the 'normal' landscape of the early modern Turkish household and a regular feature of Ottoman society. In what follows, I will briefly examine European travelers' observations of eunuch slaves and how they attempted to comprehend the place and role of the eunuch in Ottoman society. I will then explore the role or implied role of eunuchs in two of Shakespeare's plays, *Twelfth Night* and *The Tempest*—both of which have connections to the Muslim world.

Scholars attentive to the representations of race in early modern literature have lately directed attention toward the familiar and the same rather than toward the alien and the unlike. While 'otherness' and 'alterity' have been keywords in assessing early modern England's relations with foreign cultures, there has been a move toward the study of correspondences and affiliations as well. Urvashi Chakravarty urges us to reassess 'the presumption that race is fundamentally about the faraway rather than about the familiar', while Marjorie Rubright points out that paying attention to the proximate and the similar allows us to reassess how 'notions of sameness have been imagined, cast over, or wittingly or unwittingly adopted by particular groups'.[6] What if one extends Chakravarty's and Rubright's approach to this exploration of the Western representation of the eunuch in early modern Turkey? The eunuch was a servant and therefore something like the servants in European households. That, and the fact that he was formerly a Christian, meant that he was akin to the self, the same and the familiar. Yet he was also, by virtue of his castrated body and his status as convert, the alien other. He was the same and simultaneously not the same. The question is: how can paying attention to sameness 'make us more attentive to the strange'?[7]

European travel writers recognized that eunuchs were primarily servants, a category recognizable from England. Servants were familiar figures, with large English households (like large Turkish ones) employing them by the dozens if not the hundreds. In her study of domestic crime in early modern England, Frances Dolan says that crimes committed by servants against their masters conflated the familiar and the strange.[8] Servants also represented an ambiguous social class. As Mark Thornton Burnett writes:

> What exactly defined a servant in early modern England was far from universally agreed or established, and the multiplicity of definitions is eloquent testimony to the institutions' pervasive influence. Many writers argued that 'servant' was a term with a wide application and that among those who could be classed as such were players, monks, grooms, gentlemen, lords or courtiers and even kings.[9]

Anne Kussmaul argues that for some being in service was a transitional occupation rather than a permanent social status. Besides, even those who were permanently in service obtained at least part of their social status from their masters, making them a confusing social group.[10]

Of course, Turkish eunuchs were not exactly like English grooms or butlers. Their sad histories and compromised manhood set eunuchs apart and made them objects of pity. But the sympathetic response was complicated by eunuchs' special status, their high rank and their intimacy with their masters. So Sir William Harborne, English ambassador to Istanbul, in a letter to Hasan Agha (formerly Samson Rowley of Bristol, now a eunuch and treasurer to the Basha of Algiers) insists that his (Hasan's) body is 'subject to Turkish thraldom' even as the eunuch remains 'naturally loving your country [England] and countrymen'; but Harborne still addresses the Agha humbly, taking care not to reprimand him for his conversion from Christianity or for his successful career working for the Turks.[11] Much like the foreign-born janissaries who constituted the elite Ottoman military corps, these young castrates were initially sent to a special school where they were trained in court etiquette, alongside studying the Quran. Upon graduation they began as harem eunuchs with the title of *en esaghi* (meaning 'the lowest'). Some of them were fortunate or talented enough to rise to great heights and were collectively referred to as *al-aghawat* ('noblemen' / 'lords') a term that many Europeans use in their narratives. The Chief Eunuch or *kilar agha* served as messenger between the Sultan and the Grand Vizier and was rewarded with his own slaves, while the African eunuchs who guarded the mosques received large salaries. Besides, many eunuchs were part of the armies engaged in fighting with the very peoples they were born among and by all accounts they certainly did not 'experience serious inhibitions in waging war on their own infidel pagan brethren [Christians]'.[12] In the houses of wealthy Muslims 'the presence of the eunuch added to the prestige and seclusion of this domestic sanctuary.'[13] Apart from their positions as guards and protectors of inner spaces, whether the harem or the court or the sultan's person, the eunuchs were part of the religious life of Ottoman Turkey. The eunuch's duties in the harem were part of his responsibilities toward the *harim*, the sacred and the inviolable; his protection of the sultan emphasized the sacredness of kingship and his role as guardian of the shrines at Mecca and Medina was homage to their sanctity.

Slavery in the Muslim world was, in the historian Ehud Toledano's words, 'an important albeit involuntary channel of recruitment and socialization into the elite [...] [a] means of linking individuals into patronage networks'.[14] In fact, some eunuchs were not averse to their own mutilation or might even have offered themselves for castration in order to gain promotion.[15] As Robert Withers writes in *A Description of the Grand Signior's Seraglio*, 'Few or none of them are gelt and cut against their will [...] to get their consent, they promise them fair, and shew unto them the assurance they may, have (in time) to become great men'.[16] The voluntary eunuch was a fascinating and troubling figure. As Dympna Callaghan writes, men who 'willingly submit themselves to castration' 'pose something of a social threat [...] far in excess of any merely careless degeneration into effeminacy consequent upon a failure in vigilance about one's manhood'.[17] Confronting the eunuch-slave meant encountering and coming to terms with a fashioning of selfhood and of masculine subjectivity that began with a very literal fashioning of the body—a body that was deliberately disabled but that also had the potential to be mobile in the ranks of Ottoman society.

While English plays such as John Mason's *The Turk* (1610), which includes a castrated 'freeborne Christian sonne' in its cast, describe the eunuch as 'disabled of those masculine functions' and subject 'unto the vilde commaunde of an imperious Turke' (1.2), in non-literary narratives including John Withers's text, the eunuch's aberrant identity barely seems to matter. Withers devotes a long section to eunuchs when he discusses the 'inferior persons' in the harem.[18] Although he categorizes them as 'inferior', Withers repeatedly draws attention to the fact that eunuchs held positions of power and influence within and outside the seraglio and the 'ancientest, richest and, [...] highest rank' among them was appointed in 'great imployments' both at home and abroad.[19]

In Withers's narrative the word 'eunuch' becomes emptied of all connotations of deprivation or victimhood; it is quite simply an official designation. So Withers writes that white eunuchs guard and serve the Sultan and other male members of the royalty, while the black eunuchs 'are appointed for the women, and set to serve, and waite with others at the Sultanas gate [...]' that the 'Capee agha' or Chief White eunuch, 'is chief in authority and in greatest esteem with the Gran[d] Signor' and 'doth alwaies accompany the Kings person whithersoeever he goeth, both without, and within the Seraglio' while other eunuchs 'keep an exact account of all the treasure, that is brought in and taken out [of the seraglio]'.[20] The eunuch influence grew in Turkey starting in the early to mid-fifteenth century, and what these sixteenth-century European travelers were witnessing was the height of eunuch power. Between 1501 and 1623 several white eunuchs rose to occupy very high offices including that of Grand Vizier. As Seymour Drescher and Stanley Engerman write, 'As elite slaves, eunuchs represented a fundamental discontinuity in the structure of many slave systems: that slaves who were by definition property, could hold positions of power and access to high rank and influence [...] In short, eunuchs altered the social terms on which the institution of slavery was based'.[21] The high positions occupied by eunuchs fascinated and bewildered early modern Europeans. 'They are also made into great lords', writes the German captive Johaann Wild, 'The current emperor, Sultan Ahmed, has made such a chamberlain a pasha. He is now the high pasha of Constantinople and is known as Hadim Mehmed Pasha. I myself in my own time, when I came by sea from Alexandria, in the year 1610, in the month of December have seen him'.[22] Francis Osborn in his *Political Reflections on the Government of the Turks* points out that the eunuch was not considered a 'blemish' in early modern Ottoman society. On the other hand he was known for his 'moderation', 'caution', and 'circumspection' all of which were a result of his physical condition. In short, his 'imperfection' is what leads to 'honor and profit'.[23]

Commentators speculated on this inexplicable power. Osborn is of the belief that eunuchs' 'incapacity for Children gives such caution for their Fidelity, as cannot be expected from one more virile; a perfect man being in a condition to gain honour and profit by the *Change of Government*, whereas one so mutilated is capable of little more than shame or losse'.[24] Curiously, the very abnormality of the eunuch made him more predictable and hence reliable; his unswerving loyalty set up an idealized standard or norm that good subjects would do well to aspire to. Because the eunuch had lost the family and kinship ties of his birth and had no hope of setting up new ones, his loyalties could not be divided between his family and his patron. They made ideal servants, writes Withers, 'though not of great courage, yet of the greatest judgment, and fidelity: their mindes being bent on business, rather then on pleasure'.[25]

Modern scholars tend to agree with these theories. Orlando Patterson who analyses the peculiar prestige enjoyed by eunuchs right from the earliest stages of 'political eunuchism' (which, according to Patterson, developed no earlier than the eighth century, though human castration is recorded in Assyria in the second millennium BC), concludes that the eunuchs' 'genealogical isolation [...] their incapacity to reproduce themselves' meant they could not pass on their status and served to assure insecure monarchs of their fidelity.[26] Patterson also attributes the peculiar power and privilege enjoyed by the eunuchs to their intimacy with the monarch (often from the latter's earliest childhood) and compares them to the Privy Chamber officials of Renaissance English monarchs who gained prestige by virtue of the menial but intimate tasks they performed.[27] Patterson argues that the fact that eunuchs could not be assimilated into the aristocracy made them reliable as henchman to the king and their strong esprit de corps enhanced their efficiency.

The complex relationship between monarch and slave in the Ottoman and other empires was such that 'it is difficult [for the master] to dominate another person [the eunuch] when that other person is the main basis of one's power, or more frequently the sole means of communication with the basis of one's power'.[28]

The eunuch is part of the normal social and political landscape of Ottoman Turkey. European writers recognized this and while some of them saw the very acceptance of what seemed a 'vile' and 'unnatural' practice as a sign of the disturbing and repulsive foreignness of the Turks, others simply offered their commentaries as interested observers and ethnographers. They appear to be of the view that comprehending rather than condemning the tradition of eunuch slavery is important to understanding the mechanisms on which Ottoman success depend. However abnormal and unacceptable the idea of a tremendously powerful Muslim polity on the very doorsteps in Europe might be, these writers chose to recreate for their European readers those aspects of life considered to be 'normal' by the Turks. While some aspects of Turkish life certainly rendered them alien and unnatural to European readers, the complexity of their institutions, traditions, and the nuanced reasons and justifications behind them also made them a complicated, real people rather than a monstrous type. The foreign-born eunuch also becomes not just a pathetic victim, or an abnormal freak, or an absolute alien, but a telling reminder of the value of the normal and familiar qualities of service, loyalty, and faithfulness, especially when exhibited by servants and inferiors. The eunuch is also, somewhat paradoxically perhaps, a reminder of the equally valuable qualities of ambition, personal drive, and success. Understanding the eunuch, for these commentators meant considering similitude and difference, normality and abnormality, together and simultaneously.

SHAKESPEARE'S COMEDIES AND THE CASE OF THE DISAPPEARING EUNUCH

Renaissance playwrights were intrigued enough by the figure of the eunuch to include him in a number of plays. The Englishman Clem in Thomas Heywood's *The Fair Maid of the West—Part 1* (1597–1603) gets castrated and Gazet in Philip Massinger's *The Renegado* (1624) almost does, both because of their ambition to gain advancement in Muslim courts. Clem and Gazet are comic figures and castration 'becomes a source of anxiety-dispelling laughter'.[29] Carazie, who also figures in *The Renegado*, is a castrated English slave serving a Turkish princess. He helps the Christian hero, Vitelli, gain access to his mistress's chambers in the royal harem and eventually helps the lovers elope, so betraying his Muslim masters and proving his enduring loyalty to Christians. Both Gazet and Carazie serve as reminders of the power of the Turks to emasculate and convert Christian men but they also are an indication of former Christians' supposedly enduring loyalty to adherents of the religion of their birth.

Shakespeare explicitly evokes the eunuch in *Twelfth Night* (1601–1602). While the comedy is set in Illyria, a locale that mostly is a fantasy space of dreams and desire, the play still does evoke an eastern setting. *Twelfth Night*, as Constance Relihan points out, was based on the story 'Apolonius and Silla' by Barnaby Riche, set in Constantinople and Cyprus.[30] 'Allusions in the language of the play to the "sophy", "heathens" and to Heliodoruses's *Aethiopica* (to cite just a few examples) insists that its readers never entirely forget that they are experiencing a liminal realm where East and West mingle'.[31] Relihan argues that the masculinity represented by Orsino, Sir Andrew Ague-Cheek and Malvolio could 'easily be attributed to the feminizing, hypnotic quality of Constantinople' and be read with reference to Western constructions of Turkish manhood.[32] But *Twelfth Night* effectively erases eastern settings because locating 'the text's explorations of masculinity in an eastern world in which they could handily be dismissed as the aberrations of "heathens" and "renegadoes" [...] would defeat the text's interrogation of the ambiguities of hetero-and homosexual desire and gender identity'.[33]

But there is the case of Viola, the man-who-is-not-a man. Early in the play Viola declares her intention to serve as a eunuch in Orsino's court: 'Thou shall present me as an eunuch to him', she insists to the captain, 'It may be worth thy pains; for I can sing / And speak to him in many sorts of music,' (1.2.56–58). As the play proceeds Shakespeare dismisses (or forgets) Viola's eunuch identity. She simply becomes a male servant in Orsino's court, the Duke's favored 'boy.'[34] 'What kind o' man is he?' Olivia asks of Cesario (1.5.147), and he proves to be a delightful kind of man, one 'very well favored', who 'speaks shrewishly'—one she rapidly falls in love with. While Viola forgets to sing for Orsino (it is Feste who takes on the song duty in the play), her job portfolio is much like that of the eastern eunuch. Cesario serves as messenger to his master; eunuchs were often 'engaged in performing secret and not-so-secret missions for the ruler within and without the court'.[35] Cesario's status in Orsino's court (eventually in Olivia's household) comes from his intimacy with his master (and Olivia), the fact that he is their friend and confidante even as he is a subordinate. Leslie Peirce writes that 'authority [in Ottoman society was ...] increasingly a phenomenon of the inner' in the sixteenth and seventeenth centuries.[36] Like the eunuch in Turkish households, Cesario has access to Orsino's and Olivia's homes and chambers, he mediates between male and female spaces, between the world of the aristocrats and that of the servants, and between Orsino the languishing aesthete and Orsino the persistent suitor. Most importantly, he is his master's confidante and has access to his innermost thoughts, fears, and desires. The rhetoric of love is intertwined with the rhetoric of service in the play and Cesario's loyalty and love are both born of his loss of family and kinship ties, the fact that he finds himself alone in a country whose name he does not know when he lands on its shores. His intimacy with the Duke follows this loss and is born of the desire to establish new beginnings. Like the eunuch, Cesario finds there is nothing to tempt him away from his master.

In spite of these striking similarities, like the play's eastern setting Cesario as eunuch is effectively erased in the play. This serves to normalize the play as romantic comedy—if Viola had passed herself off as a castrated man, the attraction Olivia feels for him might have heightened the comic effect, but it would more likely be simply bizarre; the delightfully ridiculous would tip over into the grotesque. Right from the start it would be desire without the possibility of consummation, a love doomed to end in precisely nothing. So Olivia is simply charmed by a young man, one who 'when wit and youth is come to harvest' will become a 'proper man' (3.2.132–134). The audience of course knows that she is in love with a woman, but that kind of same-sex desire, even if it is rejected at the end for heterosexual romance, can be playfully explored, laughed at and delighted in. It can even be somewhat titillating. On the other hand, desire for a eunuch would be both unimaginable and disturbing. The grotesque and the comi-tragically incomplete instead becomes normalized by projecting it onto Malvolio—also a faithful servant, intimate, and message-bearer who is doomed to love and not be loved in return and who has no place in the comic ending which celebrates love and sexual desire. But Malvolio also exits the play; Feste, singer of songs, single and unattached, who expresses neither romantic love nor sexual desire, is perhaps the only lingering reminder of the eunuch that remains.

There are no eunuchs in Shakespeare's other comedy *The Tempest*. But what if we examine Ariel in light of the discourse of servitude, transformation, and ambiguous gender identity? What if 'eunuch' is used (in relation to Ariel) in ways similar to 'queer' in the book *Shakesqueer* where 'queerness' can refer to 'the open mesh of possibilities, gaps, overlaps, dissonances and resonances, lapses and excesses of meaning when the constituent elements of anyone's gender, of anyone's sexuality aren't made (or can't be made) to signify monolithically'.[37] For Madhavi Menon queer readings pay attention to those aspects of 'texts and ideas that address. [...] the vexed relation between sameness and difference'.[38] Similarly, understanding Ariel against the critical backdrop of the historical eunuch allows one to consider a type of identity that is ambiguous and fluid but that is also shaped by issues of violence and power.

Ariel moves between abstraction (he is called spirit about thirteen times in the play) and material presence, is simultaneously and at different times 'brave', 'dainty', 'fine', 'moody', 'tricksy', 'malignant', making him as mysterious and shifting as any of the shadows Prospero conjures up with his magic. Bryan Reynolds and Ayanna Thompson write that Ariel's origins, sexuality and future 'all evade exact terms within the play' and he even 'seems too flimsy and whimsical to grasp and hold up to critical examination'.[39] When he has been held up to scrutiny, Ariel has been read as representing the airy and intangible (his name is clearly derived from the word 'aerial'), in contrast to the earthy Caliban. Ariel has also been interpreted as signifying the artistic imagination and has been ascribed a range of identities ranging from a daemon or beneficent spirit of the neo-platonic tradition to a fairy to a magician's apprentice to an indentured servant, pliable according to some interpretations and resentful according to another. Reacting to José Enrique Rodó's 1900 reading of Ariel as symbolizing 'the mastery of reason and of sentiment over the baser impulses of unreason [...] the ideal end toward which human selection aspires; that superman has disappeared under the persistent chisel of life, the last stubborn trace of the Caliban, symbol of stupidity and sensuality' (1922), later post-colonial critics see Prospero's 'tricksy spirit' (5.1.228) as the deft, accomplished slave who learns the skills of the white master[40] or as 'an educated slave or freedman open to white creolization',[41] or as a slavish mullato. Stage depictions have also varied: the nineteenth century saw a childlike Ariel, swift of movement, delighting in service, while late twentieth century productions have implied a reluctant and hostile slave (in Michael Bogdanov's 1992 production Ariel moves at snail's pace, in Simon Russell Beale's 1993 RSC production he spits at Prospero's face when given his freedom, in Nancy Meckler's 1996/1997 production he is confined in a restrictive tabard, and in the 2016 RSC production he is a devoted servant who sadly leaves his master at the end).

Of course, Ariel's gender has long fascinated readers and audiences. Through the seventeenth century it was a 'breeches role' played primarily by young boys; the Dryden-Davenant version of the play had a girl dressed as a boy play Ariel and even gave him a female partner, though by the early eighteenth century it had become an exclusively—and much coveted—female role. In post-war productions Ariel has nearly always been a man and 'a good deal of sentimentality—and humanity—disappeared from the role'.[42] This male Ariel is either hypermasculine (e.g. Alan Badel 1951; Duncan Bell 1987) or androgynous and feminized (e.g. Ben Kingsley 1970; Mark Rylance 1982). In spite of these male depictions of Ariel, Denise Albanese says Ariel is represented in feminine terms in the play—his need for love in return for service is 'a transaction readily gendered in modern discourse as feminine'.[43] On the other hand, Christine Dymkowski reads Ariel simply as 'a sexless shape-shifter, an "it" rather than a "she" or "he"'.[44]

Of late, attention has been drawn to *The Tempest*'s Mediterranean location and the play's role in discursive constructions of the Islamic east.[45] Algiers, the home of Sycorax, was specifically the 'corsair capital' of the region described in horrific terms by Samuel Purchas in 1625 as the 'Whirle-poole of these Seas, the throne of Pyracie, the Sink of Trade and the Stinke of slavery; the Cage of uncleane Birds of prey, the Habitation of Sea devils, the Receptacle of Renegadoes of God, and Traytors to their Countrey'.[46] It is from here that Sycorax is banished to the unnamed island where she enslaves the innocent Ariel. Ariel's story of enslavement and bondage mirrors the stories of the tens of thousands of Europeans who were captured by Muslim slave traders. However, he refuses to obey Sycorax's 'abhorred commands' and is imprisoned and tortured, till released by Prospero, who re-enslaves him. The very ambiguity of Ariel's identity and his endlessly shape-shifting personality have invited readings of him as the hermaphrodite who playfully crosses boundaries and mixes opposites, so capturing the aesthetics of Renaissance drama. But unlike the hermaphrodite, Ariel's story is marked by violence. When imprisoned by Sycorax he clearly underwent tremendous physical pain—he vent his groans, Prospero tells us, 'As fast as mill-wheels strike' (1.2.281) and his cries 'Did make wolves howl and penetrate the breasts / Of ever-angry bears' (1.2.285–289)—somewhat unexpected in a spirit of the air. A reading that focuses on Ariel as eunuch (rather than a hermaphrodite) allows one to acknowledge that the violence, servitude and transformation intersect and work together in the play.

Sycorax who 'with age and envy / Was grown into a hoop' (1.2.157–158) signifies degeneration and decay, but she is also the agent of transformation. As Marina Warner argues, her brand of metamorphosis is frighteningly 'unruly mutation'.[47] The Renaissance surgeon Ambrose Paré also associated darker magical powers with metamorphosis: 'there are some such men; which when they have once addicted themselves to impious and divelish arts, can by the wondrous craft of the Devil, do many strange things, and change and corrupt bodies, and the health and life of them and the confution of all mundane things'.[48] In fact, Paré goes further to associate such powers of transformation, which paradoxically are both corrupting and 'wondrous', with castration: 'We know for certain that magicians, witches, and conjurers, have by charms so bound some that they could not have to do with their wives; and made others impotent, as if they had been gelt or made eunuchs'.[49] Similarly, Sycorax has worked her dark powers on Ariel and rendered him hapless, unfree and dis-spirited. It is up to Prospero to free him, but Ariel has already been marked as a permanent slave and he is simply pressed into service again by his new master.

Ariel's job description is remarkably like that of the eunuch-slave: while Caliban does the hard physical labor, Ariel functions as a kind of upper-class servant. He has 'substantial freedom of movement and action' and like the privileged eunuch he is Prospero's indispensable agent, spy, and messenger who embodies and enacts his master's power.[50] Ariel is oddly ageless, embodied but also invisible (the eunuch's castrated body was characterized as grotesque, but the body's sexual impotency rendered him invisible as a man and hence a fit guardian of the harem) and, like the eunuch-slave, he is powerless yet strangely powerful. He is also privileged in the local social hierarchy. While Caliban lusts for Miranda, Ariel is completely indifferent to her. He can 'meet and join,' but with nothing. As David Sundelson says 'Ariel's sexuality is stripped of grossness, he is all air'.[51] And, of course, Ariel can sing. As John Bulwer writes, castration is known to advance 'the smallnesse and sweetness of the voice'; and Ariel's voice, rises and fades magically in this isle that is 'full of noises' (3.2.136).[52]

Ariel is neither referred to as a slave nor ever describes himself as one; he is resentful of his bondage yet not openly rebellious; he might not labor solely for love, like Ferdinand does, but he often appears to delight in the tasks assigned to him and also longs for his master's approval, even his affection: 'Do you love me, master […] ?', he asks, perhaps somewhat poignantly, even after expressing resentment at being enslaved, and Prospero responds: 'Dearly my delicate Ariel' (4.1.48–49). Indeed, it is this very love and need for love that might keep him subservient. Because unlike Caliban, who at least has a memory of his mother, Ariel has no community apart from Prospero, no knowledge or memory of family and no past, apart from the horrific one Prospero reminds him of. But he does believe he has a future. Felicity Nussbaum writes that for the eastern slave 'because manumission could in some instances be earned after a specific number of years, the slaves' situation sometimes resembled that of indentured servants. Religious piety, the death of one's master or purchasing freedom were all possible opportunities for changing status'.[53] So Ariel bides his time and waits for his freedom.

If Sycorax's dark powers had transformed Ariel to hapless slave, Prospero's power further complicates that status. Because Ariel is a 'spirit' rather than more straightforwardly a slave (albeit a spirit whom Prospero bends to his will), Prospero rewrites or at least avoids confronting on a daily basis Sycorax's torture and possible mutilation, not to speak of his own act of enslavement. Ariel's (still enslaved) body is now all beauty and light and is constructed as having moved to the realm of the non-material, much like the 'cloud-capped' towers of Prospero's magic. Unreal and wondrous as Ariel is, he is normal and acceptable in the context of the workings of the magic isle. Ariel is one of the agents behind the many miracles the ship-wrecked party experiences: the lavish banquets that appear and disappear, the mysterious voices and the glittering clothes hanging off trees. Ariel's very fantastical nature is part of the normal backdrop of romance. The discourse of the grotesque, the deformed and the hostile is shifted instead onto Caliban. Caliban is the 'monster', the 'fish', 'the freckled whelp hag-born—not honour'd with / A human shape' (1.2.283–284), macabre as well as physically and mentally wounded. He is one to be tamed and subdued. However, by constructing Ariel's slavery as peculiarly privileged, his laboring body as that of a 'delicate' and 'dainty' spirit, and by both reminding Ariel of his debt to his master and by bringing 'love' into the master–slave equation,

Prospero quite effectively continues to exert power over his servant. In spite of being granted freedom at the end, Ariel's eager servitude is, in a sense, more enduring, because it is easier for the master to manage and because it provokes less guilt.

Transformation is a principle motif in *The Tempest*. The isle is a space of phantasms that appear, disappear, and change. Jonathan Bate points out that Ariel is a remarkably Ovidian character in this remarkably Ovidian play. Puck-like, he transforms himself from human to spirit to water-nymph to vengeful harpy, and even possibly to Ceres. He sings 'the great song of metamorphosis': 'Full fathom five'.[54] In constantly mutating, Ariel is simply doing what spirits (particularly daemonic ones) do. For Paré they 'turn themselves into all shapes and wondrous forms of things, as oft-times into wilde-beastes [...] into serpents, toads, owls, lapwings, crows or ravens, goats, asses, dogs, cats, wolves, buls and the like. Moreover, they oft-times assume and enter human bodies [...] yea also they transform themselves into angels of light'.[55] By changing himself and by becoming an agent of the change that Prospero seeks in his betrayers, Ariel becomes most associated with transformation in the story. However the seemingly endless and magical power of transformation is really a result of his fundamental powerlessness. It is also both a constant reminder and a cover for the violent transformation worked on him by both his masters, Sycorax and Prospero.

Prospero might seek to rewrite Ovidian transformation as moral reform and the play's reminders of the drowning, decaying body might simply be 'metaphors for the inner changes that Prospero seeks to work', but Prospero's success in this endeavor is fairly limited.[56] Caliban is associated with degeneration at worst or stasis at best—in contrast to the reformation and moral progress exhibited by the other characters. Antonio might not have changed much either and, for that matter, neither might Prospero, who in spite of his resolution to be more 'human' (interestingly urged on by Ariel's remarks on tenderness and pity), appears to feel some bitterness and resentment right to the end. Gonzalo's utopia can never fully be realized and the golden age is 'shot through with Iron Age characteristics'.[57] Shakespearean comic endings seek to deflect the extreme violence of Ovid, but *The Tempest*'s resolution remains fragile. Transformation, to the extent it takes place, is demanded and imposed on the characters and it is an effect of power in its rawest configuration. The play might envision the artistic project as enacting a transformation that is both beautiful and good (the transformation of a brazen world into a golden is after all Sidney's vision for poetry), but the fact that art is signified in *The Tempest* as magic of a somewhat dubious nature casts doubt on this enterprise. Prospero, who, unlike his spirit-slave, has fathered a child, might now, in his later years, seek to reproduce and fulfill himself through his art-magic, but the cloud-capped towers and palaces are doomed to vanish.

Ariel is of course granted his freedom. 'I shall miss thee, / But yet thou shalt have freedom', declares Prospero wistfully before letting him go (5.1.95–96). But like the eunuchs of the other 'Turk plays' Ariel's future remains unknown. He has been completely 'natally alienated' (to evoke Orlando Patterson's description of the state of slavery), remains dispossessed and solitary, at one with nothing but the elements he will join in his freedom. But the play does not dwell on any of this; it has to find its closure as a normal romance and what one is invited to imagine is a 'delicate' spirit leading a perfectly normal spirit existence, reclining in the heart of cowslips, flying with the bats and bees and living quite 'merrily, merrily' (5.1.92–93) in one idyllic, unending summer.

If the eunuch's aberrant identity is normalized in the travel narratives where his social status and professional role in Ottoman society overtake his 'abnormality', Shakespeare's comedies effectively erase or rewrite the eunuch. In *Twelfth Night* the eunuch is forgotten and this leads to a rendition of romantic desire that may not be entirely appropriate, but that nevertheless can enhance the delights of romantic comedy. *The Tempest* does not mention the eunuch at all, but Ariel, the eunuch-in-disguise, is normalized as a spirit, so fulfilling the requirements of magical romantic comedy. But locating and remembering the missing eunuch in *The Tempest* serves to complicate the rhetoric of servitude in the play as well as to recognize the violence, terror, and perhaps also the beauty that accompanies transformation.

Notes

1. Hakluyt (1600: T3^v, 500).
2. Frankle (1975: 56).
3. Biddulph (1609: F2^r, 27).
4. Blount (1650: H10^v, 186).
5. See W. G. Clarence-Smith (1996).
6. Chakravarty (2016: 15) and Rubright (2014: 25).
7. Chakravarty (2016: 17).
8. See Dolan (1994).
9. Burnett (1997: 2).

10. Kussmaul (1981)
11. Hakluyt (1589: P7^v, 180).
12. Ayalon (1999: 30).
13. Marmon (1995: 7).
14. Toledano (1998: 4).
15. See Patterson (1982: 312).
16. Withers (1650: G4^v, 112). Withers's work, written ca. 1620, though not published until 1650, is practically a translation of the French diplomat Ottavio Bon's earlier (1604–1607) very well-known writings on the Turkish seraglio.
17. Callaghan (2000: 56).
18. Withers (1650: F7^r, 93).
19. Ibid.: G4^r, 103.
20. Ibid.: G6^r–G7^v, 107–108; G1^v, 96; G2^v, 98.
21. Drescher and Engerman (1998: 191–192).
22. Johann Wild, 'Aus der Reisebeschriebung des Johann Wild', quoted in Marmon (1995: 96).
23. Osborn (1656: C10^v, 58).
24. Ibid.: C10^v–C10^r, 58–59.
25. Withers (1650: G5^v, 104).
26. Patterson (1982: 319).
27. See also Starkey (1977).
28. Patterson (1982: 335).
29. Burton (2005: 155).
30. 'Apollonius and Silla' appeared in Barnaby Riche's *Riche His Farewell to Military Profession* (1581). The story was closely based on an Italian comedy, *Gl'ingannati* (1531, 'The Deceived'), published anonymously, and a story in Matteo Bandello's *Novelle* (1554–1573).
31. Relihan (1997: 92).
32. Ibid.: 91.
33. Ibid.: 81.
34. All quotations from Shakespeare's plays have been taken from *The Arden Shakespeare: Complete Works* (2011).
35. Ayalon (1999: 17).
36. Pierce (1993: 9).
37. Sedgwick (1993: 25) quoted in Menon (2011: 6).
38. Menon (2011: 6).
39. Reynolds and Thomson (2003: 190–191).
40. See Mannoni (1956).
41. Brathwaite (1977: 48).
42. Orgel (1978: 78).
43. Albanese (1996: 73).

44. Dymkowski (2000: 35).
45. See for instance Fuchs (1997) and Hess (2000).
46. Purchas (1905, 108).
47. Warner (2000: 98).
48. Paré (1649: 669).
49. Ibid.: 668.
50. Evett (2005: 191).
51. Sundelson (1980: 43).
52. Bulwer (1653: 355).
53. Nussbaum (2007: 154).
54. Bate (1993: 245).
55. Paré (1649: 665).
56. Bate (1993: 245).
57. Ibid.: 257.

Works Cited

Albanese, Denise. 1996. *New Science, New World*. Durham, NC: Duke University Press.
Ayalon, David. 1999. *Eunuchs, Caliphs and Sultans—A Study in Power Relationships*. Jerusalem: Hebrew University Magnes Press.
Bate, Jonathan. 1993. *Shakespeare and Ovid*. Oxford: Clarendon.
Biddulph, William. 1609. *The Voyages of Certain Englishmen into Africa, Asia, Troy, Bythinia, Thracis and the Black Sea*. London.
Blount, Henry. 1650. *A Voyage into the Levant*. London.
Brathwaite, Edward Kamau. 1977. Caliban, Ariel, and Unprospero in the Conflict of Creolization: A Study of the Slave Revolt in Jamaica in 1831–32. *Annals of the New York Academy of Sciences* 292: 45–69
Bulwer, John. 1653. *Anthropometamorphosis: Man Transform'd: or, the Artificiall Changling*. London.
Burnett, Mark Thornton. 1997. *Masters and Servants in English Renaissance Drama and Culture*. London: Macmillan.
Burton, Jonathan. 2005. *Traffic and Turning: Islam and English Drama, 1579–1624*. Newark, DE: University of Delaware Press.
Callaghan, Dympna. 2000. *Shakespeare Without Women*. London and New York: Routledge.
Chakravarty, Urvashi. 2016. More Than Kin, Less Than Kind: Similitude, Strangeness, and Early Modern Homonationalisms. *Shakespeare Quarterly* 67 (1): 14–29.
Clarence-Smith, W.G. 1996. *Islam and the Abolition of Slavery*. New York: Oxford University Press.

Dolan, Frances E. 1994. *Dangerous Familiars: Representations of Domestic Crime in England, 1550–1700*. Ithaca: Cornell University Press.
Drescher, Seymour, and Stanley Engerman (eds.). 1998. *A Historical Guide to World Slavery*. New York: Oxford University Press.
Dymkowski, Christine. 2000. Introduction. In *The Tempest*. Cambridge: Cambridge University Press.
Evett, David. 2005. *Discourses of Service in Shakespeare's England*. New York: Palgrave.
Frankle, Robert J. 1975. Some Aspects of Renaissance Slavery. *Explorations in Renaissance Culture* 2: 55–65.
Fuchs, Barbara. 1997. Contextualizing *The Tempest*. *Shakespeare Quarterly* 48 (1): 45–62.
Hakluyt, Richard. 1589. *The Second Volume of the Principal Navigations, Voyages, Traffiques, and Discoveries of the English Nation*. London.
Hakluyt, Richard. 1600. *The Third and Last Volume of the Principal Navigations, Voyages, Traffiques, and Discoveries of the English Nation*. London.
Hess, Andrew C. 2000. The Mediterranean and Shakespeare's Geopolitical Imagination. In *'The Tempest' and Its Travels*, ed. Peter Hulme, William Sherman, and Robin Kirkpatrick. Philadelphia: University of Pennsylvania Press.
Kussmaul, Anne. 1981. *Servants in Husbandry in Early Modern England*. Cambridge: Cambridge University Press.
Mannoni, Octave. 1956. *Prospero and Caliban: The Psychology of Colonization*. New York: Frederick A. Praeger.
Marmon, Shaun. 1995. *Eunuchs and Sacred Boundaries in Islamic Society*. New York: Oxford University Press.
Mason, John. 1610. *The Turke, A Worthie Tragedy*. London.
Menon, Madhavi. 2011. Introduction: Queer Shakes. In *Shakesqueer*, ed. Madhavi Menon. Durham: Duke University Press.
Nussbaum, Felicity. 2007. Slavery, Blackness and Islam: The Arabian Nights in the Eighteenth Century. In *Slavery and the Cultures of Abolition: Essays Marking the Bicentennial of the British Abolition Act of 1807*, ed. Brycchan Carey and Peter Kitson. Cambridge: Brewer.
Orgel, Stephen. 1978. Introduction. In *The Tempest*. Oxford and New York: Oxford University Press.
Osborn, Francis. 1656. *Political Reflections on the Government of the Turks*. London.
Paré, Ambrose. 1649. Of Monsters and Prodigies. In *The Workes of that Famous Chirurgion Ambrose Parey*, trans. Thomas Johnson. The Internet Archive. https://archive.org/stream/workesofthatfamo00par#page/n3/mode/2up. Accessed 1 December 2016.
Patterson, Orlando. 1982. *Slavery and Social Death: A Comparative Study*. Cambridge, MA: Harvard University Press.

Pierce, Leslie. 1993. *The Imperial Harem: Women and Sovereignty in the Ottoman Empire*. Oxford: Oxford University Press.
Purchas, Samuel. 1905. *Hakluytus Posthumus or Purchas his Pilgrimes*, vol. VI. Glasgow: John Maclehose and Sons.
Relihan, Constance. 1997. Erasing the East from *Twelfth Night*. In *Race, Ethnicity, and Power in the Renaissance*, ed. Joyce Green MacDonald. Madison, NJ: Farleigh Dickinson University Press.
Reynolds, Brian, and Ayanna Thomson. 2003. Inspriteful Ariels: Transversal Tempests. In *Performing Transversally: Reimagining Shakespeare and the Critical Future*, ed. Brian Reynolds. New York: Palgrave.
Rodó, José Enrique. 1922. *Ariel*, trans. F.J. Stimpson. Boston and New York: Houghton Mifflin Company, The Internet Archive. https://archive.org/stream/ariel01rodgoog#page/n0/mode/2up. Accessed 20 November 2016.
Rubright, Marjorie. 2014. *Doppelganger Dilemmas: Anglo-Dutch Relations in Early Modern Literature and Culture*. Philadelphia: University of Pennsylvania Press.
Sedgwick, Eve. 1993. *Tendencies*. Durham: Duke University Press.
Shakespeare, William. 2011. *The Arden Shakespeare: Complete Works*, ed. Richard Proudfoot, Ann Thompson, and David Scott Kastan. London and New York: Bloomsbury.
Starkey, David. 1977. Representation Through Intimacy: A Study of the Symbolism of Monarchy and Court Office in Early-Modern England. In *Symbols and Sentiments*, ed. Ioan M. Lewis. New York: Academic Press.
Sundelson, David. 1980. "So Rare a Wonder'd Father": Prospero's *Tempest*. In *Representing Shakespeare: New Psychoanalytic Essays*, ed. Coppelia Kahn. Baltimore: Johns Hopkins University Press.
Toledano, Ehud. 1998. *Slavery and Abolition in the Ottoman Middle East*. Seattle: University of Washington Press.
Warner, Marina. 2000. "The Foul Witch" and Her "Freckled Whelp": Circean Mutations in *The Tempest*. In *The Tempest and Its Travels*, ed. Peter Hulme and William Sherman. Philadelphia: Philadelphia University Press.
Withers, Robert. 1650. *A Description of the Grand Signior's Seraglio or Turkish Emperours Court*. London.

PART III

Staged Normality and the Domestic Space

CHAPTER 10

Everyday Murder and Household Work in Shakespeare's Domestic Tragedies

Emma Whipday

Early modern conduct literature forges a link between the home and female virtue. In the domestic conduct book *A Preparative to Marriage* (1591), Henry Smith advises wives to position themselves within their homes in order to protect their chastity:

> [W]e call the wife *huswife*, that is, house wife, not a street wife like *Thamar*, nor a field wife like *Dinah*, but a house wife, to shew that a good wife keepes her house... as though home were chastities keeper.[1]

Using Biblical analogies, Smith equates domestic enclosure with female chastity, and constructs transgression in spatial terms. This Biblical association between the home and the housewife pervades early modern culture. In the rhyming domestic conduct manual *Five Hundreth Points of Good Husbandry*, Thomas Tusser writes:

E. Whipday (✉)
Newcastle University, Newcastle upon Tyne, UK
e-mail: emma.whipday@ncl.ac.uk

© The Author(s) 2019
R. Loughnane and E. Semple (eds.), *Staged Normality in Shakespeare's England*, Palgrave Shakespeare Studies,
https://doi.org/10.1007/978-3-030-00892-5_10

> Make husbandry dayly, abrode to provide,
> Make huswifery dayly, at home for to guide.
> Make coefer fast locked, thy treasure to keepe:
> Make house to be suer, the safer to sleepe.[2]

Tusser likens the gendered division of the spheres, which locates female work within the home, to household security; like Smith, he suggests that the safety of the home's inhabitants relies upon the housewife's association with domestic space.

Women on the early modern stage, particularly those belonging to the non-elite sphere, are often represented in relation to the home: from Emilia unpinning Desdemona in *Othello* to the Duchess gazing in her glass in *The Duchess of Malfi*, and from Annabella's needlework in *'Tis Pity* to the maidservant Sisly serving the adulterous Anne supper in her bedchamber in *A Woman Killed with Kindness*, their femininity is fashioned through their use of domestic objects, their accomplishment of domestic tasks, and their association with domestic spaces. Yet the material culture of housework remains 'a paradoxical blindspot in the history of early modern women'[3]; quotidian domestic items were disposable, often used until they fell apart, and have rarely been assigned cultural value. The spaces, objects, and work of the home, associated with the quotidian, the trivial, and the female, are too often culturally invisible.

Household conduct literature counters this cultural invisibility by presenting a vision of domestic life in which structures, spaces, objects, and tasks pertaining to the home are of the utmost significance, associated with both the salvation of the household members' souls and the security of the state. As Catherine Richardson argues,

> The people who consumed these manuals are often said to have been of the 'middling sort' [... and] buying one of these books offered aspirant readers a clear sense of the behaviour required of such a group.[4]

These texts posit particular kinds of household structures, and particular modes of domestic behaviour, as at once usual and desirable. In the treatise 'The Order of the Household', Dudley Fenner writes that 'the household order hath 2. parts', 'the governors of the family' and 'those which are governed by the same'[5]: the domestic sphere is here, as in much conduct literature from the period, structured around a twofold pattern of governance and submission, husband and wife, parents and children, masters/mistresses and servants, masculine authority and feminine domestic work. Despite the fact that husbands performed tasks within the home, and many wives had work beyond it,[6] conduct literature remained rooted in Tusser's fantasy of the husband providing and abroad, and the wife making 'huswifery' at home. These texts focus upon the quotidian, the conventional, and the 'normal', yet the normality these texts represent is idealised, setting up the hierarchically-ordered household, and the feminine domestic sphere, as at once ubiquitous and ideal, expected and aspirational.

In Nathaniel Rogers's 1644 treatise *A Letter, Discovering the Cause of Gods Continuing Wrath*, he uses the term 'normall' to prescribe ideal behaviour: 'the first & normall patterne prescribed in the doctrine, & recorded in the history of the sacred Scriptures'.[7] 'Normall' here implies correct, in association with 'first' or originary Scriptural behaviour; Rogers seems to be applying a term previously used in mathematics to mean 'perpendicular' (a meaning now obsolete), to human conduct (*OED* 'normal', A2, B1). The meaning of 'normal' now prevalent—'regular, usual, typical; ordinary, conventional' (A1a)—echoes Rogers's sense of normal as correct; in the extent to which it represents 'normality', conduct literature depends upon a tension between 'normal' as usual, common, or expected behaviour, and 'normal' as prescribed, idealised, or aspirational.

There is a further category of the 'normal' implied by these texts. When Smith writes that we call the wife 'housewife, that is, *house wife*' to 'show that a good wife keeps her house', his argument rests on the idea that this prescribed behaviour is a natural consequence of her marital status (she is a wife therefore she will keep her house, and as 'huswife' is defined by her ability to keep her house). Yet Smith then lists other Biblical examples of 'wives'—the 'field wife' Dinah (who is raped in a field), the 'street wife' Thamar (who pretends to be a prostitute)—at once clearly delineating the distinction between the 'housewife' and the other spatial manifestations of erring or vulnerable wives, and suggesting that this seemingly normal or usual definition of wife as housewife implies its own opposite (the wife who is sexually vulnerable, beyond the boundaries of the home). Likewise, Tusser's lines, quoted above, group household security with the possibility for household danger—the house is to be 'sure', that its inhabitants may sleep safe, yet the coffer containing household treasure must also be 'fast locked', suggesting that even the security of the house cannot prevent the entrance of thieves (who may already be inside the home). This is reiterated later in the text, when

Tusser advises that, despite locked doors and cabinets, housewives must listen at night for the noise of thieves.[8] The normative in conduct literature is here both defined and undermined by the anxiety associated with the possibility of normative household spaces, objects, and activities becoming threatening.

In 'The Uncanny', Freud suggests that the uncanny (*unheimlich*) 'is that class of the terrifying which leads back to something long known to us, once very familiar'; *heimlich* is that which is familiar, native, or pertains to the home, yet it can also suggest concealment, secrecy, or even danger, and thus *unheimlich* becomes 'a sub-species of *heimlich*'.[9] Angela McShane and Garthine Walker make a similar suggestion in relation to early modern everyday behaviour: 'the extraordinary and the everyday each informed the other' so that 'any characterisation of the normative, indeed the concept of 'everyday life', is itself essentially unstable'.[10] The genre of domestic tragedy, I suggest, places the *heimlich*, the everyday, and the normative, under pressure, by demonstrating the extent to which the domestic 'normality' prescribed by the conduct literature contains within its hierarchical structures, spatial logic, and gendered household work, the potential for extraordinary and uncanny violation. In domestic tragedies, the maintenance of the boundaries of the home prescribed by Smith and Tusser fails to protect the virtue (or the lives) of its inhabitants, as both the act of murder and its aftermath are contained within the daily life of the household; and the association between the body and virtue of the housewife and the home, may render both home and housewife vulnerable. In this chapter, I explore how household tasks, spaces, and objects are perverted through their involvement in murder and adultery in domestic tragedies. In so doing, I suggest that Shakespeare, in staging the violent homes of *Macbeth* and *Othello*, reimagines the versions of domesticity presented by earlier domestic tragedies such as *Arden of Faversham*, *A Warning for Fair Women*, *Two Lamentable Tragedies*, and *A Woman Killed with Kindness*.[11]

"A LITTLE WATER CLEARS US OF THIS DEED": HOUSEHOLD WORK AND CRUENTATION

Lady Macbeth: What's the business
That such a hideous trumpet calls to parley
The sleepers of the house? Speak, speak.

Macduff: O gentle lady,
Tis not for you to hear what I can speak.
The repetition in a woman's ear
Would murder as it fell.
Enter Banquo: O Banquo, Banquo,
Our royal master's murdered!
Lady Macbeth: Woe, alas –
What, in our house?
Banquo: Too cruel anywhere.

(II.iii.76–85)[12]

In the immediate aftermath of the discovery of Duncan's murder, Lady Macbeth's cry—'what, in our house?'—could be read as an error that betrays her guilt. Pretending surprise, she reacts as if it is the location of the crime that distresses her, and not the crime itself; a reaction for which Banquo rebukes her. Yet her reaction could also be a convincing performance of the distress of a hostess who has failed in the most basic aspect of hospitality: protecting her guests from being murdered in their sleep. Daryl Palmer argues that in Lady Macbeth's welcome to Duncan, 'the horror of the scene builds through the formulaic speeches of hospitality'; the same is true in the above exchange, as she uses the postures of hospitality in an attempt to veil her 'violent exploitation of household decorums'.[13] Lady Macbeth twice uses the term 'house', rather than 'castle', to describe her abode; she complains, like a good hostess, that Macduff's noise may wake the 'sleepers of the house', and then bemoans that a murder has taken place 'in our house'. Unlike Macduff, who declares 'our royal master's murdered', Lady Macbeth's emphasis is not upon the murder of a (governing) King in the castle of one of his (subordinate) thanes, but upon the duty she and her husband owe guests in their home.

Likewise, when Macbeth first contemplates murdering Duncan, he views it in two lights—as a treasonous murder of a king, and as an inhospitable murder of a guest:

He's here in double trust.
First, as I am his kinsman and his subject,
Strong both against the deed; then, as his host,
Who should against his murderer shut the door,
Not bear the knife myself.

(I.vii.12–16)

As Naomi Conn Liebler puts it, 'Macbeth casts regicide in the language of inhospitable behaviour'.[14] In depicting Duncan's murder as at once an act of treason and a household murder, Shakespeare draws explicitly on the conventions and concerns of domestic tragedy, which show how the concealment of household murder involves the performance of household work—men and women may both commit violent crimes, and men may transport, hide, and dismember the bodies of those they have murdered, but women clean up the blood.

In the earliest surviving domestic tragedy, *Arden of Faversham* (1592), a play based on the recent murder of Kentish landowner Arden by his wife Alice, her lover Mosby, and various accomplices, Alice takes as active a role in her husband's murder as the men she has commissioned to kill him. When Mosby and two hired killers have failed to complete the murder, Alice finishes the deed herself. Yet when, in the immediate aftermath of the crime, the men dispose of the body and then escape, it is Alice and her maid, Susan, who must clear away the evidence:

> *Alice*: And, Susan, fetch water and wash away this blood.
> *Susan*: The blood cleaveth to the ground and will not out.
> *Alice*: But with my nails I'll scrape away the blood.
> The more I strive the more the blood appears!
> (xiv.251–254)

After Alice's moment of transgressive and murderous agency, she returns to her role as housewife; disposal of the evidence becomes a surreal extension of her normal household work, yet the blood cannot be removed through usual domestic processes. Susan asks her mistress if she knows the reason, and Alice replies 'because I blush not at my husband's death' (256). This is a variation on cruentation, 'the belief that the corpse of a murdered person would bleed anew in the presence of its murderer'.[15] In James VI's 1597 *Daemonologie*, he claims that a corpse touched by the perpetrator 'wil gush out of bloud, as if the blud were crying to the heaven for revenge to of the murtherer', a 'secret super-naturall signe' appointed by God.[16] This trope was not merely figurative: as Malcolm Gaskill notes, cruentation not only 'added dramatic tension to popular pamphlets', but also 'actually featured in trials'.[17] In *Arden*, this miraculous domestic cruentation, where the house bleeds even when the body has been removed, counteracts Alice's attempts at incorporating her criminal removal of the evidence within her everyday household work, as the house itself seems to resist her betrayal of her role as wife.

In *A Warning for Fair Women* (1599), another 'true crime' domestic tragedy which charts the fatal consequences of adultery, cruentation proliferates in a variety of bodies and objects. George Browne desires to kill a London merchant, Sanders, for love of Sanders' wife, Anne; he fails to kill Sanders in the environs of his London home, and so he kills him as he walks in the countryside, attended by a friend's servant, Beane. Following the attack, Beane's still-living body bleeds in the presence of Browne—'his wounds break out afresh in bleeding' (IV.iv.135)—and Browne complains that the fifteen wounds have become 'fifteen mouths that do accuse me' (138). Beane then recovers enough to speak the name of his murderer with his own mouth. This cruentation offers a miracle, the symbolism of which is reinforced by a dumb show, representing the murder, in which the personification of Murder 'imbrue[s]' the hands of the conspirators by 'rub[bing]' them with blood (II.ii.56sd). Bloody imagery proliferates further: a maidservant named Joan has a dream that Beane suffers a nosebleed, and then experiences a nosebleed herself: 'as I was washing my hands my nose bled three drops, then I thought of John Bean[e]' (III.iii.118–120). In her dream, Joan recalls, 'I ran to my chest to fetch ye a handkerchief' (IV.iv.56); later, in the immediate aftermath of the murder, Browne dips his own handkerchief in Sanders's blood, in order to send it 'as a token to my love' (III.iii.71)—a misguided decision, as the bloody handkerchief later becomes evidence against Browne.

The handkerchief is thus transformed from normal domestic object, which in Joan's dream cleans quotidian blood, to uncanny love token carrying emblematic blood, to legal evidence bearing bloody witness to a transgressive act, as it is made *unheimlich* through its involvement in murder. As the handkerchief is transformed, so is Beane: the cruentation of Beane's living body is echoed by dreams, symbols, and portents, as the normal enters the realm of the miraculous. Patricia Fumerton suggests that 'it is often precisely in the trivial detail of everyday life that Renaissance men and women invested their lives with extraordinary meaning'[18]; in domestic tragedies, both the trivial details of everyday life, and the men and women themselves, are invested with extraordinary meaning, through the transformative act of murder.

In *Arden*, the moment of cruentation that prompts the discovery of Alice's guilt likewise proliferates, as a knife and bloody hand-towel (the murder weapon and the means by which the murder is hidden) are discovered, linking the crime to domestic objects: the servant Michael 'was so afraid I knew not what I did' (384), failing not only to hide the murder weapon, but also to hide the means by which Alice and Susan cleaned up after the murder, so that the hand-towel, another quotidian domestic object which becomes corrupted, is used to clean up after the murder, and so is transformed into legal evidence. Finally, following Alice's arrest, Arden's own body bleeds in her presence, in a literal act of cruentation: 'the more I sound his name the more he bleeds' (xvi.4). Yet the bleeding of the corpse is almost an afterthought: it is upon the blood on the floor that the narrative emphasis is placed, as it is this that proves Alice's undoing. In *Arden*, then, the idea of cruentation is transfigured, as the house itself, and the objects within it, become allied with both murderer and victim, bearing witness to the guilt of the latter and the wounds of the former. Alice cannot 'clear' her home through housewifely activities because her role as housewife has been perverted through her involvement in the murder of her husband; she has placed herself, and her home, beyond the power of normal domestic processes (xiv.353).

A comparable perversion of domestic work in the aftermath of murder can be seen in the 1601 domestic tragedy *Two Lamentable Tragedies*, in which a tavern-keeper, Master Merry, murders a neighbouring shopkeeper in the 'upper room' of his tavern. His sister, Rachel, discovers the crime, and he orders her:

> Merry: Wipe up the blood in every place above,
> So that no drop be found about the house,
> I know all houses will be searcht anon:
> Then burne the clothes, with which you wipe the ground
> That no apparent signe of blood be found.
> Rachel: I will, I will, oh would to God I could
> As cleerly wash your conscience from the deed[19]

As an unmarried sister living in her brother's household, Rachel does not govern huswifery within the domestic sphere, but rather, must perform obedience to the householder. As Catherine Richardson argues, 'the murder becomes subsumed into the routines of the household'[20]; Rachel is forced, in cleaning the home, to wipe up the blood (a task she completes more successfully than Michael, in burning the 'clothes' used in this corrupted housework). Rachel, like Alice's maidservant Susan, finds her usual household duties rendered malign and dangerous through the criminal act, and abuse of authority, of her household superior.[21] Here, as in *Warning*, bloodstains are associated with the bloody conscience of the murderer; yet Rachel makes a distinction between the two. Rachel ensures the blood is successfully washed from the house, but her brother's conscience remains stained.

In *Macbeth*, there is a similar emphasis on a perversion of housewifely duties. In the immediate aftermath of the murder, Lady Macbeth hears knocking at the gates, and her thoughts turn to the concealment of the crime:

> *Lady Macbeth:*   I hear a knocking
> At the south entry. Retire we to our chamber.
> A little water clears us of this deed.
> How easy is it then! Your constancy
> Hath left you unattended. *Knock [within]*
>   Hark, more knocking.
> Get your nightgown
>   (II.ii.63–68)

As Sarah Wintle and René Weis observe, 'her repeated insistences to her husband that he wash himself are telling assertions of the fact of intimacy and domestic relation'[22]: Lady Macbeth's instructions may relate to the specificities of concealing a murder, but they are rooted in the quotidian familiarity of a wife's instructions that her husband wash and change into his nightgown. Yet just as Rachel bemoans her inability to cleanse her brother's conscience as she cleanses his home, so Lady Macbeth finds that a little water is insufficient to clear her of this deed.

Macbeth, then, is in conversation with a wider pattern of criminal behaviour and miraculous justice. Macbeth's murder of the sleeping king leads to his realisation that he has 'murdered sleep', and Browne's transformation of a handkerchief into a bloody token prompts a counter-transformation in the cruentation of the body of his victim. Alice Arden murders her husband, on whose behalf she holds the keys of the house and with whom she inhabits the house itself, and so she can neither clear her house, nor maintain its boundaries against the watch that comes to arrest her. Lady Macbeth perverts her role as hostess in bedewing her hands with the blood of her murdered guest in order to implicate his drugged and sleeping servants, and so finds that in her own sleep, her hands are endlessly bedewed. Lady Macbeth's imagined hand-washing, then, is the extreme form of the coupled cleanliness and disposal of evidence that characterises housewives, sisters, and servants in domestic tragedy, and links the outcome of her inhospitable crime with the disrupted domesticity her act initiates.

The cruentation of Arden's home is transfigured in *Macbeth* from a literal miracle to an imaginative state, so that first Macbeth and later Lady Macbeth believe themselves unable to clean the blood from their hands. The relationship between bloody hands and guilt here echoes the dumb show in *Warning*, in which, as Ariane M. Balizet observes, 'the act of murder appears inextricable' from the dumb show 'image of bloody hands'.[23] For Alice, the unyielding blood becomes evidence that will condemn her; for Lady Macbeth, the indelible memory of the blood becomes a matter of conscience that will destroy her.

Lady Macbeth's fatal error is to underestimate the extent to which contaminating her home will destroy her peace within it. As her husband commits the murder, Lady Macbeth boasts to the audience:

> The doors are open, and the surfeited grooms
> Do mock their charge with snores. I have drugged their possets
> (II.ii.5–6)

In bringing the grooms their possets, Lady Macbeth, as mistress of the house, is showing them a significant degree of hospitable attention—and in drugging those servants so that they cannot guard the sleeping house in her stead, she renders her hospitable act malign. By opening Duncan's door and incapacitating his servants, Lady Macbeth betrays her role as housewife and hostess—and her housewifely request that her husband wash cannot restore her household boundaries that she has threatened in opening the bedchamber doors to her murderous husband. Instead, a group of thanes will soon knock at her gates to discover the murder, prefiguring the eventual entry of the army that will conquer the castle; the Macbeths' 'corruption of hospitality'[24] becomes a tragic invitation to invasive guests. Likewise, in aiming to murder her husband, Alice Arden renders all her domestic activities malign, in ways that will prove fatal to her. In the opening scene of the play, she poisons her husband's breakfast, in what Susan Staub refers to as 'a perversion of the prescribed wifely duty of providing nourishment'.[25] Furthermore, in plotting her husband's death, Alice Arden invites Black Will, a hired killer, to supper, sequesters him within Arden's counting-house, and gives him the key to it: 'thou'st keep the key thyself' (xiv.104). In committing acts of malign hospitality, both Alice and Lady Macbeth undo their identities as domestic 'huswives', and so their houses themselves turn against them. They deprive household boundaries of their efficacy and are eventually undone by the homes they have contaminated: Alice in the domestic cruentation and bloody hand-cloth that cause her arrest and execution, and Lady Macbeth in the protective battlements that bring about her death.

'CLOSET, LOCK AND KEY': CLOSETED WIVES AND LOST HANDKERCHIEFS

Iago: Awake, what ho, Brabanzio! thieves, thieves, thieves!
Look to your house, your daughter and your bags!
Thieves, thieves!
[Enter] Brabanzio above.
Brabanzio: What is the reason of this terrible summons?
What is the matter there?
Roderigo: Signor, is all your family within?
Iago: Are your doors locked?
(*Othello*, I.i.77–83)

Early modern conduct literature emphasises the maintenance of household boundaries as a key facet of the housewife's domestic work. Tusser's advice that a housewife should 'Make cofer fast locked, thy treasure to keepe' is obsessively reiterated throughout his conduct book: she must 'see dore lockt faste', 'make keyes to be kepers', and 'kepe keyes as thy life'.[26] The keys, as a symbol of patriarchal authority, may be entrusted to the wife who must guard both the house and herself, as aspects of her husband's property.[27] Keys and locks are also sexual metaphors, representing at once the male and female genitalia, and the proprietary right of a man to a woman's sexuality.[28] In *Cymbeline*, Giacomo, in viewing Imogen's sleeping body, claims he will convince her husband 'I have picked the lock and ta'en/ The treasure of her honour' (II.ii.41–42), a treasure that, by implication, belongs to her husband. Keys thus both literally enclose the wife, allowing her to reinforce the integrity of the boundaries of and within the home, and metaphorically guard the boundaries of her body, in preserving her chastity. Shakespeare plays on the significance of these household objects in the opening to *Othello*.

When Brabanzio is awakened at night by the call of 'thieves', the theft is not immediately revealed to be a human one; house, daughter and bags are each listed as vulnerable, calling into question Brabanzio's property, family, and possessions, and thus questioning his authority as homeowner, father, and head of household. In asking if Brabanzio's doors are locked, Iago suggests that these locks have proved inefficacious; the 'jewel' (I.iii.195) has already been stolen. The thief in question is read by Brabanzio as Othello, but Iago's words have a different implication: when he asks if the doors are locked, he is at once questioning whether Desdemona-as-possession is locked safe within, and whether Desdemona as a member of Brabanzio's household has betrayed the trust and authority invested in her by unlocking the doors of her home, and of her body, herself.

Desdemona threatens the boundaries of her home by unlocking its doors. The illicit use of the household keys by a wife or daughter is symbolically charged in this period. This is evident in an emblem from Guillaume de la Perrière's *Theatre of Fine Devices* (Fig. 10.1), which

Fig. 10.1 Guillaume de la Perrière, *The Theater of Fine Devices Containing an Hundred Morall Emblems* (London, 1614), Emblem XVIII. By permission of University of Glasgow Library, Special Collections

features a virtuous wife, seated upon a curtained bed, who holds a large key in front of the threshold to her home. The import of this is explained in the accompanying verse:

> The key doth note, she must have care to guide
> The goods her husband doth with pain provide.

The key is here a symbol of domestic enclosure, but it is also a quotidian domestic object which a housewife (or a daughter who, in the absence of her mother, inhabits the role of housewife) would have been expected to possess. As Georgianna Ziegler notes, the wife 'herself is the greatest of his goods, responsible for guarding that which makes her most valuable, her chastity'[29]; the key therefore becomes an object possessed by the wife on behalf of the husband, an emblem of a significant aspect of the housewifely role, and a phallic symbol of sexual proprietary rights. The tortoise on which the wife rests her foot exemplifies this; a 'favourite metaphor for the virtuous wife', it carries its own home everywhere in the form of its shell, and so can guard itself within its 'walls' whenever necessary.[30] The keeping of locked goods, the enclosure of the wife within the home, and wifely chastity, are here paralleled in both image and verse.

In Perrière's emblem, as in the conduct literature I discuss above, the prescribed 'normal' behaviour implies its own opposite: the possibility of an unchaste wife who unlocks her husband's doors and steps beyond the boundaries of her home (hinted at in this emblem by the window opening into the world beyond). Keys wielded by a wife could also be emblematic of a broader strategy of household insubordination, as in an illustration of a skimmington in the collection of engravings *English Customs* (1628), in which a wife holds a set of keys over her head, in order to beat her husband with them. In domestic tragedies, as in the opening scene of *Othello*, the keys, as everyday household objects that symbolised a wife's 'normal' responsibilities, become emblematic of the transgressive potential of a woman's proprietary rights over the boundaries of her home, and of her body.[31]

In Heywood's *A Woman Killed with Kindness* (first performed c.1603), the trope of lock and key is repeatedly linked to adultery. When betrayed husband Frankford learns of his wife Anne's affair with his household guest Wendoll, he must steal into his own house with forged keys in order to surprise them in the act of adultery. Frankford's position as husband is undermined by his use of false keys. He must follow the trajectory of a thief in order to discover what has already been stolen from him:

> This is the key that opes my outward gate,
> This is the hall door, this my withdrawing chamber.
> But this, that door that's bawd unto my shame,
> Fountain and spring of all my bleeding thoughts,
> Where the most hallowed order and true knot
> Of nuptial sanctity hath been profaned.
> It leads to my polluted bedchamber...
>
> (xiii.8–14)

Frankford lists the spaces of his home as properties owned by him: his gate, his withdrawing chamber, and finally, his bedchamber. Yet the doors to these spaces are not referred to by possessive pronouns in this litany of property: his wife's illicit locking of these doors has undone his proprietary rights. As Subha Mukherji argues, '[Frankford's] position is one of peculiar alienation [...] The key becomes at once a token of proprietorial access and of exclusion'.[32] The maintenance of household boundaries that Smith and Tusser prescribe has failed to protect the home, as the adulterer is already within its walls.

Furthermore, Frankford's 'here' in referring to each of these keys suggests that they are not merely tokens, but also stage properties. As Frankford and Nicholas cross the various boundaries of the household, Frankford loses his right to locks and keys in the drama of illicit entry. The spatial logic of the scene does not allow the audience to join with Frankford and Nicholas in crossing these boundaries, represented by the set of keys that Frankford holds, because a single doorway must become our focus: that to the 'polluted bedchamber'. This doorway is presumably mapped imaginatively onto one of the stage doors, as Frankford exits through it to discover his wife sleeping in Wendoll's arms, and then re-enters to inform both Nicholas and the audience of it. A door between the stage and the tiring house becomes a charged threshold that represents the transition from suspicion to knowledge. Yet the presence of the keys reminds the audience of the multiple thresholds of the home which have been divested of their protective capabilities, just as Frankford has been divested of his domestic authority, by Anne's betrayal. Anne's locking of the doors within the household, which should guard her virtue, in order to enclose a threat to it, is a perversion of her protective role as wife.

As with the imaginative cruentation in *Macbeth*, Shakespeare transforms the trope of the lock and key in *Othello* from the literal to the metaphorical. When, later in the play, Othello is brought to believe that Desdemona has committed adultery, he refers to her as a 'closet lock and key of villainous secrets' (IV.ii.21). This is the logical conclusion of Brabanzio's earlier construction of Desdemona as a 'jewel' that has been stolen from him[33]: Othello comes to believe that, having unlocked the doors of her father's house to enable her elopement, Desdemona's status as a chaste and key-holding wife has been perverted. It is not chastity but adultery that she keeps 'locked' inside her.

In seventeenth-century critic Thomas Rymer's famous condemnation of the play, he suggests that the play be given a new title:

> So much ado, so much stress, so much passion and repetition about an handkerchief! Why was not this call'd *The Tragedy of the Handkerchief*?[34]

Rymer complains that the 'moral' of the play is a 'warning to all good Wives, that they look well to their Linnen'.[35] Rymer's bathetic humour observes a key facet of the role of the handkerchief in the play. Whether or not a wife can look well to her linen is of great significance in a society in which chastity is associated with enclosure, locked chambers, and 'keeping'. In 'losing' the handkerchief, Desdemona unknowingly suggests that she cannot keep domestic objects guarded and enclosed. Furthermore, the handkerchief, once lost, circulates amongst those who would possess it: Cassio orders Bianca to 'take out' the work, that he also might own it. In permitting a domestic object to be distributed and potentially copied, to become, as Paul Yachnin puts it, 'reproducible, exchangeable', Desdemona raises the possibility that her body has likewise circulated.[36]

Othello believes that Desdemona has rendered her symbolic role as keeper of household keys malign and so orders Emilia: 'turn the key and keep our counsel' (IV.ii.98). The key that should guard wifely chastity and household security alike becomes, as in *Arden* and *Macbeth*, an accomplice to murder—not, here, by allowing the murderer entry, but by locking the murderer within. Othello reads Desdemona's loss of the handkerchief as a perversion of her housewifely role, and so uses his household authority—over keys, servants, and wife—to kill her.[37]

In so doing, Othello aligns himself with a stage tradition associating the circulation of quotidian domestic cloths with both transgression and evidence. As many critics have observed, one of the antecedents of Desdemona's handkerchief is Kyd's 'bloody hankercher' in *The Spanish Tragedy*. In *Arden*, Franklin confronts Alice with 'Know you this hand-towel and this knife?' (381), as the bloody hand-towel is transformed into evidence. Likewise, when Browne dips his handkerchief in Sanders's blood to transform it into a love token, he observes: 'Look how many wounds my hand hath given him,/ So many holes I'll make within this cloth' (72–73). Browne unknowingly prefigures the 'speaking wounds' of Beane's body; furthermore, his handkerchief, at once stained with Sanders' blood and punctured in a metonymic representation of his wounds, echoes the handkerchief in Joan's dream, which she fetches to stem Beane's nosebleed,[38] highlighting the quotidian status of the handkerchief as an object for cleaning innocuous blood, and prefiguring the perverted use to which the handkerchief will be put. Just as Browne fails to realise the bloody handkerchief he makes a love token will become evidence to condemn him, Othello fatally misunderstands the emblematic significance of the handkerchief.

In 'Othello's Black Handkerchief', Ian Smith argues that there has been an 'overwhelming critical tendency to associate the handkerchief with Desdemona',[39] yet if we follow Smith in reading the handkerchief 'dyed in mummy' as related to the 'textual black body' used to signify blackness onstage, and thus to the body of Othello himself, there is a further resonance. Just as Othello misreads Desdemona's metaphorical association with closets, locks, and keys as suggestive, not of chastity, but of adultery, so he misunderstands the crime that the handkerchief portends. He does not comprehend that the blood-red strawberries symbolise not the impossible 'ocular proof' of his wife's adultery, but rather, proleptically signify both his eventual act of murder, and his resulting suicide, when his own wounds bear witness to his act of self-slaughter. Shakespeare, then, at once borrows the bloody handkerchief of *Arden* and *Warning*, and transforms it: this red-spotted handkerchief is not evidence of, but the motive for, Desdemona's murder.

Grouping the strawberry-spotted handkerchief with the bloody handkerchiefs of *As You Like It*, *Cymbeline*, and *A Midsummer Night's Dream*, Balizet argues that these 'bloody or spotted tokens are consistently misread and misunderstood as evidence of something that has *not* happened'.[40] I suggest that not only is Desdemona's handkerchief misread as evidence of something that has not happened—the act of adultery with Cassio—but it also, like the handkerchief in Joan's dream in

Warning, bears witness to something that has not yet happened: the murder of Desdemona (which does not stain the wedding sheets on the marriage bed with blood) and the suicide of Othello (which does). Cruentation reminds us of the blood the murderer has spilled, but the image of the miraculously bleeding corpse also contains within it its own outcome: the blood of the murderer, spilled in justice by the state. In *Othello*, the tragic hero takes on this role himself, and famously becomes his own executioner:

> in Aleppo once,
> Where a malignant and a turbaned Turk
> Beat a Venetian and traduced the state,
> I took by th'throat the circumcised dog,
> And smote him thus.
> [*He stabs himself.*]
> (V.ii.345–349)

Othello here 'implicitly identifies' with the turbaned Turk, yet in killing himself, 'the violence is displaced onto the demonised, "malignant" Turk', as he reasserts his identity as tragic hero.[41] Completing Othello's half-line, Lodovico responds with: 'Oh, bloody period!' (349), bearing witness to the blood that is spilled as Othello dies upon a kiss. As a trivial domestic object which Desdemona 'loses', the handkerchief emblematises: how her housewifely inability to 'keep' domestic objects leaves her vulnerable to interpretation; the instability of 'chastity' once virginity has been lost[42]; and the eventual self-inflicted bloody justice that Othello's crime will necessitate.

In each of these plays, quotidian domestic objects—hand-towels, keys—become malign when used to commit and conceal a murder. Yet in each case, when the female characters wield domestic objects for nefarious purposes, so that the normal realm of household work is transformed, the domestic sphere itself turns against them. The hand-towel and the blood-stained floor bear witness to both Alice Arden's crime, and her inability to 'clear' her house after it. In *Two Lamentable Tragedies*, Rachel's house may be clear, but its association with herself and her brother proves her undoing when all the neighbours band together to knock upon the doors and arrest them. Anne locks herself in her bedchamber with the adulterous Wendoll, and forces her husband to make his way through their home with false keys, leading to her own banishment from the house. Lady Macbeth's cry of 'What, in our house?' proves prophetic—the castle, coupled with her guilt, will bring about her death, when she throws herself from its battlements. Only Desdemona is innocent of the crime her lost domestic object portends; and that is because the domestic crime it symbolises is that of her husband.

In these plays, domestic activities, objects, and spaces become significant because of their role in committing and concealing crimes, but they also bring about the discovery and apprehension of the criminals. In using everyday objects as stage properties, domestic tragedies demonstrate that the domestic sphere is worthy of the dramatic reach of tragedy. In *Macbeth* and *Othello*, household objects and household work become malign in the aftermath of murder, but these objects and tasks are also transformed into the realm of metaphor, drawing on the concerns of domestic conduct literature to emblematise the extent to which transgression perverts the spaces, objects, and roles of the household. I suggest that, in drawing on the tropes of domestic tragedy in these plays, Shakespeare creates new versions of the genre, using heightened language, foreign settings, and elite spheres to stage familiar, everyday, normal domestic worlds. From Browne and Desdemona's handkerchiefs to Alice and Rachel's cloths, Lady Macbeth's possets, and Alice and Frankford's keys, these trivial, quotidian objects bring about both tragedy and its resolution.

Notes

1. Smith (1591: E7^v).
2. Tusser (1573: C2^v).
3. Ogilvie et al. (2009: 149).
4. Richardson (2013: 176).
5. Fenner (1592: A1^v).
6. See, for example, the preliminary findings of the 'Women's Work in Rural England, 1500–1700' project at the University of Exeter (Whittle and Hailwood 2017).
7. Rogers (1644: 9).
8. Tusser (1573: S4^v).
9. Freud (1959: 368, 375).
10. McShane and Walker (2010: 4).
11. It has been suggested that Shakespeare may have been one of the writers of *Arden of Faversham,* and there has been a scholarly consensus that if

Shakespeare's hand is in the play, it can be found in scenes iv–viii (Taylor and Loughnane 2017: 489–490; see Jackson 2006 and 2014). If this is the case, then Shakespeare's experience of working on an early domestic tragedy seems to have informed his use of tragic domestic tropes in his later tragedies. I suggest that, whether or not he was involved in writing a domestic tragedy, Shakespeare was aware of, and in conversation with, the genre; for further discussion, see Whipday (2019), *Shakespeare's Domestic Tragedies: Violence in the Early Modern Home*.
12. All references to Shakespeare's works are to the *Norton Shakespeare*.
13. Palmer (1992: 173).
14. Liebler (1995: 206).
15. Lin (2012: 143).
16. James VI (1597: 79).
17. Gaskill (2000: 227).
18. Fumerton (1999: 6).
19. Anon (2013: D3^r).
20. Richardson (2006: 135–136).
21. Dowd (2011: 138–139).
22. Weis and Wintle (1991: 144).
23. Balizet (2014: 169).
24. Power (2016: 142).
25. Staub (2002: 132).
26. Tusser (1573: U4^r, V4^r, V4^r).
27. Flather (2007: 46–58).
28. Williams (1994: 759–760).
29. Ziegler (1990: 76).
30. Wiesner (1993: 25).
31. I discuss the significance of keys in *Arden of Faversham* further elsewhere; see Whipday (2015, esp. 105–106).
32. Mukherji (2006: 76).
33. Korda (2002: 133).
34. Rymer (1956: 160).
35. Ibid.
36. Yachnin (2002: 325).
37. Orlin (1994: 154).
38. Leggot (2011: 17).
39. Smith (2013: 3).
40. Balizet (2014: 24).
41. Singh (1994: 291).
42. Boose (1975: 360–374).

Works Cited

Anon. 1628. *English Customs*. London.
Anon. 2007. *Arden of Faversham*, ed. Martin White. London: New Mermaids.
Anon. 2011. *A Warning for Fair Women*, ed. Gemma Leggott. *Early Modern Literary Studies*. Hosted Resources. https://extra.shu.ac.uk/emls/iemls/resources.html. Accessed 8 March 2017.
Anon. 2013. *Two Lamentable Tragedies*, ed. Chiaki Hanabusa. Manchester: Manchester University Press.
Balizet, Ariane M. 2014. *Blood and Home in Early Modern Drama: Domestic Identity on the Renaissance Stage*. Abingdon, Oxon.: Routledge.
Boose, Linda E. 1975. Othello's Handkerchief: "The Recognizance and Pledge of Love". *English Literary Renaissance* 5: 360–374.
de la Perrière, Guillaume. 1614. *The Theater of Fine Devices*. London.
Dowd, Michelle M. 2011. Desiring Subjects: Staging the Female Servant in Early Modern Tragedy. In *Working Subjects in Early Modern English Drama*, ed. Michelle M. Dowd and Natasha Korda, 131–144. Farnham, Surrey: Ashgate.
Fenner, Dudley. 1592. The Order of Household. In *Certain Godly and Learned Treatises*. Edinburgh.
Flather, Amanda. 2007. *Gender and Space in Early Modern England*. Woodbridge: The Boydell Press.
Freud, Sigmund. 1959. The Uncanny. In *Collected Papers*, trans. Alix Strachey, 368–407. New York: Basic Books.
Fumerton, Patricia. 1999. Introduction: A New New Historicism. In *Renaissance Culture and the Everyday*, ed. Patricia Fumerton and Simon Hunt, 1–17. Philadelphia: University of Pennsylvania Press.
Gaskill, Malcolm. 2000. *Crime and Mentalities in Early Modern England*. Cambridge: Cambridge University Press.
Heywood, Thomas. 2008. A Woman Killed with Kindness. In *A Woman Killed with Kindness and Other Domestic Plays*, ed. Martin Wiggins. Oxford: Oxford University Press.
Jackson, MacDonald P. 2006. Shakespeare and the Quarrel Scene in *Arden of Faversham*. *Shakespeare Quarterly* 57 (3): 249–293.
Jackson, MacDonald P. 2014. *Determining the Shakespeare Canon: Arden of Faversham and A Lover's Complaint*. Oxford: Oxford University Press.
James VI. 1597. *Daemonologie in Form of a Dialogue*. Edinburgh.
Korda, Natasha. 2002. *Shakespeare's Domestic Economies: Gender and Property in Early Modern England*. Philadelphia: University of Pennsylvania Press.
Liebler, Naomi Conn. 1995. *Shakespeare's Festive Tragedy: The Ritual Foundations of Genre*. London: Routledge.
Lin, Erika T. 2012. *Shakespeare and the Materiality of Performance*. Basingstoke: Palgrave Macmillan.

McShane, Angela, and Garthine Walker. 2010. Introduction. In *The Extraordinary and the Everyday in Early Modern England: Essays in Celebration of the Work of Bernard Capp*, ed. Angela McShane and Garthine Walker, 1–5. Basingstoke: Palgrave Macmillan.

Mukherji, Subha. 2006. *Law and Representation in Early Modern Drama*. Cambridge: Cambridge University Press.

Ogilvie, Sheilagh, Markus Küpker, and Janine Maegraith. 2009. Women and the Material Culture of Food in Early Modern Germany. *Early Modern Women* 4: 149–160.

Orlin, Lena Cowen. 1994. *Private Matters and Public Culture in Post-reformation England*. Ithaca: Cornell University Press.

Palmer, Daryl M. 1992. *Hospitable Performances: Dramatic Genre and Cultural Practices in Early Modern England*. West Lafayette, IN: Purdue University Press.

Power, Andrew J. 2016. "Why Should I Play the Roman Fool, and Die/On Mine Own Sword?" The Senecan Tradition in *Macbeth*. In *Celtic Shakespeare: The Bard and the Borderers*, ed. Willy Maley and Rory Loughnane, 139–156. Abingdon, Oxon: Routledge.

Richardson, Catherine. 2006. *Domestic Life and Domestic Tragedy in Early Modern England*. Manchester: Manchester University Press.

Richardson, Catherine. 2013. Household Manuals. In *The Elizabethan Top Ten: Defining Print Popularity in Early Modern England*, ed. Andy Kesson and Emma Smith, 169–178. Farnham, Surrey: Ashgate.

Rogers, Nathaniel. 1644. *A Letter, Discovering the Cause of Gods Continuing Wrath*. London.

Rymer, Thomas. 1956. A Short View of Tragedy. In *The Critical Works of Thomas Rymer*, ed. Curt Zimansky. New Haven: Yale University Press.

Shakespeare, William. 2016. *The Norton Shakespeare*, 3rd ed., ed. Stephen Greenblatt, et al. New York: Norton.

Singh, Jyotsna. 1994. Othello's Identity, Postcolonial Theory, and Contemporary African Rewritings of *Othello*. In *Women, "Race", and Writing in the Early Modern Period*, ed. Margo Hendricks and Patricia Parker, 287–299. Abingdon, Oxon: Routledge.

Smith, Ian. 2013. Othello's Black Handkerchief. *Shakespeare Quarterly* 64 (1): 1–25.

Smith, Henry. 1591. *A Preparative to Marriage*. London.

Sofer, Andrew. 2003. *The Stage Life of Props*. Ann Arbor, MI: University of Michigan Press.

Staub, Susan C. 2002. Bloody Relations: Murderous Wives in the Street Literature of Seventeenth Century England. In *Domestic Arrangements in Early Modern England*, ed. Kari Boyd McBride, 124–146. Pittsburgh, PA: Duquesne University Press.

Taylor, Gary, and Rory Loughnane. 2017. The Canon and Chronology of Shakespeare's Works. In *The New Oxford Shakespeare Authorship Companion*, ed. Gary Taylor and Gabriel Egan, 417–602. Oxford: Oxford University Press.

Tusser, Thomas. 1573. *Five Hundred Points of Good Husbandry*. London.

Weis, René, and Sarah Wintle. 1991. Macbeth and the Barren Sceptre. *Essays in Criticism* 41 (2): 128–146.

Whipday, Emma. 2015. "Marrow Prying Neighbours": Staging Domestic Space and Neighbourhood Surveillance in *Arden of Faversham*. *Cahiers Élisabéthains* 88 (1): 95–110.

Whipday, Emma. 2019. *Shakespeare's Domestic Tragedies: Violence in the Early Modern Home*. Cambridge: Cambridge University Press.

Whittle, Jane, and Mark Hailwood. 2017. *Women's Work in Rural England, 1500–1700*. https://earlymodernwomenswork.wordpress.com. Accessed 12 May 2017.

Wiesner, Merry E. 1993. *Women and Gender in Early Modern Europe*. New York: Cambridge University Press.

Williams, Gordon. 1994. *A Dictionary of Sexual Language and Imagery in Shakespearean and Stuart Literature*, vol. II. London: The Athlone Press.

Yachnin, Paul. 2002. Wonder Effects: Othello's Handkerchief. In *Staged Properties in Early Modern English Drama*, ed. Jonathan Gil Harris and Natasha Korda, 316–334. Cambridge: Cambridge University Press.

Ziegler, Georgianna. 1990. "My Lady's Chamber": Female Space, Female Chastity in Shakespeare. *Textual Practice* 4: 73–90.

CHAPTER 11

Children, Normality, and Domestic Tragedy

Emily O'Brien

> I pray thee, look thou giv'st my little boy
> Some syrup for his cold, and let the girl
> Say her prayers, ere she sleep.
> (Webster, *The Duchess of Malfi*, 4.2.201–203)

The Duchess's tender solicitations on behalf of her children in the moments before her death have intrigued critics, seeming to offer a poignant glimpse into the commonplace routines of domesticity and familial care at the centre of the tragedy. Judith Haber argues, however, that despite abundant reference to these lines, 'not enough attention is given to the disruptive force of their extraordinary ordinariness'.[1] In this chapter, focusing on domestic tragedy, I seek to attend to the 'disruptive force' wrought by child characters as they introduce moments of 'extraordinary ordinariness' onto the early modern stage. These plays have long been analysed from the perspective of their tragic innovation, with special attention given to the evocation of a familiar, recognisable, everyday world in which things go terribly wrong. The plays labour to stage a version of normality which they envision as central to their moral

---

E. O'Brien (✉)
Trinity College Dublin, The University of Dublin, Dublin, Ireland
e-mail: eobrien1@tcd.ie

© The Author(s) 2019
R. Loughnane and E. Semple (eds.), *Staged Normality in Shakespeare's England*, Palgrave Shakespeare Studies,
https://doi.org/10.1007/978-3-030-00892-5_11

applicability and ability to move the spectator. The role of children in helping to conjure this sense of disrupted normality, however, has been little explored. Through an analysis of Thomas Middleton's *A Yorkshire Tragedy*, this chapter begins the process of recovering the significance of child characters in domestic tragedy.[2]

The important presence of children in early modern dramatic culture is now well established. It is frequently noted that the study of the history of childhood has 'exploded' over the last half century, with consideration given to the 'rhetorical child' as well as the 'historical child'.[3] '[C]hildren were everywhere' in early modern society, in Peter Laslett's words, and they were a familiar sight on the adult stages as well as in the boys' companies.[4] Earlier critical assumptions about children's triviality have therefore given way to scholarship that demonstrates the crucial roles played by child characters on the early modern adult stage, despite the brevity of their parts.[5] However, this work is predominantly focused on Shakespeare; the children's parts of domestic tragedy, which may similarly seem minor at first glance, remain largely overlooked despite the increased attention the genre has attracted in recent decades. In fact, children are more numerous in domestic tragedy than one might at first realise, with speaking parts for young children in *A Warning for Fair Women*, *Two Lamentable Tragedies* and *A Yorkshire Tragedy*, and with thematic or symbolic resonance in a broader range of plays.[6]

Indeed, it is surprising that the role of children in domestic tragedy has not yet been subjected to sustained critical scrutiny, given the strong focus on the early modern family and household in analyses of the genre.[7] Of the existing criticism about children in these plays, as well as in the related forms of murder pamphlet and murder ballad, most has been concerned with the crime of infanticide, but even there analysis largely focuses on the actions of the perpetrators rather than on the child characters.[8] The fact that children are not primary characters in these plays and have little dialogue means that scholars have often overlooked their potential in performance.[9] Moreover, in domestic tragedy in particular, the children's convincing absorption into the everyday rhythms of the household represented in these plays—their apparent unremarkable normality—may itself contribute to their critical neglect. As Wendy Wall notes in relation to the passage opening this chapter, then, '[t]he Duchess's words might seem so familiar in their emotional register as to need no gloss at all'.[10] However, it is precisely this quality of familiarity that has been treated as a distinguishing feature of domestic tragedy.

Existing criticism on the genre has long examined its investments in representing on stage the contemporary world of the spectators. J. P. Collier, describing these plays as domestic tragedy for the first time in 1831, aligned them on the grounds that they were 'founded upon comparatively recent events in our own country', observing that:

> it seems to have been the constant practice of the dramatists of that day, to avail themselves (like the ballad-makers) of any circumstances of the kind, which attracted attention, in order to construct them into a play, often treating the subject merely as a dramatic narrative of a known occurrence, without embellishing, or aiding it with the ornaments of invention.[11]

While there is much in this account that might be debated, Collier's apprehension of how the plays' association with actuality more broadly informs their dramaturgical and theatrical character has been affirmed by subsequent generations of scholars, who have noted, like Martin White, the 'presentation of ordinary, virtually contemporary, men and women in a clearly-drawn English setting' that results in 'something different from the usual subject matter and milieu of Elizabethan tragedy'.[12] As later scholarship on 'dangerous familiars', 'place-specific topography', and the material culture of domesticity has shown, the artificial setting of the stage means that the suggestive normality performed in these plays is indeed not simply a question of omitting embellishment or, as Collier suggested, 'the ornaments of invention'.[13] Rather, it is something that must be actively brought into being and given meaning.

As Catherine Richardson notes, '[t]he construction of a sense of what is normal on stage is difficult [...] because it depends upon creating the illusion of something that has become invisible through familiarity and stability'.[14] In these plays, the figure of the child seems particularly effective in summoning a sense of domestic normality, against which the depiction of transgression is given meaning, emotional force, and didactic potential. This is necessary because, as Rory Loughnane argues, '[a]ctions such as murder, rape, revenge, thievery, adultery, and whoring were so often performed as to become generically conventional' on the early modern stage.[15] Consideration therefore needs to be given to those apparently unremarkable vignettes of normality centred around children that actually gain force from their ordinariness in domestic tragedy. What is the import in *A Warning for Fair Women*, for example, of a domestic moment in which a 'little sonne' looks for a snack only to be met by his mother's fond disbelief that 'sir sauce' could already be hungry again (B2^v)? Or of a scene in which this little boy and his friend play games of 'crosse and pile' at the door of his house, ignorant of his father's murder (F4^r)? Or indeed in *A Yorkshire Tragedy*, of the murderer's monologue of maniacal rage being interrupted by the entry of his '*little son with a top and a scourge*' (4.93.1), complaining that his father's 'wide legs' (4.96) are getting in the way of his game?

I want to argue here that these moments of domestic normality involving children serve to make legible the plays' representations of transgression; that they require detailed analysis to unlock their broader historical and rhetorical resonance; and, furthermore, that the tangle of normality and abnormality that attends the child characters' immersion in these contexts is part of the broader aesthetic and ethical project of domestic tragedy. These plays locate their power in their niche ability to deliver 'home-borne tragedies', both 'lamentable and true' (*A Warning*, K3^v; *A Yorkshire Tragedy*, title page), insisting that particular events can be universally significant, and the child characters—at once mimetic and emblematic—play an important role in this. They share traits with their better-studied peers in Shakespearean tragedy, including an association with innocence, suffering, candid speech, and childishness, but these traits gather special significance in relation to the genre of domestic tragedy, where the focus on the contemporary household also involves the emergence of a proto-realist mode of representation.[16] The remainder of this chapter analyses *A Yorkshire Tragedy* from this perspective, examining how its child characters help to produce the impression of disrupted normality which is central to the genre of domestic tragedy, and in which the plays locate their didactic power and pathos.

A Yorkshire Tragedy, acted by the King's Men at the Globe playhouse, seems to have been performed swiftly after the crime on which it is based took place, possibly in a compilation with three other unknown short plays.[17] The circumstances detailed in the plot would have been familiar to early audiences.[18] On 23 April 1605 Walter Calverley, a Yorkshire gentleman from an old and respected family, who had gambled away most of his fortune, attacked his family. He murdered two of his young sons, who were only three or four years old and eighteen months old at the time. He also intended to murder his wife, who survived with injuries, and his third child, a baby of six months old, who was unharmed because he was away with his wet-nurse. *A Yorkshire Tragedy* represents on stage the two boys who are murdered (the younger probably in the form of a

11 CHILDREN, NORMALITY, AND DOMESTIC TRAGEDY

doll), and makes reference to the offstage baby and his nurse. The play follows closely a pamphlet written about the case, entered in the Stationer's Register on 12 June 1605, even echoing its wording in many places.[19] The pamphlet account's level of detail, especially disturbing in its description of the movements of the injured children, is compressed in this extremely brief play, producing its distinctive impression of starkness and momentum, but the detail of the little boy playing with his toy is maintained.

In the astonishing first murder scene of *A Yorkshire Tragedy*, the Husband's tortured and angry reflections upon his debt and feelings of entrapment are interrupted by '*his little son*' who enters, as the stage direction notes, '*with a top and a scourge*' (4.93.1).[20] What follows is a collision of the normal and abnormal, where an ordinary domestic moment gives way to horrific violence:

> Son: What ail you, father, are you not well? I cannot scourge my top as long as you stand so. You take up all the room with your wide legs. Puh, you cannot make me afeard with this. I fear no visors nor bugbears.
> *Husband takes up the child by the skirts of his long coat in one hand and draws his dagger with th'other*
> Husband: Up, sir, for here thou hast no inheritance left.
> Son: O, what will you do, father? – I am your white boy.
> Husband: (*strikes him*) Thou shalt be my red boy. Take that!
> Son: O, you hurt me, father.
> Husband: My eldest beggar. Thou shalt not live to ask an usurer bread, to cry at a great man's gate, or follow 'good your honour' by a crouch, no, nor your brother.
> 'Tis charity to brain you.
> Son: How shall I learn now my head's broke?
> Husband: (*stabs him*)
> Bleed, bleed, rather then beg, beg. Be not thy name's disgrace.
> Spurn thou thy fortunes first if they be base.
> Come view thy second brother. Fates, my children's blood
> Shall spin into your faces; you shall see
> How confidently we scorn beggary. *Exit with his son.*
> (4.94–112)

The normality that the child represents, spinning his top and exuding touchingly confident ownership of his domestic space, provides the backdrop for the deep abnormality of the Husband's subsequent actions.

In this scene, then, the child character, embodied by a boy actor with a long skirt and toy, generates on stage the kind of productive glimpse of normality that is characteristic of domestic tragedy. This normality gives context to the extreme violence that follows, sharpening the horror of the transgression for an audience that might be jaded by the expected bloodiness of contemporary tragedy. The little boy's entry in the midst of the Husband's furious monologue about his depravity and dissolution is unexpected, but this surprise is in turn quickly engulfed by the much larger shock of his murder.

Richardson has demonstrated 'the centrality of the physical household' to this kind of play.[21] In this scene, the stage property of the spinning top is a vital part of its representation of disrupted normality, as a material artefact of domesticity associated with childhood. *A Yorkshire Tragedy* is distinctive among the domestic tragedies because it largely anonymises the events it represents—the characters are named as Husband, Wife, and Son in the play-text—and it eschews much of the particularising detail associated with the genre.[22] The minimalist quality of the play is highlighted by the disjuncture between the induction and the rest of it; this scene seems to be an addition which is incompatible with what follows.[23] As well as its named servant characters, the induction scene is notable for its comic invocation of a number of stage properties, as Sam returns *'furnished with things from London'* (1.16.1) including 'three / hats and two glasses [...] two rebato / wires [...] a capcase [...] a brush / [...] an almanac [...] and three ballads' (1.24–27). In contrast, the rest of the play is largely bereft of such domestic objects, making the inclusion of the child's toy even more significant and its role as a material signifier more prominent.[24]

The spinning top was a popular early modern toy that had been in existence for centuries.[25] In a recent archaeological find at a church in Market Harborough, England, two hundred toys thought to date from 1570 to 1630 came to light, of which eighty-nine were spinning tops.[26] These playthings must have been a familiar sight, evocative of childhood. In Thomas More's early *Pageant Verses*, the first image is of 'a boy playing at the top & / squyrge' (ll. 9–10). The verse reads 'I am called Chyldhod, in play is all my mynde [...] / A toppe can I set, and dryue it in his kynde' (ll. 12–14).[27] Toys seem to have been an unusual sight on the early modern stage, however; they 'are rarely mentioned in Shakespeare as artefacts to be played with by children' and there are no stage directions that name toys as stage properties for child characters in his plays.[28] The spinning top that the little son brings onto the stage in *A Yorkshire Tragedy* is both a generally recognisable emblem of childhood, and an object that is personal to the boy (perhaps with associations of loving gift-giving), who is therefore presented and established as an individual with his own pre-play past and culture. The normality that it encodes, then, derives both from the toy's status as something that invokes common experience, and as something that suggests a realistic, singular child character.

The stage directions in this scene are more detailed and prescriptive than in most of the play-text, and they especially emphasise the son's smallness and young age. Wearing a '*long coat*' with '*skirts*', the little boy is evidently presented as being below the age of breeching, which took place at about seven years old, and before which 'most of his time would have been spent with his mother, nurses, or other female servants' in the domestic sphere.[29] The stage direction records that the Husband '*takes up the child by the skirts of his long coat*' (4.97.1), while simultaneously drawing his dagger with the other hand. The flimsy vulnerability of the boy's little body is emphasised in the way that his father can pick him up single-handedly and hold him high enough that he is dangling by his clothes. This movement also accentuates the violence against the child. At the end of the scene, the stage direction reads '[*e*]*xit with his son*' (4.112.1). Fatally injured, the child must be carried from the stage by his father. These images of the father lifting and carrying his son, a familiar gesture that in another context would indicate care, also figure the dreadful transformation of normal fatherly behaviour that takes place in *A Yorkshire Tragedy*.

This episode in the play thus seems to draw on continuities between the young age of the character represented and the boy actor's childish body. While the historical counterpart of the son was little more than a toddler at the time of his death, and the play presents him as some age younger than seven, it is likely that the boy actor playing him would have been at least twelve years old.[30] However, the visual contrast in age and size between the child actor and the adult actors who surround him would nonetheless serve to mark out the character's young age and vulnerability. The theatrical effect of the boy actor in an adult company, therefore, has the potential to be quite different from that of the boy actor in a children's company. In performing adulthood, the children's company performances drew attention to the 'distance between actor and role' in order to 'foreground the discontinuous relationship between age and adult male status through their very constitution'.[31] 'Paradoxically', then, as Bart van Es observes, 'the children's companies struggled to depict children'.[32] In *A Yorkshire Tragedy*, in contrast, there is continuity between the aged identities of the character and actor, and the boy actor's authentically diminutive body becomes part of the convincing depiction of the child in his domestic space, consistent with the broader conventions of domestic tragedy.

That the son is especially young is also foregrounded in what he says and does in this scene. We are given his viewpoint when he complains from the eye level of a child that his father's 'wide legs' (4.96) are getting in the way of his game. As the scene lurches from the fleeting normality of the child's play to the Husband's violence, the boy continues to attempt to interpret what he is experiencing with a poignantly childish set of references. The dialogue suggests that the Husband grimaces at the child at this point, because the son scoffs at what he perceives to be a pretence of an angry face: 'Puh, you cannot make me afeard with this. I fear no visors nor bugbears' (4.96–97). While the father uses heightened and blustering language, the boy's responses are simple and ingenuous, invoking what Catherine Belsey describes as a 'traditional [...] contrast between simplicity and rhetorical elaboration' in relation to children's speech.[33] After being struck by his father's dagger, for example, the son exclaims 'O, you hurt me, father', and a little later asks, 'How shall I learn now my head's broke?' (4.102, 4.107). Still thinking about his lessons rather than death, he is uncomprehending of the severity of his situation, creating dramatic irony and increased tension as the audience alone understands what awaits him. We are thus forced to experience this scene in part from the perspective of the child, at the same time that we maintain a third-party sense of the child's vulnerability, deepening its pathos and horror.

The son's interaction with his father in this scene demonstrates his expectation of normal contact and implies that they had a loving relationship in the past. When he is attacked by his father, the son responds with frightened bewilderment and reminds him of their relationship in childish terms of affection, telling him that 'I am your white boy' (4.99). This plea for recognition by the son evokes for spectators past moments of normal intimacy between the two characters, as the child speaks words that we imagine his father has formerly said to him. His implicit trust in his knowledge of their relationship and of their past is doubly poignant because we are aware that the boy's future will be abruptly cut off.

Both are transformed through the Husband's violence as this potentially normal encounter between father and child is revealed to be deeply abnormal. The gruesome journey of the son from 'white boy' to 'red boy' exemplifies the broader action of the play, which frames the Husband's actions in terms of reversal, first as the prodigal type who has gone from promising to dissolute, and in the later suggestion that he has been possessed (even if this is ambiguous and stays in the realm of metaphor).

The fundamental dramatic principle of this scene is indeed juxtaposition: of the *'little son'* (4.93.1) and the looming Husband who 'take[s] up all the room' (4.95–96); of the playful and free movement of the child and the father's oppressive monologue; of the wholesomeness of the boy and the wickedness of the father; of simple and rhetorical speech; of the implicit affection in the son's words and the father's violence.[34] Underlying all of these juxtapositions is the child's connection with an everyday, domestic world and the father's disruption of this through murder. The son's characterisation is consistent with that of other early modern children in the drama in this respect; he is vulnerable, innocent, speaks with candour, and functions as a 'pathos intensifier', in Michael Witmore's formulation.[35] In this scene, then, the child briefly appears as a vibrant, fully drawn character, filling the stage temporarily with the material signifiers of childhood, speaking in a language that seems convincingly childlike, and displaying behaviour appropriate to the implied domestic space. A normal moment of family life is brought into being through his entry with his spinning top, and the individual boy becomes representative of the small, ordinary world that is shattered by the Husband's actions.

However, at the same time as being instantly comprehensible as a marker of normal childhood activity, the boy and his spinning top form an image that is potently figurative. This is consistent with the manner in which the proto-realist developments of domestic tragedy are equally replete with symbolic resonance. There is a hint of implied violence in the use of the whip to propel the spinning top, a connotation evident in other literary manifestations of the toy. In *Mundus et Infans*, after presenting his spinning top to the audience, the boy announces that he can also use his 'scourge-stick' to hit his playmates on the head (ll. 76–81). Nicholas Orme notes that spinning tops were sometimes linked to the season of Lent, speculating on whether 'this was an echo of the scourging of Jesus on Good Friday, or of the whipping of penitent sinners'.[36] In *The Duchess of Malfi*, the image of the toy sparks a similar set of associations when the Duchess tells Antonio 'I have seen my little boy oft scourge his top / And compar'd myself to't: naught made me e'er / Go right but heaven's scourge-stick' (3.5.79–81). In contrast, the reference to the spinning top in Shakespeare's *The Winter's Tale* draws rather upon its suggestive precariousness, as Leontes muses on whether or not Mamillius is his child:

> [...] If I mistake
> In those foundations which I build upon,
> The centre is not big enough to bear
> A schoolboy's top.
> (2.1.100–103)

The image emphasises the tiny point upon which the object rests when spinning, and the description of it as a 'schoolboy's top' accentuates its lightness and vulnerability, qualities that might then become imaginatively transferred to Mamillius, as well as expressing the fragility of patrilineal descent and the volatility that attends such fragility. The associations surrounding the spinning top in this passage of *The Winter's Tale* thus resonate with its figuring in *A Yorkshire Tragedy* as both fathers are consumed by doubts about the paternity of their children and their legacy.[37] In both cases, although the time frames and actions leading up to the ends differ greatly, the sons will end up dying at their fathers' hands. The starkest symbolism of the top in *A Yorkshire Tragedy* in performance, then, is probably the simple action of it falling over and stopping. The top must be in motion as the son enters the stage and must then be derailed by the father, foreshadowing the little boy's life prematurely ended.

This image also illustrates the central theme of *A Yorkshire Tragedy*: disruption to the family unit, especially in terms of its impact on lineage. The son is therefore thematically crucial to the play as a reminder of what it means that the family inheritance has been squandered, and this is how the father responds to him, as an abstract idea rather than as a human being. The representation of the boy is thus both mimetic and emblematic in nature, and the broader symbolic and affective resonance is here—characteristically for domestic tragedy—rooted in the naturalistic depiction of the son at play and in his father's jarringly abnormal response to him as impoverished heir rather than child. Ariane Balizet explains that '[b]ecause of the understanding that lineage is physically manifest in the blood or "bloodline," then as now, children were often described as literal extensions of a father's blood'.[38] Katie Knowles's argument that aristocratic boy characters in Shakespeare are identified as heirs *and* as 'individuated children', however, equally applies to the son in *A Yorkshire Tragedy*.[39] He is a powerless victim of terrible violence at the hands of an adult, but for a brief moment on the stage at least, the child character's own subjectivity dominates.

As *A Yorkshire Tragedy* progresses, and the child becomes more and more wounded and finally dies alongside his infant brother, there is a shift in his representation. The second murder scene opens with '*a Maid with a child in her arms, the Wife by her asleep*' (4.112.1). This younger son was most likely represented by a property doll or some other stage property, such as a blanket, that could stand in for a babe-in-arms.[40] As Richardson notes, this scene creates a closed domestic space for women and children.[41] Opening with the intimate view of the Maid talking to the infant, telling him that 'Nothing but misery serves in this house' (5.6) and shushing him to 'Sleep sweet babe' (5.1), the space is quickly invaded by the Husband, who is carrying the bleeding body of his still-conscious eldest son. He attacks the Maid and his wife, and kills his younger son. The eldest son's only line in this scene is that which confirms his subsequent silence: 'Mother, mother, I am killed, mother!' (5.15). These same words awaken his mother (notably described as such rather than as 'Wife' in the quarto stage direction here), who responds to the sight of her murdered children with moving terror: 'O me, my children! / Both, both, both bloody, bloody!' (5.16–17).

Infants on the early modern stage are unique in their status as both characters and stage properties.[42] In the scene above, the Maid's cradling of the stage property immediately characterises it as an infant.[43] It is instilled with affective power through its position in her arms and her soothing lullaby-lament, and then through the mother's dismay. At the same time, as Chedgzoy argues, 'an important part of the theatrical power of infancy lies in its capacity to elude [...] social specificity, so that representations of tiny babies often serve as screens on to which adults may project their own fears and longings'.[44] The infant is thus imbued with a special capacity for universality and immediacy, and here attracts the audience's sympathy and emotional identification. His murder in this scene—wrested from the Maid's arms, picked up by the mother, stabbed, and thrown down again—alongside that of his brother, may intertextually recall scenes depicting Herod's slaughter of the innocents in mystery cycles, in which babies are taken from the arms of their mothers and killed.[45] This is a key antecedent for the treatment of the events in *A Yorkshire Tragedy* and for scenes of child murder in early modern drama more widely, and playwrights may have drawn on their own memories of seeing mystery plays performed.[46] The Husband is a character in this mode as he exits with the intention of murdering his third and youngest son, 'my brat at nurse, my sucking beggar' (5.41). At the same time, the infant's situation in this scene brings into focus the broader network of affective relationships surrounding the children and evokes the domestic framework of the play's setting.

The representation of the children in this scene therefore replaces the function of the spatial detail of the pamphlet to some extent.[47] The account of the murder there is harrowing as it describes at length the action happening across several rooms and the staircase of the house as the father attempts to murder his family and the women and servants attempt to prevent him. In particular, the movements and positions of the children are recounted with appalling specificity. In this passage, the mother awakes in the midst of the attack:

> The child that was wounded was all this while crying in the chamber and with his woeful noise waked as woeful a mother, who, seeing one child bleeding, the other lie on the ground (for he had laid the younger down while he strove to throw the maid downstairs), she caught up the youngest, and going to take the elder which was going toward the door, her husband, coming back, met her and came to struggle with her for the child which she sought to preserve [...] And when he saw he could not get it from her, most remorseless, stabbed at it some three or four times, all which she saved the child from by taking it on herself. [...] But he, more cruel by this resistance, caught fast hold upon the child and in the mother's arms stabbed it to the heart. [...] The child which was first wounded sought to get to the door, and having recovered the top of the stairs, by expense of blood and the greatness of the wound, having nobody to comfort it, fell also downstairs.[48]

The play compresses the action of this scene but preserves the sense of struggle, particularly over the infant's body, which is mirrored in the hemisticomythia of the Husband and Wife's dialogue. The stage directions to *strive, throw, catch up, stab* and *get* are obviously informed by the pamphlet and insist on the scene's physicality (4.7.1–4.25). The fact that the role of the infant is not performed by an actor means that

11 CHILDREN, NORMALITY, AND DOMESTIC TRAGEDY 249

there is increased possibility for the staging of extreme violence here and, because the stage property representing the infant must be continually marked as a person through its interaction with those around it, it becomes especially emotionally charged.

Both sons die in this scene but they appear on stage again when their bodies are put on display in the final scene, at which point they seem less like characters in their own right than visual ciphers. The scene opens with the Husband passing his house on his way to prison. Asking permission to speak to his wife who is inside 'alive, but much endangered' (8.2), she enters '*brought in a chair*' (8.4.1). The Husband, now repentant, expresses his expectation that he will be executed for his crimes. As the Wife responds that 'Thou shouldst not, be assured, for these faults die / If the law could forgive as soon as I' (8.31–32), the stage direction indicates '*Children laid out*' (8.32.1). The children's bodies are either brought on stage or are revealed and the Wife describes to her Husband the sight of 'our two bleeding boys laid forth upon the threshold' (8.34). Their dead bodies thus displayed at the house in which they were murdered form a tableau that exposes the crime to the world and issues a warning to spectators, both within and beyond the play-world. The threshold offers a liminal space in which the events of the individual household can be publicised and given generalised homiletic significance, so that at this point the children span the particular and the universal. In this they recall the function of the (living) children in the final scenes of female repentance in *A Warning for Fair Women* and *A Woman Killed with Kindness*, in which the child characters are similarly abstracted and used to support a moral message relating to appropriate female behaviour, enacting the broader aesthetic and ethical project of domestic tragedy.

The characterisation of the Husband and Wife is likely informed by the Patient Griselda archetype and the children now seem subordinated to an instrumental function in the resolution of the marriage.[49] Early in the scene, the Husband responds to his Wife's (apparently endless) capacity to forgive him by finding that the Devil 'glides' from him (8.18). Seeing his children, he comments on their display in sentimental terms that evoke conventional ideas of witnessing a sad scene and kisses them, saying 'I'll kiss the blood I spilt, and then I go. / My soul is bloodied, well may my lips be so' (8.51–52). All of this seems to aestheticize the children's corpses, turning them into a mechanism for the Husband's repentance to be broadcast, and obscuring his responsibility for their deaths. Remarkably, the Wife in this scene tells her husband that '[u]nkindness strikes a deeper wound than steel' (8.12) and that she is more upset to lose him now '[t]han former sorrows made me' (8.62). Even when the Master of the College explicitly reminds her of the baby who has survived—'One joy is yet unmurdered. / You have a boy at nurse; your joy's in him' (8.63–8.64)—she entirely dismisses him. In fact, not even her dismissal makes reference to the surviving child. Instead the Husband's claims on her are foregrounded: 'Dearer than all is my poor husband's life' (8.65). Although the Wife has been exceptionally forbearing throughout the play, this statement nonetheless seems disquieting and at odds with her earlier reaction to her children's deaths, when she implored:

> Why do I now recover, why half live
> To see my children bleed before mine eyes? –
> A sight able to kill a mother's breast
> Without an executioner.
> (5.70–73)

The marital bond is now depicted as superseding the maternal bond, prioritising a Christian message of forgiveness rather than one of retribution. The Wife thus invites 'the melodramatic sympathy extended especially to obedient, suffering wives' that van Es observes in demotic and domestic dramas on the adult stage.[50] In this way, the children's corpses function differently from those in revenge tragedies, for example, where they act as reminders to carry out vengeance (*The Spanish Tragedy*) or as tools for vengeance (*The Revenger's Tragedy*), and instead provide the opportunity to emphasise the Wife's constancy towards her husband, even in these dire circumstances.

This scene seems to expect that spectators will be moved, both by the tableau of the children and by the resolution of husband and wife. Although it is hard to imagine that this coming together of the couple beside their murdered children's corpses could be anything other than ghastly, the Wife's behaviour would have been accepted by early modern spectators as an expression of idealised female sacrifice and wifely devotion, and the pathos of the scene is perhaps simply no longer culturally legible.[51] The Wife's claim in this scene that her husband's unkindness has hurt her more deeply than his dagger (8.12) might be interpreted as an attempt to air a generally applicable moral lesson for the play's audience, who have presumably not murdered their children, but who are probably guilty of more routine impatience and cruelty. Lynn Robson notes the Calvinist underpinnings of the providential scheme of early modern murder pamphlets, in which human sinfulness unfurls through a chain of events, each 'linked to the one before and the one after, "every linke depends and is inyoak'd upon one another [...] for Sloth is linked with drunkenness, with fornication and adultery, & adultery with Murder"'.[52] In this way, Calverley's attack on his family, with its implications of demonic possession, is understood to be rooted in more ordinary domestic dysfunction, the seeds of which are widespread and embedded in normal life. The normality of the little son, running onto the stage with his spinning top and childlike speech, has earlier established for the audience that tragedy can play out in contexts that seem removed from such extraordinary evil. The children now act as abstracted signs of that recognisable world, their bodies displayed as a didactic symbol of the ends of sin, and their victimisation curiously displaced as emphasis is shifted from the Husband's culpability to his remorse.

Middleton recognised in the pamphlet source for *A Yorkshire Tragedy* the dramatic potential of the small child who 'came into the gallery to scourge his top'.[53] The figure of the little son with his spinning top provides a dramatic shorthand for the ordinary and benign rhythms of domestic life which are threatened from within by the Husband, and invites the audience's recognition and sympathy. This chapter has contended that the 'extraordinary ordinariness' of such child characters in domestic tragedy deserves attention for its crucial role in producing the sense of disrupted normality that characterises the genre's innovations.[54] While *A Yorkshire Tragedy* abjures much of the particularising detail familiar in earlier instantiations of the genre, distilling the moral conflict, it nonetheless relies on the disarming experience of a familiar world being devastated by sin. Like other domestic tragedies, the play's moral and emotional potential derives from this bridging of the particular and the universal, crystallised in the figure of the child. The child's normality is produced both through his emblematic status as a representative of childhood in general, and through the mimetic verisimilitude of his characterisation as an individual boy. His infant brother also provides a focus for the audience's emotional investment and establishes the broader picture of household relationships in which the children live their lives, and which are fractured in the play.

Although largely overlooked in criticism, then, the children of domestic tragedy relate in a key way to the aesthetic that develops in the genre in which proto-realist elements emerge alongside melodramatic or allegorical modes of representation. I have noted that child characters in domestic tragedy share traits with those in Shakespeare's tragedies, and that it is on the adult stages that more life-like representations of children are found, rather than on the children's company stages. The relationship between the two might also be approached in terms of the influence of domestic tragedy on Shakespearean tragedy, however, with specific reference to the portrayal of children. Close analysis of the child characters in *A Yorkshire Tragedy* shows that they are fundamental to the broader inflection of tragedy evident in these domestic plays, then, but it has the potential equally to illuminate aspects of the mainstream tradition. I argued at the outset of this chapter that the children of domestic tragedy are overdue critical attention. In *A Yorkshire Tragedy*, such attention reveals these characters to be at the heart of the genre's capacity to conjure on stage a tragic vision of disrupted normality, animating the play's homiletic impulses, stimulating its artistic invention, and forming some of its most vivid and affecting moments of performance.

Notes

1. Haber (2009: 83).
2. Unless otherwise stated, references to *A Yorkshire Tragedy* are to the edition by Stanley Wells in *Thomas Middleton: Collected Works* (Taylor and Lavagnino 2007). References to Shakespeare are to *The New Oxford Shakespeare: Modern Critical Edition* (Taylor et al. 2016).
3. Ferraro (2012: 61) and Duane (2013: 15). For a summary of the historiography of early modern children, see also Griffiths (1996: 3–4), King (2007), and Campana (2011).
4. Laslett (1983: 119). While its boundaries were variously interpreted, childhood in early modern England was 'a stage of development occurring in the early years of a human life' as well as a 'category of cultural and ideological meaning' (Chedgzoy 2007: 22). See Lamb (2009) on 'age and childhood as cultural constructs' in relation to children's company players (2009: 7).
5. Piesse (2007), Rutter (2007), and Knowles (2012).
6. The London plot of *Two Lamentable Tragedies* features a young male servant who is murdered, and the Italian plot is a babes-in-the-wood story set in Italy, with the young son of the murderer playing a

prominent role. While *Arden of Faversham* notably does not include any staged child characters (if we exclude youthful figures like the bookseller's apprentice), the absence of children in the Ardens' marriage itself becomes a preoccupation that might be interpreted in terms of a 'patrilineal crisis' at the heart of the play (Martin 2001). In *A Woman Killed with Kindness*, Anne is removed from her children as part of her punishment, and they are reunited at the reconciliation scene before her death. The term 'domestic tragedy' has been understood to refer to plays based on true crimes such as *Arden of Faversham*, *A Warning for Fair Women*, *Two Lamentable Tragedies*, and *A Yorkshire Tragedy*, as well as others not based on true crimes, such as *A Woman Killed with Kindness*, *The English Traveller*, and *The Witch of Edmonton*. Critics have noted the immediacy of the plays' English settings and subject matter, the presence of middling characters, and the focus on the individual household. The term thus describes a shifting set of texts; on resultant difficulties, see White (1982: xvii).
7. Moreover, much of this work on the family has examined the ideology of patriarchy, which as Deborah Shuger points out is a 'cultural ideal' of fatherhood (1997: 219).
8. I am using infanticide to denote child murder, rather than its specific early modern legal meaning of the murder of a new-born baby (or concealment of its death). On infanticide, see Dolan (1994: Chapter 4) and Travitsky (1993).
9. Discussing children's parts in Shakespeare, Rutter contrasts their small number of lines with their far-reaching impact in performance where they 'achieve highest visibility' (2007: xviii).
10. Wall (2006: 150).
11. Collier (1831: 49–50).
12. White (1982: xvii).
13. Dolan (1994), Greenberg (2007: 20), and Richardson (2007).
14. Richardson (2005: 146).
15. Loughnane (2013: 10).
16. On traits associated with children in Shakespearean tragedy, see, for example, Blake (1993), Belsey (2007), and Scott (2017).
17. The title page header reads 'All's One, or, One of the foure Plaies in one, called a York-shire Tragedy'.
18. See Wells (2007: 452–455).
19. See Wells (2007: 453).
20. In the pamphlet, the child 'came into the gallery to scourge his top; and, seeing his father stand in a study, looked prettily up to him, saying, "How do you, father?"'. Transcription from *Two Unnatural Murders* (1605) in Appendix C of Sturgess (1969: 312).

21. Richardson (2007: 6).
22. The title, with its geographical detail, may not have been used in performance. On *All's One* as the performance title, see Kirwan (2015: 88–89).
23. See Wells (2007: 454).
24. One exception is 4.43.1, where the Husband and Master of the College are brought wine by a servant.
25. Orme (2001: 50) and Gray (2015: 25).
26. Corless (2013).
27. See also *Mundus et Infans* (76–81) and *The Merry Wives of Windsor* (5.1.19–20).
28. Chedgzoy (2007: 26–27). Of course, any object can potentially become a toy: 'children see a wide array of objects as potential playthings, and they often manipulate and imagine discarded or unused adult artifacts or natural objects as toys' (Baxter 2005: 42). Given the apparent scarcity of toys in the drama, it is interesting that the son and his friend in *A Warning for Fair Women* also play on stage, albeit in a game resembling heads and tails rather than with a purpose-built toy.
29. Munro (2017: 86).
30. Kathman (2005).
31. Munro (2007: 84).
32. van Es (2017: 117).
33. Belsey (2007: 37).
34. As Gary Taylor and Doug Duhaime suggest, the scene is characteristic of Middleton's tragic aesthetic (2017: 87).
35. Witmore (2007: 141).
36. Orme (2001: 54).
37. In *A Yorkshire Tragedy*, the Husband worries about his children's impoverishment as well as about them not being his own.
38. Balizet (2014: 90).
39. Knowles (2012: 6).
40. See Higginbotham (2013: 104).
41. Richardson (2007: 188).
42. Higginbotham (2013: 104).
43. Higginbotham argues that 'the only markers of the fictional infant's human status were the actions and words of the players' (2013: 104).
44. Chedgzoy (2007: 22).
45. Higginbotham notes that '[t]he use of counterfeit infants in drama had roots in medieval religious plays, particularly those that present Herod's slaughter of the innocents, such as the Towneley and Coventry cycles. In these plays, women have their babes-in-arms taken from them and murdered, and the early modern plays that continue the tradition of staging infanticide evoke pathos through the display of the children's vulnerability' (2013: 110).

46. Cawley and Gaines (1986: 5.15ff.n) and Blake (1993: 304).
47. In scenes 4 and 5, it seems that 'the action is imagined as occurring in an upper room' (5.0.1n), evidence of the pamphlet's influence on the play, but the spatial plotting seems to remain fairly ambiguous.
48. Cited in Sturgess (1969: 313).
49. On Patient Griselda as a dramatic type, see Comensoli (1996: 49–64).
50. van Es (2017: 102).
51. See Peter Kirwan's review of a 2010 production, where he notes that 'the stock figure of the virtuously suffering patient heroine [...] is foreign to the sensibility of a 21st-century audience' (2010: 165). This production did not display the children's bodies in the final scene and the son was played by a man.
52. Robson (2008: 295–296), quoting John Taylor, *The Unnaturall Father* (London 1621: sig. A3r, 296).
53. Transcription in Sturgess (1969: 312).
54. Haber (2009: 83).

Works Cited

Anon. 1599. *A Warning for Faire Women*. London: Valentine Sims for William Aspley.
Anon. 1608. *A Yorkshire Tragedy*. London: Thomas Pavier.
Anon. 2002. Mundus et Infans. In *Three Late Medieval Morality Plays*, ed. G.A. Lester. London: A & C Black.
Balizet, Ariane M. 2014. *Blood and Home in Early Modern Drama: Domestic Identity on the Renaissance Stage*. New York: Routledge.
Baxter, Jane Eva. 2005. *The Archaeology of Childhood: Children, Gender, and Material Culture*. Walnut Creek, CA: AltaMira Press.
Belsey, Catherine. 2007. Little Princes: Shakespeare's Royal Children. In *Shakespeare and Childhood*, ed. Kate Chedgzoy, Susanne Greenhalgh, and Robert Shaughnessy. Cambridge: Cambridge University Press.
Campana, Joseph. 2011. Shakespeare's Children. *Literature Compass* 8 (1): 1–14.
Cawley, A.C., and Barry Gaines (eds.). 1986. *A Yorkshire Tragedy*. Manchester: Manchester University Press.
Chedgzoy, Kate. 2007. Introduction: "What, Are They Children?". In *Shakespeare and Childhood*, ed. Kate Chedgzoy, Susanne Greenhalgh, and Robert Shaughnessy. Cambridge: Cambridge University Press.
Collier, J.P. 1831. *The History of English Dramatic Poetry to the Time of Shakespeare*. London: J. Murray.
Comensoli, Viviana. 1996. *Household Business: Domestic Plays of Early Modern England*. Toronto: University of Toronto Press.

Corless, Adrienne. 2013, February 16. A Hoard of 16th- and 17th-Century Children's Toys. *Irish Archaeology*. http://irisharchaeology.ie/2013/02/a-hoard-of-16th-and-17th-century-childrens-toys. Accessed 5 September 2017.

Dolan, Frances. 1994. *Dangerous Familiars: Representations of Domestic Crime in England, 1550–1700*. Ithaca: Cornell University Press.

Duane, Anna Mae. 2013. Questioning the Autonomous Subject and Individual Rights. In *The Children's Table: Childhood Studies and the Humanities*, ed. Anna Mae Duane. Athens, GA: University of Georgia Press.

Ferraro, Joanne M. 2012. Childhood in Medieval and Early Modern Times. In *The Routledge History of Childhood in the Western World*, ed. Paula S. Fass. Abingdon: Routledge.

Gray, Douglas. 2015. *Simple Forms: Essays on Medieval English Popular Literature*. Oxford: Oxford University Press.

Greenberg, Marissa. 2007. Signs of the Crimes: Topography, Murder, and Early Modern Domestic Tragedy. *Genre* 40 (1–2): 1–29.

Griffiths, Paul. 1996. *Youth and Authority: Formative Experiences in England, 1560–1640*. Oxford: Clarendon Press.

Haber, Judith. 2009. *Desire and Dramatic Form*. Cambridge: Cambridge University Press.

Higginbotham, Jennifer. 2013. *The Girlhood of Shakespeare's Sisters: Gender, Transgression, Adolescence*. Edinburgh: Edinburgh University Press.

Jackson, MacDonald P. 2014. *Determining the Shakespeare Canon: Arden of Faversham and A Lover's Complaint*. Oxford: Oxford University Press.

Kathman, David. 2005. How Old Were Shakespeare's Boy Actors? *Shakespeare Survey* 58: 220–246.

King, Margaret. 2007. Concepts of Childhood: What We Know and Where We Might Go. *Renaissance Quarterly* 60 (2): 371–407.

Kirwan, Peter. 2010. "If the Law Could Forgive as Soon as I": A Review of *A Yorkshire Tragedy* at the White Bear Theatre Pub, London, January 2010. *Law and Humanities* 4 (1): 162–168.

Kirwan, Peter. 2015. *Shakespeare and the Idea of the Apocrypha*. Cambridge: Cambridge University Press.

Knowles, Katie. 2012. Shakespeare's "Terrible Infants"?: Children in *Richard III, King John*, and *Macbeth*. In *The Child in British Literature: Literary Constructions of Childhood, Medieval to Contemporary*, ed. Adrienne E. Gavin. Basingstoke: Palgrave Macmillan.

Lamb, Edel. 2009. *Performing Childhood in the Early Modern Theatre: The Children's Playing Companies (1599–1613)*. Basingstoke: Palgrave Macmillan.

Laslett, Peter. 1983. *The World We Have Lost: Further Explored*, 3rd ed. London: Methuen.

Loughnane, Rory. 2013. Introduction: Stages of Transgression. In *Staged Transgression in Shakespeare's England*, ed. Rory Loughnane and Edel Semple. Basingstoke: Palgrave Macmillan.

Martin, Randall. 2001. "Arden Winketh at His Wife's Lewdness, & Why!": A Patrilineal Crisis in *Arden of Faversham*. Early Theatre 4: 13–33.
Middleton, Thomas. 2007. *Thomas Middleton: The Collected Works*, ed. Gary Taylor and John Lavagnino. Oxford: Clarendon Press.
More, Thomas. 1997. *The Complete Works of St. Thomas More*, vol. 1, ed. Anthony S.G. Edwards, Katherine Gardiner Rodgers, and Clarence H. Miller. New Haven and London: Yale University Press.
Munro, Lucy. 2007. *Coriolanus* and the Little Eyases: The Boyhood of Shakespeare's Hero. In *Shakespeare and Childhood*, ed. Kate Chedgzoy, Susanne Greenhalgh, and Robert Shaughnessy. Cambridge: Cambridge University Press.
Munro, Lucy. 2017. Speaking Like a Child: Staging Children's Speech in Early Modern Drama. In *Childhood, Education and the Stage in Early Modern England*, ed. Richard Preiss and Deanne Williams. Cambridge: Cambridge University Press.
Orlin, Lena Cowen. 1994. *Private Matters and Public Culture in Post-Reformation England*. Ithaca: Cornell University Press.
Orme, Nicholas. 2001. Child's Play in Medieval England. History Today 51 (10): 49–55.
Piesse, A.J. 2007. Character Building: Shakespeare's Children in Context. In *Shakespeare and Childhood*, ed. Kate Chedgzoy, Susanne Greenhalgh, and Robert Shaughnessy. Cambridge: Cambridge University Press.
Richardson, Catherine. 2005. Properties of Domestic Life: The Table in Heywood's *A Woman Killed with Kindness*. In *Staged Properties in Early Modern English Drama*, ed. Jonathan Gil Harris and Natasha Korda. Cambridge: Cambridge University Press.
Richardson, Catherine. 2007. *Domestic Life and Domestic Tragedy in Early Modern England*. Manchester: Manchester University Press.
Robson, Lynn. 2008. "Now Farewell to the Lawe, Too Long Have I Been in Thy Subjection": Early Modern Murder, Calvinism and Female Spiritual Authority. Literature and Theology 22 (3): 295–312.
Rutter, Carol Chillington. 2007. *Shakespeare and Child's Play: Performing Lost Boys on Stage and Screen*. London: Routledge.
Scott, Charlotte. 2017. Incapable and Shallow Innocents: Mourning Shakespeare's Children in *Richard III* and *The Winter's Tale*. In *Childhood, Education and the Stage in Early Modern England*, ed. Richard Preiss and Deanne Williams. Cambridge: Cambridge University Press.
Shakespeare, William. 2016. *The New Oxford Shakespeare: Modern Critical Edition*, ed. Gary Taylor, John Jowett, Terri Bourus, and Gabriel Egan. Oxford: Oxford University Press.
Shuger, Deborah. 1997. *Habits of Thought in the English Renaissance: Religion, Politics and the Dominant Culture*. Toronto: University of Toronto Press.

Sturgess, Keith (ed.). 1969. *Three Elizabethan Domestic Tragedies: Arden of Faversham, A Yorkshire Tragedy, A Woman Killed with Kindness.* Harmondsworth: Penguin.

Taylor, Gary, and Doug Duhaime. 2017. Who Wrote the Fly Scene (3.2) in *Titus Andronicus?*: Automated Searches and Deep Reading. In *The New Oxford Shakespeare: Authorship Companion*, ed. Gary Taylor and Gabriel Egan. Oxford: Oxford University Press.

Taylor, Gary, and John Lavagnino (eds.). 2007. *Thomas Middleton: Collected Works.* Oxford: Clarendon Press.

Taylor, Gary, and Rory Loughnane. 2017. The Canon and Chronology of Shakespeare's Works. In *The New Oxford Shakespeare: Authorship Companion*, ed. Gary Taylor and Gabriel Egan. Oxford: Oxford University Press.

Travitsky, Betty S. 1993. Child Murder in English Renaissance Life and Drama. *Medieval & Renaissance Drama in England* 6: 63–84.

van Es, Bart. 2017. Shakespeare Versus Blackfriars: Satiric Comedy, Domestic Tragedy, and the Boy Actor in *Othello.* In *Childhood, Education and the Stage in Early Modern England*, ed. Richard Preiss and Deanne Williams. Cambridge: Cambridge University Press.

Wall, Wendy. 2006. Just a Spoonful of Sugar: Syrup and Domesticity in Early Modern England. *Modern Philology* 104 (2): 149–172.

Webster, John. 2009. *The Duchess of Malfi*, 2nd ed., ed. John Russell Brown. Manchester and New York: Manchester University Press.

White, Martin (ed.). 1982. Introduction. In *Arden of Faversham.* London: Benn.

Witmore, Michael. 2007. *Pretty Creatures: Children and Fiction in the English Renaissance.* Ithaca: Cornell University Press.

CHAPTER 12

Feminine Transgression and Normal Domesticity

Stephen Guy-Bray

It is the custom to classify Renaissance plays into various categories of genre: histories, romances, tragicomedies, Roman plays, citizen comedies, and so on. Most of these categories do not stand up to careful scrutiny, however. Just using Shakespeare's plays, we could ask why *Julius Caesar* is not considered a history play, for example, or why *The Two Noble Kinsmen* is not considered a tragedy. The most interesting classification might be 'domestic tragedy.' This is a term rarely applied to any of Shakespeare's plays, although in their different ways *Othello*, *King Lear*, *Hamlet*, and *Macbeth* are all tragedies which focus upon the domestic sphere. In this generic tag, however, the household referred to is understood to be a normal English household in the Renaissance. Even leaving aside the question of what that normal household in any age would look like, we can see that an obvious problem is that the domestic arrangements in *Arden of Faversham* or *A Woman Killed with Kindness* may seem no less strange to us now than those depicted in the famous tragedies I mentioned above. Nevertheless, the idea that 'domestic tragedies'

S. Guy-Bray (✉)
University of British Columbia, Vancouver, BC, Canada
e-mail: Stephen.Guy-Bray@ubc.ca

© The Author(s) 2019
R. Loughnane and E. Semple (eds.), *Staged Normality in Shakespeare's England*, Palgrave Shakespeare Studies,
https://doi.org/10.1007/978-3-030-00892-5_12

present what the contemporary audience would have seen as a familiar space may be useful. By analyzing *Arden of Faversham* and *The Duchess of Malfi*, I want to look at the ways in which the association between female transgression and what is often conceived as a safe and female space may be especially troubling.

Despite its setting in a foreign and Catholic country, *The Duchess of Malfi* depends on a solid domestic foundation, one that—*mutatis mutandis*—would not seem out of place in the England of the time. From the beginning, Webster encourages us to make connections between the home and the state of which it is part. Indeed, at the very beginning of the play's opening scene, Antonio, newly returned from France, explicitly links national and domestic order in his speech to his friend Delio:

> In seeking to reduce both state and people
> To a fixed order, their judicious king
> Begins at home.
> (1.1.5–7)[1]

The reforms intended to transform the nation must be based in the home, even if that home is the highly unusual home we call a royal palace and court. As Antonio goes on to say, the king has considered

> that a prince's court
> Is like a common fountain whence should flow
> Pure silver drops in general; but if't chance
> Some cursed example poison't near the head,
> Deathdeath and diseases through the whole land spread.
> (1.1.11–15)

As I will show, the connection between domestic and political order will turn out to be crucial for *The Duchess of Malfi* as a whole; in that play, the inability to create a safe domestic space brings about the eventual tragedy.

In the rest of this long first scene, what we initially see is a strong, if implicit, contrast between France and Calabria, as both Ferdinand, the Duke, and his brother, the Cardinal, the representatives of Calabria, are described as corrupt, the immoral centre of a diseased state. They are condemned first by Bosola (1.1.48 et seq.) and then at greater length by Antonio himself (1.1.150–179). What both stress is that Ferdinand and the Cardinal are extremely susceptible to flatterers and parasites. Speaking of Ferdinand, Delio concludes that

> the law to him
> Is like a foul black cobweb to a spider:
> He makes it his dwelling and a prison
> To entangle those shall feed him.
> (1.1.170–173)

While the French king's home establishes a moral norm that can be imitated by his subjects, Ferdinand's 'dwelling' poisons the realm as a whole.

Ferdinand's corrupt court is not the only domestic setting in the first scene, however. Increasingly, Webster stresses the Duchess's household as well, both in his choice of settings and in his choice of characters and his focus on their domestic offices. For one thing, both Bosola and Antonio are her domestic officers: Antonio is her steward and Bosola, at Ferdinand's request (1.1.204–210), becomes her provisor of horse. And crucially, it is within this domestic space that the Duchess proposes to Antonio and that the two of them become husband and wife. It is highly significant for my purposes here that the two are married in the house with the Duchess's woman Cariola as their only witness. As the Duchess remarks, 'I have heard lawyers say, a contract in a chamber / *Per verba de presenti* is absolute marriage' (1.1.463–464).[2] This is certainly a prudent choice, as the Duchess could not have publicly been married to her own steward. But it is also important in terms of the modern generic classification of the play as a domestic tragedy. This marriage presents the household as a place that is a refuge in a way that is certainly not unusual, but it also presents the household as a place with authority, a place that has the power to transform people's lives. If the Duchess and Antonio are not merely lovers but also married, and if that marriage has legal standing outside the household, then the household itself is not just a sanctuary from a hostile and corrupt world, but also, perhaps, a real alternative to that world.

That, at least, is what they hope: the play does not cooperate and eventually becomes the kind of tragedy that is now taken as characteristic of the Jacobean period. But it is important to remember that the violent events that end *The Duchess of Malfi* are set up by the domestic happiness of much of the play. Surveying the play as a whole, we may chiefly remember the generic conventions of tragedy, but the experience of reading or seeing it is different. One of the most surprising aspects of this experience is the extraordinary scene with the Duchess, Antonio, and Cariola in 3.2, a scene that Garrett A. Sullivan has argued may be 'the most convincing and touching scene of affective relations in all of Jacobean tragedy'; I cannot think of another.[3] The scene may be overshadowed by the fact that just after it Ferdinand bursts in and threatens his sister, but Webster's decision to show this intimacy should not be seen as inconsequential.

Significantly, the danger to the Duchess and Antonio (and to their children) that erupts in this scene comes principally from Bosola, who is himself a member of the household and who is clever enough to figure out that the Duchess is pregnant, but not to figure out who the father of her child is. Both he and the Duchess's brothers assume that the child is illegitimate. In part this is because a clandestine marriage seems improbable, but it is also because they cannot imagine that she has access to men of the same rank or that a marriage could be a love match. The marriage we do see in Act II (and it is clearly significant that we see the husband and wife in this marriage separately) is between the old man Castruchio and his wife, Julia, who is the Cardinal's mistress—an affair that is both adulterous and a violation of the celibacy demanded of Roman Catholic priests. Conforming to English national prejudices about the immorality of Italians and of Catholics in general, this adultery seems to illustrate normal behaviour in the society in which the play is set. Adultery is thereby normalized in this Roman Catholic context; nevertheless, Webster has given us a picture of true marital intimacy.

That the Duchess might have found a husband on her own initiative seems literally unthinkable to almost all the people around her, a point that is demonstrated more than once in the third act. Just as the second act took place at least nine months after the first, so the passage of time between the second and third acts has been at least long enough to allow for the birth of a second son and a daughter. The unusual expansiveness of the play's time scheme is one of its distinguishing features and, among other things, helps to underline the duration and the everyday quality of the marriage. There has been a good deal of critical commentary on these gaps; perhaps most interesting for my purposes here is Emily C. Bartels's suggestion that the gaps 'dramatically underscore the duchess's unprecedented freedom.'[4] While a gap of a couple of years is unusual for a play it seems to be unremarkable to this play's characters: to some extent, the play takes place in the normal, extended time of family life rather than in the highly-compressed time of dramatic representation. As well, I would argue that this unremarkable quality is stressed by the casual representation of the reunion between Antonio and Delio at the beginning of the third act, two old friends: in other words, this violation of dramatic form could remind us of the artificiality of drama in exactly the same way that the normality of the Duchess's marriage could remind us of the rules that appear to govern Italian society, here presented in typically English fashion as corrupt and immoral.

Webster's point throughout much of the play is that the Duchess's marriage is invisible to most of the people who surround her, almost hiding in plain sight. In the first scene of the third act Antonio confides to Delio that her subjects, who know of or suspect the existence of the children, see her as immoral and Antonio as corrupt,

> for other obligation
> Of love or marriage between her and me
> They never dream of.
> (3.1.35–37)

The only narrative the subjects have to make sense of the situation is a scandalous tale of the unregulated lusts of a widow, a narrative familiar from much Renaissance literature.[5] That the much simpler narrative of a man and a woman falling in love and marrying—a narrative that might seem drearily normal and predictable to us—is apparently inconceivable to virtually all of the play's characters shows that in *The Duchess of Malfi* the normal as we see it has no place, or at least not a lasting one. While the class difference between the Duchess and Antonio is important here, I would argue that this is also part of a larger inability to conceive of female agency.

When Ferdinand bursts in on the Duchess he shows that he, like the Duchess's subjects, cannot imagine that marriage is the explanation for his sister's behaviour. Webster underlines the point by having Ferdinand suggest a husband for her. What happens after he surprises the Duchess in the next scene and accuses her of having a lover is even more telling. After the Duchess, drawing on what we could call a common-sense conception of normal life, plaintively asks 'Why might I not marry? / I have not gone about in this to create / Any new world or custom'

(3.2.109–11), Ferdinand retorts that 'thou has ta'en that massy sheet of lead / That hid thy husband's bones, and folded it / About my heart' (3.2.112–114). Ferdinand's comments demonstrate that for him the implications of the Duchess's marriage chiefly concern him: the norm at this time, at least among families at the top of the social scale, was that marriage was a crucial part of the life of the family and, like the other parts of this life, was under the control of the male head of the family.

In stark contrast to his view, the Duchess's comment gestures towards another norm. For her, marriage is perhaps the most usual and even quotidian part of her life. Her marriage to Antonio, which appears to inspire horror in almost all the play's characters (a horror that eventually results in the death of many of them), is for her not something that separates her from everyone—as her brothers believe—but rather something that connects her to the world in which she lives. In marrying and having children, the Duchess makes her court into a home that resembles households all over her realm and fulfills the duty of procreation seen as one of a wife's chief duties. Nevertheless, she recognizes the practical importance of concealment. After the detection of her clandestine marriage, the Duchess comes up with a plan in which she will accuse Antonio of embezzlement as a way of hiding her connection to him. She describes her plan to Antonio with a telling allusion:

> I must now accuse you
> Of such a feignèd crime as Tasso calls
> *Magnanima mensogna*, a noble lie.
> (3.2.176–178)

The allusion is to Tasso's epic *Gerusalemme Liberata*, where a character plans to shield her fellow Christians from persecution by the Muslims in Jerusalem. The situation in Tasso's epic is analogous to the Duchess's (at least, according to the Christian standards of the day) in that in both cases there is a strong contrast between a virtuous minority and a wicked society: abnormality is normal, and thus to tell a lie in this iniquitous context can be the virtuous course of action.

One sign of this inversion of standards can be seen in Webster's peppering throughout the second half of *The Duchess of Malfi* of scenes of insanity with readily-recognizable proverbs (usefully italicized in the Norton edition) and scenes of insanity. Proverbs are part of a common stock of wisdom and suggest that life can be understood and that general patterns apply, as for instance when Bosola suggests that the Duchess is unhappy because of her rank: '*Glories, like glow-worms, afar off shine bright, / But looked to near have neither heat nor light*' (4.2.133–134). This statement is singularly unhelpful to the Duchess as it does not apply to her situation, but it is helpful to us, as in its failure to apply to her it suggests the discrepancy between individual experience and general attempts to make sense of this experience. Her unhappiness is not due to her rank, but rather to what others (including Bosola) think is appropriate behaviour for this rank. In using a common proverb, Bosola seeks to elide his own culpability. On the other hand, insanity, at least in the context of Renaissance England, gives us a society that seems completely abnormal but that has many disturbing connections to our lives. The connection between the two is clearest near the end of the play when the Doctor speaks of a man who said that he was a wolf: 'only the difference / Was, a wolf's skin was hairy on the outside, / His on the inside' (5.2.16–18). The idea that we are all wolves—and here a proverb, the famous Latin one that says '*homo homini lupus*', is certainly applicable—but that our lupine nature may be disguised, neatly epitomizes the world of the play, in which anything may be considered either normal or abnormal and boundaries of all sorts seem permeable.

With its high body count, the ending of *The Duchess of Malfi* adheres to what we might expect from Jacobean tragedy. What is unusual about the ending, however, is Delio's appeal to the survivors in the play's last speech:

> Let us make noble use
> Of this great ruin, and join all our force
> To establish this young hopeful gentleman
> In's mother's right.
>   (5.5108–5111)

As we have already been informed that the Duchess had a son by her first marriage, her son by Antonio could not be his mother's heir. Thus, as Michelle M. Dowd points out in her discussion of this plot detail, the play 'ends with a succession narrative that seems blatantly to defy the norms of patrilineality.'[6] In her analysis, the identification of Antonio's son as his mother's heir is not an authorial error or abandoned intention but rather 'part of a larger process in which bloodline is actively constructed to be a social, thematic, and dramaturgical problem.'[7] One of the main norms propping up Renaissance society was patrilineal descent. Dowd's analysis allows us to see that just as the Duchess's marriage, which is in many ways very normal, is the strangest thing in the world in which the play takes place, so too the unremarkable idea that a son would inherit his mother's possessions is an idea that could change that society fundamentally.

In contrast to *The Duchess of Malfi*, *Arden of Faversham* takes place in rural England, not far from London, and among characters that are—more or less—drawn from the middle ranks of society and that we see in private rather than public life. These are the reasons for its categorization as a domestic tragedy, and we are presumably intended to expect a normal and familiar setting. In fact, the play itself makes this claim in the Epilogue, delivered by Arden's friend Franklin. After briefly and efficiently summarizing the fates of most of the other characters, he ends with an appeal to the audience:

> Gentlemen, we hope you'll pardon this naked tragedy
> Wherein no filèd points are foisted in
> To make it gracious to the ear or eye;
> For simple truth is gracious enough
> And needs no other points of glozing stuff.
> (Epilogue. 14–18)[8]

These lines are a tissue of lies. Although the dramatist(s) followed the account of the murder in Holinshed's *Chronicles* to a considerable degree, there is still much rearranging, addition, and subtraction. What is more, a good deal of the play is in noticeably formal language.

While classical allusions are rare, much of *Arden of Faversham* (including most of the important speeches) is written in highly polished blank verse, including some of the speeches of lower-class characters. The gap between the protestations of simple truth and the artificial poetry of a good deal of the dialogue is a useful indication of the gap between what is normal theatrically and what is normal in the real life that the epilogue stakes a claim to represent.

I would argue that this gap is not created at the end of the play by Franklin's inaccurate characterization of the play, but is instead a fundamental part of the play from the beginning. *Arden of Faversham* does not take place in a stable and well-ordered world that is disrupted by the actions of an immoral woman—a point of view enforced by the play's full title (see Note 8), with its emphasis on Alice's wickedness and its punishment—but rather in a society characterized by violent upheavals.[9] As the play begins, Franklin tries to cheer up Arden with good news:

> My gracious Lord the Duke of Somerset
> Hath freely given to thee and to thy heirs,
> By letters patent from his majesty,
> All the lands of the Abbey of Faversham.
> (i.2–5)

This is indeed good news for Arden, but obviously bad news for the monks who lived at the abbey before the dissolution of the monasteries; without necessarily suggesting any sympathy for Roman Catholicism on the part of the dramatists,[10] we might also note the contrast between the collective community of a great monastic house and the individualism of a rising man like Arden.[11] Indeed, Garrett A. Sullivan has suggested that the play shows some nostalgia for the old days: 'the play [...] looks backward longingly to ideologies (nearly) lost.'[12] While the old days are not described in any detail, there is a strong suggestion that the play takes place in a somewhat anarchic time.

In any case, these opening lines present the world of the play as one characterized by momentous changes not only to the distribution of assets but also to the organization of society itself. Unsurprisingly, Arden himself does not see things this way. The sadness noticed by Franklin is caused by Alice's adultery with Mosby, whom Arden, with class bias, scornfully describes as:

> A botcher, and no better at the first,
> Who, by base brokage getting some small stock,
> Crept into service of a nobleman,
> And by his servile flattery and fawning
> Is now become the steward of his house,
> And bravely jets it in his silken gown.
> (i.25–30)

Although Arden describes himself as 'by birth a gentleman of blood' (i.36), the parallel between himself and Mosby is clear to us, if perhaps not to him or to Franklin. The profound upheavals of this period—changes that have made Arden a rich landowner—have also lifted

Mosby from a humble artisan to a richly dressed and important person. Whatever the value of this passage as historical commentary, it is certainly the case that we are being introduced to a world in which personal qualities and connections can lead to profound alterations in the social hierarchy.

Arden is offended by Mosby's presumption in wearing a silken gown, but his worst offence clearly lies in his presumption in taking Arden's wife: 'on his finger did I spy the ring / Which at our marriage day the priest put on' (i.17–18). To Arden, the appropriation of the ring that symbolizes his marriage is an unambiguous outrage. In her first soliloquy, however, Alice sees the matter very differently:

> Sweet Mosby is the man that hath my heart;
> And he usurps it, having nought but this,
> That I am tied to him by marriage.
> Love is a god, and marriage is but words;
> And therefore Mosby's title is the best.
> Tush! Whether it be or no, he shall be mine
> In spite of him, of Hymen, and of rites.
>
> (i.98–104)

The ambiguity of the antecedent for 'he' in line 99 is important: in this context, Alice clearly means to refer to Arden, but Arden's own view (which is obviously the established view of marriage as well) is that Mosby, the adulterer, is the usurper. There is a similar ambiguity in the last line quoted: Alice again means Arden when she says 'him,' but grammatically, the pronoun initially appears to indicate Mosby.

These pronoun ambiguities should not be taken either as evidence of Alice's confusion or as evidence of problems in the writing or transmission of the play. Instead, they are characteristic of the uncertainties and shifts that are normal in the world in which *Arden of Faversham* takes place. Just as both Arden and Mosby can be lifted above the rank in which they were born and thus the social hierarchy is revealed to be neither fixed nor stable, so Alice regards marriage itself—a bond typically seen as one of the basic constituents of the state[13]—as something that can be altered, even as something that one person can end simply through her own volition. In this speech, Alice refers contemptuously to the marriage ceremony as 'but words' and as 'rites' and indicates that she does not intend to be bound by them, although these particular words are often seen as the single best example of performative utterance in the language and the marriage rite itself has often been considered to be one of the most important events of a woman's life. To her, however, these words that simultaneously bring together and demonstrate the power of both the state and the church are merely words.

The dissolution of the monasteries and the introduction of divorce with which it was connected were developments that took place only a few years before the time in which the play is set (the murder took place in 1551, during the Protestant reign of Edward VI). *Arden of Faversham*'s references to both of these developments so early on stress our sense of the period as one characterized by rapid shifts and by the undermining of central institutions that had been thought to underpin what we could call normal social life. Alice's elevation of elective bonds over the bonds ratified by the state and the church is her version of the social mobility exemplified by her husband and by Mosby. The play thus takes place within a culture where the desires and ambitions of the individual may be seen to override those institutions like marriage and the social hierarchy that are intended to provide social stability. The important connection between these institutions is underlined by Alice's use of 'title' to refer to Mosby's claim to her: the word also refers to the honorifics given to high-status individuals, like the Duke of Somerset, and to the documents that indicate who owns land, documents that are especially significant in the case of valuable land like the Abbey of Faversham.[14]

Arden, Alice, and Mosby all inhabit the shifting terrain that the play presents. They are not alone in this, however. Later in the opening scene we learn that Arden's possession of the abbey lands is itself a dispossession of Greene, who comes on stage to tell Alice that he has learnt that the grant of the lands to Arden means 'that all former grants / Are cut off, whereof I myself had one' (i.461–462). Alice confirms this when she tells Greene that

> the lands are his in state,
> And whatsoever leases were before
> Are void for terms of Master Arden's life.
> (i.465–467)

It is not surprising that Arden's wealth comes at the expense of another man's, but even by this early point in the play, it seems clear that his own tenure may be insecure. The insecurity of this possession is emphasized by the fact that Mosby has already claimed to Arden that Greene offered him the lands (i.293–295). The possession of the abbey and its lands by the monastic institution, a possession that had lasted for centuries, has been revoked not once but twice, and perhaps even more times than that. A system that would once have appeared to be immutable has been replaced by a system that is constantly changing.

Alice's response to Greene's complaint is to offer him sympathy and then to present herself as an unfortunate woman mistreated by her cruel husband. When Greene takes the bait and offers to kill her husband himself, Alice gives him advice on how to do it: 'Endanger not yourself for such a churl, / But hire some cutter for to cut him short' (i.520–521). Nor is her advice limited to this practical tip, as she also offers him material inducements:

> Here's ten pound to wager them [i.e., the hired assassin] withal.
> When he is dead, you shall have twenty more;
> And the lands whereof my husband is possessed
> Shall be intitled as they were before.
>
> (i.522–525)

Even by this early point in the play, it is clear that Alice cannot possibly pay all the debts she incurs in her efforts to have her husband killed. In speaking with Mosby, for instance, she has spoken of her husband's wealth as 'the goods that shall be thine' (i.222) and only Greene could be naïve enough to think that he will get the abbey lands back. Moreover, in her efforts to ensure her husband's death Alice has promised Mosby's sister Susan to both Michael and Clarke.

It might seem reasonable to blame the difficulties that will inevitably arise from Alice's promises in this opening scene on her own faults of character, and the dramatist clearly intends us to see her as a woman who is unstable—as her irreconcilable promises to the men she wants to kill her husband demonstrate—as well as immoral. Nevertheless, Alice's view of marriage as something that can easily be abandoned and that depends on personal volition might seem like a natural response to the shifting nature of the society in which she lives. Similarly, her role in drawing together several people who apparently were not previously connected in any meaningful way and in drawing them together for an evil purpose can be seen as a microcosm of the workings—always at least potentially malevolent—of a society composed of individuals seeking their own personal gain. *Arden of Faversham* is a play in which society as early modern audiences might have conceived of it seems barely to exist. Although social class is central to the play—and thus the play could be said to give us a social hierarchy to that extent—there is almost no sense of hierarchy beyond the personal interactions that fill the play. That is, there seems to be very little in the way of an overarching structure (governmental or ecclesiastical or even financial) that binds together all the characters. Alice is arguably the main character in the play, and the play's full title focuses on her particular wickedness, but in her instability and deceit and in her desire to dissolve and reform relationships she seems to be a representative figure: the rule rather than the exception.[15] Although she is intended to appear especially wicked, her belief that existing relationships of all sorts can be dissolved at will seems an understandable response to what the play depicts as the state of affairs in mid-sixteenth century England.

Alice's adultery is a transgression that is an enduringly popular topic of literature, but the play also stresses the breaking of a bond that is now hardly thought of: the bond between master and servant. Arden's servant Michael is one of the most important characters in the play: he even (unusually for a servant) has soliloquies, in which his language is noticeably formal for a lower-class character. He is introduced in the first scene, chiefly so that Alice can promise that he will have Mosby's sister, but his most important appearances are in the third and fourth scenes. The third scene ends with a soliloquy in which Michael summarizes what he knows of the plot against Arden and speaks of his own place in this plot. We might expect a soliloquy in which Michael wrestles with his conscience, but he appears to be rather untroubled:

> Ah, harmless Arden, how, how hast thou misdone
> That thus thy gentle life is levelled at?
> The many good turns that thou hast done to me
> Now must I quittance with betraying thee.
> (iii.195–198)

The beginning of the lines suggests that Michael will show remorse, but the 'must' of line 198 does not indicate that he feels constrained by his loyalty. As the soliloquy continues, more signs of internal conflict appear. Michael contrasts what he knows to be his duty with what he plans to do:

> I, that should take the weapon in my hand
> And buckler thee from ill-intending foes,
> Do lead thee with a wicked, fraudful smile,
> As unsuspected, to the slaughterhouse.
> (iii.199–202)

In the course of this soliloquy, Michael gives as the reason for his actions the fear that if he protects his master he will be killed and the speech ends with a statement of his decision to persist: 'I am resolved, and Arden needs must die' (iii.209). What is surprising here is not this decision, but rather the remarkably flat affect of what should be a dramatic representation of a man torn between two opposing courses of action. But what seems most significant is that the soliloquy demonstrates that Michael knows the norms of society, according to which a servant should risk his own life in his master's service, and the norms of theatrical practice, in which a soliloquy should feature a dramatic conflict of some sort, but is unable either to be a faithful servant or to deliver a properly dramatic soliloquy. Alice's speeches have clearly demonstrated the dramatist's ability to write effective soliloquies, and so Michael's failure is his failure as a character, rather than the dramatist's. He assembles the materials for the speech he should give, but he cannot capitalize on them. The norms of society (and of the theatre) are known to him, but they have apparently ceased to have any real meaning.

This, at least, is the case in the play's third scene. In the fourth scene, Michael does act more like the conventional faithful retainer and manages to deliver a dramatic soliloquy with a suitable beginning: 'Conflicting thoughts encampèd in my breast / Awake me with the echo of their strokes' (iv.58–59). In the speech that follows, Michael opposes the claims of his master, to whom he owes his duty, and his mistress, who has promised him Mosby's sister. Ultimately, he is so persuaded by the horrors he imagines that he cries out: 'He comes, he comes! Ah, Master Franklin, help! / Call up the neighbours, or we are but dead' (iv.85–86). When Arden and Franklin rush in they discover that the doors were unlocked and they lock them, thus preventing the entrance of the killers and saving Arden's life. The result is an excellent example of dramatic irony: Michael has in fact done his duty and saved his master's life, but only because of his vividly imagined fears for himself. From one point of view, then, Michael has acted as a servant should, but he has done so for reasons that are self-interested in a way that is consonant with *Arden of Faversham* as a whole.

When Michael ponders the conflicting claims on his loyalty, he says that his love for Susan 'is nearer than a master's love' (iv.66). Michael sets aside his duty to his master just as Alice sets aside her duty to her husband. One bond that is unbroken, however, is the bond between the two male friends Arden and Franklin. They often appear together, and Michael's second soliloquy takes place while they are in bed together. Arden and Franklin's relationship gives the play the pair of male equals so important to much Renaissance literature.[16] Randall Martin points out that Franklin is 'an invented character' and adds that his 'viewpoint and responses establish a patriarchal norm.'[17] An important part of this norm is the homosocial bond, and in adding Franklin, the playwright creates a male couple that could be said to provide the central relationship in the play: they certainly provide its only truly virtuous one. A loving friendship between equal men was often seen as the highest possible relationship. About the same time that the play was written, for instance, Spenser placed male friendship above both the love of children for their families and a man's love for a woman: 'faithfull friendship doth them both suppresse,/ And them with maystring discipline doth tame.'[18] In *Arden of Faversham*, however, male friendship cannot provide the civilizing effects in which Spenser believed. Like the idea that a man was entitled to unquestioning loyalty from his wife and his servants, it is something to which the play refers but which has no power.

When considered together, the two plays I have discussed provide interestingly contrasting views of the relationship between feminine transgression and normative domesticity. In *The Duchess of Malfi*, the eponymous character's transgression is actually to be conventionally domestic. In remarrying against her brother's wishes and in setting up a household with a servant, the Duchess offends both against the class system and against a patriarchy that places restrictions upon female agency. In contrast, *Arden of Faversham* takes place in a domestic setting among characters who could be described as middle class. Alice's adultery and her plot to kill her husband are obviously transgressive, but what is ultimately disturbing about the play is that she seems to be not the exception but rather the rule. In this play normality is not the stable backdrop against which terrible crimes are committed: instead, what is normal is a shifting landscape in which bonds of all sorts are subject to change. Both the Duchess and Alice are transgressive from one angle, but within the context of their situations, operate normally. The Duchess's desire is to have a husband and children, a desire that would appear unremarkable in most situations, while Alice's desire to remake her life as she sees fit, seems to be typical of the England of her time. Without losing sight of the obvious differences between the plays (most notably, the Duchess is an innocent victim while Alice is a criminal), we can see that both characters fall fatally afoul of societies in which to say what is normal—and perhaps especially what is normal for women—is a harder task that might seem to be the case.

Notes

1. All references are to Michael Neill's edition of the play (2015).
2. A good discussion of marriage in the English Renaissance (including the fact that marriages were considered binding if performed in the presence of witnesses even outside a church) can be found in Dolan (2008).
3. Sullivan (2005: 113).
4. Bartels (1996: 422). For the suggestion that the second of these gaps should be seen as a metatheatrical joke, see Lopez (2003: 76).
5. See, for example, Panek (2004).
6. Dowd (2015: 79).
7. Ibid.: 80. For Dowd's excellent analysis of *The Duchess of Malfi* as a whole, see 76–116.
8. All references are to M. L. Wine's edition (1973). The full title of the first edition of 1592 is "The lamentable and true tragedie of M. Arden of Feversham in Kent Who was most wickedlye murdered, by the meanes of his disloyall and wanton wyfe, who for the loue she bare to one Mosbie, hyred two desperat ruffins Blackwill and Shakbag, to kill him. Wherin is shewed the great mallice and discimulation of a wicked woman, the vnsatiable desire of filthie lust and the shamefull end of all murderers".
9. Lena Cowen Orlin has a very good discussion of why the connections between the play and its society are important. See Orlin (1994: 74–76).
10. The play is now thought to be co-authored by Shakespeare and another anonymous dramatist; see Taylor and Loughnane (2017: 487–490).
11. For an interesting study of Arden as a character, with particular reference to his lack of a male heir, his masculinity, and his status as a landowner, see Martin (2001: 13–33).
12. Sullivan (1994: 247).
13. This idea is a commonplace in much Renaissance English writing. For a discussion, see Kerrigan (2016).
14. It is worth pointing out that the Duke was himself a rising man. Born Edward Seymour, he became prominent because of his sister's marriage to Henry VIII. He only became Duke of Somerset in 1547, shortly

before the events of the play; in 1552, shortly after those events, he was executed and his title was forfeited and not restored to his descendants until 1660. See *Oxford Dictionary of National Biography*, 'Seymour, Edward, Duke of Somerset'.

15. Alice is the largest role of any female character in the drama of the 1580s, speaking almost twice as many lines as Arden, the next largest role in the play. See Power (2017: 19–20).
16. For an excellent discussion of the importance of Franklin and of ideas of male friendship to the play, see Garrison (2014: 44–54).
17. Martin (2001: 21).
18. *Faerie Queene*, IV.ix.2.3–4, in Spenser (1912). The bibliography on male friendship in the English Renaissance is extensive. For a brief discussion that considers this passage from Spenser, see Guy-Bray (2014: 2–4) as well as the book by Garrison cited above.

Works Cited

Anonymous. 1973. *The Tragedy of Master Arden of Faversham*, ed. M.L. Wine. London: Methuen.

Bartels, Emily C. 1996. Strategies of Submission: Desdemona, the Duchess, and the Assertion of Desire. *Studies in English Literature* 36: 417–433.

Beer, Barrett L. 2004. Seymour, Edward, Duke of Somerset [Known as Protector Somerset] (c. 1500–1552), Soldier and Royal Servant. *Oxford Dictionary of National Biography*. Oxford University Press, September 2004. http://www.oxforddnb.com.ucc.idm.oclc.org/view/10.1093/ref:odnb/9780198614128.001.0001/odnb-9780198614128-e-25159 (Online edition).

Dolan, Frances E. 2008. *Marriage and Violence: The Early Modern Legacy*. Philadelphia: University of Pennsylvania Press.

Dowd, Michelle M. 2015. *The Dynamics of Inheritance on the Shakespearean Stage*. Cambridge: Cambridge University Press.

Garrison, John S. 2014. *Friendship and Queer Theory in the Renaissance: Gender and Sexuality in Early Modern England*. New York: Routledge.

Guy-Bray, Stephen. 2014. 'Fellowships of Joy': Angelic Union in *Paradise Lost*. *Early Modern Culture* 10. http://emc.eserver.org/1-10/guy-bray.pdf.

Kerrigan, John. 2016. *Shakespeare's Binding Language*. Oxford: Oxford University Press.

Lopez, Jeremy. 2003. *Theatrical Convention and Audience Reaction in Early Modern Drama*. Cambridge: Cambridge University Press.

Martin, Randall. 2001. "Arden Winketh at His Wife's Lewdness, & Why!": A Patrilineal Crisis in *Arden of Faversham*. *Early Theatre* 4: 13–33.

Orlin, Lena Cowen. 1994. *Private Matters and Public Cultures in Postreformation England*. Ithaca, NY: Cornell University Press.

Panek, Jennifer. 2004. *Widows and Suitors in Early Modern English Comedy.* Cambridge: Cambridge University Press.

Power, Andrew J. 2017. *Arden of Faversham*: Roles and Requirements. In *New Oxford Shakespeare: Critical Reference Edition*, vol. 1, ed. Gary Taylor, et al. Oxford: Oxford University Press.

Spenser, Edmund. 1912. *Spenser: Poetical Works*, eds. J.C. Smith and E. de Selincourt. Oxford: Oxford University Press.

Sullivan, Garrett A. 1994. "Arden Lay Murdered in That Plot of Ground": Surveying, Land, and Arden of Faversham. *English Literary History* 61: 231–252.

Sullivan, Garrett A. 2005. *Memory and Forgetting in English Renaissance Drama.* Cambridge: Cambridge University Press.

Taylor, Gary, and Rory Loughnane. 2017. The Canon and Chronology of Shakespeare's Works. In *The New Oxford Shakespeare: Authorship Companion*, ed. Gary Taylor and Gabriel Egan. Oxford: Oxford University Press.

Webster, John. 2015. *The Duchess of Malfi*, ed. Michael Neill. New York: W. W. Norton.

CHAPTER 13

Afterword

Frances E. Dolan

Perhaps no scholar has been more influential in discussions of early modern 'normality' than Lawrence Stone. Variations on the word 'normal' appear on 76 pages of his weighty tome *The Family, Sex and Marriage in England: 1500–1800* (1977). In it, Stone opines confidently about normal experiences, including whipping as a normal part of a childhood and 'normal adulterous pursuits'.[1] One of the reasons Stone is still both fascinating and infuriating to read is that he was confident that there was an early modern normal, that he knew it when he saw it, that we could access it, and that it was interesting, both because it was 'our' history and because it was pruriently provocative. He made bold claims, and once you see them as such, and as in dialogue with other historians, they can be generative. He also assembled a rich array of evidence we can put to our own uses. In this collection, for example, Michelle Dowd cites Stone, drawing on his evidence of how often the norm of patrilineage broke down.

Many of Stone's assertions about the normal provoked controversy, particularly his claim that relations between upper-class parents and children were 'usually fairly remote' because 'the very high infant and child

F. E. Dolan (✉)
University of California, Davis, CA, USA
e-mail: fdolan@ucdavis.edu

© The Author(s) 2019
R. Loughnane and E. Semple (eds.), *Staged Normality in Shakespeare's England*, Palgrave Shakespeare Studies,
https://doi.org/10.1007/978-3-030-00892-5_13

mortality rates [...] made it folly to invest too much emotional capital in such ephemeral beings'.[2] Throughout the seventeenth century, he claimed, one 'normally could expect' little show of emotion, especially from fathers.[3] The resistance to this claim launched many a review essay and counter history of the early modern family. Objections focused on Stone's evaluation of the surviving evidence, on what many historians scolded as uncritical uptake by literary critics (who, it was claimed, cited Stone's contentions as facts rather than arguments), and on defensive assertions about parent-child attachment as transhistorical and even natural ('everyone loves their children!').

Stone framed questions that continue to occupy scholars now and the controversy he stirred up can still alert us to what is at stake in our own chartings of the normal. What is the 'normal' relationship, for instance, between fathers and sons? We cannot begin to answer without asking which fathers and sons (Stone focused on the aristocracy because they left the most evidence) and specifying the evidence we adduce, since one body of evidence often contradicts another. In her essay here, Emily O'Brien approaches a father's murder of his sons in *A Yorkshire Tragedy* as a disruption of the 'everyday, domestic world.' This avoids the possibility that paternal violence, as long as it falls short of murder, might be part of the fabric of that world, rather than a rent in it. O'Brien describes the child as calling domesticity into being: 'conjuring' a sense of 'disrupted normality' and 'summoning a sense of domestic normality, against which the depiction of transgression is given meaning, emotional force, and didactic potential' (O'Brien). O'Brien's resonant verbs suggest that the child, agent as well as victim, creates or casts the domestic order rather than being interpellated into it. Perhaps this child is a threat to or extension of paternal power in the play, as well as the target of it. O'Brien's verbs also suggest the spectator or reader's own magical creativity, taking up the hint of the child and embroidering domestic normality around it. If 'we' are the conjurers, then, prompted by the child on stage or page, we differ from one another and so conjure up different normals.

Like Stone, contributors here turn to plays, conduct literature, 'wills, probate records, and marriage settlements' that 'document the multiplicity of practices built into the legal framework of England's patrilineal system' (Dowd); proverbs, which 'are part of a common stock of wisdom and suggest that life can be understood and that general patterns apply' (Guy-Bray); and travel narratives (Charry). The map of the normal is familiar from earlier studies—including the stage, the playhouse, the household, the school, and the neighborhood or parish among the institutions that produce, monitor, and register norms. While the church is touched on here, it does not loom large as a norm-policing institution, perhaps because it has been so well-studied, from its homilies to the operations of church courts.

Material culture—including theorizations of the lives, stories, and agencies of objects—has become a crucial part of our understanding of early modern life. In these essays, Mazzio demonstrates the norming and informing impact of the ruler and measuring square, and Hanson of the register or gradebook. Johanson argues that 'Almanacs, diaries, and the continued use of books of hours, as well as the increasing consumption of personal time-keeping devices through the end of the sixteenth and into the seventeenth century, all indicate that early modern individuals thought about tracking, and tracked, their use of time.' Sanders helps us see, touch, and smell the leather in jerkins and shoes. I want to draw particular attention to O'Brien's passing reference to the possibility that children scourging their tops were imitating the scourging of Jesus. Their tops were then 'scriptive things,' in the phrase Sanders borrows from Robin Bernstein's work on twentieth-century American children's culture, things that carry stories in them, moving persons through spaces and dictating actions. In this case, a toy scripts the daily, domestic re-enactment of torture.

In this volume, we find agential things and instrumentalized people (including heirs, servants, and slaves). While these essays do not attend to animals or plants, partly because essays with that focus find homes in differently organized collections, the 'normal' built environment they address is one we are learning to see as a kind of text, with writing on many surfaces, as coterminous with a green world that both surrounds and permeates it, and as a space of intimate interactions and identifications between humans and animals, animated by sentience distributed across self–other, person–thing, animal–vegetable–mineral divides.

While our understanding of early modern England has changed dramatically since Stone wrote almost half a century ago, many of these essays share with him and other older studies of the old normal an association of the normal with the domestic and the everyday. Edel Semple mentions 'the familiar and the banal,' 'the recognizable and relatable,' the everyday, quotidian, ordinary, and common, as well as a 'localized setting' and 'trivial concerns.' Julie Sanders addresses the 'normal, tangible, understandable,' 'everyday activities and their attendant sensory geographies,' and 'everyday tangible lives' constituting 'a rich repository of staged normality.' For both Semple and Sanders this normality cluster—'the normal—common people such as servants, domestic items, everyday concerns, habitual actions'—works to secure identifications between spectators and characters. We also find here 'social temporal norms' (Johanson) and 'the normal, extended time of family life' (Guy-Bray); 'everyday whims of affect and personality' (Dowd); the 'small, ordinary world' of 'normal contact' and 'normal intimacy' (O'Brien); as well as 'the quotidian, the trivial, and the female' and thus the 'too often culturally invisible' (Whipday).

Various scholars have demonstrated that the early modern household was a node in networks of global trade, experimental science, and knowledge transmission, rather than a bounded and 'private' space, and that women's domestic labor entailed power, skill, knowledge—and violence.[4] The very food on the table, to take one much-discussed example, often came from someplace else, directly or indirectly. A much-quoted passage from Gervase Markham's *The English Housewife* (1649) urges that the housewife's diet should 'proceed more from the provision of her own yard, than the furniture of the markets, and let it be rather esteemed for the familiar acquaintance she hath with it, than for the strangeness and rarity it bringeth from other countries.'[5] Yet, as Kim F. Hall has shown, praise of the determinedly English home, English diet, and English physic tended to ignore how cosmopolitan English gardens and pantries already were by the seventeenth century. Hall argues that the housewife plays a crucial role not just in overseeing consumption and domestic production but in naturalizing or normalizing imports: 'It might be that the woman's "familiar acquaintance" is the very thing necessary to remove the threat of strangeness: as substances pass through the English home and are transformed from raw material to "food," they lose their foreign taint'.[6] That process often suppressed a history of exploitation and expropriation, bleaching out the blood, for example, that went into producing white sugar.

This research unsettles easy assumptions about what the early modern normal looked like or what can be taken as a given, uncovering the striking shifts that have emerged in the wide gap of time between now and then as well as the sometimes unexpected ways early modern norms (and processes of crafting and defending them) continue to shape our own possibilities. While Whipday here discusses the uncanniness of early modern life, she also discusses 'a perversion of housewifely duties' in domestic tragedies. Does everyday murder pervert 'the spaces, objects, and roles of the household' or is it a reminder of the uncanniness, and inherent violence, of a norm that is no longer familiar? Might it even alert us to the ways violence remains a norm in homes and on streets? Stephen Guy-Bray raises the question of marital intimacy as both normal and strange in the unsettled world of *The Duchess of Malfi*. But what exactly does early modern marital intimacy entail and whom does it include and exclude? The intimacy between Antonio and the Duchess in the *Duchess of Malfi*, as Wendy Wall has pointed out, usually includes the maid Cariola.[7] While Stone associated the family and household with the nuclear family of a married heterosexual couple and their children, we are increasingly aware that servants such as Cariola were also family. Same-sex friendship often had more prestige, and was more saturated with emotional and erotic expectations, than marriage.[8] In short, too tight a connection between family and sex on the one hand and marriage on the other, or between the household and marriage, has been exploded and opened out. We now see what central figures the maid in *A Yorkshire Tragedy*, or the servants Brinda Charry discusses, were in this period.

While the old normal studies paid little or no attention to race, new work on race and ethnicity is transforming our understanding of the early modern world. The stage itself seems to have played an important role in shaping what audiences could recognize as familiar. Ania Loomba, for example, points out that 'By 1600, eighteen to twenty thousand visits were made each week to London playhouses. The bulk of these visitors got their images of foreign people from the stage, rather than from books or real-life interactions. Thus the theatre deeply shaped English imaginings of outsiders.'[9] Those outsiders were not just impersonated on stage but were inside the playhouse, inside the household, both as inhabitants and as ghosts haunting the comestibles created through their labor. Edel Semple's reading of *Sir Thomas More*, and the xenophobic riot with which it starts, registers the increasing presence of strangers in London. 'Strangers' were also inside the conceptualizations of norms and how to measure them. Carla Mazzio shows here how, in *Antony and Cleopatra*, Shakespeare exposes 'the limits of Roman measurements and 'norms' in the face of a more capacious Egyptian history of, and approaches to, measurement.' The play needs Egypt, then, to interrogate Western standards in part because the two can best be understood in relation. Just as the research I have discussed above has offered us a strange new perspective on the domestic, so the scholarship on race and ethnicity Brinda Charry engages and advances here offers new knowledge of how familiar the alien was in English homes and streets, the proximities and intimacies—rather than oppositions or distinctions—that formed the texture of early modern life.

What Mazzio refers to as 'an as-yet-unwritten prehistory of norms' is coming into being, advanced by her own contribution here. Valerie Traub argues that early modern anatomy and cartography shared not only a 'graphic idiom' and a 'spatial epistemology' but a 'logic of the grid,' which imposes normative order on the objects of knowledge it positions in space (and in relation to one another). Moving past the emphases on discovery and difference, conquest and otherness, that have animated many accounts of the period, Traub instead traces a prehistory of the concept of normality and its attendant notion of a fundamental shared, abstract universal human nature. Traub's discussion of the grid depends on an innovative approach to form as social as well as literary. The grid operates as a conceptual container, an empty space to be filled in with evidence of human diversity. But this container is not neutral, of course. As Traub shows, it imposes distinctions and hierarchies on the persons it graphs. No one is outside the grid. The strange and the familiar alike become objects of representation and through that representation, objects of knowledge.[10]

This collection contributes to such efforts to estrange what was once taken as normal in the early modern period and to think about how the norms that emerge then still bear on us today. We have to begin by tackling the fact that, as Rory Loughnane argues in his introduction, the normal as we define it is not yet an early modern concern. As Michael Warner puts this in *The Trouble with Normal*, 'One reason why you won't find many eloquent quotations about the desire to be normal in Shakespeare, or the Bible, or other common sources of moral wisdom, is that people didn't sweat much over being normal until the spread of statistics in the nineteenth century. Now they are surrounded by numbers that tell them what normal is' and invited to compare themselves to that norm.[11] But there was measurement before statistics, as Mazzio demonstrates in her discussion of two 'once commonplace but now obsolete idioms for deviations from the norm: "out of square" and "enormous."' Kristine Johanson also contributes to a prehistory of norms, by questioning whether there was an early modern investment in time management and in the self-regulating, time-managing subject. Elizabeth Hanson emphasizes that, prior to the nineteenth century, the normal was what one should do rather than what one usually did (see also Whipday on the tension between the common and the aspirational at the heart of conduct literature). Bracingly, Hanson refuses to be bound by the evolution etymology so often seems to imply, challenging the presumption that 'a meaning is not culturally available until all determining historical conditions have converged on the word in question.'

According to Warner, 'The point of being normal is to blend, to have no visible difference and no conflict'.[12] And yet, these essays draw our attention to what stands out as well as blends in. Of the figures who are eccentric or enormous, not abnormal as much as out-standing or egregious, we might start with Shakespeare himself. 'Of course,' Gamboa writes, 'Shakespeare is not exceptional [...] but he stands apart.' We find here also the enormity of Antony (Mazzio); the 'widely-acknowledged extraneousness' of the Latin scene in *Merry Wives* (Hanson); the martyr (Semple); the smell and feel of leather (Sanders); the child (O'Brien); the female heir who was nevertheless 'a remarkably common figure' (Dowd); and the eunuch (Charry). These last two figures showcase the central role of the oxymoron, yoking apparent contraries, in *Staging Normality*. Dowd argues that variations on the legal norm of primogeniture were so common in Shakespeare's England that those variations effectively became the norm, and refers to 'normative deviance,' 'normal disorders,' and 'normative patrilineal disorder.' O'Brien describes the child as at the center of 'the tangle' of the normal and the abnormal. Semple argues that *Sir Thomas More* stages 'rebellion, disobedience, and deviancy' not as aberrant but as 'part of the normal fabric of society and indeed human life itself.' For Stephen Guy-Bray, 'abnormality is normal' in the worlds of *Malfi* and *Faversham*.

As Dowd shows, the female heir as depicted on stage simply does her job as heir, shoring up patrilineage by providing an alternative mechanism of transmission when the male line fails (as it so often did). The lack of a male heir is not the female heir's fault; instead, she is a solution to a problem. The female heir, then, participates in a representational pattern Kathryn Schwarz traces by which 'women pose a threat when they willingly conform to social conventions.' Schwarz focuses not on depictions of women who resist or break gender norms, as studies of female willfulness and transgression often have, but on those who purposefully and intentionally fulfill them and thereby reveal the dependence of heterosocial order on their willing participation. As Schwarz puts it: 'The suspicion that a virtuous woman might act for your own good is every bit as vibrant as the fear that a vicious woman might kill you in your bed'; sometimes it is a virtuous woman who feels wholly justified in killing you in your bed for the greater good of the heterosocial order.[13] Like Schwarz, Dowd turns her attention away from transgression, exploring how romances stage how 'norms are creatively enabled, sustained, and redefined.'

Brinda Charry, too, considers a figure who both stands out and fits in. 'Their sad histories and compromised manhood set eunuchs apart and made them objects of pity,' she points out, but also reminds us that eunuchs were servants in a world in which many people had been servants and employed them. They stood apart for their bright futures as well as their 'sad histories,' since they could rise higher than many other kinds of servants. In this collection, eunuchs remind us of the intimate terms on which servants lived with their masters, the threat that formed part of that intimacy, and the spread of the slave trade in this period.

How does dramatic form manage the challenge of enormous figures such as the female heir and the eunuch? We might view both norms and genres as contracts that serve one another. In an influential argument, Fredric Jameson claimed that 'genres are essentially contracts between a writer and his reader.'[14] Kristine Johanson argues here that norms are contractual: 'understanding what "normal" or "normality" signifies in a given situation is contingent upon an agreement between an individual and their community. What is read as "normal" depends upon the relationship between that individual and that society' (Johanson). Many of the contributors here experiment with various verbs to describe exactly what plays do in relation to norms. For Johanson, Shakespeare's drama 'participates in constructing those temporal norms it investigates and interrogates.' Carla Mazzio places Shakespeare's *Antony and Cleopatra* into dialogue with a rich and unexpected set of other plays, demonstrating 'the paradoxically generative potential and constitutive status of the square for a range of "deviant" dramatic subjectivities.' Brinda Charry argues that Shakespeare's comedies 'effectively erase or rewrite the eunuch.' Michelle Dowd considers how Shakespeare turns to an old form—lost child plots from Roman comedy—to creatively uphold and reimagine 'the presumed norms and stability of patrilineage.' In doing so, the romances help to 'manage, sustain, and actively promote a kind of legal normality' during a period of acute socioeconomic pressures, offering 'a comforting, conservative narrative that compels a kind of new normality into existence.' We find here, then, accounts of how Shakespeare exceeds norms, interrogates them, manages, invigorates, compels, and promotes them. In a wonderfully fruitful formulation, Elizabeth Hanson suggests that 'Shakespearean comedy is a particularly sensitive and productive site for developing ideas and feelings that anticipate new versions of normal.' In its conclusion, a play like *Merry Wives* might respond 'to an order that has not yet arrived' (that is, the modern, quantifying normal). Staging normality, then, can help to invent and disseminate it. Sometimes, that's the trouble.

Notes

1. Stone (1977: 164, 282).
2. Ibid.: 105.
3. Ibid.
4. See Wall (2002, 2015), Korda (2002), and Cowen Orlin (2007).
5. Markham (1986: 8).
6. Hall (1996: 182).
7. Wall (2006: 162).
8. Of the many important studies of early modern friendship and same sex attachments, I want to draw particular attention to Laurie Shannon's *Sovereign Amity: Figures of Friendship in Shakespearean Contexts* (2002).
9. Loomba (2002: 8).
10. See Traub (2009) as well as her work in progress, *Mapping Embodiment in the Early Modern West: A Prehistory of Normality*.
11. Warner (2000: 53).
12. Ibid.: 60.
13. Schwarz (2011: 12).
14. Jameson (1975: 135).

Works Cited

Cowen Orlin, Lena. 2007. *Locating Privacy in Tudor London*. Oxford: Oxford University Press.

Hall, Kim F. 1996. Culinary Spaces, Colonial Spaces: The Gendering of Sugar in the Seventeenth Century. In *Feminist Readings of Early Modern Culture: Emerging Subjects*, ed. Valerie Traub, M. Lindsay Kaplan, and Dympna Callaghan. Cambridge: Cambridge University Press.

Jameson, Fredric. 1975. Magical Narratives: Romance as Genre. *New Literary History* 7 (1): 135–163.

Korda, Natasha. 2002. *Shakespeare's Domestic Economies: Gender and Property in Early Modern England*. Philadelphia: University of Pennsylvania Press.

Loomba, Ania. 2002. *Shakespeare, Race, and Colonialism*. Oxford: Oxford University Press.

Markham, Gervase. [1649] 1986. *The English Housewife*, ed. Michael R. Best. Kingston and Montreal: McGill-Queen's University Press.

Schwarz, Kathryn. 2011. *What You Will: Gender, Contract, and Shakespearean Social Space*. Philadelphia: University of Pennsylvania Press.

Shannon, Laurie. 2002. *Sovereign Amity: Figures of Friendship in Shakespearean Contexts*. Chicago: University of Chicago Press.

Stone, Lawrence. 1977. *The Family, Sex and Marriage in England: 1500–1800*. London: Weidenfeld and Nicolson.

Traub, Valerie. 2009. The Nature of Norms in Early Modern England: Anatomy, Cartography, and King Lear. *South Central Review* 26 (1/2): 42–81.

Wall, Wendy. 2002. *Staging Domesticity: Household Work and English Identity in Early Modern Drama*. Cambridge: Cambridge University Press.

Wall, Wendy. 2006. Just a Spoonful of Sugar: Syrup and Domesticity in Early Modern England. *Modern Philology* 104 (2): 149–172.

Wall, Wendy. 2015. *Recipes for Thought: Knowledge and Taste in the Early Modern English Kitchen*. Philadelphia: University of Pennsylvania Press.

Warner, Michael. 2000. *The Trouble with Normal: Sex, Politics, and the Ethics of Queer Life*. Cambridge: Harvard University Press.

Author Index

A
Abate, Corinne S., 16
Adelman, Janet, 63
Agha, Hasan (Samson Rowley), 196
Ahmed, Sara, 40, 60
Albanese, Denise, 203
Althusser, Louis, 9
Amussen, Susan D., 85
Appadurai, Arjun, 124
Arab, Ronda, 123
Archer, Ian, 15, 168
Aristotle, 23, 35, 36, 40–42, 44, 47, 48, 52, 55, 58, 60–62
Ascham, Roger, 62
Austin, John, 11
Ayalon, David, 208

B
Balizet, Ariane M., 224, 230, 246
Barber, Lester E., 156, 191
Barish, Jonas, 149
Bartles, Emily C., 262
Bate, Jonathan, 206
Baumlin, James S., 104
Baxter, Jane Eva, 254
Beckett, Samuel, 2
Beckman Taylor, Paul, 105, 106
Belsey, Catherine, 244, 253
Benese, Richard, 52
Bennett, Susan, 124
Bernstein, Robin, 111, 119, 124, 279
Biddulph, William, 193, 207
Bland, Robert, 42, 60
Blount, Henry, 194
Boas, Frederick S., 148
Bolens, Guillemette, 105, 106
Bon, Ottavio, 208
Bonfield, Lloyd, 190
Bono, Barbara J., 48
Boose, Linda E., 233
Boulton, Jeremy, 123
Bourdieu, Pierre, 75, 77, 78, 82
Bradbury, Nancy, 95, 105
Brathwaite, Edward Kamau, 208
Brietz Monta, Susannah, 167
Bulwer, John, 204, 209
Burke, Peter, 15, 101
Burnett, Mark Thornton, 195
Burrows, John, 105

C

Cahill, Patricia A., 46, 47, 59, 61
Callaghan, Dympna, 15, 196
Campana, Joseph, 252
Canguilheim, Georges, 8, 9, 25
Carlyle, Joseph, 25
Cavell, Stanley, 9–11, 25
Cawdrey, Robert, 34, 58
Cawley, A.C., 255
Chakravarty, Urvashi, 194, 195, 207
Charles V, 94
Charry, Brinda, 22, 193, 281, 282, 284
Chaucer, Geoffrey, 2, 94, 104, 106
Chedgzoy, Kate, 247, 252
Chekhov, Anton, 4
Cicero, Marcus Tullius, 60, 62, 85, 106
Clarence-Smith, W.G., 207
Cohen, Adam Max, 105, 106
Cohen, Simona, 104
Cohen, Walter, 73
Collette, Carolyn P., 95, 105, 106
Collier, John Payne, 239
Comensoli, Viviana, 255
Comte, Auguste, 8
Condren, Conal, 106
Conley, Tom, 37, 38, 43, 59
Cooper, Helen, 190
Craig, Hugh, 75, 105
Craik, T.W., 148
Crane, Mary Thomas, 63
Crawford, Patricia, 190
Crawforth, Hannah, 123
Cressy, David, 15, 147
Croce, Mariano, 8

D

Dekker, Thomas, 111, 118, 120, 125
de la Perrière, Guillaume, 226
De Pizan, Christine, 94, 106
Dessen, Alan C., 148, 149
Dohrn-van Rossum, Gerhard, 104, 105
Dolan, Frances E., 15, 16, 23, 195, 207, 253
Donatus, 178
Donne, John, 56, 63
Doran, Gregory, 17
Doty, Jeff S., 106
Dowd, Michelle M., 16, 21, 123, 190, 191, 233, 265, 274, 277, 284
Downie, Penny, 17
Draper, F.W.M., 85
Drescher, Seymour, 197
Drumm, Thomas L., 26
Duane, Anna Mae, 252
Dudley, Robert, 49
Durkheim, Emile, 8
Dustagheer, Sarah, 123
Dymkowski, Christine, 203

E

Elizabeth I, Queen, 119
Engel, William E., 104
Engerman, Stanley, 197
Epstein, Andrew, 2
Erasmus, Desiderius, 85
Erickson, Amy Louise, 16, 174, 190
Erickson, Peter, 24, 85
Euclid, 52
Evanthius, 178
Evett, David, 209
Ewald, François, 8

F

Fenner, Dudley, 216
Ferraro, Joanne M., 252
Fitzpatrick, Joan, 168
Flather, Amanda, 233
Fleming, Juliet, 16
Ford, John, 4
Forman, Valerie, 180
Foucault, Michel, 9, 25, 35, 38, 58, 59

Frankle, Robert J., 207
Freeman, Elizabeth, 104
Freud, Sigmund, 3, 218
Fuchs, Barbara, 190
Fumerton, Patricia, 15, 112, 124, 155, 163, 221

G
Gabrieli, Vittorio, 168
Gaines, Barry, 255
Gamboa, Brett, 21, 24, 283
Garrison, John S., 275
Geroulanos, Stefanos, 25
Ginzburg, Carlos, 3, 24
Glasser, Richard, 105
Glennie, Paul, 104, 105
Goldberg, Jonathan, 104
Gould, Timothy, 11
Gray, Douglas, 254
Greenberg, Marissa, 253
Greenblatt, Stephen, 147, 155
Greene, Gayle, 15
Greene, Robert, 155
Griffiths, Paul, 252
Gurr, Andrew, 168
Guy-Bray, Stephen, 22, 275, 278, 281, 283

H
Haber, Judith, 237, 255
Hackel, Heidi Brayman, 149
Hackett, Helen, 190
Hailwood, Mark, 232
Hakluyt, Richard, 207, 208
Hall, Kim F., 24, 280
Hamling, Tara, 16
Hanson, Elizabeth, 7, 20, 85, 279, 283, 285
Harborne, William, 195
Harkness, Deborah, 123
Harris, Jonathan Gil, 104, 149

Harrison, William, 114
Hawkins, John, 193
Heidegger, Martin, 9, 10, 12
Helgerson, Richard, 86
Henry IV, 98
Henry V, 18, 47, 62, 94, 98, 104, 115, 139, 146, 164
Henry VI, 98, 101, 103
Hentschell, Roze, 123, 124
Heraclitus, 2, 10, 23
Hess, Andrew C., 209
Heywood, Thomas, 20, 111, 112, 118, 120–122, 124, 168, 199, 227
Higginbotham, Jennifer, 254
Highley, Christopher, 123
Hill, Tracey, 153, 167, 169
Hindle, Maurice, 24
Hiscock, Andrew, 191
Holinshed, Raphael, 114, 157, 163, 266
Hollingsworth, T.H., 190
Holmes, Sherlock, 3
Houlbrooke, Ralph, 14
Howard, Jean E., 153
Howard-Hill, T.H., 166, 168
Hoyle, R.H., 85
Huang, Alex C.Y., 123
Humphrey, Chris, 105
Hunt, Simon, 15, 155
Hutson, Lorna, 58
Hyman, Wendy Beth, 105, 106

I
Ibsen, Henrik, 4, 24
Ingold, Tim, 39, 40, 60
Iyengar, Sujata, 57, 61, 186

J
Jackson, MacDonald P., 233
Jaffee, Michele, 62

Jameson, Fredric, 284
Johanson, Kristine, 20, 105, 279, 280, 282, 284
Jones, Ann Rosalind, 16, 135
Jonson, Ben, 18, 120, 122, 124
Jowett, John, 166–169

K
Kahn, Coppélia, 15
Kalas, Rayna, 59
Kaplan, Steven, 15
Kastan, David Scott, 106
Kathman, David, 254
Kegl, Rosemary, 72, 73, 85
Kermode, Lloyd Edward, 153, 168
Kerrigan, John, 274
King, Margaret, 252
Kinney, Arthur, 123
Kirwan, Peter, 254, 255
Knowles, Katie, 247, 252
Korda, Natasha, 16, 149, 233, 285
Kott, Jan, 140, 148
Kussmaul, Anne, 195, 208
Kyd, Thomas, 4, 230

L
Lamb, Edel, 252
Landreth, David, 79, 86
Laslett, Peter, 14, 238
Lefebvre, Henri, 9, 10, 25
Le Goff, Jacques, 104, 105
Leo Africanus, 54, 63
Levine, Laura, 24
Levine, Nina, 169
Liebler, Naomi Conn, 220
Lin, Erika T., 233
Lindley, David, 106
Loomba, Ania, 24, 34, 58, 62, 281, 285
Lopez, Jeremy, 274

Loughnane, Rory, 25, 57, 58, 63, 104, 105, 146, 161, 162, 190, 191, 239, 282
Lowe, Eleanor, 124

M
Macfarlane, Alan, 14
Manley, Lawrence, 169
Mannoni, Octave, 208
Marcus, Leah, 84, 86
Marcus Aurelius, 23
Marlowe, Christopher, 4
Marmon, Shaun, 208
Marston, John, 48
Marx, Karl, 85
Mason, John, 197
Masten, Jeffrey, 24, 37, 57, 59
Matchett, William, 148
Mazzio, Carla, 13, 16, 19, 20, 57, 61, 279, 281, 282, 284
McGavin, John J., 124
McLaren, Dorothy, 190
McMillin, Scott, 168
McNeill, Fiona, 16
McShane, Angela, 218
Meads, Chris, 167
Melchiori, Giorgio, 78, 85, 124, 156, 163, 168
Menon, Madhavi, 202, 208
Middleton, Thomas, 4, 18, 113, 238
Miller, Arthur, 4
Miller, D.A., 60
Miola, Robert, 177, 190
Montaigne, Michel de, 91, 104
More, Thomas, 21, 151–153, 161, 165, 166, 242, 281, 283
Morelli, Giovanni, 3
Muir, Kenneth, 84
Mukherji, Subha, 167, 228
Mulcaster, Richard, 78, 82
Munro, Lucy, 254
Murray, Mary, 190

N
Nashe, Thomas, 122
Neill, Michael, 167, 168, 274
Nelson, T.G.A., 190
Netzloff, Mark, 168
Northbrooke, J., 104
Notaro, Michael R. Jr., 59

O
O'Brien, Emily, 16, 22, 278–280, 283
Odell, George C., 85
O'Neill, Eugene, 4
Orgel, Stephen, 50, 208
Orhonlu, Cengiz, 208
Orme, Nicholas, 245, 254
Osborn, Francis, 198, 208

P
Palfrey, Simon, 84
Panek, Jennifer, 274
Paré, Ambrose, 204, 206
Parker, Patricia, 177
Paster, Gail Kern, 169
Patterson, Orlando, 198, 207, 208
Paul, Joanne, 104
Paynell, Thomas, 52
Piesse, A.J., 252
Pink, Sarah, 124
Plato, 35, 42, 44, 58, 61
Plautus, 177, 178
Pliny, 54, 63
Plutarch, 35, 47, 58
Polito, Mary, 124
Porter, Chloe, 132
Potter, Ursula, 85
Power, Andrew J., 233, 275
Prior, Mary, 100, 190
Prynne, William, 5, 24
Puttenham, George, 42–44, 48, 49, 60

Q
Questier, Michael, 168
Quinones, Ricardo, 103

R
Rabinow, Paul, 8
Randall, Martin, 161, 273
Rappaport, Steve, 168
Relihan, Constance, 200, 208
Reynolds, Edward, 40, 41, 60
Richard II, 20, 91, 94, 95, 98–100, 103
Richardson, Catherine, 16, 216, 222, 239, 242, 247, 253
Ricoeur, Paul, 10
Robson, Lynn, 251, 255
Rocklin, Edward L., 149
Rodó, José Enrique, 202
Rogers, Nathaniel, 217
Rosen, Stanley, 11, 12, 23, 26
Rosenberg, Marvin, 148
Rotman, Brian, 62
Rowland, Richard, 111, 115, 116, 124
Rubright, Marjorie, 195
Rutter, Carol Chillington, 252, 253
Rymer, Thomas, 229

S
Sacerdoti, Gilberto, 63
Salvatore, Andrea, 8
Sanchez, Melissa E., 24
Sanders, Julie, 20, 123, 124, 280
Sauter, Michael J., 105
Schwarz, Kathryn, 283
Scott, Charlotte, 253
Sedgwick, Eve, 208
Semple, Edel, 21, 57, 104, 190, 279, 281
Shakespeare, William, 2–4, 6, 7, 12–15, 17, 18, 20–22, 24–26, 34,

35, 39, 45–50, 52, 57, 58, 61, 63, 72, 74, 84, 85, 89–91, 93–100, 102–104, 106, 115, 116, 119, 121, 123, 124, 130–132, 135–149, 166, 174–178, 180, 181, 184, 186, 188–190, 194, 200, 202, 207, 208, 218, 220, 225, 229, 230, 232, 233, 238, 242, 246, 247, 252, 253, 259, 274, 281–285
Sharpe, J.A., 85
Shuger, Deborah, 253
Sidney, Philip, 49, 50, 62, 206
Simon, Joan, 86
Sinfield, Alan, 156
Singh, Jyotsna G., 162, 233
Sipiora, Phillip, 104
Smith, Henry, 215
Smuts, Malcolm, 123
Spenser, Edmund, 52, 57, 61, 63, 91, 273, 275
Spring, Eileen, 177
Stallybrass, Peter, 16, 135
Starkey, David, 208
Staub, Susan C., 224
Stern, Tiffany, 93, 104–106
Stillman, Robert, 49
Stolberg, Michael, 169
Stone, Lawrence, 14, 26, 174, 176, 277
Stretton, Tim, 190
Strindberg, August, 4
Stubbes, Philip, 5, 24
Sturgess, Keith, 253
Sullivan, Garrett A., 124, 262, 267

T
Tally, Robert, 123
Tasso, Torquato, 264
Taylor, Gary, 254
Tennant, David, 17
Terence, 177

Thompson, Leslie, 149
Thrift, Nigel, 104, 105
Toledano, Ehud, 196
Torczon, Vern, 104
Tory, Geoffroy, 37, 38, 43, 44, 59
Traub, Valerie, 15, 24, 37, 57, 59, 61, 282, 285
Travitsky, Betty S., 253
Trebitsch, Michel, 10, 25
Tusser, Thomas, 215–218, 225, 228

V
Van Es, Bart, 244, 250

W
Walker, Garthine, 218
Walker, Greg, 124
Wall, Wendy, 16, 80, 83, 84, 86, 238, 281, 285
Warley, Christopher, 86
Warner, Marina, 204
Warner, Michael, 282
Weber, Max, 2
Webster, John, 4, 23, 261–264
Weissman, Ronald F.E., 15
Wells, Stanley, 252–254
Westphal, Bertrand, 110, 123
Whipday, Emma, 22, 233, 281, 283
White, Martin, 239, 253
Whitney, Charles, 168
Whittle, Jane, 232
Wiesner, Merry E., 233
Wild, Johaann, 198, 208
Williams, Gordon, 233
Williams, Grant, 104
Wilson, F.P., 104
Wilson, Harry Bristow, 85
Withers, Robert, 196
Withington, Phil, 168
Witmore, Michael, 245

Wittgenstein, Ludwig, 1, 2, 11, 24, 146
Wood, David Houston, 93, 104
Woodbridge, Linda, 15
Woods, Gillian, 158, 167–169
Wrightson, Keith, 14, 123

Y
Yachnin, Paul, 229

Yates, Frances A., 58
Young, Jennifer, 123

Z
Zaller, Robert, 190
Ziegler, Georgianna, 227
Zimmerman, Susan, 15, 147

Subject Index

0-9
1 Henry IV, 21, 139
2 Henry IV, 83, 115
3 Henry VI, 20, 95, 105

A
Abnormal, 2, 6–9, 13, 19, 34, 59, 97, 159, 199, 241, 245, 246, 265, 283
Admiral's Men, 121
adultery, 187, 218, 221, 227, 229, 230, 239, 251, 262, 267, 271, 273
All's Well That Ends Well, 12, 104
antitheatricalism, 5–7
Antony and Cleopatra, 20, 34, 39, 46–48, 50–52, 54, 57, 58, 61–63, 281, 284
A Preparative to Marriage, 215
Arden of Faversham, 18, 22, 121, 123, 218, 220, 232, 233, 253, 259, 260, 266, 268, 269, 271–273
Arte of English Poesie, The, 42, 61

Attention, 2–7, 9, 13, 15, 19, 21, 23, 41, 47, 51, 54, 61, 63, 72, 75, 86, 91, 96, 98, 113, 114, 116, 117, 119, 122, 123, 125, 135, 138, 145, 152, 155, 166, 184, 186, 194, 195, 197, 202, 203, 224, 237–239, 243, 251, 252, 279, 281, 283–285

B
Bankside, 111, 124
Bermondsey, 110, 118
Blackfriars theatre, 118
Blame Not Our Author, 44, 61
Boar's Head, 18, 111, 116
Book of Common Prayer, 70

C
castration, 196–198, 200, 204
childhood studies, 74
children, 74–78, 82, 176, 180, 198, 216, 237–255, 262–264, 273, 277–279, 281

Clerkenwell, 110, 111
comedy, 48, 71, 72, 81, 139, 141, 142, 153, 156, 175, 177, 178, 181, 182, 184, 200–202, 207, 208, 284, 285
Common, 3, 11–13, 15, 21, 34, 43, 46, 63, 69, 74, 77, 93, 100, 132, 152, 155, 156, 163–165, 169, 174–178, 180, 182, 184, 187, 190, 217, 243, 260, 263–265, 278–280, 282, 283
conduct literature, 22, 215–218, 225, 227, 232, 278, 283
conventions, 3, 5, 14, 21, 24, 130, 131, 133–137, 144–146, 164, 220, 244, 262, 283
conversion, 196
Coriolanus, 12, 124, 146
Cymbeline, 6, 13, 21, 136, 137, 175, 177, 178, 185–189, 225, 230

D

death, 13, 14, 21, 45, 48, 53, 59, 100, 135, 137–139, 142, 147, 148, 152, 160, 164, 165, 174, 179, 181, 185, 205, 220, 224, 225, 232, 237, 243, 244, 253, 264, 270
Description Of England, 114
domestic life, 216, 251
domestic murder, 220, 245
domestic tragedy, 18, 218, 220–222, 224, 232, 233, 237–240, 242, 244–246, 249, 251–253, 259, 261, 266
Drama, 2–6, 15, 18–24, 44, 46, 48–50, 57, 58, 63, 90, 93, 97, 103, 111, 112, 118, 119, 123, 124, 135, 144, 145, 158, 166, 169, 174, 175, 203, 228, 245, 248, 254, 263, 275, 284

dramatic form, 187, 189, 263, 284
dream, 26, 148, 188, 221, 230, 263
Duchess of Malfi, The, 22, 216, 237, 245, 260, 261, 263–266, 273, 274, 281

E

Early modern, 2–7, 12, 14–16, 19, 20, 22–24, 35–37, 39, 40, 43, 46, 47, 52, 55, 57–59, 69–71, 74, 75, 79, 83, 85, 89–91, 94, 97, 103, 104, 111–113, 118–121, 123, 124, 146, 147, 149, 151, 167, 174, 176–178, 180, 181, 186, 187, 189, 190, 194, 195, 197, 198, 215, 216, 218, 225, 237–239, 242, 245, 247, 248, 250–254, 271, 277–283, 285
early modern toys, 242
Eastcheap, 115
Edward III, 7
Edward IV (1 and 2), 111–113, 116–118, 120, 124
Egypt, 19, 20, 34, 50–57, 61–63, 194, 281
England, 12–17, 39, 43, 46, 55, 58, 70, 90, 91, 98, 106, 158, 162, 174–177, 180, 184, 187, 189, 190, 193–196, 232, 242, 252, 260, 265, 266, 271, 274, 278, 279, 283
English Customs, 227
English dictionarie: or, An interpreter of hard English words, 46
English language, 59, 74, 78
eunuch, 22, 194–202, 204, 207, 283, 284
everyday, 1, 2, 4, 6–11, 13–16, 18, 19, 21–23, 110–112, 114–116, 118, 119, 122, 123, 152, 154, 155, 158, 161, 163, 166, 174–177,

189, 218, 220, 221, 227, 232, 237, 238, 245, 262, 278–281

231, 232, 238, 240, 242, 249, 251, 253, 259, 261, 262, 273, 279–281

F

Faerie Queene, The, 61, 63, 91, 275
family, 14, 21, 54, 75–77, 83, 110, 136, 152, 157, 158, 160, 161, 165, 167, 174, 176, 177, 181, 182, 198, 201, 205, 216, 225, 226, 238, 240, 245, 246, 248, 251, 253, 263, 264, 278, 280, 281
Five Hundreth Points of Good Husbandry, 215

G

gender, 4, 16, 22, 24, 37, 39, 40, 48, 50, 52, 57, 80, 97, 103, 176, 200, 202, 203, 283
genre, 50, 115, 124, 130, 133, 136, 139, 141, 142, 145, 149, 177, 218, 232, 233, 238–240, 242, 251, 252, 259
geometry, 39, 43, 46–48, 50–54, 58, 61–63, 84
Gerusalemme Liberata, 264
ghosts, 21, 130, 131, 135–137, 145, 281
Globe theater, 62

H

Hamlet, 13, 16–18, 20, 21, 24, 89, 134–136, 259
heiress, 21, 175–180, 182–185, 187–189
historiography, 52, 53, 252
Holinshed's *Chronicles*, 114, 266
household, 16, 22, 23, 76, 120, 151, 157, 194, 201, 216–229,

I

Ill May Day, 153, 154
inheritance, 16, 21, 174–181, 183–185, 188–191, 246

J

Julius Caesar, 13, 144, 259

K

King Lear, 21, 84, 139, 148, 177, 259
King's Men, 240
Knight of the Burning Pestle, The, 160

L

Latin, 7, 20, 26, 34, 35, 40, 44, 48, 49, 60, 61, 72, 74, 77–81, 83–85, 97, 178, 179, 265, 283
leather, 20, 110–114, 116, 118–123, 279, 283
legal norms, 175
London, 18, 24, 85, 92, 109–113, 117, 118, 120, 121, 123, 124, 151, 153, 154, 157, 161, 162, 164, 165, 221, 226, 252, 255, 266, 281
lost-child plot, 21, 175, 177, 178, 180–182, 184, 185, 187–189
Love's Labour's Lost, 49, 144

M

Macbeth, 6, 21, 22, 136, 137, 143, 218, 223, 224, 229, 232, 259
magic, 202, 205, 207

marriage, 14, 16, 23, 61, 62, 79, 97,
    142, 156, 176, 182, 184–186,
    231, 249, 253, 261–266,
    268–270, 274, 278, 281
martyr, 60, 165, 283
masculinity, 19, 20, 35, 36, 39, 40,
    43, 44, 46, 49, 50, 55–57, 61,
    63, 123, 200, 274
Measure for Measure, 13, 123, 142,
    143, 149
mediocrity, 83
Merchant of Venice, The, 121, 142,
    145, 148
Merchant Taylor's School, 76
Merry Wives of Windsor, The, 20, 72,
    119, 254
metaphysics, 40
middle class, 72–75, 80, 83–85, 273
militarism, 46
mimesis, 130, 141, 144, 145
Much Ado About Nothing, 24, 144
Munday, Anthony, 160
Mundus et Infans, 245
murder, 17, 121, 133, 147, 148,
    218–224, 229–232, 238–242,
    245, 247, 248, 251, 253, 266,
    269, 278, 281
Muslims, 196, 264

N
neighbourhood, 110, 111, 113, 117,
    122, 124
normality, 2–9, 11, 12, 16–19, 21–23,
    50, 59, 69, 74, 79, 83, 84,
    98, 111, 115, 129, 136, 141,
    143, 145, 146, 152, 157, 165,
    166, 175, 189, 199, 217, 218,
    237–244, 251, 252, 263, 273,
    277, 278, 280, 282, 284, 285

O
ordinary, 1, 2, 5, 7, 11–13, 15, 18,
    21, 23, 24, 26, 34, 45, 54, 70,
    83, 84, 130, 143, 145, 146, 152,
    155, 156, 158, 160, 162–164,
    166, 169, 174, 217, 221, 239,
    241, 245, 251, 279, 280
Othello, 22, 216, 218, 225, 227, 229,
    231, 232, 259

P
Pathology, 8, 11
*Patient Man and the Honest Whore,
    The*, 160
private life, 158
Privy Council, 21, 151, 158
property, 16, 73, 121, 174, 176, 186,
    189, 197, 225, 226, 228, 242,
    247, 249
props, 122, 131, 145

R
realism, 4
Red Bull, the, 111
Renaissance, 52, 58, 103, 105, 124,
    135, 178, 193, 198, 199, 203,
    204, 221, 259, 263, 265, 266,
    273–275
rhetoric, 1, 2, 34, 36, 37, 41, 43, 48,
    52, 53, 55, 174, 187, 201, 207
Rhetorica ad Herennium, 1
Richard III, 21, 136, 137
riot, 21, 152–154, 156, 165, 281
Romances, 175, 177, 178, 189, 190,
    259, 284
Roman comedy, 178, 184, 284
Rose theatre, 20, 109, 110, 112, 114

S

school, 10, 14, 20, 26, 72, 74–82, 85, 115, 178, 196, 279
self-fashioning, 89
self-regulation, 18, 90, 94, 103
servants, 21, 152, 161, 162, 165, 167, 168, 195, 198, 199, 201, 205, 216, 224, 229, 243, 248, 279–281, 284
sexuality, 4, 37, 79, 202, 204, 225
Shoreditch, 20, 110, 111, 116
Sir Thomas More, 21, 151–153, 161, 162, 165, 166, 281, 283
slavery, 193, 194, 196, 197, 199, 203, 205, 207
social norms, 91, 93, 96–100, 103, 156
Southwark, 20, 109–112, 114, 116–118, 123, 124
Spanish Tragedy, The, 35, 58, 230, 250
spectators, 21, 109, 114–119, 122, 129–149, 162, 239, 244, 249, 250, 280
spirit, 13, 15, 42, 115, 135, 147, 198, 202, 204–207
stage properties, 16, 18, 228, 232, 242, 247
subjectivity, 9, 15, 90, 93, 94, 96, 97, 102, 103, 197, 247

T

Taming of the Shrew, The, 20, 95
Tempest, The, 22, 177, 194, 202, 203, 206, 207
Tilney, Edmund, 151, 154, 159, 166, 168
time, 1, 6, 9, 14, 17, 20, 39, 45, 50, 55, 57, 59, 71, 77, 79, 80, 84, 90–106, 111, 112, 114, 116–118, 120, 121, 123, 124, 132, 135, 138, 141, 147, 154, 157, 159, 160, 176, 177, 179, 181–184, 186, 187, 196, 198, 205, 239, 240, 243–245, 247, 248, 260, 262–264, 267, 269, 273, 274, 279, 280, 283
Timon of Athens, 4, 161
transformation, 45, 202, 204, 206, 207, 223, 243
Turks, 194, 196, 199, 200
Twelfth Night, 22, 144, 194, 200, 207
Two Lamentable Tragedies, 218, 222, 231, 238, 252, 253
Two Noble Kinsmen, The, 13, 149, 259

V

Vitruvian man, 37, 48

W

Warning for Fair Women, A, 22, 218, 221, 238, 239, 249, 253, 254
Welsh language, 74, 81
Westminster, 158
What You Will, 48
Winter's Tale, The, 21, 138, 148, 173–175, 177–182, 184–187, 189, 246
Woman Killed with Kindness, A, 22, 216, 218, 227, 249, 253, 259
Work, 3, 5, 8–11, 14–18, 22–25, 42, 51, 53, 57, 58, 60, 63, 72, 80–83, 90, 93, 100, 101, 111, 121, 123, 137, 144, 149, 152, 155, 156, 158, 163, 166, 168, 175, 191, 204, 206, 208, 216–218, 220–222, 225, 229, 231, 232, 238, 253, 279, 281, 285

Y

Yorkshire Tragedy, A, 22, 238, 240–244, 246–248, 251–254, 278, 281